D1565943

Specters of the Atlantic

Specters

DUKE UNIVERSITY PRESS   DURHAM AND LONDON   2005

IAN BAUCOM

of the Atlantic

FINANCE CAPITAL, SLAVERY, AND THE PHILOSOPHY OF HISTORY

© 2005 Duke University Press
All rights reserved
Printed in the United States
of America on acid-free paper ∞
Designed by Amy Ruth Buchanan
Typeset in Janson by Keystone
Typesetting, Inc.
Library of Congress Cataloging-
in-Publication Data appear on
the last printed page of this book.

For Gabriel, Leah, Kiran, and Camden

Contents

Acknowledgments

My work on this book has coincided almost exactly with my time in Durham, and my first thanks are to my many generous colleagues in the Duke English department whose intellectual example and warm friendship have made life here so pleasurable and rich. Irene Tucker has left Duke but I count the two years we spent as colleagues in the English Department and the friendship we have continued since as among the finest gifts of this place to my life. Charlie Piot, with whom I have talked and thought about the Atlantic more than with anyone else I know, has contributed far more to this book than I have had occasion to tell him, as have the other faculty and graduate students involved over the years in Duke's Atlantic Studies Research Group. To him and to them my thanks. My single most engaging year at Duke has undoubtedly been that I spent as a Fellow at the Franklin Humanities Institute in the "Race, Justice, and the Politics of Memory" seminar. All the members of that seminar (Srinivas Aravamudan, Charlie Piot, J. Kameron Carter, Sheila Dillon, Grant Farred, Thavolia Glymph, Susan Thorne, Evelyn Higginbotham, Hortensia Calvo, Alessandro Fornazzari, Stephane Robolin, and Leigh Raiford) read and commented on a draft of the first section of this text, and I am deeply grateful for all they taught me and for the sheer pleasure and intellectual delight of that year. I am particularly grateful to Srinivas and Charlie, who convened us and whose dexterities of intellect continue to give shape to much of my thinking. There are many others at Duke and elsewhere who have lent their wisdom and their criticism to this book as it has moved toward completion. I cannot name them all but would like to thank, in particular, Alberto Moreiras, Jed Esty, Ranji Khanna, Genevieve Abravanel, Christian Thorne Miano, Simon Hay, Greg Dobbins, Sarah Lincoln, Joan Dayan, and Phil Weinstein. In completing the manuscript I have benefited from the support of a summer research grant from the National Endowment for the Humanities, a Duke Arts and Sciences Research Fellowship, and a New Research Fellowship from the office of the Provost at Duke. I have also had the opportunity to deliver portions of the manuscript as lectures on a variety of occasions and am particularly grateful to the faculty of the Johns Hopkins English Department, the University of Miami English Department, the University of Tennessee English Department, the University of California, Irvine, English Department, and the English Departments of the University of Edinburgh and the University of Birmingham for their many insightful and productive responses to earlier versions of my argument. Without the early support of Ken Wissoker and the sterling assistance of Courtney Berger at Duke University Press the publication of this book would not have been possible. Without the thoughtful and detailed criticisms of the two anonymous readers of the manuscript it could not have acquired the coherence I hope it now has. Without the unabating love of my wife, Wendy, I would not have had the wherewithal to write it. And without those little four, Gabriel, Leah, Kiran, and Camden, I simply would not be. This book is for them: thank you for all the scampering wildness and jollity that awaits me each day.

*

Portions of the material in chapter 5 of section one ("Please decide: The Singular and the Speculative,") and the conclusion were previously published in slightly different form in my essays "Cryptic, Withheld, Singular," *Nepantla: Views from South* 1, no. 2, and "Specters of the Atlantic," *South Atlantic Quarterly* 100, no. 1 (winter 2001), respectively.

Part One

"NOW BEING": SLAVERY, SPECULATION,

AND THE MEASURE OF OUR TIME

It is said that the dialectical method consists in doing justice each time to the concrete historical situation of its object. But that is not enough. For it is just as much a matter of doing justice to the concrete historical situation of the [present] interest taken in the object. And *this* situation is always so constituted that the interest is itself preformed in that object and, above all, feels this object concretized in itself and upraised from its former being into the higher concretion of now-being.

—Walter Benjamin, *The Arcades Project*

Each "now" is the now of a particular recognizability. In it, truth is charged to the bursting point with time. . . . It is not that what is past casts its light on what is present, or what is present its light on what is past; rather, image is that wherein what has been comes together in a flash with the now to form a constellation.

—Walter Benjamin, *The Arcades Project*

CHAPTER 1

Liverpool, a Capital of the Long Twentieth Century

The minute book for the Lords Commissioners of the Admiralty for the month of July 1783 contains an absence, an item of business unattended to, a petition unacknowledged, an appeal for justice unaddressed. The petition came in the form of a letter and a bundle of accompanying documents that were sent to the Lords Commissioners sometime in the first few days of that month.[1] There is, to be sure, no contemporaneous record that the letter was ever opened or read in the surviving log of correspondence to and from the Commissioners assiduously kept by the Admiralty's clerks, nor in the equally fastidious minutes of the Commissioners' daily meetings.[2] That the letter was indeed sent is, nevertheless, attested to by its author, who mentioned it to several of his other correspondents at the time it was dispatched.[3] It is a harrowing document.

This book is a history of that unacknowledged letter, the events it recounts, the appeal it makes, the business the Lords Commissioners left unfinished in not responding to it, the silence it writes into the histories of empire and the modern, and the efforts that have been made to broach that silence. A history of a gap in the archive, this book also assembles a counterarchive, an archive that, over the past two hundred years, has collected itself around this piece of writing and the event whose history it attempts to write. This is, as might be expected, a variegated archive: a convoluted assortment of letters, bits of journalism, court documents, financial records, snippets of biography, speeches in Parliament, obituary notices, novels, insurance contracts, collections of poetry, pieces of art, nineteenth- and twentieth-century essays in art history, and a wide range of treatises in social, cultural, and political theory — all of which have, in some way or another, been party to, born upon, or found themselves haunted by the event whose news that initial, unacknowledged letter sought to communicate. That this counterarchive constitutes more than an effective history of that event, that secreted within it are the trace elements and perhaps also some of the secrets of our own contemporary experience of history and the modern, that the materials assembled within it might be to a long twentieth century what Walter Benjamin discovered the artifacts gathered within the Parisian arcades to be to the nineteenth, is also, as the title of this chapter suggests, part of my argument. As is it my argument that to read this archive *so* — to read it as *worth* reading, *worth* uncovering, *worthwhile*, because the utterly singular history it assembles can be seen to find its general equivalent in a reassembled history of the modern — is to risk repeating in abstract form (and in the form of abstraction) the profound human damage it so convolutedly documents.[4]

But those arguments come later, not only after the process of assemblage is complete (or, at least, after I have completed my own necessarily particular, necessarily partial, acts of assemblage), but after one or more of the pieces have begun to fall into place. Perhaps, then, these are not so much arguments that come after the archive as ones that can begin to articulate themselves only after the work of archiving has begun, arguments that can situate themselves, or discover themselves, only in the interstices of the elements assembled here, arguments that can enact themselves as aftereffects of the work of assemblage, arguments, thus, that will find themselves serially disassembled and reassembled as that archive unfolds itself.

∗

To begin then: with silence. But also with chatter, with the endless business of an empire that in 1783 found itself passing from what historians identify as its first to its second stage, with the phenomenal busy-ness of the naval masters of a global military power that was just on the point of losing thirteen of its colonies on the American mainland even as it was exerting a broadened hegemony over the Caribbean. Indeed, the reader's first impulse on encountering the Lords Commissioners' silence on the matter of a civil dispute arising from the voyage of a Liverpool slave ship some two years earlier (a civil dispute that had already been taken up and, apparently, settled at trial earlier that summer) is to attribute that silence to the many, infinitely more pressing matters of state that must have occupied the Commissioners' attention during that decade of great defeats, victories, and uncertainties. The minutes, however, do not support that reading. The dominant sense they convey is not of epic history or the grand narrative but of the minutiae of imperial management, the trivial daily business of global rule, the submemorable chatter of sovereignty by committee. The Lords Commissioners do not emerge from these records as the architects of history, but as its petty clerks, accountants, and small claims adjusters. They did, certainly, find time to direct the movement of ships from one Caribbean, Mediterranean, or North Atlantic port to another, but they seem to have spent the better part of their days paying bills, awarding pensions, managing personnel, investigating minor crimes, and overseeing the upkeep of the fleet.

In the two-week span from July 2 to July 16 — the fortnight during which the unexamined letter was most likely to have arrived — they found time, among other things, to appoint a Mr. Landers as schoolmaster to the *Irresistible*; assign pursers and a master of arms to the *Terpsichore*, the *Helena*, and the *Europa*; order their victualing agent in Jamaica to dispose of his wares in a manner "most advantageous to his Majesty"; pay off a wide range of bills of exchange (in amounts ranging from the 19,000 pounds owed to a Mr. Robbins, naval storekeeper of the East Indies, to the 15 pounds and 15 shillings due the clerk of the House of Commons); refuse to honor numerous other bills (including one submitted by Mr. Lewis, the crown's agent for prisoners of war in Jamaica); debate and order the further investigation of a letter from a Mr. Armstrong of Uppingham who claimed to have invented a waterproof paint; entertain a report on the deleterious effects of copper on iron bolts (the report suggested that copper degraded the bolts, causing ships' planking to fall off); and order, pursue, and ratify the court-martial of Thomas Morley, boatswain of the *Bombay*, for "conveying out of" his ship "certain coils of rope."[5]

This last case is something of an anomaly, however, at least for the brief period in question. For on the matter of justice, the Commissioners' interest was more frequently compensatory than punitive. Indeed, they seem to have spent the majority of their time calibrating a fine and exact scale of recompense for those far-flung workmen of the empire whose bodies had been wounded in the service of the crown. On the single day of July 3, 1783, the Commissioners took the time to address six such cases:

> To the widow of Captain George Wilkinson (late of the *Ville de Paris*) and her four children: 100 pounds a year and half pay.
>
> To a Lieutenant Furnival, who had received a wound in his shoulder from the "rebels" the previous May: 5 shillings a day and half pay.
>
> To Lieutenant John Willis, "who had the misfortune to lose his right thigh in action against the French and Spanish Fleets" the previous October: 5 shillings a day and half pay.
>
> To William Smith, Master in the Navy, "who, in an action with the French frigates in July 1778, had the misfortune to have his left foot shot off": half pay.
>
> To Thomas Sutton, clerk in the storekeeper's office in Jamaica, who lost his sight by a "violent inflammation" in January 1782: 40 pounds.
>
> To Captain John Thomas, who had received "many dangerous wounds," including "one through his lungs, one through his bladder, and has now seven balls lodged in his body which cannot be extracted": 150 pounds a year and half pay.[6]

There is something more than a little macabre about this list, something unnerving that exceeds the finicky mince of bureaucratic language, the formulaic translation of the loss of a foot, a thigh, a lung, or a bladder into a misfortune. If such formulations unnerve because of the obvious incommensurability of "misfortune" with "had his left foot shot off," then it is the imperturbable search for an alternate, alinguistic grammar of commensurability, the casual pursuit of a financializing, decorporealizing logic of equivalence that so confidently translates a lieutenant's foot into 5 shillings a day, a clerk's eyes into a one-time payment of 40 pounds, a captain's bladder and lungs into 150 pounds plus half-pay for life, that lends the counting-house scene chronicled in this record book its fully surreal quality. To my mind that surrealism attaches less to the exquisite-corpse or Frankenstein-like quality of the proceedings, less to the image of a composite imperial body being stitched together (and priced) as this foot is added to this thigh, this bladder, this lung, this set of eyes (and the bill for the whole is presented to the Admiralty) than to the triumph, over the whole enterprise, of this monetarizing anatomization of the body — the triumph, over an embodied knowledge of history, of something like double entry bookkeeping.[7] The specter of money and money management hangs over the entire minute book, a text which functions to convert history, for the most part, into a calculable matter of credits and debts, to reduce the vast business of empire to a column alternately labeled debt or misfortune and another labeled payment, with, in the debt column, not only a list of accounts due but a schedule of wounds received, bodily parts lost, lives surrendered, and in the paid-out column an undifferentiated array of numbers. In switching from the business of settling their 19,000 pound account with Mr. Robbins, Naval Storekeeper in the East Indies, to signing off on the 150 pounds for Captain Thomas's bladder and lungs, the Lords Commissioners were thus not switching business at all, merely applying the logic of one case to the particularities of the other:

Debt/Misfortune	Payment
To Mr. Robbins, Naval Storekeeper, E. Indies	19,000.0s.0d
To Mr. Cuthbert, Naval Storekeeper, E. Indies	12,000.0s.0d
To Clerk of the House of Commons	15.15s.0d
To John Willis, right thigh	5 shillings per diem
To William Smith, left foot	5 shillings per diem
To Thomas Sutton, eyes	40.0s.0.d
To John Thomas, bladder, lungs	150.0s.0d

If they had paused to pull back from the business at hand, the Lords Commissioners might have been troubled by something else also. For what haunts this record book, what haunts the accounting procedures and the econometric logic of justice explicit in the Lords Commissioners' attempt to do justice to those who had suffered on the empire's behalf, is not only the specter of a modern principle of bookkeeping and a modern system of finance capital capable of converting anything it touches into a monetary equivalent, but the specter of something else such financial protocols made possible, something the Admiralty would decidedly not have wished to associate with its loyal, suffering, subjects: the specter of slavery, the slave auction block, the slave trader's ledger book; the specter, quite precisely, of another wounded, suffering human body incessantly attended by an equal sign and a monetary equivalent.

And perhaps that is the reason why the Lords Commissioners did not attend to the letter that Granville Sharp had sent them. For if they had opened that letter, if they had read it, what they would have discovered related there was not something wholly alien to their way of doing business but something, rather, that would have seemed like a grotesque parody of their own activities, something relating the tale of a British ship, its trans-Atlantic voyage to the Caribbean, the loss of life aboard that ship, and the monetary amount a British court had parsed as just compensation to those whom it determined to have suffered this loss. That the ship, the _Zong_, was not a Royal Navy but a merchant vessel, that the dead were not British sailors but the 132 slaves the ship's captain had thrown overboard, that the petitioners were not bereaved family members but those drowned slaves' Liverpool owners who had sued their insurance agents for the underwritten value of the slaves and convinced a jury in the Guildhall Court that in drowning the slaves the ship's captain, Luke Collingwood, was not so much murdering them as securing the existence of their monetary value — all these things might, of course, have convinced the Lords Commissioners that the matter was none of their business, nor, in any important sense, that of the empire's.

*

"Liverpool, a capital of the long twentieth century," I have claimed, though, of course, not yet established. It is a queer claim, even with the qualification that I do not thereby intend that Liverpool is _the_ capital of this extended period of historical time but should be numbered _among_ the shipping, trading, and financial entrepôts that I understand to have dominated and ushered into existence our long contemporaneity, and even if the type of argument this claim suggests is more than familiar from the two essays to which it alludes: Walter Benjamin's "Exposé" of 1935, "Paris, the Capital of the Nineteenth Century," and his 1939 revision of the essay which serve as introductions of sorts to the materials that compose his _Arcades Project_. Paris makes an immediate, if disputable, sort of sense, not only as the capital of the nineteenth century but, potentially, as the capital of any number of other historical periods. Paris, capital of the nineteenth century; Paris, capital of the eighteenth century; Paris, capital of modernity — the idea is not, on the face of it, ridiculous. What remains is for that idea to substantiate itself, to define the contours of its argument, to tell us how and why we might accede to it, or quarrel with it.

*

As concerns Benjamin's claim, the fundamental argument is clear enough. As he quite pithily put it in a letter he wrote to Gershom Scholem in May 1935, an exploration of "the fetish character of commodities [stands] at the center."[8] The two exposés, if more oblique in their presentation of Benjamin's interests, are equally insistent on the centrality of the commodity form not just to nineteenth-century Parisian life but to an increasingly global culture system whose key principle was the production of exchange values, whose chief labor was the production of those commodities in which such exchange values were "petrified," whose central activity was the display, inspection, collection, and consumption of these commodities, and whose signature aesthetic object was, for Benjamin, the allegorical fragment. Allegory, he suggested, enacts the central logic of commodification by conferring on its subject matter an abstract signification analogous to the economic value that capital processes of exchange confer upon the commodity. "The key to the allegorical form," as he puts it in the 1939 exposé, "is bound up with the specific signification which the commodity acquires by virtue of its price. The singular debasement of things through their signification, something characteristic of seventeenth-century allegory, corresponds to the singular debasement of things through their price as commodities."[9] Thus, the nineteenth century emerges as a definable epoch because it is in that century that the commodity is not merely "enthroned" as an article of consumption and display but that moment in which even those who are economically excluded from the circuits of consumption, even "the masses [who are] forcibly excluded from consumption, are imbued with the exchange value of commodities to the point of identifying with it."[10] And Paris identifies itself as the capital of that commodito-centric century because in the boulevards cleared by Haussman, in the World Exhibitions the city staged ("World exhibitions are places of pilgrimage to the commodity fetish"), in the allegorical poetry of Charles Baudelaire (and the "flaneur's gaze" that poetry turns upon "the streets of Paris"), and, above all, in the Arcades, those "centers of commerce in luxury items," Benjamin discovered the French metropolis to be staging itself as the world center of commodity fetishism.[11]

Hence, if only in outline form: Paris, capital of the nineteenth century. Liverpool, a capital of the long twentieth century, is less evident.

*

But it is Liverpool in which I am, nevertheless, interested — and this despite the fact that the long twentieth century within which I want to situate the Merseyside metropolis begins to emerge into visibility in the final decades of the eighteenth century, and despite the fact that the voyage of the *Zong* (the voyage that is to this text what the Parisian thoroughfares were to Benjamin's *Arcades Project*) was not a voyage that began in Liverpool. For though it was owned by a group of Liverpool merchants, the *Zong* had not actually departed from the Liverpool docks for that trans-Atlantic passage whose murderous history Granville Sharp had sought to bring to the attention of the Lords Commissioners of the Admiralty. Instead, sometime in summer 1781, five Liverpool merchants — Edward Wilson, James Aspinal, William Gregson, and his two sons James and John — had dispatched a ship to the "Guinea" coast of Africa to take on board a cargo of slaves, which the vessel's captain was ordered to then convey to Jamaica for sale. On reaching the African coast some weeks later, the captain was offered the sale not only of slaves but of a ship. He purchased the vessel for his employers, sent them news of his actions, and transferred to the new ship's deck his vessel's surgeon, Luke Collingwood. Collingwood took command of the newly acquired ship, the *Zong*, and with the support of his chief mate, James Kelsall, set about purchasing a cargo of slaves from the holding pens of the slave factories then maintained by the London-based Company of Merchants Trading to Africa.[12] There were at the time numerous such factories, or forts, littered along the Guinea coast, often at a distance of just a few miles from one another.[13] From the limited evidence that survives of Collingwood's purchasing activities he seems to have done business with several of them, though principally with Fort William at Anamabo, which the Committee of Merchants had built in 1753 with the assistance of a large fund of money made available by Parliament, and whose retiring Governor, Robert Stubbs, Collingwood took on board as a paying passenger to Jamaica. For his new responsibilities, Collingwood was to be paid 100 shillings a month (approximately 5 pounds) and the sale price of two slaves (for which he could expect something in the range of 30 pounds "per head": the amount at which each slave had been valued for insurance purposes by Wilson, Aspinal, and the Gregsons in the contract they drew up with their underwriter, Thomas Gilbert).[14]

These then are the principal names of the Britons involved: Luke Collingwood, surgeon and captain of the *Zong*; James Kelsall, chief mate and later chief witness in the trials that were to follow the voyage; Robert Stubbs, one-time governor of the slave fort at Anamabo and, later, also a witness before the court; Edward Wilson, James Aspinal, William, James, and John Gregson, Liverpool merchants, slave traders, co-owners of the *Zong*, and, in time, plaintiffs before the courts; and Thomas Gilbert, Liverpool merchant, marine-insurance underwriter, and defendant at trial.

Of the 440 slaves purchased by Collingwood and crowded into the hold of the *Zong* no names survive.

the poem makes them up

*

The names of the slaves may not survive, but the value put upon them and the ship that was to carry them to Jamaica by their Liverpool owners does. By the terms of the insurance contract drawn up with Gilbert, the total value of Wilson, Aspinal, and the Gregsons' investment in the *Zong* and its cargo was as follows:

For the *Zong* itself:	2,500
For 440 slaves, valued at 30 pounds per head:	13,200
Total insured value:	15,700[15]

*

Four hundred forty slaves. Four hundred forty items of property valued at 30 pounds each. Thirteen thousand two hundred pounds. Four hundred forty human beings. We know almost nothing of them, almost nothing of Captain Collingwood's conduct in "acquiring" them, almost nothing of their entry, as individuals, into the trans-Atlantic slave trade. Not as individuals. As "types" they are at least partially knowable, or imaginable. Indeed what we know of the trans-Atlantic slave trade is that among the other violences it inflicted on millions of human beings was the violence of becoming a "type": a type of person, or, terribly, not even that, a type of nonperson, a type of property, a type of commodity, a type of money.

The logbook of the *Zong* does not survive. Here then is an outline list of what was so numbingly typical taken from the log of the *Ranger* — a Liverpool slave ship that loaded a cargo of slaves while anchored off the slave fort at Anamabo and sailed for Jamaica in convoy with a vessel owned by and named for the Gregson family. It is a long and a repetitive list, one whose reiterative predictability both requests the eye not so much to read as to skim and one whose flattened pathos solicits the reader's indulgence for horror banalized, horror catalogued. So I ask, do not skim, read:

> January 23, 1790: The *Ranger* weighs anchor in the Anamabo roads, and engages in transporting various goods from Fort William to the ship.
>
> January 24: The captain sends his sailmaker to repair the sails of the *Gregson*, over which he also has command.
>
> January 25: The *Ranger*'s carpenter is engaged in building the "barricadoes"

which will serve to pen the slaves in the vessel's hold; more goods loaded from the shore.

January 28: The *Ranger* purchases its first slaves: one man and one woman.

January 29: The captain sends the *Gregson* upcoast for fresh water.

January 31: Christian Freeze, a crewman, is discovered embezzling rum from the *Ranger*'s cargo hold; he insults Mr. Woods (the second mate) and has his rum allowance suspended for eight days.

February 4: One slave purchased: a man.

February 5: The captain orders the crew to check and clean their guns; purchases one woman.

February 7: One woman.

February 9: One woman.

February 13: Two men.

February 14: Canoe sent upshore for water; one man and one woman.

February 15: One man.

February 17: First child purchased, a boy; the captain also buys a woman.

February 18: The *Ranger*'s cooper is occupied making anchors.

February 19: The boatswain and several other crew members are caught embezzling rum by boring a hole into a puncheon of rum with a gimblet; they speak mutinous words to Mr. Woods, the second mate. No record of punishment.

February 20: Three men are purchased.

February 21: The captain dismisses the boatswain from service, he departs the ship.

February 24: One man, one woman.

February 25: Thunder in the distance, lightning, distant appearance of a tornado.

February 27: Loading water; one man and one woman.

March 1: Two women, two more children, girls.

March 4: One woman.

March 5: Two men.

March 6: One man.

March 7: Crew engaged in drying the sails; one man.

March 8: One woman.

March 9: One man, one woman.

March 10: The cooper is still working on anchors.

March 11: One man.

March 12: The captain orders the slavehold cleaned; the crew spends the day "taking care" of the slaves.

March 13: One man.

March 14: One girl.

March 15: One boy.

March 17: One woman.

March 20: The captain barters two women and an anchor for a quantity of rum; sends a party ashore for firewood.

March 21: Receives four puncheons of rum in exchange for the previous day's barter.

March 22: One man.

March 26: Bad weather, heavy surf, impossible for the "natives" conveying slaves to "come off" the shore.

March 28: The captain dispatches a quantity of firewood to the *Gregson*.

March 30: One man.

April 1: Two men.

April 2: The day is spent cleaning the slavehold and "taking care" of the slaves.

April 4: The captain orders the sails dried; one man.

April 9: The *Ranger* sails upcoast in search of trade.

April 12: The captain sends aboard the *Gregson* nine women and three girls and transfers sundry goods between the two ships.

April 13: The captain sends aboard the *Gregson* four anchors, one cinch hawser, one five-and-a-half pound gun, and twenty-six male slaves.

April 14. The *Ranger* completes its transfer of goods with the *Gregson*.

April 15: Trading for gold

April 18: Trading for gold.

April 19: Trading for gold.

April 24: Trading for gold; one woman.

April 25: Trading for gold.

April 26: One man.

June 2: One slave is traded for gold.

June 4: One slave is traded for gold.

June 5: The captain sends wood, water, sixteen puncheons of rum, and twelve and a half ounces of powder to the *Gregson* for two boys, six women, and three men.

June 8: One man.

June 10: The *Ranger* returns to Anamabo.

June 12: The captain sends aboard the *Gregson* ten men, nine women, four boys, and one girl.

regularity w/ which *talk a/b purchasing people*

June 16: The day is spent stowing bread and water casks.

June 19: The day is spent stowing beans; the captain sends a quantity of beans to the *Gregson*.

June 23: The *Ranger* completes its watering.

June 24: The crew spends the day washing out the male slaves' hold.

June 26: The *Ranger* weighs anchor and departs for Jamaica.[16]

Five months, almost to the day. For the crew, if we can reconstruct a portrait of their lives from these scant details, five months of boredom; one hundred fifty days, all but one or two of them at anchor, with little work to do other than the odd labor of sail drying or wood fetching; one hundred fifty days of restlessness broken up by the intermittent raid on the ship's rum supply, the stray talk of mutiny, the intimidating of the human cargo mounting up below the decks. For the captain the greater stress of finding work to keep his men occupied, diverting them from rebellion, holding the crew in line and his ship in place as he builds his cargo with frustrating slowness, one or two slaves at a time, and works the calculus of profit and risk: too long at the coast and the talk of mutiny may convert itself into a real rebellion, the weather may change, the distant tornadoes may move closer in and trap him; too little time and he will not have accumulated enough slaves, will not secure the profit he has promised his employers. For the slaves? For the women and men carried across the surf and penned in the holds below the deck? For that first child, that boy? For those human beings whose individual tragedies enter the log as little more than a chain of numbers: one man, one woman, one man, one woman, one woman, two men, one boy? For them: nothing out of the ordinary, nothing to single them out, nothing to cause the captain to record anything more about them after he has first made note of their purchase, nothing to draw the attention of the historian or the archivist to this document, this voyage, this cargo. For them, nothing unusual, nothing to make their terror, their captivity, their sorrow particularly interesting, memorable, worth writing about. Nothing momentous. Just the typical.

*

The *Zong* and its cargo of four hundred forty slaves sailed from the coast of Africa on September 6, 1781. What subsequently took place aboard that ship, what marked its voyage out for Granville Sharp's particular attention, what convinced him that these slaves' experience of the middle passage was anything but typical, what has made this voyage the subject of this book as opposed to any of the thousands of other such voyages, was to become widely known within the next few years, not only to Sharp but to Olaudah Equiano (who, in fact, first brought news of the voyage to Sharp's attention), Lord Mansfield (then Chief Justice of the court of King's bench and the most influential jurist of the late eighteenth century), the London newspapers that covered the appeal trial over which Mansfield presided, a British reading public, a broad range of abolitionist organizations, the House of Commons, and, of course, the *Zong*'s Liverpool owners.[17] At this point, at the moment of the *Zong*'s sailing, however, it is less what was or was to become known (or at least entered into evidence) that defines the British knowledge of the *Zong* than what was *not* known, could not be known, only imagined. All knowledge is, of course, to some extent imaginary, and neither Sharp, Mansfield, nor anyone else at the trial, the eyewitnesses included, could ever be said truly, fully, to have known what took place on the ship. The boast of evidence, however, is that it limits and constrains the promiscuity of the imagination, weds imagination to a liturgy of facts, records, documented events. If to know is always, in part, to imagine, then evidence demands that imagination bind itself to the empirically demonstrable. And certainly the Liverpool owners of the *Zong* had some facts at their disposal that September, though, indeed, rather few, little more than the name of the ship and its captain. What is so striking, then, is not what they knew at this point but what they were asked to imagine. Or perhaps more accurately, what is so striking is how credible that imaginary knowledge was to both the owners and the marine underwriter who insured the ship and its cargo for over 15,000 pounds.

The Liverpool merchants had never seen the *Zong* or the slaves Captain Collingwood had purchased on their behalf. They had paid for both the ship and many of the slaves with a form of money equally dependent on an act of mutual credibility: an ocean-crossing bill-of-exchange like those which sustained the trans-Atlantic slave trade and made of it as much a trade in credit as a trade in commodities. These were promissory notes which the merchants would have agreed to honor, with interest, some six or twelve months later (much like the bill the naval storekeeper to the East Indies had submitted to the Lords Commissioners for payment). And though neither party to the insurance contract that was later the basis for the case could, at the time that contract was signed, have possessed anything more than an imaginary knowledge of the property they had agreed to value at 15,700 pounds, they could and did legally bind themselves to credit that knowledge and, by that act of crediting one another's imagination, brought that value into legal existence. The ensuing trials were, at least in this sense, a wild abnormality, abnormal for their empiricism, abnormal for the effort they made to substitute *evidence* (primarily in the form of Kelsall's and Stubb's eyewitness testimony) for *credit* as the basis for a knowledge of the slave trade.

Indeed, to the extent that the case of the *Zong* was to help define the struggle between slave traders and abolitionists in the late eighteenth century, the way in which that struggle was waged suggests that it was not only a struggle between competing theories of right (the slaves' right to human dignity and the slavers' right to trade), but one between competing theories of knowledge, a struggle between an empirical and a contractual, an evidentiary and a credible epistemology.[18] As such, this struggle both extends and replays what scholars in recent years have taken to be the central epistemological drama of the long eighteenth century, the drama — emerging from the social rivalry of the old landed and the new moneyed classes — in which, as mobile property displaced "real" property, and the imaginary value of stocks, bonds, bills-of-exchange, and insured property of all kinds increasingly trumped the "real" value of land, bullion, and other tangibles, the concepts of what was knowable, credible, valuable, and real were themselves transformed. Such transformations, J. G. A. Pocock was one of the first to argue, generated a wide array of epistemological shifts in British public life, shifts in the ways that eighteenth-century Britons struggled to make sense of and devise new forms for these novel structures of knowledge.[19] One of the most important of these new forms, as Michael McKeon and other scholars have indicated, is the novel itself, a genre, to simplify matters entirely, whose ontology is to the precursor genres of genealogical history and genealogical romance what mobile property is to landed property and whose theory of knowledge is to a classical historical epistemology what credibility is to evidence.[20] The *Zong* trials and the abolitionist debate more generally, I am suggesting, define another scene in which such struggles were played out, which in turn implies that what was on trial at court was not only the conduct of the *Zong*'s captain, owners, and insurance-underwriter but something like the "novelization" of a collective imaginary, the novelizing protocols which permitted the owners, the underwriter, and, eventually, the Guildhall court itself to credit the fiction of value encoded in the *Zong*'s marine insurance policy.

The more restricted point I want to make is not that there was, in the late eighteenth century, no material evidence of the slave trade in Britain. That clearly is not the case. Indeed, much of what follows constitutes an attempt to read the ways in which the business of slavery made itself abundantly evident in British life, particularly in the lives of the Liverpool merchants who were to profit so handsomely from the *Zong*'s 1781 voyage. Such evidence exists and existed at the time. The point, rather, is to note how much of the trade, particularly the financial life of the trade and the theory of value that made it possible, depended if not precisely on the absence of such evidence, then on its belatedness. The evidence came later: after a voyage was complete; after the slaves had been sold; after the record keeping, the account adjusting, and the other work of documentation upon which historians rely for their own imaginary reconstruction of events. But the value already existed, prior to and independent of the evidence that what was valued in fact existed. Time and distance are part of the explanation. The time it took to complete the vast triangular circuit of the trade dictated that merchants must conduct much of their business on credit. But for such a system of credit to operate both a theory of knowledge and a form of value which would secure the credibility of the system itself had to be in place. Central to that theory was a mutual and system-wide determination to credit the existence of imaginary values. Central to that form of value was a reversal of the protocols of value creation proper to commodity capital. For, here, value does not follow but precedes exchange (not, to be sure, as the classical Marxist account has it, in the form of that use value that is held to preexist the moment of exchange, but as what Marx understood to be the end product rather than the originary moment of capital: as money value, value in the guise of the "general equivalent").[21] Such value exists not because a purchase has been made and goods exchanged but because two or more parties have agreed to believe in it. Exchange, here, does not create value, it retrospectively confirms it, offers belated evidence to what already exists. The 15,700 pounds attached to the *Zong* had acquired a legal reality long before the ship could ever make harbor in Jamaica, long before Collingwood could unload and sell his cargo of slaves as so many commodities on the Caribbean marketplace. The value existed the moment the insurance contract was signed.

This, then, is the larger, or at least the more abstract, point at issue: if, for Walter Benjamin, the nineteenth century is the century that enthroned the commodity, then the long twentieth century I have in mind is that which makes sovereign the value form legally secured in the *Zong*'s marine insurance contract.

There is a corollary to this point. If, for Benjamin, the nineteenth century inherits or continues the seventeenth, then the fundamental assumption of my reading of the long twentieth century is that it inherits or extends the long eighteenth.

But to provide some sense of what such claims, particularly the latter, might mean, some sense of what conception of historical time they encode, some sense of how that coding of time renders the contemporary contemporaneous with its noncontemporary "past," some sense, then, of what it might mean to suggest that the present is more than *rhetorically* haunted by the specter of the *Zong*'s 1781 voyage, we need to obtain a fuller understanding of the philosophy of history embedded in Benjamin's text. For, though the particular "past" which I understand the "present" to inherit or continue differs from that past which Benjamin discovered continued in a nineteenth-century present, my fundamental concept of how time thus extends, survives, or repeats itself is essentially Benjaminian.

*

The key to Benjamin's understanding of the nineteenth century's continuation or repetition of the seventeenth lies in his reading of the centrality, to both periods, of allegory and in his conception of the essentially allegorical nature of that process by which capital produces exchange values and, hence, commodities. As the passage I have cited from the 1939 exposé suggests, the link between allegorization and commodification lies in the "debasement," by both procedures, of the "thingliness" of the things on which they go to work.[22] Whether allegorically construed or circulated as a commodity, things, in both systems, signify not themselves but some superordinate "value"—whether that value is understood as a meaning or an exchange value. In thus acquiring value, or "signification," things, as Richard Halpern puts it in his insightful reading of Benjamin's argument, find their "concrete, thingly nature . . . temporarily extinguished. . . . Thus the commodity is, in essence, practical allegory—allegory in the sphere of social practice. The commodity devalues its own thingly existence, as does allegory, in order to signify an invisible realm of values."[23] While such an analysis implies, for Benjamin, the contours of what might be identified as a counterallegorical (and hence also a melancholic) critical project, a project, in part, devoted to recovering or redeeming the thingly life of all those things collected in the *Arcades Project*'s "Convolutes,"[24] a project directed, as Susan Buck-Morss has it, to forging a theory and a "language of objects" which could restore or "awaken" the "meaning which lay within [them]," it also implies the need for a philosophy of history which can account for the repetition *in* the nineteenth century, or, indeed, the triumph *over* the nineteenth century, of the seventeenth century allegorical protocols Benjamin had traced in *The Origins of German Tragic Drama*.[25]

On this score, Benjamin is a little less clear. From conversations he had with Asja Lacis at the time he was completing *The Origins* and beginning to draft his first plans for *The Arcades Project*, it is clear that he understood his work on the nineteenth century less as a departure from than a continuation of his seventeenth-century research and that what held the two projects together was their common interest in allegory.[26] Why allegory should emerge as the dominant mode of both periods, or what, consequently, the form of the relation is between these two periods is less evident. Some provisional answers are available from the scattered comments of the exposés, Halpern's reading of Benjamin, and a later twentieth-century text equally interested in a Marxist reading of allegory, Fredric Jameson's *The Political Unconscious*. The Jamesonian explanation, or explication, of such repetitions emerges from his theory of genre, specifically from his suggestion that while particular genres arise as the means of resolving, or at least coding, the concrete experiences and ideologies of their particular historical moments, as genres survive the moment of their fashioning, they survive by carrying within themselves, as a sort of ghostly aftereffect, the signature ideologies of their formative moments, which they then rewrite onto the subsequent historical moments in which they are redeployed. It is on the basis of such an understanding that Jameson defines his method of genre critique as a model devoted to the analysis of "formal *sedimentation*":

> What this model implies is that in its emergent, strong form a genre is essentially a socio-symbolic message, or in other terms, that form is immanently and intrinsically an ideology in its own right. When such forms are reappropriated and refashioned in quite different social and cultural contexts, this message persists and must be functionally reckoned into the new form. . . . The ideology of form itself, thus sedimented, persists into the later, more complex structure.
>
> The notion of the text as a synchronic unity of structurally contradictory or heterogeneous elements, generic patterns and discourses (what we may call, following Ernst Bloch, the *Ungleichzeitigkeit* or non-synchronic "uneven development" within a single textual structure) now suggests that even Frye's notion of displacement can be rewritten as a conflict between the older deep-structural form and the contemporary materials and generic systems in which it seeks to inscribe and to reassert itself.[27]

Bloch, we know, was one of Benjamin's most regular companions and interlocuters during the years in which Benjamin was drafting and researching *The Arcades Project*.[28] And there is a certain neatness to suggesting that the form of relation between the seventeenth and the nineteenth centuries on which Benjamin's analysis of allegory lies is the temporal form of the "nonsynchronous," the Blochian notion of the noncontemporaneity of the contemporary to itself.[29] One of Jameson's achievements in *The Political Unconscious* is to deduce from this form a general theory of historicist interpretation, a historicist hermeneutic which allows us to honor the Lukácsian injunction to situate literary texts within the "historical peculiarity" of the "age" in which they are produced while simultaneously to recognize that such historical situations (or ages or periods) are not sui generis but host to prior such moments, not autonomous but invested by a range of pasts which are not, in fact, past. The political unconscious of Jameson's title is in this sense also a political *uncanny*, a return into a subsequent historical moment of the repressed substrate of a prior historical situation. One of Jameson's contributions to literary criticism is to demonstrate how such historical and political questions encode themselves within literary form, particularly generic form (which functions as something like the indestructible, or at least undestroyed, carapace of ideology, the ideological exoskeleton through which antecedent ideologies, seemingly hollowed out by the passing of time, continue to occupy the attention of the present).

Absent from Jameson's account, however, is a theory of causality for such recurrences. He brilliantly decodes the effects and the import of generic persistence or repetition but, however valuably he alerts us to the ways in which generic repetition signals the political restaging of some earlier ideological contest, he does not tell us why a particular genre should survive, recur, repeat itself within, or find itself inherited by some subsequent historical moment, why a later moment should find itself compelled to reengage the ideological struggles of an earlier moment and thus find itself, as Bloch has it, "nonsynchronously" present to itself. This omission is both generally and particularly acute if Jameson's theory is applied to Benjamin's meditations on allegory. The omission is generally acute because it leaves us no closer to knowing why the nineteenth century should inherit the seventeenth (via the recurrence of allegory). It is particularly acute because if Benjamin is right to so closely associate allegorization with commodification, then neither this particular discovery nor Jameson's more general framing of the principle behind such discoveries can explain why, in this case, the *repeated* generic instance (*nineteenth-century* allegory) should temporally coincide with the *original* rise to dominance of the ideology it is said to encode (the ideology of commodity capital) rather than signaling the belated *return* to dominance of that ideology. Or, to put things a little more clearly, as Halpern has it, "an historical impediment stands in the way: the fact that baroque allegory precedes the thoroughgoing commodification of culture."[30] Allegory, in other words, may be the dominant genre of both the seventeenth and the nineteenth centuries (at least for Benjamin), but it is only the later moment (on his account) which is dominated by that commodity ideology the genre is held to encode.

How are we to account for this anachronism without canceling the link — crucial to both Benjamin and Jameson — between political ideology, capital logic, and aesthetic form? Halpern offers an elegant solution, one which effectively reverses the cruder theories of causality sometimes attributed to a Marxian analytic of "base and superstructure": "The commodity thus cannot offer a historical-materialist 'explanation' of allegory. Instead, it occupies the inverse position: it is not what underlies allegory but what exceeds it, surpasses it. The commodity renders allegory obsolete by perfecting and globalizing the latter's logic of representation. Under mature capitalism, allegory is no longer simply a literary technique but is rather the phenomenology of the entire social-material world."[31] Allegory, read thus, is not the literary "effect" or merely even the literary counterpart of a full-blown commodity capitalism. It is, rather, something closer to an epistemological condition of possibility: a mode of representation which enables and clears the ground for a form of capital which is an intensification and a wider practice of it. Commodity capital is not, thus, the antecedent "cause" of which allegory is the aesthetic "effect." Rather, as Halpern eloquently puts it, "the commodity is, in essence, practical allegory — allegory in the sphere of social practice."[32]

Two brief points and some anticipatory observations follow from this. The first point is that, with this reading in place, we are somewhat closer to understanding the form of the relation that obtains between Benjamin's seventeenth and nineteenth centuries. For on this account the nineteenth century does not repeat the seventeenth in some attenuated or residual form. Rather, the later moment repeats the earlier by intensifying it, expanding it. This in turn implies that the transition from the prior to the subsequent moment is not one in which a once dominant mode survives in residual form but one in which the once emergent restages itself as the now dominant. The second point, however, is that even with the assistance of this clarified version of the philosophy of history implicit in Benjamin's exposés (a philosophy of history that I would parse so: as time passes the past does not wane but intensifies; as history repeats itself it repeats in neither attenuated nor farcical form but by "redeeming" the what-has-been, "awakening" it into a fuller, more intense, form), we still lack an explanation for why, specifically, the nineteenth century should stage itself as an intensified form of the seventeenth; why, more generally, the sequence from emergent to dominant should find itself interrupted (in this case by the intervening eighteenth century); why, indeed, we are talking about a historical "repetition" rather than a continuous historical development. That what Benjamin has in mind is a theory of repetition is evident from the exposés, particularly the 1939 version, which concludes with the assent he offers to Auguste Blanqui's *L'Éternité par les astres*, a book which, Benjamin approvingly notes, "presents the idea of eternal return ten years before *Zarathustra*," a book which says for him what much of the succeeding pages of *The Arcades Project* will say again: "There is no progress.... The Universe repeats itself endlessly and paws the ground in place. In infinity, eternity performs — imperturbably — the same routines."[33] That this still quite mystical assertion of historical repetition requires some fuller explanation is equally evident.

*

First, though, the anticipatory observations I promised, observations which, once again, assume the form of a set of homologies between the "argument" Benjamin deduces from the materials in his archive and the arguments I understand to emerge from the interstices of the materials archived in this book:

— As Benjamin's nineteenth century repeats or inherits the seventeenth century by intensifying it, so the long twentieth century under discussion here extends or inherits the eighteenth by intensifying it.
— As commodity capital is to the nineteenth century's intensification of the seventeenth, so finance capital is to the long twentieth century's intensification of the eighteenth.
— As allegory is to commodity capital in Benjamin's paired moments, so "speculative discourse" (under which title I include both some versions of theoretical and some versions of novelistic discourse) is to finance capital in the long eighteenth and long twentieth centuries.

*

If for Benjamin, as I have been suggesting, the nineteenth century repeats the seventeenth by intensifying it, that process of intensification, as I have further argued, must somehow take account of its eighteenth-century interruption. There is another way of putting this. If, in Halpern's terms, nineteenth-century commodity culture enthrones a seventeenth-century allegorical "logic of representation" as the "phenomenology of the entire social-material world," what happens to that logic of representation, that phenomenology, over the course of the intervening century? What takes place in the eighteenth century to defer the rise to dominance of the commodity form? What then occurs in the transition from the eighteenth to the nineteenth century that enables the belated triumph of this phenomenology? And what, if the suggestions I have outlined are defensible, takes place in the twentieth century to permit an eighteenth-century species of finance capital and its accompanying or enabling "logic of representation" to enthrone itself in intensified form? These questions imply that what is at issue is not only a historical process of repetitions and intensifications but a history of oscillations or, indeed, an oscillating history. And it is, in fact, the concept of oscillation that can resolve the problems I have been underlining in Benjamin's philosophy of history, an oscillating history of capital that can account for that pattern of repetitions, interruptions, and intensifications through which the seventeenth century encounters itself in the nineteenth and the long eighteenth century "perfects" itself in the long twentieth.

The idea that oscillation is central to a history of modern capital is no more my own than is the notion of a long twentieth century which finds itself heir to a long eighteenth. Rather, I borrow both concepts from Giovanni Arrighi, whose *The Long Twentieth Century: Money, Power, and the Origins of Our Times* serves as the counterpart to Benjamin's *Arcades Project* as a fundamental pre-text for the argument assembled here.[34] A hybrid grafting of Arrighi and Benjamin, that argument exists, however, not simply to demonstrate that the strong intuitions which inform Benjamin's repetocentric philosophy of history find themselves confirmed by Arrighi's oscillatory history of capital, or that Arrighi's Braudelian analysis of capital's long and short *durées* requires something like Benjamin's cultural materialism if it is to reveal the ways in which the oscillating forms of capital inform and are informed by the shifting phenomenologies and recycled generic protocols of cultural practice. Indeed, however closely Benjamin and Arrighi's analyses and periodizations of capital map onto one another (and to my mind they map extremely closely), my purpose here is less to draw that map than to mark some of the ways in which it charts a trajectory from a largely obscure eighteenth-century atrocity to a present in which the capital and phenomenological protocols which are that atrocity's conditions of possibility have not waned but intensified, a present in which that "past" survives not as a sedimented or attenuated residue but in which the emergent logics of this past find themselves enthroned as the dominant protocols of *our* "nonsynchronous" contemporaneity. The *Zong* may be absent, in name, from these pages of my text, but its specter haunts everything I have to say here.

And yet, to understand how this might be, we need to keep the *Zong* frozen in place just a little longer, keep it just visible at the margins of *these* speculations, keep it in mind at that moment in which Captain Collingwood hauled in his anchor, unfurled his sails, and began his voyage, the voyage of his crew, and the voyage of that still "typical" cargo of four hundred forty human beings penned behind the barricadoes of his slave hold.

*

Arrighi's *The Long Twentieth Century: Money, Power, and the Origins of Our Times* is, as its title suggests, a history of the present, a history of a present whose "time" is not what we might think it to be, a present whose present time is not singular but plural, not present to itself alone but to a cycle of "times" it accommodates within itself. Time does not pass, it accumulates: such is another way of glossing Arrighi's argument, as it is another way of paraphrasing the "argument" of Benjamin's *Arcades Project*, the lesson of its philosophy of history *and* the argument of this book. Above all, for Benjamin, time accumulates in things, even, or particularly, those commodified things whose commodification entails not only the assignation of an exchange value but the willed repudiation of the time stored within them, the denial of their capacity to function as Proustian aide-mémoire, Marxian record keepers of the time it took to make them, the value of that labor time, the collective past-life it encodes, or even, or indeed much less, as "practical" souvenirs of an antecedent phenomenology. Benjamin's project is to restore this past-time to things, to refuse to acknowledge it as lost, to recover the time accumulated within the commodities accumulated for display in the Parisian temples of commodity culture: the World Exhibitions, Haussman's consumer-friendly boulevards, the arcades. The time accumulated within things, even by the terms of this sparse outline, is thus neither singular nor even, entailing as it does a heterochronic mix of the personal time of memory, the collective time of labor, and the long durational time of the phenomenological. The commodity thus accumulates not one time, but several, including, as I have been arguing, an anterior time that the present time stores and intensifies but which it does not so much continue as repeat.

For Arrighi, time also repeats itself. And for him, too, the evidence of such repetition is manifest in the warehouses and store windows of capital accumulation. Where he departs from Benjamin, but also where his history of capital can help make sense of Benjamin's version of eternal return, is in his suggestion that these warehouses and shop windows are but one of the two fundamental types of place in which capital accumulates, that, indeed, the accumulative protocols of commodity capitalism alternately precede and follow another practice of accumulation, an accumulation of value not in the factory zones and the shopping and consumption districts of capital, but in its quarters of high finance, its stock exchanges, its bond, credit, and currency markets, the money zones that Arrighi, following John Ruggie, calls capital's "spaces-of-flows."[35] From this elegantly simple observation Arrighi is able to construct a comprehensive history of capital periodized around a series of long *durées*, which he calls "systemic cycles of accumulation." On his account, the full history of capital encompasses four such cycles: "A Genoese cycle, from the fifteenth to the early seventeenth centuries; a Dutch cycle, from the late sixteenth through most of the eighteenth century; a British cycle, from the latter half of the eighteenth century through the early twentieth century; and a US cycle, which began in the late nineteenth century and has continued into the current phase of financial expansion."[36] Each of those cycles, in its turn, plays out, over the course of its duration, the successive component elements of Marx's general formula for capital: MCM', where M stands for money capital, C for commodity capital, and M' for the more intense, freer form of money capital that follows the transformation of money into commodity and commodity into money once more.

> Marx's general formula for capital (MCM') can therefore be interpreted as depicting not just the logic of individual capital investments, but also a recurrent pattern of historical capitalism as a world system. The central aspect of this pattern is the alternation of epochs of material expansion (MC phases of capital accumulation) with phases of financial rebirth and expansion (CM') phases. In phases of material expansion money capital "sets in motion" an increasing mass of commodities (including commoditized labor-power and gifts of nature); and in phases of financial expansion an increasing mass of money capital "sets itself free" from its commodity form, and accumulation proceeds through financial deals (as in Marx's abridged formula MM'). Together, the two epochs or phases constitute a full *systemic cycle of accumulation*. (6)

Benjamin's seventeenth and nineteenth centuries, by this account, are better understood not as "periods" in their own right, but as the midpoints (the commodity moments) of the larger cycle within which they are encompassed. The seventeenth century stands thus as the midpoint of the Dutch cycle that runs from the late sixteenth century through the majority of the eighteenth, while the nineteenth century defines the midpoint of the British cycle that extends from the end of the eighteenth century into the beginning of the twentieth.

If Arrighi's general model holds true we could predict that the two commodity moments of interest to Benjamin would each be preceded and followed by a money phase, a moment in which capital accumulates, primarily, not in the commodity form but in the paper, credit, stock, or other speculative forms of finance capital. If Arrighi's model, in its turn, is reread through Benjamin, then we could further predict that each of those money phases would coincide with or be accompanied and enabled by a series of epistemological transformations and the emergence — or reemergence — of a set of cultural forms which dialectically *encode and make possible* these reorientations of capital. Arrighi's history of capital, I am thus suggesting, provides the grounds for a historicization of Benjamin (and the cultural artifacts which occupy his attention), while the methodological framework of Benjamin's analyses of aesthetic and cultural forms provides the grounds for an epistemological counterhistoricization of Arrighi (and the cycles of accumulation which occupy his attention). The story that each tells, in other words, is only half of the story. Something like the full account depends, as ever, on the dialectical play between the pair of them, or, indeed, between these pairs: Benjamin and Arrighi; cultural artifact and capital form; epistemology and mode of accumulation; repetition and oscillation.

But Arrighi's side of the picture needs to be made a little clearer in order to set that dialectic to work and to see how it might be redeployed to an examination of the voyage of the *Zong*, the historical moment in which it sailed, the insurance contract I take to be a paradigmatic document of the cultural, epistemological, and capital protocols of that hypermonetarized, hyperspeculative moment, and the intensified repetition of that moment within our own exorbitantly financialized present. I indicated above that Benjamin's seventeenth and nineteenth centuries are better understood, from Arrighi's perspective, as the midpoints of a Dutch and a British cycle of accumulation and that their commoditocentrism should thus be grasped as subsequent and prior to the enveloping money phases of capital. These money phases, with which Arrighi's "systemic cycles of accumulation" begin and end, are best understood, however, not simply as the brackets of a given cycle but by being bracketed alongside one another. For, arrayed so, they permit us to see both how one cycle transforms itself into another *and* how each subsequent cycle largely repeats the history of the prior (while expanding and intensifying its theater of address).

In rough schematic form that array of cycles, including the beginning of a new cycle Arrighi suggests might be underway (though under whose sovereign dominance — if anyone's — is unclear), would look something like this[37]:

Genoese cycle	*Dutch cycle*	*British cycle*	*American cycle*	*?*
1450–1650	1560–1780	1750–1925	1860–Present	1980–
MCM′	MCM′	MCM′	MCM′	MCM′

As the approximate dates that Arrighi provides for the beginning and ending of these cycles suggest, the transition from one moment to the next is not absolute. It involves, rather, a moment of overlap as capital hegemony shifts from a Genoese-funded Spanish Empire to Holland, from Holland to Britain, and from Britain to the United States. During these moments of overlap (as one MCM′ cycle nears its close and another begins to emerge) the general Marxist formula that Arrighi has adapted to his purposes assumes its abridged form, MM′. A fuller schematization of Arrighi's account would thus need to include these moments:

Genoese cycle	*Dutch cycle*	*British cycle*	*American cycle*	*?*
1450–1650	1560–1780	1750–1925	1860–Present	1980–
MCM′	MCM′	MCM′	MCM′	MCM′
	MM′ phase	MM′ phase	MM′ phase	MM′ phase

As these MM′ phases — these transitional moments in which, as Arrighi has it, capital accumulation proceeds virtually exclusively through "financial deals" — correspond to a series of overlaps between Arrighi's cycles, they mark out four crucial periods in which finance capital exerts its dominance over an ever-expanding capital world system. The period from the end of the sixteenth century to the beginning of the seventeenth; the mid and final decades of the eighteenth century; the decades spanning the end of the nineteenth and the beginning of the twentieth century; and the final few decades of the twentieth century thus define themselves as the highest moments of finance capital, moments in which capital seems to turn its back entirely on the thingly world, sets itself free from the material constraints of production and distribution, and revels in its pure capacity to breed money from money — as if by a sublime trick of the imagination.

∗

As Arrighi notes, these four moments are also, fairly exactly, the moments that economic historians tend to associate with the dominance of finance capital, as they are the moments in which capital hegemony serially shifts from one metropolitan center to another in the wake of massive capital flight: first from the Genoese-funded markets of the Spanish empire to Holland following the signing of the Treaty of Westphalia and the emergence of a dominant Dutch banking class; then from Holland to London's Exchange Alley as the Dutch banking and finance monopolies collapsed over the course of the eighteenth century and the Dutch East India company was superseded by an array of British chartered companies; and once more from Britain to Wall Street as the British empire reached its zenith and began its decline. The Nasdaq market had not emerged to its current prominence at the time Arrighi was conducting his research, though its emergence certainly corresponds to the renewed money phase of accumulation toward which he predicts capital is headed. That this Chicago exchange might preside over a delocalized, deterritorialized global cycle of accumulation seems equally feasible.

Whatever the predictive virtue of Arrighi's model, its discourse of anticipation is clearly grounded in his theory of repetition. By the terms of that theory, as I have indicated, repetition functions through oscillation, or indeed through a variegated sequence of oscillations. The most fundamental repetition in his history is obviously that by which each succeeding cycle of accumulation imitates or repeats the history of the cycle that it succeeds.[38] As one MCM' cycle bleeds into another, however, the repetition of the entire process is broken down into a sequence of smaller alterations in the dominant regime of accumulation, alterations which take the form of a constant oscillation between monetary and commodity capital, a continuous moving back and forth between forms which leads Arrighi to suggest a general rule for the history of capital: "The system seems to be moving 'forward' and 'backward' at the same time. . . . Old regimes [of accumulation] do not just persist [or vanish]. . . . Rather, they are repeatedly resurrected as soon as the hegemony that superseded them is in its turn superseded by a new hegemony."[39] It is this general pattern of repetition through oscillation, this pattern by which apparently "late" or "mature" finance capital constantly finds itself succeeded by the more "primitive" commodity form that it, in its turn, has just succeeded, that I am suggesting can help us to make sense of Benjamin's discovery of the deferred repetition of a seventeenth-century allegorical phenomenology within the commodity culture of the nineteenth century.

It is not, however, only the general pattern of repetition outlined in Arrighi's text that deserves mention. The particular obsession of his text, the close attention he gives to those liminal moments in which the general pattern of capital development finds itself serially interrupted by the special case, the interest he sustains in those hyperfinancialized moments that recur between one cycle and another also bears emphasis. For if it is one of these moments that our present inhabits, one of these pure money moments from which, as Jameson has it, our present derives its "historical peculiarity," its "cultural logic," then, by Arrighi's account at least, such a moment is by no means original to the late twentieth century, not at all a unique and final stage of capital development qualitatively unlike anything that has come before it. This moment is instead something closer to an uncanny moment. It is a moment of repetition, a moment in which the past returns to the present in expanded form, a moment in which present time finds stored and accumulated within itself a nonsynchronous array of past times. Our present moment is, thus, more than structurally like the antecedent high finance moments whose value forms and capital logics it recuperates. It is a moment which does not merely resemble that equally financialized moment in which the *Zong* sailed. Our time, I want instead to suggest, is a present time which, in a fully Benjaminian sense, inherits its nonimmediate past by intensifying it, by "perfecting" its capital protocols, "practicalizing" its epistemology, realizing its phenomenology as the cultural logic "of the entire social-material world." "It is not," as Benjamin has it, "that what is past casts its light on what is present, or what is present its light on what is past; rather . . . what has been comes together with the now to form a constellation."[40]

*

"The universe repeats itself endlessly," Benjamin avers, following Charles Blanqui. The "men of the nineteenth century [find] the hours of their apparitions . . . fixed forever . . . always bringing back the very same ones."[41] "The entire system," Arrighi insists, "seems to be moving forward and backward at the same time . . . Old regimes do not just persist [or vanish] . . . they are repeatedly resurrected."[42] "The notion of the text as a synchronic unity of structurally contradictory or heterogeneous elements, generic patterns and discourses," Jameson argues, " . . . [suggests] a conflict between the older deep-structural form and the contemporary materials and generic systems in which it seeks to inscribe and reassert itself."[43] Thus three different versions of eternal return; three aprogressive analyses of those processes by which modernity unfolds its nonsynchronicities within collective time consciousness, capital history, and textual form; three interinformative accounts on which I have based my conception of the long twentieth century and from which I deduce the following arguments in the rest of the book.

The hyperfinancialized late twentieth century and early twenty-first, like Benjamin's nineteenth century, Arrighi's regimes of accumulation, and Jameson's textual object, is not contemporary with itself alone. It accumulates, repeats, intensifies, and reasserts the late eighteenth. The hour of *its* apparitions is fixed by this prior hyperspeculative moment. If the past this present inherits is thus — as I have earlier suggested — not the past that haunts Benjamin's "men of the nineteenth century," then the form of the relation between either of these two "presents" and the pasts by which they are haunted is nevertheless the same. It is the dialectical form by which the later moment finds its conditions of possibility in the earlier moment even as the earlier moment finds itself "awakened" by the later; the dialectic through which the present realizes itself by retroactively detonating the cultural and epistemological charge latent within the moment that has preceded it; the dialectic whereby "what has been comes together with the now to form a constellation." There is then, by this account, no such thing as a fully discrete or isolated "present" or "past," just as there is no discrete late twentieth century or early twenty-first to speak of, only a nonsynchronous contemporaneity in which an older deep-structural form inscribes, reasserts, and finds itself realized: an inordinately long twentieth century boundaried at either end by one of Arrighi's transitional periods of pure money capital.

My long twentieth century is thus both consistent and inconsistent with Arrighi's. It is consistent to the extent that in either case "the long twentieth century" functions as a collective name for all four of Arrighi's cycles of accumulation, as a corporate way of naming modernity as capital's sixteenth-to-twentieth-century long durée. And my usage is consistent with Arrighi's to the extent that, like him, I simultaneously intend it to designate a particular final cycle within that long durée, a cycle marked out at either end by a transitional moment of high finance capital. My use differs from Arrighi's, however, in my dating, or bracketing, of this cycle, and in the territory with which I associate it. For Arrighi this more particular long twentieth century runs from the late nineteenth century to the end of the twentieth. It follows the lapse of the "British" cycle of accumulation, is coterminous with what he calls the U.S. cycle, and is precipitated by the flight of capital from British to American financial markets. On my account, this more specific long twentieth century runs from the mid–eighteenth century through the "present." It is precipitated by the flight of capital from Amsterdam to London, conjoins the British and U.S. cycles in a single Atlantic cycle of accumulation, enshrines commodity capital at its nineteenth century midpoint, and enthrones speculative epistemologies and value forms at either end of its long durée. Its historiography partially corresponds to what is sometimes called the New British history and sometimes Atlantic history.[44] Its cultural theory emerges from a range of recent works in black-Atlantic, trans-Atlantic, and circum-Atlantic cultural studies.[45] Its philosophy of history, as I have been suggesting, derives from Benjamin. Its time consciousness is hauntological.[46]

Thus, on my account (if only, still, in outline form): the long twentieth century.

*

And Liverpool is one of its capitals, the voyage of the *Zong* one of its "arcades," the *Zong*'s insurance contract one of its allegories.

*

The book that follows constitutes my attempt to justify these claims and to explain more fully what I mean by them by tracking a critical path through the circum-Atlantic archive of discourses and texts that has built up around the massacre over the past two centuries. For though the Lords Commissioners of the Admiralty never responded to Sharp's letter, their silence did not cause the event to disappear. Thanks to the work of Sharp, Equiano, and their colleagues, accounts of the event quickly became a staple of abolitionist discourse on both sides of the Atlantic. The fashionable metropolitan magazines offered their thoughts on the massacre. William Wilberforce brought it before Parliament's attention in the 1806 debates on the abolition of the slave trade. In 1840, J. M. W. Turner's canvas *Slavers throwing overboard the dead and the dying* took its inspiration from the event. And in recent years the case of the *Zong* and the scene of drowning and terror it names have again resurfaced, first as a brief episode in general histories of the Atlantic slave trade and the African diaspora and then, particularly over the past ten years, as a sort of haunting spirit in a broad array of literary, sociological, historical, and philosophical texts devoted to an exploration of what Paul Gilroy has called the black Atlantic world. *Specters of the Atlantic* joins those recent texts but argues more directly than any of them that the event and its representations are central not only to the trans-Atlantic slave trade and the political and cultural archives of the black Atlantic but to the history of modern capital, ethics, and time consciousness.

The book has three parts broadly correspondent with its three primary interests in this triad of modern economy, ethics, and philosophy of history. The first part (" 'Now Being': Slavery, Speculation, and the Measure of Our Time") provides a history of the massacre, the ensuing court cases, and the business and social dealings of the group of Liverpool merchants who were the co-owners of the ship (two of whom were at some point in their careers mayors of Liverpool). It identifies the moment of the massacre with one of those periods of finance capital that Arrighi argues begin and end a long-durational cycle of capital and suggests, consequently, that the massacre and trials bring to light what I am calling an Atlantic cycle of accumulation and a long twentieth century defined at either end by the rise of finance capital and the speculative culture apposite to such an order of abstract accumulation. As I have begun to make clear, I regard the voyage of the *Zong* as historically and interpretively central to that long twentieth century in much the fashion that Walter Benjamin understood the Parisian arcades to be crucial to and exemplary of the nineteenth. I pursue this Benjaminian analogy throughout the first part of the book both to ground the theory of time central to my reading of a late-twentieth and early-twenty-first-century "now" that houses within itself an eighteenth-century "what-has-been," and to investigate what a Benjaminian historical materialism might resemble when its objects are not the allegorical cultural forms of commodity capitalism but the speculative cultural forms of finance capitalism. I read the *Zong*'s insurance contract as a central such artifact of speculative culture, in part by aligning what I take to be the "theoretical realism" fundamental to the forms of knowledge and value that contract (and insurance more generally) exists to secure with the "suppositional," "abstract," or "exchangeable" types of character, object, and social encounter that recent novel theory has discovered in an eighteenth-century novelistic discourse designed, in Deidre Lynch's terms, to train readers to negotiate the financial revolution's new world of speculative transactions and mobile property. In concluding this first section I discuss what it might mean to read the case of the *Zong* (and, more generally, the Atlantic slave trade and the "speculative" revolution of Atlantic capital) as, in Kant's terms, a "signum rememorativum, demonstrativum, prognostikon" in which modernity finds itself demonstrated, anticipated, and recollected; I relate such a reading (which, at a minimum, asks us to consider trans-Atlantic slavery an "event" of equal significance to the French Revolution in the philosophical discourse of modernity) to a larger Kantian and post-Kantian event theory (particularly as developed by Benjamin and in work by Slavoj Žižek and Alain Badiou); and I conclude by counterposing this mode of reading to one that in

Gayatri Spivak's terms attends not to the general or episystemic "truth" of this event but to its singularity.

The second part of the book ("Specters of the Atlantic: Slavery and the Witness") returns to the concept of the "singular," now in order to frame the singular in relation to an ethics of "melancholy realism" and a discourse of romantic, testamentary witness that I understand to articulate themselves as long-durational countermodes of the "theoretical realism" examined in part one. Beginning with the discourses of witness manifest in the court proceedings on the massacre and the bundle of materials Sharp sent to the Lords Commissioners in a failed attempt to open a murder investigation of the *Zong* drownings, the second portion of the book thus argues that if the case of the *Zong* can be seen to exemplify the advent and triumph of an abstract, speculative, hypercapitalized modernity, then Sharp's book of evidence, the trial transcripts, and a broad array of antislavery discourse also bear witness to the emergence, internal to the speculative culture of our long contemporaneity, of the figure of the interested historical witness *and* so testifies to the emergence, internal to a Euro-Atlantic modernity, of a testamentary counterdiscourse on and of modernity: a recognizably romantic counterdiscourse; a melancholy but cosmopolitan romanticism that sets itself, in Michael Lowy and Robert Sayre's evocative phrase, "against the tide of modernity."

Subject to (if set against) this modernity, the *type* of witness Sharp and his fellow abolitionists call into life, the type of witness whose most recent incarnations include Derrida's "third," the type of romantic, interested, melancholy *and* cosmopolitan witness whose long-twentieth-century career I now trace, is, however, more than contingently or analogically related to the *particular* witness Sharp determines to be. Rather, this witness (figured as a type of modern historical observer, actor, and judge, and recently conceived by Derrida and others as *the* type of the ethical actor in history) is, I argue, if not exclusively then crucially Atlantic in its provenance; crucially if not exclusively haunted by the specter of the trans-Atlantic slave trade. I pursue this argument in a series of chapters on the *Zong* trials, abolitionist and human rights discourse, British romantic poetry and historical romance, the fact and fiction nexus in modern European epistemology, and Scottish Enlightenment conjectural historiography and moral philosophy. I conclude the second part with a reading of Turner's *Slavers throwing overboard the dead and the dying* and a brief reconsideration of the Derridean witness as both an agonist to the disinterested judicial "third" who oversees the advent and administration of Hegel's "universal and homogeneous state" *and* as a successor figure to the schizophrenic "spectator" of eighteenth- and nineteenth-century sympathy theory.

In a short final part of the book ("'The Sea is History': On Temporal Accumulation"), I offer an overview of the theory of history the first two parts of the work have articulated, largely by exploring the concept of "temporal accumulation" as I see it developed in a diasporic philosophy of history and a series of recent black-Atlantic meditations on this (or such an) event (central among these are Fred D'Aguiar's novel *Feeding the Ghosts*, Edouard Glissant's *Poetics of Relation*, Derek Walcott's *Omeros*, M. NourbeSe Philip's *Zong!*, and Paul Gilroy's *The Black Atlantic*). Time does not pass, these materials suggest, it accumulates. In making that argument and spelling out some of what it might imply, I explore the ways in which a diasporic philosophy of history (as developed, among other places, in Glissant's speculations on the "poetics of duration" and Walcott's explorations of the long "Atlantic now") revises our dominant conceptions of the genealogy and temporal logic of the modern by rearticulating a quasi-Benjaminian ethics of "now being" and so causes us to encounter a form of history in which, as Toni Morrison puts it, "all of it is now, it is always now," even for "you who never was there," even for all of those of us to whom the slaves thrown from the deck of the *Zong* can appear as little more than specters of the Atlantic.[47]

The flaneur plays the role of scout in the marketplace. . . .
[He] flatters himself that, on seeing a passerby swept along
by the crowd, he has accurately classified him, seen straight
through to the innermost recesses of him—all on the basis
of his external appearance. . . . The typical characters seen
in passersby make such an impression on the senses that
one cannot be surprised at the resultant curiosity to go
beyond them and capture the special singularity of each
person. But the nightmare that corresponds to the illusory
perspicacity of the aforementioned physiognomist consists
in seeing those distinctive traits—traits peculiar to the
person—revealed to be nothing more than the elements
of a new type; so that in the final analysis a person of the
greatest individuality would turn out to be the exemplar
of a type.

—Walter Benjamin, *The Arcades Project*

Haussman's activity is linked to Napoleonic Imperialism.
Louis Napoleon promotes investment capital, and Paris
experiences a rash of speculation. Trading on the stock
exchange displaces the forms of gambling handed down
from feudal society. The phantasmagorias of space to which
the flaneur devotes himself find a counterpart in the phantasmagorias of time to which the gambler is addicted.

—Walter Benjamin, *The Arcades Project*

CHAPTER 2

"Subject $"; or, the "Type" of the Modern

The city of Liverpool may be one of the capitals of a long Atlantic twentieth
century, but it is not the only such city. There are several. London is one. New
York is another. Cape Town and Philadelphia, as Thomas Pynchon's *Mason
and Dixon* reminds us, are a third and a fourth.[1] Joseph Roach's New Orleans
belongs on this list, as do Boston, Charleston, and Kingston: the capitals of
Ian Steele's *English Atlantic*.[2] The slave factories of the "Guinea" coast have

functioned as something like the industrial peripheries of these cities, and Liverpool as both a capital in its own right and as a hub of their common transport system. What all these places have in common is not only that they are Atlantic port cities but, in the phrase Arrighi borrows from John Ruggie, that they have all functioned as "spaces-of-flows" for an Atlantic cycle of accumulation, as the commodity entrepôts and finance zones of this long twentieth century's oscillating regimes of accumulation.[3]

The original, generic models for the spaces-of-flows, Arrighi argues, are the sixteenth-century Bisenzone fairs run by the Genoese merchant bankers who preceded the Dutch as the dominant lender class of European and imperial capital. Through these fairs — wandering bazaars of capital set up in one European city after another to channel the continental and imperial distribution of commodities and credit — the Genoese merchants were able to establish the model for a capital system "defined by the flows of precious metals, bills of exchange, [governmental] contracts . . . and money surpluses which linked these places to one another."[4] Serving to link one place to another and so to define the operative territories of capital, the geographies of circulation that supersede and interrupt the borders of the nation-state, these spaces-of-flows thus belong less to the particular cities or states they link or to the individual places in which they happen to have come to rest than to the expansive territories of circulation they govern. They exist by serving the needs of sovereign polities but exist to serve the sovereign principles of exchange they embody, the financial flows they regulate, the capital imperative which they incarnate and whose chief purpose is the conversion of endless variety into a single, general equivalent: money. Not surprisingly, their chief moments of dominance coincide with Arrighi's four transitional periods of high finance capital, those MM' phases in which capital sets itself free to breed money from money. Another way of narrating Arrighi's history of capital is, in fact, to tell it as the story of these spaces-of-flows: their wandering from one place to another; the temporary habitation they have taken in and *as* the commodity catchment and high finance zones of the Spanish Empire, Holland, Britain, and the United States; the successive cycles of accumulation they have set in motion as they wander from one place to another; the shifting geographies of circulation that have established themselves around their peregrinations.

Institutionalized for early modernity in the Bisenzone fairs of the sixteenth century, these spaces-of-flow consolidate in the seventeenth and eighteenth centuries around the chartered companies of Holland and Britain and in the Amsterdam and London stock exchanges that rose to prominence in large part by speculating in these companies' fortunes. Indeed, as Arrighi makes clear, the rise of these joint-stock chartered companies were as vital to the Dutch and British cycles of accumulation that he documents (and to the Atlantic cycle I have in mind) as the bullion and money-lending operations of the Bisenzone fairs were to the Genoese and Spanish cycle.

> Chartered companies were the medium through which the Dutch capitalist class established *direct* links between the Amsterdam entrepôt on the one side, and producers from all over the world on the other side. Thanks to these direct links, the ability of the Dutch capitalist class to centralize the commercial transactions that mattered in Amsterdam, as well as its ability to monitor, regulate, and profit from the disequilibria of world trade, were greatly enhanced. At the same time, chartered companies played a decisive role in the rise of Amsterdam to the status of world financial center. For investment and speculation in the shares of chartered companies — first and foremost of the voc — were the single most important factor in the successful development of the Amsterdam Bourse into the first stock market in permanent session.[5]

Substitute London for Amsterdam, a British for a Dutch capitalist class, and London's Exchange Alley for the Amsterdam Bourse, and you have a fairly exact description of the role played by chartered companies (the Royal Africa Company, the South Sea Company, and the Hudson Bay Company foremost among them) in helping London to identify itself as Amsterdam's successor and to establish itself as one of the Atlantic's dominant spaces-of-flows.[6] Substitute for the chartered company the multinational corporation (the third primary institutional form around which Arrighi's wandering spaces-of-flows have established themselves), New York for London, and Wall Street for Exchange Alley, and the cycle of repetitions up to this point is complete.[7] London, at the beginning of an Atlantic cycle of accumulation, and New York at its end, thus define themselves quite clearly as capitals of this long twentieth century. But, the question remains, Liverpool? Clearly its role differs in some respect or degree.

The difference is in fact one of degree rather than one of kind: a difference that corresponds to the degree to which the economic functions which had been concentrated in London at the beginning of the eighteenth century were significantly distributed to, or duplicated within, a series of other British and Atlantic port cities by the end of the century. As these competitor cities broke the monopolies of the London-based chartered corporations and the other businesses which had secured its turn-of-the-century hegemony, they managed not so much to eclipse London as to repeat it elsewhere, to scatter, multiply, and serially recenter among the port cities of the Atlantic rim the commercial and financial operations which had initially been concentrated only in London, to substitute for what had been a solitary space-of-flows something like a circum-Atlantic archipelago of flows. When most successful, as in the case of Liverpool, the cities of this ocean-circling archipelago imitated quite exactly the model that had permitted London to emerge as the Atlantic's first dominant space-of-flows, the initial "first-city" of what more specialized economic histories call the "Financial Revolution" in Britain. As that revolution founded itself on the convergence of the British state's turn-of-the-century war-making needs; on the emergence of a banking system capable of debt funding the state's military adventures; on the rise of joint-stock companies trading with the East Indian, West Indian, and continental American possessions the crown was alternately acquiring and defending; on the development of a marine insurance industry competent to underwrite and so render manageable the risks of such cross-oceanic commerce; and on the rise of a money market speculating in the bonds, stocks, and other financial instruments of state, bank, and corporation, so cities such as Liverpool were to inherit and repeat this financial revolution in the form of slave-trading partnerships, insurance corporations, and banks.[8] By the end of the eighteenth century, there were counterparts of the South Sea Company, Lloyd's, and the Bank of England in Liverpool: intimately intertwined trading partnerships, insurance corporations, and lending agents with vast trans-Atlantic and inter-archipelagic networks of interest. To be sure, the Liverpool companies did not operate under those famous names, though one of the Liverpool names associated with all three of these businesses is at least a little familiar to us. It is the name of a family under whose signs of business Liverpool emerged as one of the capitals of an Atlantic world system, a family under whose purview were concentrated virtually all the commodity-distributing, debt-servicing, insurance-brokering, and money-managing functions of the commercial elites who are the sovereigns of Arrighi's spaces-of-flows. The name is Gregson, of the insurance firm of Gregson, Case, & Co., the William Gregson, Sons, and Co. Bank, and Gregson, Wilson, and Aspinal, trading partners and co-owners of the *Zong*.[9] If Liverpool is one of the capitals of the long Atlantic twentieth century, a Bisenzone trading fair of this cycle of accumulation, then in the final decades of the eighteenth century, the Gregsons were not only citizens of this Atlantic metropolis, but its Genoese masters.

*

Among the group of merchants who owned the *Zong* and claimed title to the 440 slaves penned within the ship's hold, and who, in the final months of 1781, were awaiting delivery of the 13,200 pounds sterling those slaves represented (though not, in all probability, with any undue degree of anxiety: the insurance contract they had signed having already underwritten the legal existence of this vast sum), the three Gregsons, William, James, and John, were undoubtedly the most influential party. Of these three men, the father, William, and his son, John, were the two most active in both the business and public life of the city. To say this is, of course, to assume some reliable standard of meaning for the notions of influence and activity, to assume that they adhere to and can be rationed out by some dependable scale of measure. The scale I have in mind is, in fact, the rather arbitrary scale of archival history, the scale that measures out volumes of action and degrees of influence by the quantity of documents a life leaves behind. Edward Wilson, James Aspinal, William, John, and James Gregson are, none of them, famous men. The two hundred years that has not so much passed between our time and theirs as accumulated itself within the cargo holds of our contemporaneity has, nevertheless, worn away much that is specifically rather than typically knowable about these men. Or, when it has preserved some particular trace of them, it has done so quite casually, haphazardly, preserving only a fragment here and there and littering its slight cache wherever it will. To say that William and John Gregson were the most active and influential members of this slave-trading partnership is in fact largely to say that they left more, or more discoverable, paper fragments of themselves behind, that a sift of Liverpool's eighteenth-century archives finds more flecks and traces that bear their particular names than the names of their colleagues. For the remainder of the portrait I want to construct of them, their city, and its place within that hyperspeculative moment that inaugurates our long contemporaneity, we must speculate on the basis of the typical.

If such a procedure carries its own somewhat over-obvious ironies, then it is a further irony that it was one of the businesses in which William Gregson and his sons were involved that formulated the modern science of knowledge devoted to resolving the terms of the relationship between what is particularly and what typically knowable. The insurance business in which the Gregsons were partners, from which they derived much of their wealth and on whose legal authority to secure the real existence of imaginary values the legal battles over the *Zong* were to depend, was a business that could only operate once its actuarial science had invented the "typical" (typical risk, typical life expectancy, typical value of a given commodity) and subordinated to the greater, because more abstract, truth of the typical all the vagaries and waywardnesses of the particular. Insurance, a quintessential business of finance capital and a foundational business of the financial revolution in Britain, is that enterprise through which the typical triumphs over the particular. It is the business that trades in, invests in, and speculates on the typical, lays all its bets on the typical, and profits from this investment. Insurance's condition of possibility is a way of seeing within the particularities of any given contemporary life, commodity, or venture it is called on to underwrite, the typical structures of mortality, exchange, or history that circumscribe these things and operate as their historically peculiar circumstances. Insurance, then, as I discuss at greater length in the sections that follow, is something like an applied, if simple-minded, historicism, a "setting-to-work," for the market, of the historicist capacity to situate an individual work, object, or event within the determining historical circumstances of its age, to discover in the individual not what is exceptional *to* but what is typical *of* a given historical moment.[10] The actuary tables foundational to insurance practice are not just a set of numbers. They are, as Lukács says of Sir Walter Scott's superbly historicized characters, the "embodiment of historical-social types"; "the typically human terms in which great historical trends become tangible"; or, one might say, the expression of historicism not as a literary but as a financial practice.[11]

If, through the historicizing operations of this study, the Gregsons can come to us more as typical than as particular figures (typical of their class, typical of their time, typical, as Lukács has it, of the historical peculiarities of their age, and typical, as I want to suggest, of a capital culture that extends from their age to our own), if we can thus know them primarily as they, in their capacity as traders, could know the slaves they bought and sold, that is, not so much individually as from the aggregate of historical circumstances they embody, then the irony is that in knowing them so we also know them and their affairs much as they, in their work as insurance brokers, knew the individuals, commodities, and ventures they were willing to underwrite. We know them, that is, primarily as the typicalizing mind of insurance knows the world. To know them in this way is also of course to know them as characters in a novel, to know them as those typical representatives of a time that Fredric Jameson, in his reading of Lukács, insists the realist novel exists to create and to teach us to read.[12] This, in turn, indicates not only that we have something to learn about the bidirectional flow of insurance and historicism but that the argument I earlier sketched, the argument that suggested that the verdict of the Guildhall court could have been what it was, that a jury could find that the insurance value attached to the *Zong* and its slaves was real, and payable, because both the imagination of the court and the forms of value it credited as real had been novelized, requires its own dialectical adjustment. For the joint investment of insurance, historicism, and the novel in the concept of the typical should at least lead us to entertain the possibility that the typicalizing mind of the eighteenth-century novel, the historicist mind of insurance, and the actuarial mind of historicism do not simply happen to emerge at the same historical moment but to some degree license, depend on, and ensure one another — or, perhaps more to the point, that what insures our capacity to deduce from the scant surviving particulars of the family, business, and civic life of William Gregson and his sons a typical knowledge of the speculative finance culture of eighteenth-century Liverpool is a complex mix of historicist method, actuarial science, and novelized critical imaginary which helped to permit the emergence of that finance culture in the first place and which our own hyper-financialized "present" inherits from this eighteenth-century "past."

I am not suggesting that William Gregson and his sons are characters in a novel or composites drawn from some late-eighteenth-century actuarial table, only that this is one of the primary ways that we know how to know them, that this is a way of knowing fundamental to the speculative revolutions of Arrighi's moments of high finance capital, and that it is, in part, the persistence of this way of knowing from the late eighteenth century to the late twentieth that at once enables the historicizing operations of this text *and* identifies the present moment of its writing less as a successor present to the late eighteenth century than as a moment in which that "past" finds itself inherited.

*

If the late twentieth century inherits, repeats, and intensifies the late eighteenth, then it does so quite precisely, James Chandler suggests, by resituating as one of the dominant epistemologies of "its" age a historicist sensibility that was a dominant feature of eighteenth-century intellectual practice. It is not, on this account, simply history that repeats itself, but historicism. On a general level of abstraction Chandler's argument indicates that history repeats itself not as a sequence of recurrent events but through the reanimation of antecedent intellectual methods and genres of knowing. The eighteenth century, he more particularly argues, carries itself *into* and writes itself *upon* the late twentieth century precisely to the extent that this "subsequent" moment reappropriates and refashions the generic protocols of that historicist method which helped to define eighteenth-century intellectual culture. This is, obviously enough, a Jamesonian argument, one which relies both on Jameson's analysis of the uncanny, nonsynchronous persistence of generic forms from one moment to another and on the conception of historicism as a "genre" of knowledge. It is also, and equally evidently, an argument which corresponds with my account of the dialectical recuperation and intensification of an eighteenth-century what-has-been within a late-twentieth-century "now" — and is thus, also, at the broadest level, amenable to a Benjaminian reading of history. Where Chandler differs from the account I have thus far provided is in his field of evidence and his object of emphasis, in his suggestion that we should look to the workings of historicist method rather than to the operations of finance capital for evidence of a "repetition" between "the post-French-Revolution period in Britain and the critical categories of our own moment" (a "repetition" that I have further been suggesting we should regard less as a repetition from one moment to another than as the rearticulation at either end of a single, long-durational moment of a common and period-defining set of epistemological and capital protocols).[13] That the field of evidence which is Chandler's object of inquiry and the field which I have thus far emphasized can, in fact *should*, be articulated in relation to one another; that the concurrent rise of historicism and finance capital at either end of a "long twentieth century" should be regarded as something other than a coincidence; that historicism and finance capital serve as one another's mutual, dialectical, conditions of possibility; that finance capital, a particular type of historicism, *and* a particular form of novelistic discourse collectively articulate a "theoretical realism" which I hold to be the key component of the speculative culture with which the long twentieth century begins and ends, are also parts of my argument.

For the moment however, I want to emphasize just two points. The first is that like "the novel," the term "historicism," contains a number of variant subforms, two of which are central to my account: the "romantic historicism" that is Chandler's primary object of inquiry, which he suggests arises at roughly the same time *as* and is formally analogous *to* the historical novel, and which he indicates is recuperated by the "new historicism" of the late twentieth century; and what, for convenience, I will call an "actuarial historicism," which arises in the half century immediately prior to a romantic historicism, is roughly analogous in its fundamental epistemological protocols to the early- and mid-eighteenth-century realist novel (and, in Michael McKeon's terms, to that "naive empiricism" characteristic of the early realist novel), and finds itself refashioned and rearticulated within the "High Theory" (both structuralist and deconstructive) of the quite recent "past."[14] Actuarial historicism, the realist novel, and high speculative theory operate within the epistemological domain of "theoretical realism" and can be seen, in varying ways and to varying degrees, to function as counterparts and secret-sharers of finance capital. Romantic historicism, the historical novel, and the new historicism, conversely, articulate themselves as antagonists of a globalizing finance capital. To the extent that they are "realist," they share a melancholy realism.[15]

The second point worth emphasizing is that despite their differences, what holds a romantic and an actuarial historicism together — what, indeed, permits us to speak of them as variant forms of a common genre — is their common investment in the "period," the "situation," and the "type." To "historicize" any given event, text, or phenomenon, as Chandler maintains, is, at first glance, to place that thing within its determinate moment, to "situate" it, in Lukács's terms, within the "peculiar historical" confines of "its age," and then to read the character of that thing as, to some lesser or greater degree, determined by its situation, to read it thus as both a type for and typical of its situation (the immediate and connotatively thick-descriptive form of the period or age).[16] In order to do so, however, a historicist method requires a detailed knowledge of the situation, period, or age in question. More fundamentally, it requires the very *concept* of the situation or period of time as an abstract category of analysis. A fundamental preliminary to the act of placing an object within its situation, Chandler thus suggests, is the invention of the categories of the situation and the period themselves. Absent those categories historicist method could not exist. Historicism's fundamental task is then dual: to place objects within their situations and to invent situations and periods of time in which to place objects.[17] Its tendency, however, is to mask this second (in fact, preliminary) operation, to treat situations not as artificial forms of time which it has invented but as natural entities it has discovered. The construction of the category of the situation and the period and the work of detailing the content of particular situations or periods are, nevertheless, historicism's precondition. And it is in the early and middle decade of the eighteenth century, according to Chandler, that we can see the preconditional category of the "situation" beginning to emerge. He discovers this within a set of enterprises devoted to documenting the "state" of Britain within a given time frame, generally a single year, as is the case with the series of volumes *The Political State of Great Britain*, first published in 1711, and subsequent annuals such as William Burke's series *The Annual Register: Or a View of the History, Politics, and Literature of the Year*, which Burke began editing in 1758.[18] But the same situationalist mindset also apprehends the reduced time frames of the month (particularly in the form of the metropolitan periodicals fundamental to the emergence of a public sphere whose animated, contentious discourse constellated itself around an ongoing autohistoricizing portraiture of the contemporary state of society) and the day: above all in the newspapers whose parallel-column printing of the news contributed, as Chandler following Benedict Anderson argues, to a simultaneity and contemporaneity effect utterly apposite to a historicist framing of time.[19] To this list of those cultural forms whose typicalizing, situational discourse licenses the emergence of a historicist consciousness, Chandler also adds that novelistic "commitment to contemporaneity" that J. Paul Hunter associates with the early English novel, and I would add the practice of insurance, whose actuarial science and invention of the "average" and the typical perhaps most clearly reveal a preromantic historicism's intimate entanglements with the operations of finance capital.[20]

If historicist practices begin, both literally and figuratively, with the invention of situations, the situation itself, however, depends on the invention of the typical and the type. And this is true of all the variant forms of historicism, not just that appropriate to insurance proper. For the explanatory power which a historicist account desires from its particularized historical situations is a power directly indexed to its capacity to reveal that the particular object which it considers and which it has placed within its determinate moment, is, to some significant extent, typical of that moment. At the same time, however, because the contours of the "moment" itself need to be defined — because periods, as per Chandler's argument, are made, not found — the situation itself has to be typified. And to accomplish this, to define the situation that will then be taken (at least in part) to define the objects it circumscribes, historicist method first requires a series of concrete "types," an array of typical events, lives, texts, what-have-you, from which to deduce the "broad historical trends" typically representative of a given moment, period, or situation. This, of course, demands a wildly circular, not to say tautological, form of reasoning. Or perhaps, and less pejoratively, it implies that historicism must work both inductively and deductively at once, that it operates, simultaneously, from the outside in (as it accounts for the nature of some particular thing by reading that thing as something coded or written by its circumambient situation) and from the inside out (as it constructs the surrounding situation which will be taken to account for some thing by reading the nature of that situation off an imbricated set of typical events, texts, or lives).[21] In either case — and as Chandler reveals the problem "as to which comes first, the characters or the age, the bodies or the type" is hopelessly vexed —

historicism must be understood not only as a means of accounting for phenomena by situating them within their moment and as a mode of constructing moments that account for phenomena, but also as a genre that typicalizes phenomena as exemplary representatives of their moments by deducing moments from a range of always-already typical phenomena.[22] Historicism, to put it most briefly, thus entails not only the two-way production of situations but the two-way generation of types.

This is important for at least two reasons. The "figure . . . of the culturally representative type" is vitally significant to Chandler because it is the enduring significance of the typical to historicist method that provides him with the crucial link between a postrevolutionary romantic historicism and a broadly contemporary historicist practice.[23] The typical is *the* link that secures his genealogy of historicism, that permits him to trace a line of connection from Scott to Jameson via Lukács. "Thus," he notes, "when Jameson takes up the key question of 'typicality' in Lukács's theory of the historical novel he stresses that for Lukács, 'realist characters are distinguished from those in other kinds of literature by their *typicality*; they stand in other words for something larger and more meaningful than themselves, than their own isolated individual destinies.' "[24] The typical which Jameson finds in Lukács, who in his turn had discovered it in Scott, then becomes for Jameson, Chandler insists, the crucial concept "that links precisely the issues of historical situationism and historiographical constructivism into a single problematic, which Jameson associates, precisely, with Lukács' account of the historical novel and with the emergence of what might be properly called a 'Marxist Criticism.' "[25]

A central, recurrent, ideologeme in Chandler's history of the generic persistence of historicism from the late eighteenth century to the late twentieth, the typical is also crucial to my account, both because I follow Chandler in indexing an overarching historicism to the figures of the situation, the period, and the type, and because a more specific history of the typical is crucial to the distinction I have made between an actuarial and a romantic historicism.[26] Both of these are discourses on and of the type, but they construct different types of "type." The types on which and with which an actuarial historicism goes to work function as the measurable, abstract, aggregate representatives of what are taken to be contemporaneous, *extant* phenomena: the "Britain" whose contemporary state is gauged in a series of annual registers as the implied aggregate of all the news and events these texts report; the London criminal class, whose "culturally representative type" is Defoe's Moll Flanders; the sugar, tobacco, slaves, indeed the full range of eighteenth-century commodities which, in the memorable phrase of John Weskett's 1781 *A Com-*

plete Digest of the Theory, Laws, and Practice of Insurance, "have at some time become the subjects of insurance," and which exist for insurance not as individual material things but as the numeric contents of one or other table of "averages."[27] The romantic type, conversely, functions as the representative of something that no longer exists, something that once existed but, by the moment it enters historicist awareness, is now lost: most famously, perhaps, the "Highlanders" who inhabit Scott's texts not as the representative types of a contemporary Scotland but as the typical representatives of a lost time, as a "horde of ghosts," in Saree Makdisi's terms, "issuing forth from the past."[28] In either case, the type is the form of existence of an amaterial, nongraspable entity, a substitute. In one case the type substitutes an average abstraction for a variegated array of actually existing things ("Sugar" for all the actual sugar granules circulating through the circum-Atlantic economy, "Moll Flanders" for all the pickpockets roaming the streets of London); while in the other case the type substitutes a representative phantom for an entity which once existed but is now lost (Scott's "Old Mortality" for all those Covenanting Scottish Presbyterians vanquished in the Highlands). As representative substitutes, both the actuarial and the romantic type are thus implicated within a representational economy of exchange, though again, in quite different ways: the actuarial type endorses the exchange of the "real" for the "theoretical" life of things by avowing the real existence of theoretical abstractions (hence "theoretical realism"); the romantic type, oppositely, implicitly resists the exchange of life for death by seeking to return dead things to life and insisting on the affective reality of the exemplary ghosts it calls from the vasty deeps (hence what I am calling "melancholy realism").

It is as the former, actuarial type of "type" that I am suggesting the *Zong* slaves would have existed for William Gregson, for a finance capitalism trained to acknowledge the real existence of the abstract value they represented and for the insurance contract that endorsed that value prior to its confirmation in some "actual" market of commodity exchange. *And* it is as such a type of "type" that I am arguing Gregson and the slaves, in part, exist for us, as, through the historicizing operations of this text, I attempt to abstract some measure of their "real" existence from the general "historical trends" of their moment, attempting at once to know them by reading their "isolated, individual" destinies off the typical situations in which they were encompassed and to know their moment by positing the voyage of the *Zong* as precisely the type of event in which the "peculiar historical characteristics" of that moment are revealed.

*

The problem of the typical, as we shall see, is not only a problem of method (for historicism), business (for insurance), or characterization (for the novel). It is also a problem for memory and for ethics, a problem most intense, in the case at hand, on the far side of the voyage of the *Zong*, a problem for Granville Sharp in his letter to the Lords Commissioners, for William Wilberforce in the 1806 slave trade debates in the House of Commons, for J. M. W. Turner in his celebrated 1840 canvas *Slavers throwing overboard the dead and the dying*, and for a wide range of later artists and writers, all of whom, in their different ways, have struggled to understand what it means to remember the events that took place aboard the *Zong* as a singular or as a typical atrocity. The minor ironies I have been discussing pale before the more brutal irony that for most of these figures, and frequently for this text also, the value of the *Zong* to an ethics of historical memory depends on its being remembered as an abstractly typical rather than a singular atrocity, that, in this case at least, historical memory tends to insure the value of what it remembers by submitting *its* knowledge of the world to the mind of insurance, by discovering in the par-ticularities of this event "the typically human terms in which great historical trends become tangible."[29] To find that William Gregson survives his death as little more than one of those typical lives he spent his career buying, selling, underwriting and, if he was a consumer of his age's novels, reading about, is one thing: only the slightest revenge for irony. To discover that so many projects of remembrance have held the fate of the slaves aboard his ship worth recording because of the "great historical trends" their deaths typify is quite another. For the more the value of such recollection depends, to paraphrase my own earlier formulation, on "seeing within the particularities of this event the typical structures of knowledge, exchange, or history that circumscribe it, operate as its historically peculiar circumstances," and situate it within the great historical trends of its moment, is the more this form of remembrance models its theory of value on the evaluative protocols of that insurance busi-ness which underwrote the value of these slaves to their "owners" and de-manded that that value would survive their deaths.

This irony, this ironic triumph of what Hegel more generally called "the cunning of reason" (that operation by which, as the Absolute works itself out through history, the "too trifling value" of the "particular" and the "individ-ual" invariably find themselves "sacrificed and abandoned" to the "general idea [that] . . . remains in the background") is something this text must strug-gle to keep in mind even as it seeks to understand the events that took place on the *Zong* by situating them within the "great historical trends" of their ex-tended "moment."[30] And perhaps that minor reformulation is in fact key.

Perhaps a necessary if not a sufficient means of eluding this "cunning" is to reverse flow, to read not *from* the event *for* the trend, not from the particular in order to derive the typical, but to read the other way around, to read the typical in order to make sense of this particular, the trend to begin to comprehend this event. Or indeed, as ever, to read as best as possible both ways at once; to read, that is, dialectically; to work the "trifling" particular and the general idea against one another as we reenter the archive and reexamine the sift to discover what traces the *Zong*, its slaves, and its owners have left behind.

*

The Gregson family enters the Liverpool archives at almost exactly the moment in which the city truly begins to establish its presence as one of the Atlantic's dominant spaces-of-flows. Their ascendance largely mirrors the city's, their family's biography recapitulates its eighteenth-century history. And at the heart of both the family's rise and the city's was the trans-Atlantic slave trade.

William Gregson's name first appears in the archives of the slave trade in 1744, when, as a young and entirely obscure merchant with an interest in a rope-making business, he purchased the fourth largest share of the just built slave ship *Carolina*. In electing to invest his capital so, Gregson would neither have been acting uncommonly nor, quite yet, typically. The *Liverpool Merchant*, which had left harbor on October 10, 1699, and unloaded a cargo of 220 slaves in Barbados the following September, was the first ship the city had outfitted for the slave trade.[31] Over the next quarter century Liverpool's involvement in the trade grew slowly. By 1725 there was an average of just three Liverpool-based voyages a year carrying five to six hundred slaves. By 1730, however, those numbers had doubled, and by 1740 tripled once again. By 1744, when Gregson made his investment in the *Carolina*, the ship would have been one of about thirty Liverpool vessels engaged in the trade.[32] From his perspective, Gregson had chosen his vessel well. The *Carolina* departed from the Liverpool docks on August 8, 1744, made a successful voyage to the African coast, loaded a cargo of 348 slaves and departed for Kingston, Jamaica, which it reached on March 19, 1745. Two hundred and eighty-four slaves survived the voyage. Sixty-four did not. But the profit from the sale of those who did, even divided among the ship's five investors, was enough. Gregson took his share and, the records indicate, reinvested it three years later in the eighth and smallest share of the *Elizabeth* and, for the first time, signed on as the primary owner of a slaving vessel, the *Blackburn*.[33] It was a pattern he was to follow for the rest of his life.

His rise as a slave trader during those years was anything but slow. In 1748, the year after he had purchased a majority interest in the *Blackburn*, Gregson became the primary owner of a second ship, the *Clayton*. One year later he acquired two more vessels, the *Nancy* and the *Salisbury*. In those three years alone his ships acquired 1,009 slaves for transport to the Caribbean. In the years that followed the numbers only went up.

In 1750 Gregson's ships loaded and transported 880 slaves.
In 1751: 400 slaves.
In 1752: 1,580 slaves.
In 1753: 637 slaves.
In 1754: 1,004 slaves.
In 1755: 1,056 slaves.
In 1757: 465 slaves.
In 1758: 1,361 slaves.
In 1759: 795 slaves.
In 1760: 440 slaves.

Over the course of the decade, Gregson's vessels had transported over 8,000 slaves. The pace of the next 10 years was equally frenetic. His captains bought and transported another 7,000 slaves. Over the full span of his slave-trading career, Gregson was to be the primary owner of 19 slave ships, which performed a total of 52 voyages and carried 19,183 people into captivity. But even those numbers represent less than half his total involvement in the trade. The Lloyd's shipping lists, which are the primary source of information for his trading activities, indicate that over the course of his life Gregson invested as both a majority and a minority owner of slaving vessels. In total, they record that he was either a primary or a secondary investor in 177 voyages which carried 60,996 slaves, of whom 51,082 survived the middle passage.[34]

*

The consequences of the subtraction are appalling.

Nine thousand, nine hundred and fourteen of the human beings who were taken aboard ships Gregson either owned or co-owned did not reach the Americas alive.

All of them, and none of them, typical human beings.

*

Meanwhile — while these fatal totals accumulated; while one man, one woman, one man, one girl after another swelled the tallies; while one singular, absolute human life after another was written off as a cost of business or a successful investment; while the numbing parade of numbers by which we demographize, degrade, and seek to grasp history passes before our eyes — William Gregson was growing rich. And so was his city and the regional economy it had begun to dominate. As Gregson increased his involvement in the slave trade, so did the other merchants of the city. Between 1725 and 1750 Liverpool slaving vessels embarked on 444 voyages carrying over 120,000 slaves. Over the next quarter century those numbers tripled again, a growth sparked both by the vast profits to be made and by the abolition in 1750 of the Royal Africa Company's chartered monopoly on the trade.[35] Henceforth the trade was under the official control of the newly established Company of Merchants Trading to Africa, a holding corporation run by a committee of nine merchants representing the cities of London, Bristol, and Liverpool, each of which were entitled to appoint three delegates.[36] The establishment of this tri-local Company of Merchants, which received an annual grant of ten thousand pounds from Parliament to maintain the west African slave factories previously under the control of the Royal Africa Company, served as something like a governmental license for capital devolution, an official permit for that process through which, by exploiting their growing dominance in the slave trade, Bristol and Liverpool were to establish themselves as London's new commercial counter-cities. A formal, if belated, license for Bristol and Liverpool to break London's monopoly, the Company also represented the strategy through which the government sought formally to link these three trading and commercial centers not only to itself and to one another but to the slave coast of Africa and the Crown's holdings in the Caribbean and the Americas. An Atlantic cycle of accumulation may not begin in 1750, but it and the archipelagic network of port cities that were to preside over its rise and to function as its spaces-of-flows certainly assume greater form and visibility with the establishment of this Company of Merchants that was to be to the second half of the eighteenth century what the Royal African and South Sea Companies had been to the first.

Liverpool certainly profited from the founding of the Company. By midcentury it was already providing close to half of all the British ships involved in the slave trade.[37] Over the next fifty years Liverpool-owned vessels were to perform the triangular circuit of the trade over three thousand times, to carry just over a million slaves across the Atlantic, to return the profit from their sale to Britain in the form of rum, sugar, and other colonial commodities, and to reinvest the proceeds from these goods in yet more slaving ventures.[38] The enormous amount of money to be made in the trade produced vast riches for scores of the city's great merchant families and, according to contemporary accounts, a general frenzy among the population at large. An anonymous pamphlet of 1797, whose author had estimated the profit on each slave sold in the Americas to bring a return of just less than 30 percent on a speculator's initial investment, describes a city near unanimous in its desperation to claim some share of the riches: "This great annual return of wealth may be said to pervade the whole town, increasing the fortunes of the principal adventurers, and contributing to the support of the majority of the inhabitants; almost every man in Liverpool is a merchant, and he who cannot send a bale [for exchange on the slave market] will send a bandbox, it will therefore create little astonishment, that the attractive African meteor has from time to time so dazzled their ideas, that almost every order of people is interested in a Guinea cargo."[39]

Even those without a direct stake in some voyage or another profited amply from the trade. The ship-building industry in Liverpool exploded, as did textile manufacturing in adjacent Manchester and the road- and canal-building interests which provided the transportation links between the Liverpool port and the manufacturing base which produced the bulk of the commodities it brought to the African market to exchange for slaves. In 1739, Manchester had exported 14,000 pounds worth of goods. By 1760, its export trade stood at 100,000 pounds; by 1779, seven years after the Bridgewater Canal linking Manchester to Liverpool was opened, the figure was over 300,000 pounds. Thirty percent of that total was shipped to Africa for the slave market. Fifty percent went directly to the Caribbean and the Americas.[40] Important as the Bridgewater Canal was (it cut transportation costs between Manchester and Liverpool by over 80 percent), it was only one of scores of building projects that utterly transformed the city over the second half of the century. Over that time the city built a series of canals to Leeds, Bolton, Oldham, and Halifax, another to the Severn, Dee, and Trent rivers, and linked all its northern canals to the Thames through the Grand Junction Canal. It constructed four massive new docks (the Salthouse dock, George's dock, the King's dock, and the Queen's dock); widened legions of the city's streets, built the churches of St. Thomas, St. Paul, and St. John; and erected a set of lighthouses, the Liverpool Infirmary, and an asylum for the blind.[41]

And in 1754, just as this orgy of construction was getting underway, the Corporation of Liverpool (the city's governing body) rewarded themselves for their recent success in securing a third of the seats on the governing committee of the Company of Merchants by building a new Exchange. The Exchange, which also functioned as the city's town hall, was an elegant building, a rise of Doric and Corinthian columns capped by a pillared dome, a recognizable, neoclassical, period piece, but also a copy of London's Royal Exchange, an architectural boast of Liverpool's new status as London's financial double. The Exchange's architects may have been commissioned to offer proof of the city's success in reproducing London, but they had also been instructed to place a "local" signature on the edifice. The Corporation ordered a set of friezes attached to the façade of the Exchange and commissioned for those friezes images of the city's success, emblems of its rise and place in the world, bas-reliefs of what had generated the vast amounts of money circulating through Liverpool and accumulating within it: a set of African heads, circling the Exchange.[42]

*

The details of Eric Williams' *Capitalism and Slavery* may have been contested by succeeding generations of economic historians, his portrayal of an entire national economy built on Britain's involvement in the slave trade deemed too exhaustive in its claims.[43] The eighteenth-century merchant and political classes of Liverpool, however, were under no illusions about what had secured their city's rise, its emergence as one of the dominant commercial and financial centers of the age. The slave portraits decorating and surrounding the Exchange speak mutely but eloquently to the origins of this exorbitantly plentiful regime of accumulation. They suggest something else also. Bolstered to the walls of the city's Exchange, casting their frozen glance over a port city that had greater traffic with the "Guinea" coast than it did with the interior of England, these slave heads imply that over the course of the eighteenth century Liverpool was less the island's city than the ocean's, that the economy over which it presided and whose circuits of exchange it regulated was less national than transmarine, that the cycle of accumulation for which its Exchange was an orchestrating space-of-flows was less British than Atlantic. Any mid- or late-century citizen who failed to appreciate this knowledge had only to examine the façade of the city's Exchange to be reminded. Though, indeed, they need not have done even that. Like their countrymen throughout an island that was increasingly being remade not only in London's image but in Liverpool's, they need only have retrieved one of the coins from their pocket or purse, only have held in their hand this "guinea," to encounter a reminder of the oceanic trade that had become fundamental to Britain's prosperity even as it linked the nation's capital culture to an extranational, circum-Atlantic geography of exchange.

The African heads circling the Liverpool Exchange bear witness to the enormous profitability of a circum-Atlantic trade in commodities, a triangular trade we are accustomed to thinking of almost exclusively as a trade in *goods*: a trade in textiles and other midlands merchandise on the first vector of exchange, of human property in the passage from Africa to the Caribbean and the Americas, and of rum, sugar, coffee, and tobacco from the far side of the Atlantic back to Britain. There is nothing wrong with this picture. It is an accurate outline representation of the major circuits of the commodity culture that, in terms of pure temporal longevity, dominated this as any other cycle of accumulation. What it disregards, however, is something else the African heads on the Liverpool Exchange at least metaphorically figure: the finance culture that preceded, enabled, and secured this circuit of cross-Atlantic commodity exchange; the bank, stock, credit, insurance, and loan-driven money forms of value that underwrote this cycle of accumulation, presided over its rise, and, as Arrighi's general model predicts, have returned to dominate what Braudel calls its moment of "autumn." The trade in commodities may be the most tangible form taken by the trans-Atlantic slave trade and the long twentieth century it has bequeathed us, but its conditions of possibility are the speculative, abstract, money-into-money trades that Liverpool, in duplicating London, inherited from the turn-of-the-century financial revolution. And chief among these were the trades in insurance, stocks, bills, and all the variant forms of "paper money" derived from the establishment of a modern, credit-issuing system of banking.

∗

In a brief section from the first chapter of *Tarrying with the Negative* entitled "Money and Subjectivity," Slavoj Žižek continues his discussion of the shift from a pre-Enlightenment subject he designates as S to a Kantian subject he designates as $ ("the move from S to $ entails a radical shift in the very notion of the subject's self-identity: in it, I identify myself most to that very void which a moment ago threatened to swallow the most precious particular kernel of my being") with these comments:

> It would be of great theoretical interest to establish the conceptual link between this genesis of self-consciousness and the modern notion of paper money. In the middle ages money was a commodity which so to speak guaranteed its own value: a gold coin — like any other commodity — was simply worth its "actual" value. How did we get from that value to today's paper money, which is intrinsically worthless, yet universally used to purchase commodities? Brian Rotman

demonstrated the necessity of an intermediate term, the so called "imaginary money . . . deictically rooted in the signature of a particular named payee." . . . In order to arrive at paper money as we know it today this deictic promise with concrete dates and names has to be depersonalized into a promise made to the anonymous "bearer" to pay the gold equivalent of the sum written on the paper-money — thus, the anchoring, the link to a concrete individual was cut loose. And the subject who came to recognize itself as this anonymous "bearer" is the very subject of self-consciousness . . . [a subject that] has to relate to itself, to conceive of itself, as (to) an empty "bearer" and to perceive his empirical features which constitute the positive content of his particular "person" as a contingent variable. This shift is again the very shift from S to $.[44]

The visual homology between Žižek's two versions of $ may be a little too nice, but the question he raises is a serious one, not least because it permits him to imply, if not fully to articulate, a counternarrative for the emergence of the modern subject and, hence, also a counterground for the origins of that philosophical discourse "on and of modernity" whose two-hundred year durée is probably the most familiar form of that extended eighteenth- to late-twentieth-century contemporaneity that I am arguing we continue to inhabit.[45]

If modernity, or at least the modern subject posited by Enlightenment philosophy, can be said to begin sometime in the final decades of the eighteenth century, if it begins with the emergence of that mode of subjectivity that Žižek designates $, then our standard accounts, and the account with which Žižek has been working up to that moment in which he indexes the emergence of this cancelled subject to the rise of paper money, generally identify its rise (and define the "historical situation" that serves as its historical condition of possibility) with the events surrounding the French Revolution.[46] Žižek, as I have said, has essentially followed this explanatory tradition up to the moment in which he turns his attention to the rise of paper money. And he has done so largely by following Hegel's account of the role that revolutionary terror played in reformulating the subject's alienation of itself in its dealings with the social substance of the state. Neither Hegel's full argument nor Žižek's account of it require rehearsing here. The crucial point for Žižek is that faced with the absolute terror of the revolutionary state and the state's arrogation of the right to claim the power of its subjects' lives purely in the name of a collective moral and ethical imperative, the subject finds itself for the first time obliged to contemplate a "non-equivalent exchange."[47]

Under prior feudal, sacral, or courtly regimes of public virtue, the subject,

Hegel suggests, alienated itself, surrendered its right to self-possession, in exchange either for honor, the promise of Heaven, or some other reward. "However," as Žižek insists, "when we reach the apogee of this dialectic, 'absolute freedom,' the exchange between the particular and the universal Will, the subject gets nothing in exchange for everything. . . . The historical epoch which stands for this moment of 'absolute freedom' is, of course, the Jacobinical Reign of Terror" (23). Under that Jacobinical regime of "absolute freedom," the subject is required to alienate itself to the sovereignty of the state not in the name of some compensation or promise of reward but in the name of an abstract collective project of freedom. Nothing else is offered in exchange for the right to continued existence the subject forfeits in the name of that project. The subject negates its right to possess itself and secures nothing but the state's demand for that negation in return. As Hegel argues, however, that negation of self-possession, that canceling of the singularity of the subject before the collectivity of the "Universal Will" does not so much annul subjectivity as reconfigure it. The subject, henceforward, becomes an anonymous, interchangeable bearer of a universal will-to-freedom, internalizes this collective categorical imperative, relates to itself not as to a particular desiring will but as to the self-addressed addressee of a universal project, typicalizes itself, so to speak, as an abstract representative of the universal.[48] Hence the pre-Enlightenment subject S abnegates its individual particularity, motive, desire, and will and recodes itself as the Kantian subject $: a canceled particular, a "barred" singular that addresses itself not by name but in the name of Man and the Rights of Man.

That this subject $ is not only an analogue of the typical form of personhood available to the theoretical realism of an actuarial historicism but an analogue of that abstract value form typical of finance capital seems evident. Žižek's observation implies more, however, than an analogic relation between these sets of terms (the Enlightenment subject $, the typical subject of eighteenth-century novelistic, public sphere, and actuarial discourse, and the period's dominant value form). It implies that at least the first and last of these terms (Kant's $ and finance capital's $) might be causally related to one another or, more precisely, that the individual whose particularity is negated by the address of finance capital might compete with the individual negated by revolutionary terror as the paradigm of modern subjectivity, and, hence, that it is to finance capital rather than to the French Revolution (or to finance capital in partnership with the revolution) that we should look for the birthplace of the modern subject, the origins of a philosophical discourse on and of the modern, and the origins of our long contemporaneity.

Žižek does not mention Burke in the course of this discussion. Unsurprisingly perhaps—we certainly do not tend to think of Burke as one of Žižek's intellectual precursors. But this is, nevertheless, a Burkean argument, at least in its etiology of the modern subject if not in its ultimate appraisal of the health or desirability of that subject. Burke's *Reflections on the Revolution in France*, as J. G. A. Pocock has taken pains to stress, stages its famous defense of the local, the customary, and the inherited in opposition not to a unitary regime of abstraction but against a double logic of speculative reason: the speculative, universalizing, anticustomary logic of an Enlightenment theory of the human and the speculative operations of a non-property-based, credit-driven, restructuring of capital.[49] In either case, whether manifest as Enlightenment reason or finance capital, the true culprit for Burke is a departicularizing, degenealogizing mode of speculation which operates by creating a set of equivalences between entities and abstracting from those now-equivalent entities a "general equivalent" which permits their endless and boundless interexchangeability: the general equivalents in these cases being "man" and "money."[50] Burke's self-appointed task, then, is to defend the discrete character and the specific historical embeddedness of what are, for him, ultimately nonfungible entities. Thus custom and landed property are, in effect, opposed to abstract theory and the bourse, to those speculative spaces-of-flow trading in concepts on one hand and paper money on the other.

Abstract reason and Exchange Alley, on this account, are not merely analogues of one another. They predicate one another, serve as mutual conditions of possibility within that overarching speculative revolution which organizes abstract reason as a method for generating conceptual general equivalents and licenses a finance capitalism that has learned to profit from the trade in abstract values. If either abstract reason or finance capital do, however, establish any sort of causal precedence over the other with regard to the emergence of a novel modern subject, then it is, Burke intermittently suggests, the latter which enables the triumph of the former, finance capital which secures the exchange economy of theoretical reason. The decoupling of public personhood from those inherited and landed forms of property which tie individuals to a fixed, traditional community of obligations and the concomitant collapse of a republican practice of virtue as the fate of a citizenry is increasingly attached not to the defense of local interests (and the interests of the locale) but to the speculative rise and fall of the value of paper monies function, Burke suggests, as the preconditions for the invention of an abstract, anonymous, mode of personhood invested not in the inalienable claims of the locale but in the well-being of an anonymous collective.[51]

It is not simply revolutionary terror, Burke suggests, which alienates the subject from its signature particularity and binds it to a collective will. It is the market. It is not only the Place de la Révolution, the tumbril, and the guillotine which convinces a populace to surrender its right to self-possession. The blade, rather, permits the state to confirm what the market has already accomplished. It signals the dystopic completion of a project whose original motivation is not fear but desire, a project which convinces the subject to invest itself in a co-lateral network of interests by tying that investment to the positive rather than the negative promise of a "non-equivalent exchange," by convincing subjects to exchange ownership of themselves and their fates for the speculative riches they hope will accompany their investments.[52] Rather than finding itself enriched by this "non-equivalent exchange" (a phrase which strikes me as definitive of the ideology and, when "successful," of the operations of finance capital), the subject, Burke suggests, finds itself annulled, cancelled, barred. The guillotine may confirm that erasure, but it is a belated messenger. The terror it represents is at once irresistible and pointless: a grand theatricalization of what has already been accomplished, a belated introduction of a quivering, denuded humanity to the "fatal beauty" at the far end of the speculative sublime, a spectacle of demystification in which the beguiling "Lady Credit" who presided over the century's capital imaginary unveils herself as the guillotine's gorgon harpy ("In the groves of *their* academy [the "sophisters, oeconomists, and calculators"], at the end of every visto, you see nothing but the gallows").[53] Thus, by way of an extended paraphrase, Burke. That Žižek has some similar account in mind, one that aligns him not only with Burke but, again surprisingly, with J. G. A. Pocock — whose work over the past several decades has amounted to a systematic elaboration of this Burkean insight — is evident from the scattered comments in which Žižek suggests that this finance-capital-generated subject $ "*emerges the very moment when the individual loses its support in the network of tradition. It* [this subject $] coincides with the void that remains after the framework of symbolic memory is suspended."[54]

The problem of the modern subject however is not only one of its origin and rise but one of its spread, not only one of its local emergence but one of its global reproduction. Žižek's brief comments ask us not simply to reveal how this subject $ originates but to indicate how it becomes modernity's typical mode of subjectivity, how it is universalized, how it travels from the speculative zones of an original set of metropolitan spaces-of-flow and secures for itself, and for the "modernity" it indexes, an ever more global theater of address. Kant's answer is to link the universalization of this subject, and hence of both modernity and the promise of "progress," to the recurrent "spectacle" of the French Revolution, the "event" whose extrametropolitan dissemination he insists will secure that subjective identification with a collective project of freedom on which a progressive and cosmopolitan modernity depends. As he has it in his essay "An Old Question Raised Again: Is the Human Race Constantly Progressing?":

> This event consists neither in momentous deeds nor crimes committed by men whereby what was great among men is made small or what was small is made great, nor in ancient splendid political structures which vanish as if by magic while others come forth in their place as if from the depths of the earth. No, nothing of the sort. It is simply the mode of thinking of the spectators which reveals itself in this game of great revolutions, and manifests such a universal yet disinterested sympathy for the players on one side against those on the other. . . . Owing to its universality, this mode of thinking demonstrates a character of *the human race at large and all at once*: owing to its disinterestedness, a moral character of humanity, a least in its predisposition, a character which not only permits people to hope for progress toward the better, but is already progress insofar as its capacity is sufficient for the present.
>
> . . . That event is too important, too much interwoven with the interest of humanity, and its influence too widely propagated in all areas of the world to not be recalled on any favorable occasion by the nations which would then be roused to a repetition of new efforts of this kind.[55]

Reproduced as a sublime spectacle, recovered through the mechanisms of spectacular remembrance in one place and one time after another, the revolution, Kant avers, will progressively commit a greater and greater portion of humanity *not* to the duplication of a set of deeds or actions but to a mode of thinking, a form of sympathy, a willingness to negate the full table of individual wills and desires in exchange for a collective and universal project of freedom. It is thus that, by Kant's terms, the modern enlightened subject will universalize itself, that what Žižek designates Kant's subject $ will enter into global circulation wherever the sublime spectacle of the revolution is circulated and recollected.

Burke and Žižek imply something else. They suggest that it is not by remembering the French Revolution that "humanity at large" will normalize itself as a homogeneous, interchangeable, typical collectivity. It is, they instead argue, through the global spread of another revolution coincident with and fundamental to that revolution, through the global reproduction of a financial revolution first headquartered in Europe's metropolitan spaces-of-flow, that the speculative subject of "modernity" will become the typical subject of the globe and that the "modernity" philosophically indexed to the existence of this subject will progressively "universalize" itself. It is not, on this account, a global memory of the French Revolution that serves as a cosmopolitan modernity's precondition but the global circulation of paper money, the global implication of metropolitan and extrametropolitan subjects in the massively co-lateralizing networks of finance capital, the global extension of *this* speculative revolution that secures the increasingly universal existence of a "modernity" coterminous with what I have been calling the long twentieth century.

How does this "modernity" universalize itself?

In more ways than I am competent to answer. But one of the ways in which it does so, one of the primary ways in which it inaugurates its claims upon the global, one of the crucial ways in which this speculative revolution disseminates itself, is through the development of an Atlantic cycle of accumulation. And the engine of that speculative regime of accumulation was the trans-Atlantic slave trade. And among the capitals of that regime was William Gregson's Liverpool. And the ground zero of his city was the Liverpool Exchange and the transnational paper money market it regulated.

∗

How did the trans-Atlantic slave trade license the global spread of finance capital? How did its value forms, the epistemology appropriate to those value forms, the mode of public subjectivity consequent on that speculative epistemology, license an Atlantic cycle of accumulation that came to find one of its headquarters in the city of Liverpool? How do such questions bear upon the *Zong* massacre and the riches William Gregson and his partners claimed the massacre had secured for them? How do Žižek's value form and subject $ haunt the legal proceedings and actuarial imaginary that attended that event? How does the juridical encoding of that value form render this event an utterly paradigmatic, utterly typical, utterly foundational event of our long twentieth century?

By way of answer I return again to the Liverpool archives, both for what is particular to them and for what the particular documents they contain typify. I have in mind two sources that I have already mentioned: William Gregson's shipping records and that anonymous 1797 pamphlet on the frenzy of desire the slave trade had elicited among the city's inhabitants. The bulk of the pamphlet is concerned with detailing how profit is extracted from the three-way trade in commodities. At its close, however, its author pauses to consider the novel money forms which had both licensed this trade and emerged at the center of a supplementary economy which created wealth by speculating in and trading on the circulation of these money forms:

> It may be advanced, that this return [on an investment in a trading voyage] is not regular and successive; it is admitted, that a return cannot be made annually on the same ship with certainty, because in some instances an African voyage exceeds twelve months. . . . [Nevertheless] those capital houses [which are the primary financiers of the trade] . . . must be allowed to have yearly regular returns, uniform successive annual adventures producing successive annual remittances; this fact the more clearly appears from the modern method of treating and remitting a Guinea cargo: no sooner is an account sales closed [in the Caribbean or the Americas] than the nett proceeds are remitted by bills, which bills are accepted by what is now termed guarantee, and instantly circulated on a faith in the acceptor, and endorser only; these bills are notwithstanding established on a credit extensive as they appear precarious, three years is their present average run, which it is said is intended to be still increased one year more. This proceeding, while it benefits the factor and guarantee [the sales agent in the Caribbean or the Americas], appears to place the receiver in a very equivocal situation, when we consider the state of public credit, and the instability which commerce lately experienced in houses of the first eminence and reputation in the kingdom: [Nevertheless] these bills are numerous in the town of Liverpool, and in general circulation on a discount, therefore answer the purpose of receiver in the first instance, being taken in payment on the faith of acceptor and indorser without hesitation or diffidence.[56]

Despite its awkward syntax this is an extraordinary description of what the author calls the "modern method of treating and remitting a Guinea cargo." For within just two or three sentences the pamphlet not only sketches the financial system that had been invented to transform the irregularity and unpredictability of a single slave voyage into a "regular, successive" and even network of capital circulation, it also encapsulates the fundamental logic of the financial revolution that had transformed British life over the course of the century, thereby indicating how something like Marx's full formula for capital could collapse into its abridged money-into-money form as the commodity trade of the "Guinea cargo" found itself enabled by and giving way to a trade in the financial instruments with which that cargo is remitted. For the Liverpool merchants, at the heart of all of these processes was the need for what the pamphlet calls the "capital houses" most thoroughly invested in the trade to at once systematize and accelerate trans-Atlantic profit flows, to subordinate the trade's uneven calendar of capital return to their regular diet of capital need. And what made it possible for them to extract and reinvest capital from the trade at a quicker and more systematic rate was a credit-driven national and international banking system that had grown ever vaster and more complex since the establishment of the bank of England in 1694 and, more particularly still, the cross-Atlantic and intrametropolitan circulation of paper money in the form of bills of exchange.[57]

The system, as sketched by the pamphlet, was fairly simple: on reaching the slave markets of the Caribbean or the Americas, a vessel would assign its cargo to a local factor or sales agent. These were often, but not always, business partners of the ship's British owners. William Gregson and his sons seem to have dealt primarily with agents provided by Thomas Case, one of their regular business associates in Liverpool. That factor would then sell the slaves (by auction, parcel, scramble, or other means) and then, after deducting his commission, "remit" the proceeds of the sale in the form of an interest-bearing bill of exchange. This bill amounted to a promise, or "guarantee," to pay the full amount, with the agreed-upon interest, at the end of a specified period, typically from one to three years—though there were also shorter-term bills dated for three to six months. The Caribbean or American factor had thus not so much sold the slaves on behalf of their Liverpool "owners" as borrowed an amount equivalent to the sales proceeds from the Liverpool merchants and agreed to repay that amount with interest. The Liverpool businessmen invested in the trade had, by the same procedure, transformed what looked like a simple trade in commodities to a trade in loans. They were not just selling slaves on the far side of the Atlantic, they were lending money across the Atlantic. And, as significantly, they were lending money they did not yet possess or only possessed in the form of the slaves. The slaves were thus treated not only as a type of commodity but as a type of interest-bearing money. They functioned in this system simultaneously as commodities for sale and as the reserve deposits of a loosely organized, decentered, but vast trans-Atlantic banking system: deposits made at the moment of sale and instantly reconverted into short-term bonds. This is at once obscene and vital to understanding the full capital logic of the slave trade, to coming to terms with what it meant for this trade to have found a way to treat human beings not only as if they were a type of commodity but as a flexible, negotiable, transactable form of money. Absent this financial revolution in the business operations of the slave trade, absent this seemingly banal invention of a "modern method of remitting a Guinea cargo," absent this contract to treat human beings as a species of money, there would have been no incentive for Captain Luke Collingwood to do what he did, to confidently massacre 132 slaves aboard the *Zong*, secure in the conviction that in doing so he was not destroying his employer's commodities but hastening their transformation into money.

Collingwood's actions may seem to constitute the *reductio ad absurdum* of this "modern method," its foreseeable, perhaps inevitable, last proposition. The increased money to be made from it, however, both predated and survived his act. For by this simple shift in debiting and crediting procedures, the profit the Liverpool merchants could make from a slaving voyage was no longer restricted to the positive difference between the price they had paid to acquire slaves in Africa and the price they fetched in Charleston or Kingston, but was augmented by the rate of interest guaranteed by the bill the factor had assigned to them. As the pamphlet attests, the advantages of this procedure were not unidirectional. "Benefit" flowed in all directions. The benefit to the factor came from his ability to defer or spread out payment to the Liverpool capital houses over the full period of a bill's "run" rather than intermittently or all at once (which might not be possible if he had other significant debts outstanding at the time of sale) and thus to regularize his cash flow. The first benefits to the Liverpool investors came from the interest on the bill and from the greater speed with which they received a return on their investment in a slave voyage. If they had simply invested the sales proceeds in a cargo of sugar or rum (which, to be sure, merchants continued to do — this "modern method" of "remitting a Guinea cargo" supplemented but did not replace the older triangular trade in commodities), their "return" would have been delayed by the time it took to purchase and load this cargo in the Caribbean and the additional time it took to unload, distribute, and sell it in Britain. The factor's bill, on the other hand, could be sent back to Britain on the next available ship.

Once back in Britain these bills proved yet more flexible. They could be held and the interest and eventually the full payment collected once the note came due. Or, as seems regularly to have been the case, the bills themselves could be sold at a discount if the traders to whom they had been assigned experienced their own cash shortfall. By managing the holding and sale of their bills, the city's capital houses could, like their distant factors, regularize their cash flow, holding when they were liquid and selling when their own schedule of debts came due. By selling their bills they also increased the circulation and creation of value throughout the city's economy. Whoever purchased a bill at discount stood to gain both whatever interest remained and the full amount of the bill once it expired, or they could sign it over to yet another party in payment for some goods, service, or a debt of their own.[58] And this indeed seems to be what happened as these bills entered into circulation and became one of Liverpool's and the Atlantic's fundamental forms of money and, because of the interest they paid, one of the era's primary investment vehicles. Liverpool, unlike the more famous cities which have played home to Arrighi's spaces-of-flows, may not have had a stock market, but its market in trans-Atlantic bills of exchange functioned in much the same way, effectively linking the city's capital culture and the fate of its citizens' finances to the circum-Atlantic circulation and exchange of paper money. Liverpool's credit market may indeed have had as great an appeal as it did because the risk associated with this trade in bills was not, as it had been in turn-of-the-century London, concentrated in the prospects of a handful of giant companies (whose fate, at least in the case of the most prominent of those companies, the South Sea Company, had been tied to their monopoly interests in the trans-Atlantic slave trade) but was distributed across the full network of metropolitan capital houses and trans-Atlantic factors.

There was, however, risk — risk directly equal to the extent of the system. The more bills of exchange there were on offer, the more Liverpool's capital houses had their fortunes staked on the guarantees these factors had made them, the more the city was trading its goods and services in exchange for these bills, the more Liverpool's economy depended not only on the system of credit to which it was addicting itself but on the credibility of the Caribbean and American factors who had remitted the bills in the first place. The entire system, that is, depended on the reliability of the "guarantees" the factors had made to pay the premium and the interest on the bills. If a factor in Kingston found himself unable to meet his debts, a trader or a shopkeeper in Liverpool holding too many of his bills could go bankrupt. As these trans-Atlantic bills entered into wider and wider circulation, more and more people who were linked to this system of credit, "extensive as it is precarious," thus found themselves depending on the value of an initial promise made by a person unknown to them and more and more dependent on the credibility and perspicacity of the person from whom they were receiving the note. They could know, or hope to know, something of the person signing the bill over to them. They could hope that that person had known enough of the person from whom they had received the bill to underwrite its "guarantee" of payment. But they had little other means of protecting themselves or their investments.

As bills traveled from one hand to another, each succeeding possessor canceling the name of the previous holder and writing her or his name in as the party to whom the initial endorser now owed payment, the business of credit became not simply a financial transaction but the business of reading the solvency or character of each preceding party on this relay of exchange. The four, or six, or ten degrees of separation that distanced the present holder of a bill from its initial issuer exerted a sort of inflationary pressure not only on the financial value of the note but on the system of credibility that permitted each succeeding party to believe that they could trust the promise of the person giving them the note *because* that person had been wise to trust the promise of its previous owner that the promise originally given was sound (in the case where a bill had changed hands only three times.) Bills of exchange, then, circulated on and extended a double economy: an economy of monetary value and an economy of trust whose foundation was the credibility, the character, the trustworthiness of the person signing the bill over *and* the value of the trust that person had placed in the previous holder. To accept a multiply circulated bill of exchange was not only to accept a form of paper money but to express trust in one's own ability to read character and trust in the capacity of one's fellow citizens to do likewise. If the system were to survive, it depended not only on the soundness of the slave markets of the Caribbean but on the stability of this network of mutually invested trust and, ideally, on some means of training individuals in how to read one another's character, trustworthiness, and credibility. An accounting innovation, a "modern method of remitting a Guinea cargo," clearly was not, by itself, enough. For that method to survive and extend itself, it required a complementary social practice and a complementary practice of social reading, a habit of intersubjective analysis that would train readers to read not only the face value and negotiable worth of the bills they were exchanging but the credibility of their partners to these exchanges and the credibility of this system of exchange itself. Commodity culture, Benjamin reveals, is the practical expression of a particular phenomenology of things. The same is true of the speculative culture of finance capitalism. A system of credit encompasses more than just a set of accounting protocols, more than just a table of debts. It demands a phenomenology of transactions, promises, character, credibility.

∗

Slavoj Žižek's sketch of an anonymous, interchangeable modern subject constitutively negated by its implication in the circulation spheres of finance capitalism, I earlier argued, finds its unlikely complements in Edmund Burke's discussion of the speculative epistemologies of the French and financial revolutions of the eighteenth centuries and in J. G. A. Pocock's analyses of the social transformations that attended the financial revolution's invention of abstract, mobile property. Their full accounts of course differ — primarily with regard to the desirability of that negativity and of the modes of desire on which that negative depends — but they nevertheless share the sense that the various paper money innovations of eighteenth-century finance capital (the development of an extensive system of credit foremost among them) reflected the broader social, political, and epistemological spectrum of the "moment." It is Pocock's work, however, which provides the most extensive analysis of this dialectic and which has proven most immediately influential for those literary and cultural critics (primarily a number of recent theorists of the novel) who have sought to explain the relation between this speculative revolution, the period's novel modes of subjectivity, and the rise of an array of discursive forms which accompanied, enabled, or attempted to decode (and to train their addressees to decode) this new world of imaginary values and things.

The fundamental outlines of Pocock's argument are fairly similar to the story that for Žižek Hegel tells, though in Pocock's case the virtuous mode of public personhood interrupted by an eighteenth-century revolution was not feudal but republican, not secured by the subject's exchange of allegiance for the promise of reward but by the civic-patriot's possession of heritable property, and not overthrown by the invention of the abstract categories of Man and the Rights of Man but by the invention of abstract property and the replacement of a "landed" with a "monied" interest in the seats of political power. For Pocock, as for Burke, the engine of this revolution was not the guillotine but a system of public credit which radically transformed both the circuits of sovereign power (primarily by detaching the state's war-making capability from the loyalty of the aristocracy and attaching it instead to a range of debt-financing mechanisms and, so, to the pliability and the self-interest of the state's creditors) and the network of social relations which integrated the body politic (by offering to replace a vertical system based on genealogical hierarchies of status, deference, and obligation with a lateral system of "relations between debtors and creditors").[59] Credit and the other forms of paper money, on Pocock's account, thus altered the real mechanisms of power within the state by displacing an aristocratic class fraction from its dominant position of influence and replacing it with a more broadly anonymous monied interest and by substituting for a system of hegemony grounded in genealogical identity a more complex system regulated by debt-entanglements and the constant shifts of collectively held and serially recirculated instruments of value. Credit invented a "new image of social personality," a new social person no longer "anchored in the land" but attached instead to a series of negotiable promises, calculations, and speculations; a person no longer readable through reference to a table of inherited status but only as legible as the entire complex system itself.[60] Perhaps as significantly, credit enshrined the imagination as a new force at the heart of economic, political, and social life.

And it is on this point that Pocock begins to sound weirdly, uncannily, like Žižek:

> Government stock is a promise to repay at a future date; from the inception and development of the National Debt, it is known that this date will in reality never be reached, but the tokens of payment are exchangeable at a market price in the present. The price they command is determined by the present state of public confidence in the stability of government, and in its ability to make repayment in the theoretical future. Government is therefore maintained by the investors' imagination concerning a moment which will never exist in reality. The ability of merchant and landowner to raise the loans and mortgages they need is similarly dependent on the investors' imagination. Property — the material foundation of both personality and government — has ceased to be real and has become not merely mobile but imaginary. . . . When the stability of government in the present became linked to the self-perpetuation of speculation concerning a future, something happened which forms an important part of the history of ideas concerning unlimited acquisition and accumulation. Government and politics seems to have been placed at the mercy of passion, fantasy, and appetite, and these forces were known to feed on themselves.[61]

This vision of a public culture subordinate to the reign of fantasy, desire, imagination, and appetite may approximate Žižek's, but Pocock is of course far from urging his readers to enjoy the "symptoms" of such a condition or from suggesting that eighteenth-century civic discourse thoughtlessly accommodated itself to the sovereignty of the imagination and speculative desire. Instead, he argues, even those eighteenth-century polemicists of paper money such as Defoe and Montesquieu who were most favorably disposed to the new finance capitalism, even those who seem to have grasped (though of course they could not have expressed it in quite this way) that the new paper money had mastered the trick of abridging Marx's full formula for capital (by substituting something like the formula Money—Imagination—Money for Marx's Money—Commodity—Money) sought to contain its potential excesses. "Such thinkers," Pocock asserts, "had recognized that, in the credit economy and polity, property had not only become mobile but speculative: what one owed was promises and not merely the functioning but the intelligibility of society depended upon the success of a program of reification. If we were not to live solely in terms of what we imagined might happen—and so remain vulnerable to such psychic crises [as those exemplified by] . . . the South Sea Bubble and the Mississippi Company—experience must teach us when our hopes were likely to be fulfilled, and *confiance* teach us that we might create conditions in which their fulfilment would be more likely."[62] For Pocock, this "program of reification" produced a new form of public discourse, one devoted to teaching the public how to negotiate and make intelligible this new order of things; how to decode the arrangements of this suddenly more complex, shifting, social system; how to read the newly crucial trade in promises, speculations, and desire; how to interpret the credibility and the creditworthiness of the "new social persons" with whom society's deindividualized individuals were increasingly called on to transact public life. It produced a discourse devoted, above all, to training society's members to credit the existence of the abstract, imaginary, speculative values and things that had come to dominant social life.

It is in the service of this project (the vast social project of what I have been calling a theoretical realism) that a range of scholars influenced to a lesser or greater extent by Pocock's work have begun to argue the early- and mid-eighteenth-century novel shaped itself and sought to shape its readership. The "questions of virtue" and "questions of truth" that Michael McKeon indicates the early novel existed to resolve are precisely the sort of problems that Pocock indicates the financial revolution created. The social "nobody" at the center of Catherine Gallagher's *Nobody's Story: The Vanishing Acts of Women Writers in the Marketplace, 1670–1820*, corresponds *both* to Pocock's "new social person" made abject from a traditional register of social coding and entangled in a co-lateral network of speculative desires, promises, and exchanges, *and* to Žižek's subject $: the evacuated, anonymous, addressee of finance capital.[63] That later correspondence emerges not through Gallagher's direct engagement with Žižek but by sharing with him his key source on the "development of money, representation, and subjectivity": Brian Rotman,

whose *Signifying Nothing: The Semiotics of Zero*, Gallagher identifies as foundational to her analysis.[64] For Gallagher, however, the early novel is more than a
literary form which enthrones the anonymous, interchangeable subject of
finance capital as its chief protagonist (though that is, she maintains, one of
its critical accomplishments, one she first associates with the title character of Aphra Behn's *Oroonoko*, whose enslaved and infinitely exchangeable
body functions as something like the allegorical ground for that more general
form of abstract, negated subjectivity-as-*disembodied value* that she suggests
the novel exists to imagine and to put into public circulation).[65] For Gallagher,
however, the eighteenth-century novel does more than traffic in such subjects
after the fact. It serves to do more than report on the effects of finance capital
by refitting its subjects for aesthetic consumption and display within the pages
of a book. The novel, she argues, also helps secure the imaginary of the new
"credit economy and polity" by endorsing the validity and expanding the
circulation networks of fictional truths.

The speculative epistemology which Pocock finds finance capital to have
enthroned in political and economic life finds its dialectical counterpart, Gallagher suggests, in the contemporaneous "emergence into public consciousness of a new category of discourse: fiction."[66] Gallagher's argument is not
that there were no literary fictions prior to the early-eighteenth-century
novel, but that prior to the emergence of novelistic discourse the epistemological status of such work was limited to two options: "referential truth
telling and lying." [67] The novel altered this arrangement by inventing a new
category of reference, reifying the category of "fiction" as its solution to the
dilemmas Pocock outlines, constructing self-consciously "fictional" works
that were nevertheless understood to communicate "real" truths. "Far from
being the descendant of older overtly fictional forms," Gallagher argues, "the
novel was the first to articulate the idea of fiction for the culture as a whole . . .
what Ian Watt has called 'formal realism' was not a way of trying to hide or
disguise fictionality; realism was, rather, understood to be fiction's formal
sign."[68] The real fiction Gallagher has in mind corresponds fairly precisely to
the theoretical realism that I have identified with the overarching epistemology of finance capital and that I have been suggesting characterizes both its
value forms and its actuarial historicism. It is also the case, Gallagher insists,
that the "fictional" realism of early novelistic discourse might not only *correspond* to the imaginary epistemology of finance capital but help *secure* that
epistemology and train a body of readers to negotiate the world of values and
things it regulates, that the novel, by training readers to embrace the fictional,

might thus also represent a key component of that program of reification Pocock insists was needed to render a society of paper money "intelligible" to itself. She demonstrates this point throughout her text, most efficiently, perhaps, in a subtle reading of one of Samuel Johnson's dismissive comments on the novel. "The man whose faculties have been engrossed by business, and whose heart never fluttered but at the rise and fall of stocks," Johnson suggests in a *Rambler* essay, "wonders how the attentions can be seized or the affections agitated by a tale of love."[69] To which Gallagher responds:

> Here the man of business and the feminine or feminized sentimental reader of love stories are juxtaposed in a way that reveals their abstract similarity: both hearts "flutter" to a set of signs that, although not personally addressed to them, seize and agitate them, inviting or discouraging an investment for a defined term. Each has entered that suppositional mental space where beings who are nobody in particular (the conglomerate shareholders' mind represented by the variation of numbers attached to a stock, and the fictional lovers) provisionally solicit identification. As readers, they both speculate. The release into the culture of strongly marked overtly suppositional identities, belonging to nobody and hence temporarily appropriate to anybody, therefore, should be seen as one among many modes of facilitating property exchange and investment in the period, of creating the speculative, commercial and sentimental subject.[70]

Gallagher is not alone is offering this revisionary, quasi-Pocockian reading of the eighteenth-century novel and the role it performed in creating and training the imagination of the speculative subjects of finance capital. Deidre Lynch's *The Economy of Character: Novels, Market Culture, and the Business of Inner Meaning* is similarly influenced by Pocock, similarly inclined to associate the early- to mid-eighteenth-century novel with his new " 'world of moving objects.' "[71] For Lynch, as for Gallagher, this implies a strategic reading of novelistic discourse or, more precisely, a reading of the novel as a form of strategic discourse, "a coping mechanism" for the suddenly bewildered inhabitants of a new, complex social order founded on what I have been calling the negotiably co-lateral (rather than the immutably heritable) identities of its subjects.[72] The early novel, as Lynch's title suggests, trained Britons to cope by teaching them to read "character" — by which she intends not deep interiority or psychological depth but the external, material surface of the early novelistic protagonist (the "flat" "impersonal" character of a subject viewed and evaluated from without rather than from within).

Character of this sort proved valuable to the period's readers, Lynch argues, by providing "a rubric that licensed discussion of the order of things in a conversible, commercial society . . . *character* in its most abstract sense was a tool geared to analysis of the basic elements of the town-dweller's contemporaneity."[73] Novelistic character engaged the contemporary order of things on two main fronts, by inventing two types of "type." First it invented a general, fictional "type" broadly reminiscent of Gallagher's evacuated and exchangeable "nobody," though if anything, even closer to Žižek's anonymous, interchangeable subject $; a type of person further analogous to Pocock's "new social person," someone who, in the paradigmatic form of "the touring gentleman . . . the premier protagonist of many eighteenth century narratives, aspire[d] to typicality, to the kind of blankness that would allow him to be anyone and everyone."[74] Such typical "circulating protagonists," Lynch argues, performed a double social function: they facilitated the sort of readerly identification with and belief in "suppositional," "fictional" entities that Gallagher documents; and, by means of their picaresque tours of the new social terrain, they gave "readers the wherewithal to conceptualize society as a whole."[75] They "assuage[d] fears that the social is of unlimited and hence inapprehensible extension. Like the conversible gentleman, the protagonist in this style acts as broker of differences. His social work demonstrates how people are connected."[76] To this general fictional type (*the* type of the aggregate subject of finance capital), the novel, Lynch indicates, added a second sort of type: not only the generalizable, average, new social person, but also the typical representative of a specified rank of person active in commercial society — the typical banker, shopkeeper, suitor, trading partner, or other "sort" of person whose character and credibility readers were increasingly called on to interpret if they were to transact social life successfully. For readers who in their social life had to "negotiate the experience of a marketplace" peopled by an increasingly unknown body of contemporaries and trading in increasingly imaginary entities and values, but who "believed themselves, as literate Britons, to be the beneficiaries of a symbolic environment that was founded on principles of perspicuity and accessibility in which truths could be self-evident," "*such* characters," Lynch argues, "represented for their readers devices for thinking about typicality as such, for thinking about how, by expediting the diffusion and uniform legibility of information, printed characters supplied the social order with its impersonal mechanisms of coherence and comprehensibility."[77]

In summarizing these arguments, I inevitably simplify them, disappointing their greater subtleties. The main point, however, is clear. As allegory is to the commodity culture of Benjamin's nineteenth century, so what I have been calling theoretical realism is to the speculative culture of the long twentieth century that inaugurated itself with Britain's financial revolution. The credit financing that both accompanied the slave trade and, in partnership with the trade, fueled an Atlantic cycle of accumulation entailed more than a revolution in accounting procedures. It demanded an epistemological revolution, one which, as the work by Pocock, Gallagher, and Lynch makes clear, transformed the epistemological by fantasizing it, altered the knowable by indexing it to the imaginable. If the epistemological was transformed so too were the ontological and phenomenological convictions of society revolutionized as both the thingly and the perceptible quality of things found themselves fictionalized but credited as no less real for their increasingly theoretical existence. The subject too, as Žižek and Pocock in their different ways suggest, embarked on a new, abstract, anonymous, and speculative career. The genealogical subject, the localized subject, and the subject of courtly, religious, or republican regimes of virtue found themselves competing with the new colateral, mobile, abstract subject of speculative projects and desires. As this type of subject emerged within literary, financial, and historicizing discourse, the typical itself emerged as both the primary discursive category of the overarching theoretical realism that lends this historical moment its specifically historical character *and* as an abstract commodity in its own right, an investment vehicle in whose fortunes commercial society (with the assistance of the insurance industry) taught itself to speculate. At the heart of this revolutionary moment, then, were not only the credit networks and money forms whose metropolitan emergence and extrametropolitan extension function as one of the *Zong*'s primary historical situations, but also those discursive forms — the novel central among them — that accompanied and enabled the rise of this finance capitalism by providing it, in Pocock's terms, with its "program of reification."

In tracing the rise of the early novel we have thus come less distance than it might seem from the eighteenth-century Liverpool that functioned as one of this cycle of accumulation's primary spaces-of-flow, from the operations of the Liverpool businessmen who served as its Genoese masters, or even from the events that took place aboard the *Zong* and in the courtrooms in which the meaning and the value of Captain Collingwood's actions were adjudicated. If we are to understand how that massacre and trial (and also the insurance contract which links them) not only belong to but in fact *typicalize* their historical moment—and so too, if my reading of the extension-through-intensified-repetition of this moment into our own is tenable, how they function as types of our own long, nonsynchronous contemporaneity, as an "arcade" in which our long twentieth century encounters its repeating image—then we must come to terms with the ways in which the *Zong* engages not only the histories of property, value, and capital but how, by engaging these, it also engages and haunts the ontological, phenomenological, and epistemological histories of "its" moment. We must understand, that is, how, in the terms I have been using, the *Zong* names both a "real" event in the history of our long twentieth century and one whose real nature was licensed by the novel theories and fictions the eighteenth century first understood *as* real.

*

We do not know what novels William Gregson and his sons or partners read, or even if they read novels. Eighteenth-century novelistic discourse, and the average, abstract, typical characters that people that discourse, were not, however, limited to the printed book. Typical characters and real fictions circulated throughout the eighteenth-century social habitus and occupied the attention of both those who were and those who were not print literate. On the page, as Lynch argues, such character, or the habit of reading such character, frequently attached itself to the legibility of the human face. What was true for novelistic prose was also, in this case, true for visual culture, most prominently, perhaps, in Hogarth's various didactic series "The Harlot's Progress" and "The Rake's Progress" (series whose titles capture their investment in detailing recognizable social types as fully as, say, Defoe's *Moll Flanders* and Smollet's *Roderick Random*, their rough print counterparts) and in his popular catalogues of representative faces.[78] Canonized in Hogarth, the practice of training readers to read character and type off the surface of the face also assumed less distinguished cultural forms. Among these was one William Gregson and his sons might well have witnessed, or at least read about in the pages of Liverpool's main newspaper, *Gore's General Advertiser*, which, on September 9, 1784, contained the following announcement:

For two Evenings in the Oratorio Week.
An entire new Exhibition.
The Lovers of rational and intellectual Entertainment are respectfully
informed, that, by desire,
At Mr Forshaw's Great Room, Dale Street,
Liverpool,

On Wednesday and Friday Evenings next,
Will be delivered,
The celebrated, Serious, Comic, and Satyric
DISSERTATION UPON FACES.
As repeatedly performed at the Theater-Royal, Chester, Liverpool,
Shrewsbury, &c. with universal applause.
Written, and to be delivered, by Mr. Cowdroy.

Part I.

An occasional Exordium	The two faces of a Bum-bailiff.
The Face of an Alderman	The Face of a County Parish Clerk
The Face of a Poet	The Emblematical figure of a dancing-master
The Face of a Nabob	The two Faces of a Music-Master, and the striking effects of a Discord on his Muscles
The two Faces of a Lawyer	The two Faces of his Client, with the striking effects of a Law-suit on his Figure and Countenance

Part II.

The Face of Hyder Ally	The Face of a Man a week before and three weeks after, Marriage
The Face of a Highwayman	The Married Man's Coat of Arms
The two Faces of a Lottery Office-keeper, (before and after the drawing,) with his Motto	The Faces of two Politicians contrasted
The Face of a Naturalist	A Dialogue between three English characters, A Debtor, a Porter, and an Old Soldier, on the subject of an Invasion
The Face of an Astronomer	The two Faces of a modern Politician
The Face of a Learned Pedant, with his speech as President of a Debating Society . . .	The Face of an unlearned Pedant

**The Faces, Figures, &c. entirely new, and painted by that admired artist, Mr G. Wilkinson, whose professional abilities are sufficiently evidenced in his productions at the Theatre-Royal, Drury-lane, London, and at the Theatre of Sir Watkin Williams Wynne, Bart.

To Begin at eight O'Clock
Admission, Front Seats 2s — Back Seats 1s.
Tickets to be had at Mr. Gore's.[79]

*

"By desire. . . . Will be delivered. . . . Faces"; or, to rephrase things according to the rule of grammar: "Faces will be delivered by desire." Supplement the word "faces" with the figures that Lynch's work has taught us the eighteenth-century face metonymically evoked, and you have as succinct a formulation of that general process I have been describing as one could imagine. "Characters will be delivered by desire," "Types will be delivered by desire," "New social persons will be delivered by desire"; "Subject $ will be delivered by desire." The desire in question, as that last Žižekian substitution implies, is, of course, the speculative, phantasmagoric desire under whose rule Pocock indicates finance capital had placed political and social life. If such a regime of desire "delivers" such types of person, however, the desire of such persons, if they were to negotiate social life, was that they be delivered precisely the sort of "dissertation" on faces, characters, and types that Lynch suggests the novel existed to provide and that, with lesser subtlety, Mr. Cowdroy's "new exhibition" promises. If there is an obvious incommensurability between the seriousness of the dilemma that, with the support of Lynch, Gallagher, Pocock, and Žižek, I have been indicating such an "exhibition" offers to address, and the evidently merry-minded "comic and satyric" quality of the exhibition itself, then the very popular-cultural quality of the "dissertation upon faces" reveals something of the extent (*and* the public awareness of the extent) to which social life had constellated itself around a series of "entirely new faces, figures, &c." whose characters required painting. It was not only, such a performance suggests, the stockjobbers of London's Exchange Alley who needed to learn how to read a social terrain transformed by the wash of paper money or who could appreciate (and for an evening display and delight in their ability to appreciate) the fact that they inhabited a moment in which society had been stocked by a new cast of social types, but anyone who could afford to invest one or two shillings in an evening's "intellectual entertainment."

*

One last word about that "entertainment." As a mode of social satire, its comic effects would have licensed a double act of recognition. They would, that is, have permitted the audience to recognize discrete social types and allowed them to recognize themselves as bemused connoisseurs of such acts of recognition, enjoying the knowledge that their moment was not only one which derived its "character" from the new types of characters it had made, but one which also derived its historical peculiarity from the general, popular, inspection, and display of these typical characters. A performance of this sort is thus not simply available for subsequent historicist analysis, it is itself a historicizing operation — not, to be sure, in the mode of romantic historicism but, because what engages its attention are the aggregate, extant, types of character circulating throughout the social habitus, a performance which constructs itself (like the novels Lynch studies) as a species of what I have been calling actuarial historicism.

*

It is impossible to know whether one or other of the businessmen who had invested in the *Zong* attended Cowdroy's Dissertation upon Faces. William Gregson and his son John were, however, almost certainly in attendance at a similar if more exclusive event one week later: a ball held at the Liverpool Exchange on September 16, 1784, to celebrate the successful completion of the Oratorio week with which the Dissertation upon Faces had coincided. I suggest this with some confidence because of what can be known about the family's career during the four decades that separate these festivities from William Gregson's initial and highly profitable decision to invest in the slave trade in 1744. During the years since he purchased that first share in the *Carolina*, his and his family's fortunes had risen virtually without interruption. There would have been one brief moment of hazard, one short period during which William Gregson's argosies might have threatened to bankrupt him. In 1747, operating presumably with the profits from the successful voyage of the *Carolina*, Gregson invested as the minor of eight owners of the *Elizabeth* and, for the first time, as a majority shareholder (in the *Blackburn*). The latter decision proved to be ill-fated. The *Blackburn*, loaded with a cargo of 339 slaves, was captured by the French.[80] That Gregson was not bankrupted by the loss of the ship, in which he had clearly invested the greater portion of his available capital, was due in part to the successful voyage of the *Elizabeth* but also, in all likelihood, to the ship's insurance policy. (We know from the *Zong* trials that Gregson was in the habit of insuring his investments, and his eventual co-founding of the insurance firm of Gregson, Case, and Co. indicates his familiarity with the importance of insurance to the profitable prosecution of the slave trade.) Whatever the reason that he was able to survive the loss of the

Blackburn, his involvement in the trade continued not only unabated but with ever greater intensity. And as the number of vessels in which he invested mounted, so too did his fortunes.

At some point the former rope-maker purchased "free burgess" status for himself and his three sons, thus enfranchising both himself and them as Liverpool electors and rendering himself and his sons eligible for local office. It is unclear exactly when he first did so (an 1833 parliamentary report on municipal corporations indicates that in 1780 Gregson settled an outstanding bill of 218 pounds to the Liverpool council for these purchases) but it must have been fairly shortly after he first began to invest in the trade.[81] By the middle 1750s William Gregson had joined the forty-one free burgesses who composed Liverpool's governing Corporation and had assumed an active life in city politics. He served on many of the Corporation's committees, sponsored or cowrote numerous bills (including a perhaps particularly motivated decree in February 1759 calling on *Williamson's Liverpool Advertiser* to temporarily cease publishing its "list of the ships that enter outwards and sail from this port every week" — the news apparently having regularly fallen into the hands of the French captains eager to capture Liverpool vessels) and continued to consolidate his business and family life.[82] He established a regular set of partnerships with other prominent slave-trading families, including his sons and the Wilson and Aspinal families whose sons were to join him as co-owners of the *Zong*, and also with the family of Thomas Case, who owned a plantation in Jamaica, was a partner in a slave-brokering firm in Kingston, and whose son George was to marry William Gregson's daughter.[83]

The alliance with the Cases — who were among the older, more established families of the Liverpool elite, their wealth coming not only from the still new slave trade but from local collieries which they owned — not only permitted Gregson to link himself to virtually every financial sector of the circum-Atlantic trade, it also offers some testimony to Gregson's social skill.[84] Socially ambitious and, evidently, an astute businessman, Gregson must also have been an accomplished politician. For in 1762, eighteen short years after his climb began, Gregson's fellows on the Liverpool Corporation elected him the city's mayor. As was the custom, he held the office for a year and seems to have accomplished little of note other than presiding over the Courts of Passage and Sessions, attending services at St. George's Church and then hosting the obligatory Sunday brunch at the Exchange, lending his energies to the ongoing work of widening Liverpool's streets, extending its canals, and modernizing it docks, and, of course, securing the continuing influence and fortune of his family.[85] Here again he proved successful. His son-in-law George Case became the second member of the extended family to be elected mayor in 1782. Two years later, Gregson's son John followed suit, assuming the mayoralty in 1784.

It is here, then, that we find them, on the evening of September 16, 1784. John Gregson is mayor, apparently a more active and perhaps also civic-minded one than his father. His primary, if modest, accomplishments for his year in office include his decision, perhaps in honor of his father's humble beginnings, to become the first subscriber for a scheme to establish a set of Sunday schools for poor children, particularly those employed in the city's "rope-walks and tobacco warehouses," and to order the Corporation to do the same. He committed himself for 1 pound, the Corporation for 21.[86] The outrage stirred up by abolitionist organizations and in certain quarters of the London Press as a consequence of the *Zong* cases heard in court the previous summer has not prevented John Gregson from winning the Liverpool mayoralty. The city has just completed its festive Oratorio week (which included performances of *The Messiah*, *Judas Maccabaeus*, and a series of other works by Handel identical to those which had been performed in Westminster Abbey in May of that year) and, at John Gregson's instructions, the Corporation is feting itself at the city's Exchange with what *Gore's General Advertiser* admiringly called "a novelty unknown here before, A Fancy Ball."[87] By fancy ball the newspaper intends a fancy dress or masquerade ball for the mayor, the forty-one Corporation members — William Gregson and George Case, as ex-mayors, among them — and their invited guests.

A full description of the ball does not survive but a catalogue of the roles the revelers assumed did appear in the newspaper:

> The principal characters at the fancy ball were, a Sultana; an elegant figure; a Turk; an Algerine; America, by a Lady, who displayed the 13 stripes; 3 Spaniards; a Boatswain, well supported; 2 or 3 Jews, good; 2 Harlequin and Columbine characters; a Market Girl, with flowers; 2 Counsellors; 2 Friars; 2 Mungos; the *Child of Hale*, well attended by an excellent Nurse; a German Merchant; Collegians; a House-maid with a sweeping brush, a Good Girl, with fowls in a basket; a Country Clergyman; 2 Devils; Eve; a Conjurer; Douglas; Diana; an Ancient Briton; Mother Shipton; a Farmer, well supported; Shepherds; Shepherdesses; Sailors; Dominos of all sorts, &c. &c.[88]

It is a little surprising to read that this was the first masquerade ball held in Liverpool. If it was, or even if those attending believed it to be the first, their costuming anxiety must have been at least a little intense, at least somewhat marked by the need to demonstrate that as members of the city's elite they could successfully ape the habits of the London whose financial double Liverpool could, by 1784, almost boast to be, but which it continued to trail socially. Liverpool's anxiousness to pose itself as a second London, an anxiety evident in the architectural design of the Exchange itself, was on display throughout the Oratorio week. An account in *Gore's General Advertiser* indicated that "various entertainments had been introduced, to render the *fete* as complete, as a Town so far removed from the metropolis can be supposed to admit." Such entertainments included the decisions to replay in Liverpool the exact program of music performed some months before at Westminster Abbey and to cap the week with another import from London, a masquerade ball. Both the city's pretensions to be a northern London, and its anxieties that it was not, are on display in all these actions.[89] But so too is another economy of display, a desire to render exterior and visible an internal truth of sorts, to demonstrate in the sensory realms of architecture, sound, and fashion that the city *was* what these displays insisted it to be: another London, one of the capitals of a semiglobal world system, one of the age's orchestrating, governing spaces-of-flow.

The masquerade ball held on the floor of the Liverpool Exchange captures that mix of imitation and revelation almost perfectly, allegorizing with a sickening exquisiteness what the trans-Atlantic slave trade had allowed Liverpool to become, how it had become that thing, and what it further aspired to be. If eighteenth-century Liverpool is, as I have been arguing, one of the founding capitals of our long twentieth century, it was perhaps never more intensely so than on a night such as this, at this exact place and moment, at this masquerade ball held on the floor of the Liverpool Exchange, where, under the fixed glance of the slave heads fastened to the building as a decorative motif, the principal characters of the city could dress themselves in imitation of the characters assumed by their doubles in London. Liverpool's Oratorio week masquerade may thus have been, in the restricted sense, "a novelty unknown here before," but it was simultaneously a novelty typical of its novel and novelized moment. The performance of masquerade — the reciprocal acts of exchanging the identifiable particularity of the self for a type of self ("a Turk," "a German Merchant," "a Counsellor") and of trying to read the real identity of one's fellows from the external characters thus presented to the world — itself allegorizes the processes by which subjectivity is both coded and decoded in such a moment. The masquerade ball is the Exchange's, and a moment of hyperintensified speculative exchange's, almost ideal festivity. It belongs to the same "program of reification" as the early novel and Mr. Cowdroy's dissertation on faces. It is precisely as novel, and no more novel, than either of these. Where else could the ball have been held but on the floor of the Liverpool Exchange?

Wandering across the floors of that Exchange, circulating from one knot of "characters" to another, the principal families of the city would have found themselves performing, perhaps known themselves performing, their moment, their city, and their city's shared sovereignty over its moment with a ghastly perfection. And presiding over their merriment, hidden somewhere in that list of characters catalogued in the next morning's gossip column, was both a type of man whom we can know as no more and no less than as an abstractly typical representative of his typicalizing moment (*a* speculator, *a* slave-trader, *a* banker, *an* insurance underwriter, *a* politician) and as a man whose name we know: John Gregson, mayor of Liverpool, co-owner of the *Zong*; and somewhere not too far from him, another *such* character, his father, William.

> The world dominated by its phantasmagorias—this, to
> make use of Baudelaire's term, is modernity.
>
> —Walter Benjamin, *The Arcades Project*

> Fashion: "Madam Death! Madam Death!
>
> —Leopardi, "Dialogue between Fashion and Death"

CHAPTER 3

"*Madam Death! Madam Death!*"

CREDIT, INSURANCE, AND THE ATLANTIC CYCLE

OF CAPITAL ACCUMULATION

Among the figures not present, at least in costume, at John Gregson's masquerade ball was one who would, nevertheless, have been one of the presiding spirits of that dance and of the Exchange in which it was held: Lady Credit, who, in her wanderings through the pages of editorial correspondence, didactic pamphlets, and periodical essays, had been a staple of public sphere discourse since the early decades of the century and who was one of that discourse's primary contributions to a program of reifying, enabling, and decoding the extension and effects of the financial revolution that I have been suggesting we must read as one of the *Zong*'s organizing "circumstances."[1] Lady Credit was not, to be sure, the only "character" through whose adventures public sphere discourse (which term I use in a fairly standard and uncomplicated Habermasian sense) engaged its speculative moment.[2] Samuel Johnson's *Rambler* essay, as Gallagher suggests, indirectly accommodates the typical gentleman to the fictionality of market values by figuring those values as analogues of the suppositional identities of novelistic characters. More canonical (though it is hard to be more canonical than Johnson: more commonly known, perhaps) are Addison's series of *Spectator* character-sketch essays, introduced in *Spectator 2*, which, in Christian Thorne Miano's words, "work by mapping out the social types of mercantile England — the rude country squire, the thrifty trader, the gallant — in order to show how these potentially conflicting classes might be reconciled in a culture of politesse, as long as each class can be taught to disregard its own particular interests."[3] Mapping these types, the *Spectator*, as the various arguments by Lynch, Žižek, Gallagher, and Pocock suggest, is simultaneously mapping the representative mode of subjectivity proper to finance capitalism's speculative culture. Lady Credit, nevertheless, remains public sphere discourse's central contribution to the phenomenologization of finance capital and a key figure in that process by which an "originary" metropolitan financial revolution was able not only to capture and train a British social and cultural imaginary but to link itself to a staggered series of imitator revolutions throughout the port cities of the Atlantic archipelago and, thus, to that process by which Atlantic finance capital staked its claim to the modernization of the globe.

Lady Credit — whose classically capricious, seductive, anxiety-producing shadow falls over the 1797 pamphlet's nervous meditations on Liverpool's "precarious," "equivocal" system of trans-Atlantic credit — became, as I have mentioned, a staple of public discourse in the early decades of the eighteenth century. Her career as the imaginative embodiment of paper money in all its forms (bills of exchange, bank notes, stock coupons) rises in time with the early history of the insurance, banking, stockjobbing, and war-debt-financing activities of London's Exchange Alley and peaks, infamously, at the moment of the South Sea Bubble. Indeed, the wild swell and burst of that bubble was frequently taken to typify her power to create and destroy wealth by the sheer caprice of her affections, or, perhaps more accurately, by the capricious sway she held over the public imagination, the power she held to make the public imagine her real or unreal. Lady Credit's vulnerability before the fickle swings of the imagination, her insubstantiality apart from the trust alternately vested in and withdrawn from her, was the very secret of her power. Her changeability was the source of her ability to change society's fortunes. Garbed in her robes, credit was grasped less as a financial practice than as the collective self-image mirrored in the glass society held up to itself, the beguiling effigy in whom the public saw its self-estimate revealed. She was a word for the public estimation of the value of the promises an increasingly "financialized" society had given itself, the "guarantees" it had been offered and accepted, the trust it had invested. She was the figure in whom that collective saw itself reflected, by whom the public was rewarded when it imagined her most substantial and by whom they were punished when they withdrew their trust.[4]

The financial scheme that generated the bubble for which Lady Credit was deemed responsible was certainly imaginative in its design, the promises it made, and the trust it requested, entailing as it did a plan to settle the massive debt the government had run up during the wars it had fought from 1688 to 1719 (the dates, respectively, of King William's accession and the most recent of the Stuart uprisings). It plotted this by requiring creditors holding seven and a half million pounds in government bonds to exchange these guaranteed, long-term, but low-interest annuities for stock in the South Sea Company, which had risen to prominence in 1713 by acquiring the *asiento*, a monopoly contract from the Spanish government to supply the Spanish Caribbean with slaves.[5] In theory, everyone was to profit from the exchange: the government by retiring its debt; the company by massively increasing its capitalization and creating an incentive for a suddenly massive body of investors to drive up the value of its stock; and the creditors by exchanging the 4 to 5 percent they could earn on their bonds for the potentially far greater earnings of a soaring stock. The success of the scheme depended, again in theory, on the company's financial soundness and the profitability of its slave trading ventures. In practice, as Defoe, Addison, Cato, and a legion of other commentators observed, the scheme rested on the behavior of Lady Credit, that coy "mistress" whom Defoe held to be the "invisible je ne scay quoi" of "all our commerce and all our public transactions," that "emblem of a something though in [herself] nothing," that "beautiful virgin" whom Addison allowed "had the same virtue in her touch, which the poets tell us a Lydian king was formerly possessed of . . . that she could convert whatever she pleased" into gold.[6] It depended on this enchantress's ability to capture the public's imagination, to convince them to trust the promises her South Sea agents had made on her behalf, to agree to imagine that the value of the stock she had enticed them to acquire was as real as she was herself. As it turned out the value of the stock had precisely that degree of reality, rising from 170 per share on March 1, 1720, the month before the scheme was put into effect, to a high of 950 four months later and then, just three months after that, collapsing back to 170, bankrupting thousands in the process and threatening to bring the entire economy down in ruin.[7] In the seven months of its exorbitant rise and fall nothing significant had changed in the commercial dealings of the company. A value the public imagined to be real, and which it had conjured into being by that act of imagination, simply no longer seemed believable.

The South Sea scheme may have failed but the system of credit on which it was built, the "imaginary" theory of value and Žižekian regime of desire on which Terry Mulcaire indicates it rested, survived and indeed prospered.[8] Exchange Alley continued to be a center of stock speculation. Successive governments continued to convert their debts into financial instruments. The expenses of the Royal Navy, in particular, continued to be a prop for the London financial markets. In 1749, at the close of the Seven Years War, Henry Pelham, First Lord of the Treasury, permitted the government's creditors to exchange over three million pounds of debt accrued by the navy and its victualing agents for government stock with a 4 percent return, which sale of government issue promptly drove up the value at which these stocks were bought and sold on the London Exchange.[9] This particular set of transactions, by no means the only of its sort, bears mention because it again reveals how what standard economic histories identify as "Britain's" financial revolution, what Arrighi associates with the rise of a "British" cycle of accumulation, and what even those literary studies most attuned to the cultural and epistemological shifts attendant on the emergence of this new world of mobile property continue to associate fairly exclusively with the history of the "British" novel and the "British" public sphere, entailed more than the transformation of a national economy, a national social system, and a national imaginary.

An eighteenth-century financial revolution may have been centered in Britain, but it was centered there only by concentrating in first one and then in three or four British cities the money-managing operations of a quasi-global economic system, or, indeed, an overlapping set of systems: an Anglo-Irish-Scottish-Welsh system of capital, social, and imperial exchange that a revisionary New British History has recently begun to examine; an Anglo-Indian-Pacific system channeling the flow of bodies, commodities, capital, and power along a London-Bombay circuit of exchange; and the Anglo-Atlantic cycle of accumulation of primary interest here. If London was, finally, *the* British capital of the eighteenth century, it was so because it was the sole place in which all these circuits fully intersected, the site where these circular geographies of capital overlapped. The networks of credit that fed the revolutionary potential of each of these capital geographies — even as they defined their extent and sprawl — linked London, however, to what were quite clearly a set of transnational financial terrains.

And throughout the eighteenth century one of the primary such territories of credit, perhaps "Britain's" most important credit territory, was that territory stretched between the outposts of the triangular trade, that circum-Atlantic territory of slave trading and imperial war making that generated so great a share of both the credits and debts for sale first on London's and then on Liverpool's exchanges. The debts the Royal Navy ran up as it pursued a British hegemony over the Caribbean and fought to maintain imperial sovereignty over the American continent; the soldiers' and sailors' payrolls dispatched to Lord Cornwallis and Admiral Rodney as they waged war on the colonial patriots and pursued the French from one Caribbean port to another; the constantly accumulating debts of compensation paid out to the wounded and the families of the dead; and, above all, the interest-bearing bills of exchange that were consigned to naval storekeepers in Kingston, victualing agents in Barbados, and quartermasters in Newfoundland served as a constant source of enrichment to the financial revolution: an always open trans-Atlantic factory of debt. And as it produced ever greater quantities of debt, put ever more paper money into circulation, more thoroughly addicted the national economy to the speculation and trade in financial instruments, this modern method of war financing increasingly transformed the cities in which it was headquartered. Like those modern methods of profiting from the slave trade pioneered at the turn of the century by the stockjobbers of London's Exchange Alley and perfected at its end by the Liverpool capital houses, these means of funding (and exploiting the funding) of the imperial war machine reinvented the economic and social life of Britain's major port cities, making them less the capitals of a national economy than the dominant relays in a transoceanic circuit of exchanges, less the storehouses of the nation's wealth than the financial catchment zones and epistemological flashpans of an Atlantic cycle of accumulation.

The Liverpool method of remitting a guinea cargo may have still felt "modern" in 1797, but it was thus by no means original to the capital houses of the Merseyside metropolis. It extended a system rather than inventing it, restaged a revolution rather than sparking it, repeated for Liverpool what London had earlier accomplished. And as this system of credit migrated to Liverpool, linked the operations of Liverpool's capital houses to the financial culture of London's Exchange Alley, and connected both not only to one another but to a circum-Atlantic network of financial exchanges, its restless practitioners sought ever further methods of refining its procedures, an ever greater number of points at which to apply its Midas touch along the trade routes and perimeters of this network, an ever more total, pervasive, and saturating distribution of this "method" of imagining value, crediting the imagination, and trading credit. For the participants in the Liverpool slave trade this meant that credit — whose ever more extensive theater of address frequently seemed coterminous with the extension of "modernity" itself — was not just something to be traded between merchants in Liverpool and factors in the Caribbean and American slave markets, but something central to each transaction along the trade's full relay of exchanges, something that would permit them to "modernize" and homogenize the entire system, something that would enable them to bring each point of exchange into full unimpeded conversation with the financial and imaginative currency of the rest.

*

The Liverpool capital houses, accordingly, ordered their captains not just to sell slaves on credit once they reached the American or West Indian end of their voyages but, whenever possible, to buy slaves on credit in the first place. The firm but cautious instructions given by Robert Bostock, a prominent Liverpool slave trader, to Peter Berne, captain of the *Jenny* as he was about to embark on a voyage on July 2, 1787, provide a fair outline of this way of conducting business:

> Sir, Having appointed you to the command of the ship *Jenny* and the vessel being now compleat and ready for the Sea you are to embark on the first favourable opportunity of a fair wind to proceed in the most Expeditious manner to the windward Coast of Africa and if you can't dispose of three parts of your cargo there you may run up to the Isles of [*illegible*] to try what you can do there but you must reserve about 40 slave goods for Wm Cleveland as you will see by his indent and send your boat to Acquaint him of your Arrival and let him have the goods as soon as possible; *who ever you Barter with must take these notes of hand payable at such a date for fear of any Dispute* in good Merchantable Slaves if it should so happen that you could not Dispose of the whole of your cargo at one of these places above mentioned you are to Proceed down to Cape Mont or Elsewhere on that part of the Coast; but you are not to trust any goods to the natives there on Any Acct whatsoever in forfeit of your Commission and Priviledge hereafter mentioned for trusting goods there has been the oversetting of many voyages as when you trust them you never see them again. . . . After you have Purchas'd your Cargo of Slaves you are to Proceed to the Island of Barbadoes where I will have letters lodg'd for you in the Hand of Mr. Wm Barton and if it should so happen in your Arrival at that Island the letters should have Miscarried you are to Proceeed to the Island of Grenada where I have letters lodg'd for you in the Hands of Mr Campbell & Co. and

with Mr Munro, McFarlane & Co. . . . *You must sell your cargo of slaves to either of those houses that is to say which will give you the Best Price and the Shortest sighted Bills as I have a guarantee for both houses.* If Mr Campbell & Co. sell your cargo the Bills is to be drawn on JP Baillie in London if the other on Mr Hugh Houstown& Co. of Glasgow. *You must get your Bills at as Short Sights as you can. . . . You are not to sell your cargo of slaves with any house whatsoever but that I have a guarantee for. . . . You are to get your Bills drawn in my favour and in small sums not exceeding 250 pounds but the smaller the better (as they save Commission and Stamps and not only that but are ready payment.*[10] (Emphasis added)

The basic logic of Bostock's instructions is familiar, particularly as his directives attend to his dealings with his trustworthy ("guaranteed") factors in Barbados and Grenada, the short-term bills he wants his captain to receive from them (from which instruction we can deduce that Bostock might have been experiencing cash-flow problems that could best be met by bills that would come due quite rapidly), and his desire for "small sum" bills that he can rapidly circulate as payment to his creditors at home. What these instructions add to the portrait of the finance capitalism of the slave trade, however, is their description of the extension of debt financing to the African coast.

Bostock was apparently indebted to William Cleveland (presumably a slave dealer on the coast), a debt he ordered his captain to discharge by handing over trade goods equivalent to the purchase price of forty slaves. The more intriguing instruction, however, concerns the "notes of hand payable at such a date" that he directs Captain Berne to issue as payment in exchange for the "good Merchantable slaves" he is supposed to acquire. The mixed logic of the directive to "Barter" slaves in exchange for these bills suggests something of the mixed economy of the trade at the coast (one still conducted as much in the trade of slaves for goods as in an exchange of slaves on credit). It also hints at a moment of transition from one economy to another. At the time of Bostock's writing the heteroglossic rhetoric which permits him to draw on the transaction grammars of two different economic systems would have captured the heterodox situation on the coast quite exactly. There *were* credit networks in situ on the African coast, primarily those between British traders such as Bostock and the assorted European slave dealers resident in Africa and those that linked the operations of the Company of Merchants Trading to Africa and the British government (which had agreed to underwrite the Company's expenses in maintaining the coast's major slave factories).[11] A large portion of the surviving correspondence between the Company and the government held in the archives of the British Treasury comes, in fact, in the form of debt notices submitted by the Company to the state, including one for the construction of Fort William at Anamabo, the "factory" from which Luke Collingwood acquired the bulk of the slaves he loaded aboard the *Zong*. (The bill, for 7,623 pounds, contains among its breakdown of expenses for brick, lime, wood, and "white men's salaries," a lengthy footnote explaining the rate of "Exchange" by which expenses accrued in "Coast Money" — cowrie shells, presumably — had been converted into pounds on the basis of "Information [provided by] Persons of Credit . . . upon the Coast." The company set the rate of exchange at 60 percent. Whether it actively profited by manipulating this currency market is unclear, though the nervousness with which the issue is addressed — it is the only aspect of the bill that receives a detailed explanation — certainly suggests that the idea, if not pursued, had at least been entertained.)[12]

But between the European traders and the African agents they relied on to bring slaves to the coast there was a less settled scheme of trading on credit. The very lack of trust Bostock evinces in his letter for the "natives" in the Cape Mont region, coupled with the sense the letter gives that past traders had worked out some sort of system of entrusting goods on credit, reveals the need that merchants such as Bostock would have felt for both a greater knowledge of the African traders with whom they were dealing and a more efficient, reliable, and profitable means of trading with them. The knowledge, at least, existed in a variety of forms, primarily the travel narratives and amateur ethnographies which served not only to titillate and inform a domestic reading public but to perform for the traders active in the African outposts of this Atlantic cycle of accumulation much the same function that the novel performed in Britain, that is, to equip readers not simply to read a social ensemble but to negotiate its world of mobile property, whether that mobile property came in the form of the slaves themselves or in the increasingly heterogeneous array of commodities, monies, and credit arrangements through which they could be acquired. Of the legion of such texts, few were more explicit in their appreciation of the value of ethnographic insight to commercial behavior and of the value to Anglo-African commerce of a more extensive credit- and money-based economy than B. Cruikshank's *Eighteen Years on the Gold Coast of Africa*.

Cruikshank appears to have spent a large portion of his African years in the region of the Anamabo castle and slave factory — a good deal of his account is devoted to a history of what he calls the kings of Anamaboe — and to have occupied his time studying the integration of the indigenous and trans-Atlantic economies of this contact zone. He was, on the whole, delighted with the extensiveness of the trade in commodities. "[All] was cheerful bustle and activity. There was not a nook or corner of the land to which the enterprize of some sanguine trader had not led him. Every village had its festoons of Manchester cottons and China silks, hung up upon the walls of the houses, or round the trees in the market-place, to attract the attention and excite the cupidity of the villagers. In the principal towns on the main line of communication with Ashantee, extensive depots were formed, where every species of goods suited to the traffic might be got in abundance." Nevertheless, he was convinced that the wealth to be forced from a simple trade in goods was severely limited so long as "their [the indigenes] absolute wants were few and their desires moderate."[13] To intensify both want and desire, he suggests, some other system was necessary, some system that would tie wealth not only to the accumulation of things and desire not only to this or that cotton or silk, a system that would attach both riches and desire to the abstract concept of wealth itself. And for this, he indicates, two things were necessary: a system of "simple credit" (35) and a general "medium of circulation."[14]

Both were forthcoming during his years on the coast. Credit, he suggests, inevitably followed the commodity trade along the main line from the coast to the interior, rapidly converting each of the commodity entrepôts he discovers into outposts of an ever-expanding finance network as "agents employed to sell goods in the interior upon [a] merchant's account" increasingly released their wares on credit. "Credit," he approvingly notes, "soon became general."[15] And as it spread so too did "artificial want"; an ever greater flow of wealth along the lines of the trade routes; an "improving . . . social condition" for the inhabitants of the entrepôts that were becoming local versions of Arrighi's Bisenzone fairs; and a general "steadiness and consistenc[y] of social progress" toward that modernity that for Cruikshank is indexed by the social transformations that are necessary to, and a necessary consequence of, the spread of money capitalism.[16] "The natural result of this system of trust" he insists, "was the extensive diffusion of property throughout every class of society . . . The advantages of this system of general credit . . . in creating artificial wants, and in forming new habits, and thereby exciting to their gratification by industrious exertion, far outweighs the temporary injustice and abuses which the spirit of progress invoked by it must ultimately redress."[17]

This might be the polemic of a Whig apologist for the novel forms of mobile property transforming public life in England. Indeed, it belongs to the same tradition of public sphere discourse. It reminds us that that public sphere and the financial revolution which both enabled it and was one of its primary obsessions were not restricted to London; that the extensive diffusion of (imaginary, mobile) property that characterized this hyperfinancialized moment effected both the metropolitan centers and the furthest frontiers of this cycle of accumulation; that the system of trust that was this capital network's condition of possibility extended to and transformed the habits and imaginaries of London stockjobbers, Liverpool merchants, African traders, and Caribbean factors alike. Trust was, indeed, the system-wide currency upon which the system depended and which it had learned to trade, trust expressed both in the literal monetary credit parties requested from or extended to one another and through the abstract confidence everyone had to have in the system itself, the belief they were required to invest in the credibility of its forms of value and the value of its guarantees. For the system to work most profitably and most efficiently it needed not only a standard set of exchange mechanisms with which to translate the value of pounds, textiles, slaves, "coast money," dollars, sugar, and tobacco into one another, but a standard imaginary, a standard grammar of trust, a standard "habit" of crediting the "real" existence of abstract values. The genius of credit, as Cruikshank clearly realized, was that it could secure both these standards at once, that by the spread of its apparently banal accounting tricks it could extend ever further the transactional protocols and epistemologies of value that had become the standards of the financial revolution.

Cruikshank, like Lady Credit's paradigmatic Whig apologist and her typical Tory skeptic, was also aware that the individual acts of trust fundamental to a general system of credit could be misplaced. In Britain, the cost of such misplaced trust was, at worst, bankruptcy for the defaulted creditor and imprisonment for the defaulting debtor. On the gold coast, Cruikshank indicates, it was enslavement. Credit did not only follow the slave trade. Nor did it simply enable the purchase of slaves. By frequently producing debtors unable to settle their debts, credit produced slaves: a class of debtors whose bodies or whose relations' bodies functioned as their "guarantee" of last resort. Cruikshank presents himself throughout his account as someone opposed to the slave trade (hence the talk of "injustices and abuses" in the midst of his general encomium to credit) but if the picture he paints is at all accurate it suggests that the slave trade did not simply increase its profit margins by introducing a credit economy to the west African coast but nourished its very existence on a diet of coastal credit: "It could not be but that much of this credit was misplaced . . . whatever the cause, the result was the same — the implication of the innocent relations, who have been made available to raise the funds to liquidate the debt, either by bondage as pawns, or by actual sale."[18] The full catastrophe and evil of the slave trade, I earlier suggested, included its ability not only to turn human beings into a form of property but to treat them as a species of money, to regard them, on the point of sale in the new world, as the account deposits for a network of interest-bearing bonds. That transformation, clearly, did not await the completion of the middle passage.

Treated as human collateral against the payment of a debt before being transformed on the far side of the Atlantic into the reserve deposits for a systemwide trade in bills of exchange, slaves, as Cruikshank further indicates, intermittently functioned as actual units of currency, the standards of measure necessary to that finance capital whose "advantages," he feels certain, "far outweigh the temporary injustices . . . invoked by it." The spread of a system of "simple credit," he insists, was *the* secret of the "spirit of progress" animating the capital reconstruction of coastal society. But for that system of credit to work most efficiently, it required "a test of computation," or what Marx calls a general equivalent: a standard measure of value in whose terms the values of the range of commodities and currencies available for exchange or credit acquisition could be expressed. "Slaves," Cruikshank reveals, "for some time, as being the staple of commerce, held the most conspicuous place as a test of computation, and an article was ordinarily reckoned at the value of one, two, or more slaves."[19] However, like the "clipped" or "adulterated" coins whose utility as units of measure were the subject of fierce contemporaneous debate within Britain, slaves were of limited utility as the basis for a monetary system. "The immense variety of circumstances which depreciated their value or otherwise made it of such a relative quality, that even the classification into prime, good, bad, and indifferent, conveyed but a doubtful and indefinite idea of their true worth"[20] To complete the system of credit by which slaves were produced, acquired, sold, and finally transformed into the reserve deposits for the large and small "bills" circulating across the Atlantic and throughout its metropolitan capitals, the trade on the coast required some other money form to measure the value of the slaves, goods, and currencies accumulating within its entrepôts, some less autoreferential "coast money" against which to measure the money value of the slaves themselves.

"The introduction of the cowrie-shell and its application to this purpose," as Cruikshank puts it, "supplied the desideratum."[21] "A commodity capable of great subdivision, and in constant use as the circulating medium of an extensive district of the country" (43), the cowrie shell became the coast's ideal "general equivalent," *the* "computational" standard with which to express the value of its commodities and, perhaps more importantly, with which to record its schedules of credits and debts; *the* currency, as the bill presented by the Company of Merchants indicates, that made it possible to calculate and so truly implement a territory-wide system of credit. Closing the chapter of his text devoted to the financial practices of the gold coast, Cruikshank can barely restrain himself from shouting this "coast money's" praises:

> The reader will have some idea of the utility of this article as a circulating medium, when we state that the annual importation of cowries is steadily increasing, and that it at present amounts to one hundred and fifty tons per annum. When he is further informed that a ton of good cowries is equivalent to three hundred and sixty dollars, that two thousand four hundred shells go to the dollar, and that there are consequently eight hundred and sixty-four thousand cowries in a ton, he will more readily comprehend the facilities of exchange, and the great encouragement it gives industry. . . . Every branch of trade and industry known to the people has been influenced in an extraordinary manner by adopting this currency.[22]

Indigenized in the form of the cowrie shell no less than in the guinea, the finance capitalism of the trans-Atlantic slave trade found in this "circulating medium" the means of bringing the trade along the African coast into full conversation with a circum-Atlantic language of value, the medium through which the "modern method of remitting a guinea cargo" could also become the modern method of acquiring one. With the adoption of this coast money and the establishment of a Company-regulated currency exchange, Captain Bostock, if he had wished, could have ordered his Liverpool bookkeeper to settle his west African debt with William Cleveland by signing over to him bills of exchange guaranteed by his factor in Barbados. The financial revolution once concentrated in London's Exchange Alley had thus, by the end of the eighteenth century, migrated from one outpost of the Atlantic archipelago to another. The Liverpool merchants who were among the Genoese masters of this extended territory of flows, and in whose capital houses much of its wealth accumulated, were accordingly freed to enrich themselves not just as commodity traders but as finance capitalists, speculators in those forms of paper money and mobile property that were the distinctive value forms of their contemporaneity. Credit had become to them what Arrighi suggests the chartered company had been to London earlier in the century: the medium through which the Atlantic capitalist class established direct links between the British entrepôts on one side and trading partners from all over the world on the other. Thanks to these direct links, the ability of the Atlantic capitalist class to centralize the commercial transactions that mattered in Britain, as well as its ability to monitor, regulate, and profit from the disequilibria of world trade, was, to put it mildly, greatly enhanced.[23]

*

No wonder then that for every bill the Company of Merchants submitted to the Treasury there is another letter requesting that the flow of cowrie shells to the slave coast continue unimpeded, such as the one from June 17, 1776, appealing for permission to import 5,600 weight of cowries ("for the use of the forts") from Britain's trading rivals in Holland (presumably the Dutch East India Company — which would have acquired the shells in South Asia), or that the Treasury was happy to grant these petitions even when, as in this case, they quite clearly prejudiced the interests of the East India Company.[24]

*

No wonder also that the Africans whose lives were bought, sold, and accounted for in the easily subdivisible units of this "circulating medium" did not share Cruikshank's estimate of its "extraordinary influence." Among the slaves, Jan Hogendorn and Marion Johnson suggest in their marvelous study *The Shell Money of the Slave Trade*, the cowries developed a rather more disturbing iconography. "The shells, so it is said, came from the off-lying waters, where they fed on the cadavers of less desirable slaves thrown into the sea as their food. The bodies, or sometimes dismembered limbs, when pulled ashore were covered with attached cowries. Though macabre, this tradition as allegory is right on the mark — slaves certainly did in an economic sense 'feed' the shell trade."[25]

*

That there is more than allegorical truth to this iconography; that the money forms of the trans-Atlantic slave trade could attach themselves not only to the slaves who reached the markets of the Caribbean alive but also to those drowned along the way; that a sufficiently credible imagination could see in a drowned slave a still existent, guaranteed, and exchangeable form of currency; that a British court could hold the majesty of the law to endorse *this* act of the imagination; that the attorneys for William Gregson and his partners could convince a jury that by throwing 132 of the *Zong*'s less desirable slaves into the sea Captain Collingwood had not so much murdered a company of his fellows as hurried them into money, is also, as we shall see, unsurprising — perhaps even the inevitable consequence of that epistemological revolution (most commonly expressed as an accounting procedure) which had permitted Britain's capital houses to convert "their" slaves into paper money.

*

All of the slave traders' wealth was not, of course, paper. Nor did the paper money they had accumulated solely breed more money. It also reexpressed itself in the world of things, disabstracted itself, and took on new material form. How did John Gregson and his cohorts spend their money, retranslating their abstract wealth into the realm of material accumulation? John Gregson we know gave one pound to help establish a network of local Sunday schools. He, his father William, and his brother-in-law, George Case were willing to spend more serious amounts on their housing. Case purchased a home on the west side of the Athenaeum on Church Street, "for . . . years the resort of what may be called the 'upper crust' of Liverpool mercantile society," and seems also to have owned and enlarged an already substantial mansion called Breckfield House.[26] Not to be outdone, his father-in-law William purchased a stately house and an accompanying piece of property fronting a Baptist cemetery on Everton road, rebuilt the house and "fitted [it] up in a style of magnificence."[27] To Gregson's mind refitting the house and grounds apparently entailed pushing back the road that ran between his property and the facing "Necropolis, or city of the dead," as the Baptist cemetery was styled. "The overseers of the highways," as J. A. Picton, Liverpool's premiere nineteenth-century local historian put it, "willing to oblige so magnificent a personage, consented to alter it, so as to give adequate space in front of the mansion. Hence the awkward curve in the road as it now exists."[28] That "awkward curve" and the sculpted well that sits as an island in its middle (it is called Gregson's Well) are virtually the only specific, visible trace of the Gregsons that has survived. (The house no longer exists.) It seems, however, a fitting monument. For what Picton tactfully avoids mentioning, but what is visibly evident, is that in giving Gregson "adequate space" the road builders were obliged to run the new line of the road *through* the narrow cemetery grounds whose "every available nook and corner," as Picton allows, "had to be economised for the purposes of interment."[29] Gregson's Well and the "awkward curve" he ordered in the road sit where the dead once lay — sit, it seems overwhelmingly likely, in place of the bodies disinterred to make room for William Gregson's aesthetic proclivities. History's ironies, as ever, are the most brutal, the most inescapable, the most literal minded, and the most precise. For even in his home, William Gregson's magnificence was built on the dead; his house itself was a visible display of the multiple exchanges he had extracted from them.

*

If the members of the Guildhall jury that rendered the initial verdict on the *Zong* case could order Gregson and his partners paid for the slaves Captain Collingwood had drowned because their minds were sufficiently of the age, if they could deliver this judgment because their imaginations were sufficiently credible to see in a drowned slave a still existent, guaranteed, and exchangeable form of currency, then the accounting procedures through which their age most commonly expressed its speculative epistemology was clearly, by itself, not enough to account for the jury's decision. A system of credit, no matter how extensive, could serve as a necessary but not a sufficient condition for the jury's ruling that Collingwood had conferred a credible and recoverable quantum of value on the slaves he had drowned. Something else was required: fundamentally, that novel epistemology appropriate to a revolutionary new world of speculation and speculative transactions; that epistemology derived from a modern banking system which had taught eighteenth-century Britons to value the existence of imaginary things by training them to credit the power of the imagination to bring a new world of objects and values into existence. But something else was also necessary: a social form through which that epistemology could not so much find itself expressed as rendered obligatory, legally binding, enforceable in law. Credit transactions, stockjobbing, and paper money may have taught eighteenth-century Britons to *recognize* the existence of imaginary values. The novel may have trained them to *believe* that such fictive values could express the same "truth" as its fictional characters, even as it equipped them both to *read* the character of the individuals whose promises and money they increasingly had to take on credit and to *evaluate* the credibility of that general system of value that had encircled society and collateralized the fates of each of its members in the desire and credulity of all the others. But to recognize, read, and suspend disbelief in such value was not yet to be obliged to accept its reality when its existence came into dispute or when the tangible object to which such value was nominally attached passed out of existence. The contract law that covered credit transactions partially ensured the enforceability of the period's imaginary exchanges of value. But the absolute enforcement of the "real" existence of imaginary values required the presence of a social practice which did not simply bind parties to their contracts but one which entirely sundered the expression of value from the existence of things, a social practice which guaranteed that value was neither inherent in things nor void with their loss but was the secure product of the imagination and agreement. And the name for that practice is insurance.

*

The genius of insurance, the secret of *its* contribution to finance capitalism, is its insistence that the real test of something's value comes not at the moment it is made or exchanged but at the moment it is lost or destroyed. In a pure commodity culture (if there ever was such a thing), that value would cease to exist the moment the commodity ceased to exist, the moment there was no longer something to exchange, the moment Marx's paradigmatic yards of cloth, burnt up, no longer existed to express the value of the shirts for which they could have been exchanged. However, in a money culture or an insurance culture value survives its objects, and in doing so does not just reward the individual self-interest of the insured object's owner, but retrospectively confirms the system-wide conviction that that value was *always* autonomous from its object, *always* only a matter of agreement. Insurance value, a more durable precisely because a less material, contingent, or mutable form of value than either use value or exchange value, does not await the moment of loss to become real. It exists the moment an object is insured and effectively abridges Marx's full formula for capital at that moment, conferring upon that object a value that neither depends on its being put to use or entered into exchange as a commodity but results purely from the ability of two contracting parties to imagine what it would have been worth at that imaginary future moment in which it will have ceased to exist. Indeed, with regard to its value, the object has ceased to exist the very moment that future becomes imaginable. The insurance that covers an object has not ensured that it will survive destruction. Anticipating that future moment of destruction, insurance proleptically visits its consequences upon the object. It annuls the object, abolishes it as a bearer of value, and so frees value from the degradation of thingly existence.

If the object in question is a commodity, insurance further liberates its value from the need to be tested and expressed in an actual marketplace exchange. In place of the "real" markets to which commodities are brought for exchange, insurance substitutes an imaginary market to which the commodity would have been brought, from which it would have received its exchange value, and treats this purely speculative market as if it actually exists and has already conferred value on the commodity. Imagining a typical exchange that might have taken place, insurance indicates that an actual, literal exchange is no longer necessary. Simply to have imagined that exchange is to have created the value. (And it is in this, in its capacity to imagine typical markets and typical lives and to confer upon them the capacity to express "real" truths, that insurance is surely at its most novelistic.) Insurance thus does not confer a monetary value upon lost things, it sets the money form of value free from the life of things, insures *its* existence, instantly speeds whatever it touches to the money form of value. It does not ensure things, it ensures a form of value, serves as that form's word of guarantee. Absent the security insurance provides, finance capitalism could not exist. The world of things would stage its revenge on value each time some object or another was destroyed, would refasten value to embodied things and make one as mortal as the other. Licensed by insurance to utterly detach value from the material existence of objects, however, finance capital is free to speculate in and profit from its imaginary markets, imaginary transactions, imaginary valuations, and to exchange both use values and exchange values for the indestructible money form.

∗

It is hard to remember that, as a legal matter, the *Zong* case was not a murder case. Captain Collingwood's actions were not on trial. A form of value was. And because this was not a murder case but an insurance case, that form of valuing things — by annulling them, canceling their capacity to bear value, dismissing the question of either their intrinsic or their exchange value — could not but have emerged victorious. For what else were Collingwood's actions than this abstract form of value literalized? What else was the plaintiff's argument that the value of their "things" had survived the moment of their destruction but the very definition of insurance? What else could William Gregson, his sons, and their partners have expected but that they would walk out of court holding the tokens of that form of value their insurance contract had long since detached from the lives of the human "things" they had insured?

∗

Seven months after securing their victory in the Guildhall courtroom, John and William Gregson would have been anticipating another: John's election as mayor. The election at which he triumphed was held, as always, on October 18, St. Luke's day, also known in Liverpool as Liberty Day, the day the city celebrated William III's restoration, in 1695, of its original charter of governance (which had been temporarily abrogated during the rule of Charles II).[30] The election of a mayor by the forty-one members of the Corporation, whose existence and whose right to govern the city William III had recognized, was, thus, as much a celebration of local custom as it was a political event. The Corporation elected not only the mayor, it elected its own membership (which meant in practice that the same small group of men was essentially always in office): a prerogative which Charles II had abolished, William had restored, and the Corporation was eager to defend. (In 1791 the Corporation successfully defeated a challenge to its rule—brought to the court of King's Bench in London by a self-styled "Common Council" which had sought to open the city's electoral and governmental system—by convincing Justice Kenyon that the law should favor the city's "immemorial usages" and "customary modes" rather than the novel democratic theory of the "Common Council."[31]) In repeatedly electing one of its own as mayor, the Corporation could therefore represent itself as devoted not to guarding its own privilege but to preserving local custom and "usage" against the encroachments of a leveling, homogenizing modernity; an ironic practice, to be sure, for the elite of a city that was one of the capitals of the globe's "modernization," but also, perhaps, a predictable one, allowing the members of the Corporation, at least, to partially exempt themselves from the bewildering changes they were otherwise fostering. Hence the Corporation's determination to hold its elections on Liberty Day, the day the city's immemorial usages had been reestablished, by Royal Charter, as local law.

Hence also their devotion to pursuing the custom, a few days before Liberty Day each year, of setting out on horseback to tour the city's time-honored municipal boundaries, a set of "stones, placed at irregular intervals," commonly referred to as the Liberties.[32] The practice was for the outgoing mayor, the members of the Corporation, a collection of friends, a band of music, and a troop carrying the city's regalia, to tour the Liberties as a way of keeping the city's local history and identity "in public remembrance."[33] Following the tour—which included reading aloud from incisions cut into the surface of these stones the names of the city's previous mayors—the party would decamp to a tent pitched at Lowhill for a celebratory feast. The Gregsons would have enjoyed many of these, few perhaps, as piquantly as the one held in 1783, seven months after the Guildhall verdict and just a few days before John

Gregson's election. The menu for that meal does not survive, but a bill presented to the Corporation for a subsequent Liberty Day feast by Jane Barrow, keeper of the Lowhill Coffee-House, does, and it gives a fair sense of how the Gregsons and their fellows were accustomed to feting themselves in defense of their city's peculiar "Liberties":

To roast and boiled beef	1 (pound) 13 (shillings) 6 (pence)
Hams fowls & tongues	2 15 0
Veal Pies	0 8 0
Pidgeon Pies	0 15 6
Potted and fresh Shrimps	0 11 0
Milk Punch	2 18 6
Rum and Brandy Punch	1 15 0
Wine	0 17 6
Brandy	0 16 6
Rum	0 19 0
Ale, Porter &c.	1 8 0
Labourer's Wages, Canvas, Cartage	1 12 0
	16 (pounds) 9 (shillings) 6 (pence)[34]

The assiduity with which this practice was observed, the city's customs and usages defended, and its stones of memory preserved bears comparison with this comment from a 1758 letter sent by a parliamentary committee dispatched to investigate the conditions of the slave forts kept by the Company of Merchants Trading to Africa. The report is, on the whole, favorable, except when it comes to describing the "Insults and Intrigues of the Natives to obstruct the Proceedings of the English" in building a fort at Anamabo (the fort from which Collingwood loaded the *Zong*'s cargo of slaves). "In respect to this particular Fort of Annamaboo," it turned out, the insults and intrigues of the natives, amounted to a refusal to collect or quarry rock for construction on the fort: "Stone might be had," the report irritatedly notes, "but it depends on the pleasure of the Superstitious Natives, who deem many of their Rocks Sacred . . . [and] it would be the utmost folly to Undeceive them."[35]

∗

The fort was, nevertheless, built and the "sacred rocks" of the "superstitious natives'" incorporated into the walls of its holding pens. Against this loss of their Liberties there was, needless to say, no insurance.

∗

The Liverpool Corporation eventually lost its liberties also. The charter of William III was revoked in 1835 under the Municipal Corporations Reform Act.[36] The custom of "riding the Liberties" lapsed in the same year. Contemporary political history clearly had much to do with this change (one can read it as a local version of Chartist history). I find it hard however to resist the suggestion that the fate of the Anamabo rocks and the Liverpool Liberties were linked, that their vanishing is part of the same historical process, that, in minuscule form, the loss of liberty the Liverpool slave merchants visited upon the slaves was belatedly visited upon them as the loss of their peculiar Liberties to a modernity indifferent to local custom, usage, or superstition. Regardless of the direct and indirect causal logics at work, however, the vanishing of either of these sets of sacred stones again allegorizes the more general dematerializing logic of the moment, allegorizes that war on thingliness which characterizes the speculative culture of finance capital, and which, I have further argued, finds its ultimate expression in the practice of insurance.

*

A finance capitalism that traces its origins to the establishment of a modern system of banking in the later decades of the seventeenth century may, by the eighteenth century, have become literally unimaginable without the support insurance provided it. Absent the slave trade, however, eighteenth-century insurance could not have been what it was — either as a means of ordering imaginary value or as a foundation for accumulating bankable wealth. The cowrie may have fed the slave trade, but the slave trade fed the insurance industry which in its turn nourished the financial revolution which inaugurated an Atlantic cycle of accumulation. The role that insurance played in securing Britain's turn-of-the-century financial revolution is fairly straightforward. If insurance value, as I have suggested, is a general epistemological precondition and guarantee for finance capitalism, the practice of insurance, as P. G. M. Dickson makes clear throughout his history of the financial revolution, was crucial both to "stimulat[ing] investment in domestic and foreign trade" (by reducing the risk of such investment) and to providing speculators with another major industry in which to invest.[37] Barely existent through the seventeenth century, and extremely loosely organized at the beginning of the eighteenth by a range of ad hoc brokers and underwriters, insurance had, by the 1720s, taken on a far more coherent form. Its four centers were the consortium of underwriters based at Lloyd's Coffee House, the Sun Fire Office, the Royal Exchange Assurance Corporation, and the London Assurance Corporation — the last three of which had major stock presences on

Exchange Alley, the last two as chartered companies established by a 1720 act of Parliament. (The potential wealth to be made from the insurance trade was sufficient to convince agents for the Royal Exchange and London Assurance companies to give King George a "gift" of 600,000 pounds in exchange for his support in granting the charters, an investment which, at least in the short run, proved worthwhile: in the first year that they were traded on the Exchange, the stock of the two companies rose from an initial price of 5 guineas to over 250 pounds per share.)[38]

All four of the bodies around which the new industry clustered occupied themselves with the primary forms of insurance of the period, some of which, such as life, fire, and marine insurance (*the* major source of insurance business) involved fairly standard guarantees of compensation against the loss of life or property, but many of which were more imaginative. Insurers sold tontine loans — a form of group life insurance — to consortiums of purchasers in exchange for a fixed capital amount which was then invested in the shares of publicly held companies whose dividends were paid to the investors as long as one of them was alive. Each investor's share of the total dividends, in other words, increased as her or his fellows died off, with the last one living receiving the entire amount. Through the purchase of these loans investors were thus able to speculate both on the market and on their own and their fellows' mortality, profiting either when the market was up or when one or more of their business partners died or, ideally, both. Positively insured against the death of a business partner, the customers of Britain's eighteenth-century insurance underwriters could also negatively insure themselves against the risk of their other investments. Lottery insurance (the concept of which had been borrowed from John Law, the exiled Scottish financier who had also invented the model on which the South Sea scheme was based when, in 1719, he convinced the French government to exchange its debt for shares of the India and Mississippi Companies trading on the Parisian Bourse) was particularly popular throughout the 1720s, both for those whose losing lottery tickets were insured against total loss and for the state, which raised much of its revenue through lotteries and encouraged any practice which would stimulate the sale of tickets.[39] The industry's fundamental entanglement with the practical affairs of eighteenth-century finance capitalism came, however, in less creative forms, primarily through the floating of insurance company stock and the day-to-day accounting procedures through which insurance underwriters, like the slave-trading clientele who provided the bulk of their business, managed most of their business dealings on credit.

A standard eighteenth-century marine insurance contract involved three parties: a ship's owner or one or more of its investors; a broker, hired to negotiate a contract by the party seeking insurance; and an insurance underwriter (in fact almost always a set of underwriters). A broker charged with the task of securing 10,000 pounds of insurance on a vessel and its cargo would typically secure that cover from a collection of underwriters (no single one of whom would want to make themselves liable for so great a risk) in exchange for a premium that generally amounted to 10 to 20 percent of the total insurance value (half of which was often returned if the voyage came off without a loss). Collectively, the underwriters were thus owed a premium of 1,000 to 2,000 pounds. But the brokers, who earned their living on the commissions they made from each contract they negotiated, rarely handed over a cash payment from the owners to the underwriters. Premiums were, instead, accepted on credit in the form of the now-familiar bills of exchange.[40] The advantages of this system were largely identical to those derived from the credit financing of the slave trade itself. The interest-bearing bills increased the value of the premiums while permitting brokers and underwriters alike to manage their cash flow and to circulate a means of payment throughout the wider economy. As D. E. W. Gibb indicates in his history of Lloyd's, this system of credit payment also served to guarantee the security of insurance contracts themselves:

> The real reason for the security of a Lloyd's policy in the eighteenth century lay in the long credit that underwriters gave to brokers. They seem never to have allowed less than twelve months credit and sometimes as much as three years. Unless a man's underwriting was very unprofitable he was always owed a considerable sum by the brokers, and the brokers' balances were a floating reserve which must have proved valuable if the underwriter were ever forced into insolvency by some staggering total loss. That accounting system, which had grown up at Lloyd's no doubt for the convenience of brokers and their clients, was at the same time a safeguard to any merchant who found he had a defaulting underwriter on his policy. It mitigated the mischief after the mischief was known.[41]

The security of their contracts safely underwritten by their willingness to accept payment on credit, insurance underwriters were thus freed to pursue and to expand their business, to bank or circulate the premiums which they had been promised, to augment their own wealth even as they increased the quantity of paper money steadily accumulating within the circum-Atlantic economy. Each time a slaving contract was signed, each time a premium was promised and accepted on credit, between 10 and 20 percent of the insurance value of the trade was instantly converted into paper money, an advance contract of sorts on the still greater amounts of negotiable debt generated in the slave markets of west Africa and the Caribbean and serially recirculated throughout the port cities of the Atlantic archipelago.

For the first half of the century, the bulk of that insurance-generated paper money would have accumulated within London. Over the last fifty years of the century, however, the insurance industry, while remaining vibrant in London, also wandered upcoast to serve the needs of the Liverpool slavers who had begun to dominate the trade and whose city was rapidly becoming another countercapital of this cycle of accumulation. As Liverpool-based brokers and underwriters began to add their tallies of credit and debt to the city's economy, and so increased yet further the degree to which economic life was transacted through the trade's money forms, their way of conducting business would have further increased the need for a set of social reading practices which could enable both the immediate and the collateral parties to this trade to evaluate the credibility of their counterparts' promises and to confirm the valuation they had placed on those things whose worth they wished reexpressed as an insurance value. In other words, insurance, no less than credit financing, extended a dual economy of credibility and speculative value, demanding the establishment of a novelized public imaginary as it systematically co-lateralized the well-being of subjects, not only in the trustworthiness of their fellow's paper money but in the trustworthiness of one another's character and one another's ability to read the credibility of character.

For the brokers and underwriters this need was most immediately manifest at the moment a contract was signed. As Gibb's history of Lloyd's reveals, the primary challenge for an insurance broker was not finding an underwriter with whom to sign a contract (there were more than enough underwriters seeking trade) but evaluating the fiscal and ethical credibility of those offering to do business lest they sign a cargo of goods over to someone unable or unwilling to pay off its potential loss. "[They] had to guess correctly the means of the different underwriters, distinguish between the strong men and the weaklings, and see to it that, if possible, no policy sent out . . . was signed by a man of doubtful standing. . . . [They had to] know their men . . . watch their methods . . . detect the first sign of recklessness in an underwriter."[42] The challenge to the underwriters was similar but also more complex, partially because they had to accurately evaluate the character of the brokers who brought them business and signed over their bills of exchange in payment for a contract *and* to evaluate the trustworthiness of the merchants who were represented by those brokers and who claimed to have in their possession (though, in the case of marine insurance, often not in Liverpool or London) the goods they wished insured. And, as was the case with those individuals who despite being at one or more remove from an original transaction had nevertheless come into possession of the bills of exchange signed by the "factors" of the Caribbean slave markets, this need to evaluate credibility and read for character did not stop with the signing of a contract. If anything it intensified as it restaged itself at each moment of a bill's recirculation, each moment of ever-greater remove, each moment of an ever more extensive coimplication of all those parties whose names might appear on the circulating bills but whose characters became ever more a matter of speculation, ever more apprehensible only as one of those "types" that Lynch suggests the contemporary novel was teaching Britons to read.

The task of the underwriters involved more, however, than the initial exertion of this work of evaluation. To the general social work of evaluating character they were charged with the specific work of valuing society's goods, setting a valuation on things that would at once accurately define their worth and survive their loss. In the lexicon of the eighteenth-century insurance business this was known as "averaging," and it required a social reading practice as reliable and complex as that fundamental to the evaluation of character. Credit, for its successful operation, may have required a novelistic education in the reading of society. Insurance demanded this too. But it also required something like the practice of a historicist cultural theory. The fundament of that interpretive practice was the "intelligence" which John Weskett identifies as crucial to the welfare of insurance in his 1781 *Complete Digest of the Theory, Laws, and Practice of Insurance*, the first text to attempt to systematize British insurance and a manual of sorts to that situated cultural study on which it depended.[43] By "intelligence" Weskett intends the full body of knowledge requisite to the profitable pursuit of a career in underwriting: the knowledge of ship sailing and docking times provided for the London insurance community by Lloyd's lists and published for their Liverpool counterparts in *Gore's General Advertiser*; the knowledge of market conditions and commodity prices in the full range of maritime entrepôts; the knowledge of the hazard levels associated with each of the 100 or more commodities most commonly insured in the maritime trade; the knowledge of both the particular domestic and foreign political events that might affect a given commodity trade and of the broader historical trends impinging on Britain's involvement in international commerce; the knowledge of conditions of commodity scarcity and oversupply prevailing at each of the port cities to which a cargo might be brought for sale; the knowledge of currency exchange rates and the shifting value of a cargo of goods as expressed in Spanish, American, Dutch, French, and British coin; the knowledge of the trustworthiness of individual merchants consigning a cargo to the sea and of their willingness to submit a fraudulent claim; the knowledge of the behavior of captains, their willingness to sail in the company of a Royal Navy escort (when such was provided) or to bolt escort in the interest of arriving first at an undersupplied market; the knowledge of the incidence of privateering along particular trade routes and of the weather hazards of these; the knowledge, in a word, of the full set of historical circumstances which might operate as a given cargo's situation, and in Lukács's terms, lend it its typical, hence measurable, hence riskable or untouchable character. Blending all this knowledge, the intelligence (what I have earlier called the "mind") of insurance could hope to historicize the particular, situate the individual voyage or commodity within its moment, and from the thick descriptive protocols of this historicizing operation evaluate its character and, more profitably, convert this evaluation into a number — the demanded premium which functioned as a numeric expression and condensation of the sum total of knowledge generated by this cultural theory. As a stock valuation is the market's expression of its heterological cultural analysis of the character of a corporation, so premiums functioned as the numeric outcome of the "intelligence" of insurance's historicizing "theory" of trade.

The task of insurance was not, however, only to evaluate a trade in advance of its accomplishment but to set a valuation on that trade's objects against the eventuality of their loss, indeed to define this (anticipated) loss as a condition of their value, to define value as loss value. And to secure this valuation (and so, also, to secure the release of value from the hazards of the thingly, material existence of the commodity), insurance, according to Weskett, requires an identical intelligence but directs that intelligence not toward an actual knowledge of what "is" but to a speculative knowledge of "what would have been."[44] It accumulates its knowledge of the circumstances in which the individual thing (voyage, cargo, trade, commodity) is situated but then, rather than bringing these circumstances to bear on its evaluation of that individual thing, substitutes for the individuality of the thing its typical or average character and identifies this typical, average abstraction as that thing's immaterial value. The strong analogies between this procedure, the typicalizing operations characteristic of the early novel, and the recuperation of typicality as the central category of a preromantic historicist method suggest that the problem of the "average" which Weskett identifies as the central problem addressed by his "theory" of insurance may indeed also be the central theoretical problem which both an early-eighteenth-century pragmatic historicism and the eighteenth-century novel seek to resolve.

If, when they turned their attention to the case of the *Zong*, the Guildhall jury ruled in favor of a form of value, a mode of abstract speculation, and the validity of the concept of the "average" on which that form and that mode depended, then the "intelligence" which permitted the jury to do so was clearly not unique to the insurance practice which had established the immediate terms for this legal proceeding. The jury was, rather, operating with a form of intelligence entirely apposite to that overarching "theoretical realism" that characterized the epistemological protocols of the "age"; a form of intelligence which permitted both the historicizing and the novelistic practices of the period to endorse a similar conception of persons, events, and things: a conception in which, as Jameson has it in his reading of Lukács's reading of novelistic "characters," as a consequence of their "typicality: they stand . . . for something larger and more meaningful than themselves, than their own isolated individual destinies."[45] The point is not, therefore, that either an emergent historicist sensibility or the rise of novelistic discourse are somehow to be blamed for the jury's ruling, but that both they *and* that theory of insurance which emerged at roughly the same time commonly express a refusal of the absolute, singular, individual, isolated lives of persons, events, or things — indeed posit themselves as the mode of expression for a world of persons, events, and things whose meaning is never intrinsic but always indexed to "something larger and more meaningful than themselves," something apprehensible only by way of the average and the typical. This implies that like insurance, such historicist and novelistic discourses are themselves indexed to substitutionary loss (as opposed to a romantic historicism and the romantic novel, which are indexed to the recuperation of the lost)[46] and that even the most memorable individual characters they create or the most striking moments they situate accrue what we might think of as meaning value precisely to the extent that they annul their objects' singularity. It means that all of these discourses ensure the value of their objects by visiting a speculative destruction on them equivalent to that from which insurance derives its average values and that is in their shared propensity to ground value in the loss of the singular and the invention of the average and the typical that an early novelistic and an actuarial historicist imaginary participate in and help to secure the triumph of that speculative epistemology which was the condition of possibility for the court's ruling.

*

If the eighteenth century manifests itself in crucial respects as the century of the typical and the average; if the *Zong* trials reveal the moment in which that average finds itself and the speculative epistemology it expresses legally enthroned as the obligatory value form of finance capitalism; and if the *Zong*'s insurance contract thus fashions itself as an analogue of those Parisian arcades that Benjamin found to concentrate within themselves the dominant capital and epistemological protocols of *their* capital moment, then, as Weskett's definition of the average makes clear, the key to that contract, moment, mode of speculation, and speculative epistemology is that procedure by which value detaches itself from the life of things and rearticulates itself in the novelistic theater of the typicalizing imagination. And at the definitional heart of that procedure (which is itself the very type of its typicalizing age) there is, Weskett's text indicates, a typical set of events from which an insurance culture derives its organizing protocols, a typical set of circumstances from which the concept of the average is determined, a typical situation that reads like both a description of and an invitation for the *Zong* massacre. There is another way of putting this. The typical and the average, I have been arguing, are the primary categories within which finance capital and the speculative culture apposite to the triumph of such a regime of abstract accumulation express their operation. Finance capital and its culture of speculation finds itself at once secured and articulated by that theory and practice of insurance that exists to reexpress the (after)lives of persons and things not as themselves but as a suppositional, aggregate mode of being in the world. Insurance thus underwrites the hegemony of the average and the typical. It secures these, however, much as the law secures the abstract principles it exists to ensure: by defining for itself a set of material precedents, typical cases from which (in full tautological casuistic form) to derive its general principles of operation. In the late eighteenth century, as Weskett's text indicates, all these precedents from which an insurance culture derives its operative protocols are drawn from the field of marine insurance.

There is of course nothing surprising about this. Britain's global hegemony from this moment to the middle of the nineteenth century was an oceanic hegemony, its capitalism a transmarine capitalism, and its speculative culture one secured, as the jingo cadences have it, by the assurance that "Brittania rules the waves." Ruling the waves, Britain also derived its rules of sovereignty from its maritime hegemony, not just its naval dominance of the Atlantic, Mediterranean, and Indian Oceans, but from the rules of commerce that made of these oceans the primary territories of its regime of capital accumulation. Absent the flow of commodities crisscrossing the trade routes of these marine expanses, Britain could not have maintained its hegemony. Absent the development of a marine insurance industry, it could not have *established* that hegemony. The British empire was built on its capital reorganization of the globe. That capital organization demanded, however, that the particular investments of an imperial merchant class be insured and that the value of the investments thus insured be recognized as recuperable and real even in, or exactly in, the event of their loss. How? By defining, in advance of any given risk commerce might run, a typical set of test cases which could be appealed to (after the event of loss) as the source of a guarantee that what might have been lost was not in fact lost but insured and, thus, that speculative investment in the practices of imperial commerce could continue unabated.

Marine insurance, unsurprisingly, supplied these precedents. The concept of averaging (or general averaging) unified their principles of operation. And the principle of the general average, in its turn, defined for itself *a* representative test case, *a* typical precedent from which the entire exfoliated practice of recognizing the continued existence of lost things and the real nature of speculative values depended. At the heart of what I have been calling an Atlantic cycle of accumulation is finance capital. At the heart of finance capital is insurance, particularly, in the eighteenth century, marine insurance. At the definitional heart of marine insurance is the concept of the average. And at the heart of the average is a representative test case which reads like an invitation to the *Zong* massacre:

> Whatever the master of a ship in distress, with the advice of his officers and sailors, deliberately resolves to do, for the preservation of the whole, in cutting away masts or cables, or in throwing goods overboard to lighten his vessel, which is what is meant by *jettison* or jetson, is, in all places, permitted to be brought into a general, or gross average: in which all concerned in ship, freight, and cargo, are to bear an equal or proportionable part of what was so sacrificed for the common good, and it must be made good by the insurers in such proportions as they have underwrote.[47]

This is the first sentence of Weskett's definition of the "general average," the major of the three types of averaging with which insurance concerns itself. The three types—all of whose protocols, like Weskett's general theory

of insurance itself, assume marine insurance as their normative ground—
are the "simple average," which "consists in the extraordinary expenses incurred" by a ship; the "petty average" which pertains to such minor affairs as
harbor towing expenses, and "general average" which pertains to "expenses
incurred . . . for the preservation of the ship" and, as the most fundamental
issue addressed by the practice of averaging, those "damages sustained" by the
ship or its cargo.[48] The situation that Weskett envisions in this introduction to
the concept of the general average, the paradigmatic situation from which
insurance practice deduces its full range of valuing procedures, is identical to
that with which he has earlier introduced the basic notion of the average and
from which he derives his account of its protocols: "Average and contribution
are synonymous terms in marine cases and signify a proportioning of a loss to
the owners of goods thrown overboard in a storm. . . . [Its fuller definition] is
as follows—Average means the accidents and misfortunes which happen to
ships and their cargoes, from the time of their lading and sailing, 'till their
return and unlading. . . . When goods arrived damaged, the first thing requisite is, to find out the true quantum of the damage or loss, or the diminution in
value which they have sustained; and then *to apportion that loss on what would
have been the value of the goods if they had arrived safe and undamaged*." [49]

To speak of the average is thus to speak of insurance's most complex work
of valuation, as it is to speak of a general damage or loss theory of value, of that
full range of circumstances that might degrade a good's thingly existence,
without—if it was insured—affecting its ultimate "value."[50] The average begins with damage or loss, computes the extent of loss, and then substitutes, as
a sort of prosthesis for what has been lost, the "what would have been." Average is then the word insurance gives to that paradigmatic finance-culture procedure by which lost singulars find themselves reexpressed as speculative but
exchangeable typicals. And *its* paradigm, *the* "typical" situation from which its
protocols are deduced, is the *Zong* massacre—not to be sure as a unique event
but, precisely, as a type of event, a paradigm of that typical event that the
theory of the average establishes as its general precedent and test case. Such,
certainly, was Collingwood's determination when, in October of the year that
Weskett's *Digest* was published, he called together his officers and crew, informed them that their ship was in distress, its water and food supplies running out, and, having sought their advice, as he was obliged to do, "deliberately resolve[d] . . . for the preservation of the whole. . . . [to throw] goods
overboard" with the intention of justifying his acts under the law of jettison
and claiming average compensation for "what was so sacrificed" on the basis
of "what would have been the value of the goods if they had arrived safe and

undamaged." The *Zong*, then, was not an aberration, not some wildly exceptional event which could nevertheless, somehow, just barely, be encompassed or made sense of by the dominant cultural logic of its age, not some anomaly that with the greatest of imaginative effort could be contained within the bounds of a logic that Lord Mansfield, in the appeal hearing held subsequent to the Guildhall verdict, implied Collingwood's actions had stretched just this side of the breaking point ("It is a very uncommon case," Mansfield pronounced from the bench of his court, "it shocks one very much.")[51] Nor was it simply a case to which the moment could valiantly bring its mind, a boundary event to which this finance culture could somehow manage to apply the historical peculiarities of its intelligence, method, epistemology, or imagination. It was, instead, the very type of the type of case which that moment's value theory had identified as its test case, the type of the type of event in which that moment found the full range of its cultural, capital, and imaginary protocols concentrated, *the* typical sort of loss event from which this typicalizing age deduced its speculative procedures, average theories, theoretical realism, and money forms of value.

The *Zong*, thus, was not only a name for a late-eighteenth-century *legal* case. It was, as James Chandler has taught us to reunderstand the word, an eighteenth-century case par excellence; a situation which a casuistic jurisprudence ("casuistry," Chandler reminds us, is, most simply put, "a discipline for dealing with the application of principles to cases") could submit to the test of "a general normative scheme," precisely, if tautologically, because it defined the type of situation *from which* that general normative scheme could deduce itself.[52] The case, like the historicist situation ("The relation of cases and casuistries to the notion of the situation has always," Chandler argues, "been close"; contemporary New Historicism, he further observes, tightens the fit by means of the "anecdotes" that serve as its test "cases"), thus generates a bidirectional interpretive practice, "a two way-movement in which now the general normative scheme, now the particular event or situation, is being tested." It produces a process of simultaneously reading the meaning and value of the particular off the grammar of the general *and* construing the general from the representative particular. And it is as such a situation, as such a two-way case, that the *Zong* at once falls within, and can be made sense of by, the general normative schemes of its typicalizing moment while defining the very type of situation on which the normative schemes of that (long, repeating) moment depend.[53]

*

Weskett may have argued that, with regard to insurance practice at least, this is not true, that though finance capital might depend on insurance, though insurance might rely on the notion of the average, and though the concept of the average might have defined as its typical situation a captain throwing goods overboard and so identified such acts of jettison as the test case for its average theory of value, his theory does not imagine slaves to be included among those jettisoned things, does not envision some Captain Collingwood to be the master sacrificing his goods to the sea. A maritime trade built on the transport of slaves and an insurance industry heavily financed by the slaves it included among the commodities it was willing to underwrite cannot, however, claim such innocence.

*

There is one more thing to be said about Weskett's text, one more general point to be made about the work it performs not only as a digest of insurance theory and practice but as a guidebook to that finance culture which found in the insurance and average values that underwriters like Weskett placed on things an absolutization of its general theories of value and modes of speculation. Weskett's *Digest* provides both a theory for the practice of insurance and serves as a monument to its success. It is both an abstract of how insurance might continue to be practiced and a display of what that practice has already accomplished. And among the objects of success it displays, the most significant are the tables and lists of those forms of human personhood, historical event, and commodified object that, by 1781, insurance had succeeded in drawing within its empire of value. I will not cite all of these, a selection will suffice.

In the section of his text devoted to "Lives" (a section entirely composed of annotated premium tables), Weskett includes the following:

> By a table of Mr Thomas Simpson, in his *Treatise of Annuities* . . . it appears that out of 1280 new-born infants, 410 die within the first year; and that of the 870 remaining, 170 die within the second year; and so on, as is below exhibited: — according to which, the premium to insure the life of a newborn infant for one year would be 410×100/1280 or 32 and 40/1280 per cent. and the premium for the life of a one year old appears to be 170×100/870 or 19 570/870 per cent. And so on, as in the following Table:

No. that die	Out of	Of the Age	Premium per cent for the next year
170	870	1	19 and 570/870
65	700	2	9 and 220/700
35	635	3	5 and 325/635[54]

In his section on "General Averages," Weskett includes, among the items in his list of "all the particulars which fall under the denomination of general average," and thus qualify as recompensable damages or losses, not only the predictable (such as "All that is thrown overboard, or damaged by a jettison for a ship's safety" and "The value of any goods or stores taken away or plundered by privateers") but the bizarre: "Charges (in Roman Catholic countries) of carrying the Holy Virgin home, offering thanks, and what is given to the poor."[55]

In his list of "the great variety of commodities which at different times *become the subjects of insurance*," Weskett includes:

Under Class 1. Least Hazardous: Alabaster, Beads, Brass, Bricks, Bugle, Bullion, Cane, Canvas, Coals, Coin and Medals, Copper, Copperas, Coral, Cork, Cowries, Culm, Deals, Elephants Teeth, Gold and Silver Plate, Horn Ware, Iron, Lead, Liquors, Logwood, Mahogany, Marble, Masts, Oil, Ores, Pewter, Pinch, Plank, Staves, Stone, Tar, Tiles, Timber, Tin, Wooden Ware.

Under Class 2: Common Hazardous: Brushes, Butter, Candles, Cards, Catlings, Cattle, Chariots, China, Coaches, Cochineal, Crockery, Feathers, Glass, Glue, Hair, Hats, Hogs Bristles, Hops, Horse Furniture, Hosiery, Household Furniture, Kelp, Leather Manufactures, Lime, Linens, Matts and Matting, Painters Colours, Parchment, Plaster of Paris, Quills, Rice, Rosin, Sedans, Silks, Slaves, Soap, Tallow, Tarras, Tobacco Pipes, Tortoiseshell, Toys, Vellum, Vermicelli, Wax, Wearing-Apparel, Whalebone, Woolens, Yarn.

Under Class 3: More Hazardous: Flax, Hemp, Hides, Skins, Sugar, Tobacco. . . . [56]

*

What do all these things have in common: alabaster, beads, brass, bricks, newborn infants, coral, cowries, one year olds, glass, glue, hair, oil, goods seized by pirates, lime, linens, goods thrown into the sea, parchment, quills, carrying the Virgin Mary home, rice, rosin, two year olds, sedans, silks, slaves, soap, vermicelli?

What do all the things in this grotesque Borgesian list have in common? The money form, the invisible equal sign that insurance places alongside each one of them, the speculative epistemology that over the course of the century drew each of them within its ever expanding territory of address, converted each of them into not only a type of thing, person, or event, but into a negotiable type of money, attached to each of them a premium, an insurance evaluation, and an average value, imagining for each of them an afterlife within the speculative territory of the "what would have been" and treating this imaginary existence as the condition of their worth. Each item added to the list, each item that "at some time or another became the subject of insurance," signaled another victory for finance capital, a further demonstration of the flexibility of its imagination, a further extension of its empire of value. Like the lieutenant's foot, clerk's eyes, captain's bladder and lungs converted into so many compensatory shillings, guineas, and pounds by the Lords Commissioners of the Admiralty, these candles, silks, infants, holy processions, and slaves entered the list of "things" on which the money form had gone to work, that it could subject to itself, that it could convert into an ocean-crossing network of loans, debts, bonds, and bills of exchange, an archipelagic eddy of circulating paper money, a circum-Atlantic cycle of accumulation.

What do all these things have in common? The financial entrepôts of an Atlantic cycle of capital accumulation; the shipping ports whose vessels carried these "things" from one center of the Atlantic archipelago to another; the Exchanges in which the profits generated by their transport and sale continued to accumulate; the credit networks that had transformed these "goods" into paper money; the marine insurance industry whose "typicalizing" theory of value had licensed and secured the existence of this trans-Atlantic finance capitalism.

*

And Liverpool was one of this world's capitals. And the Gregsons were this city's mayors. And the voyage of the *Zong* was one of the "arcades" in which it put itself on display.

To articulate the past historically does not mean to recognize it "the way it really was." It means to seize hold of a memory as it flashes up in a moment of danger. Historical materialism wishes to retain that image of the past which unexpectedly appears. . . . Only that historian will have the gift of fanning the spark of hope in the past who is convinced that *even the dead* will not be safe from the enemy if he wins.

This is how one pictures the angel of history. His face is turned toward the past. Where we perceive a chain of events, he sees one single catastrophe which keeps piling wreckage upon wreckage and hurls it in front of his feet. The angel would like to stay, awaken the dead, and make whole what has been smashed. But a storm is blowing from Paradise; it has got caught in his wings with such violence that the angel can no longer close them. This storm irresistibly propels him into the future to which his back is turned, while the pile of debris before him grows skyward. This storm is what we call progress.

— Benjamin, "Theses on the Philosophy of History"

CHAPTER 4

"Signum Rememorativum, Demonstrativum, Prognostikon"

MODERNITY AND THE TRUTH EVENT

"We desire a fragment of human history and one, indeed, that is drawn not from past but future time, therefore a predictive history."[1] Thus writes Kant, in the first sentence of his essay "An Old Question Raised Again: Is the Human Race Constantly Progressing?" The "fragment of human history" he has in mind, the revelatory object he wishes to snatch from future time "as a possible representation a priori of events which are supposed to happen then" is among the more extraordinary and complex figures of his philosophy of history, one that offers to make him less the precursor antagonist whose modern "time consciousness" Walter Benjamin will drastically reverse 150 years later (as many standard accounts of Benjamin's work suggest) than an anterior interlocutor whose work functions, quite precisely, as a representation a priori of the Benjaminian work to come.[2]

If Benjamin's *Arcades Project* is the fragment of human history which Kant may be said — perhaps to his great surprise — both to anticipate and to desire (not as an event, to be sure, but as a meditation on the reiterative temporality of events), these first sentences of Kant's essay are not sufficient to make this clear. For despite the striking similarity of his concept of the representation a priori (not to mention, in the phrase which immediately precedes this formulation, his notion of "a divinatory historical narrative of things imminent in future time")[3] to the Benjaminian notion of the redemptive, messianic future-present which retroactively redeems the contemporary present as its what-has-been Kant's account has not yet established as its point of view that "future time" which will code the present as its past, thus discovering the future fully "imminent" in the past-present, and so severing this philosophy of history from that "horizons of expectation" discourse that Reinhart Koselleck identifies as the Enlightenment's prime contribution to a modern consciousness of time.[4] Koselleck's argument is well known, and it certainly accommodates these sentences by Kant within its general discussion of a future-oriented Enlightenment time consciousness licensed by the growing gap "societal modernization" opens between the anterior and the lived "space[s] of experience" and an anticipated, transformed-and-transforming future which functions, in Habermas's gloss on Koselleck, as the present's ever more rapidly approaching "horizon . . . constantly subject to being overlaid with utopian conceptions."[5] Benjamin's prime contribution to the philosophy of history, Habermas argues, is, in fact, to overturn precisely this conception, to reverse flow by identifying as the present's key "horizon" not the future but the past (hence the backward-looking "angel of history"), to offer to transform the "present" (as both a "space of experience" and a period concept) by snatching for it predictive, messianic, typological fragments of human history not from future time but from time past.[6]

The Kant/Benjamin opposition thus seems, at least so far, to hold. The "future," however, does not wait the 150 years that pass between Kant and Benjamin to finds itself replaced by the "past" as the present's governing horizon of expectation. That reversal — what we might think of as Kant's proleptic Benjaminian turn (or, to repeat his phrase again, his a priori representation of Benjamin) — comes a scant few pages later in his text when he comes to identify his desired fragment of human history not with an event to come but with one that has already, if still quite recently, passed.

> There must be some experience in the human race which, as an event, points to the disposition and capacity of the human race to be the cause of its own advance toward the better . . . Therefore, an event must be sought which points to the existence of such a cause and to its effectiveness in the human race, undetermined with regard to time, and which would allow progress toward the better to be concluded as an inevitable consequence. This conclusion could then be extended to the history of the past (that it has always been in progress) in such a way that that event would have to be considered not itself as the cause of history, but only as an intimation, an historical sign (*signum rememorativum, demonstrativum, prognostikon*) demonstrating the tendency of the human race viewed in its entirety, that is seen not as individuals (for that would yield an interminable enumeration and computation), but rather as divided into nations and states (as it is encountered on earth.)[7]

The event Kant has in mind, he then goes on to clarify, is the sublime spectacle of the French Revolution: the occasion for "disinterested sympathy it affords," the power it possesses to make of itself "a phenomenon in human history [that] is not to be forgotten . . . [an event that] is too important, too much interwoven with the interest of humanity and . . . too widely propagated in all areas of the world to not be recalled on any favorable occasion by the nations which would then be roused to a repetition of new efforts of this kind."[8] The crucial turn (the Benjaminian volte-face) in this sequence from Kant's opening desire for "a fragment of human history . . . drawn not from past but from future time," to his discovery of that future in a past event that is "not to be forgotten," is the phrase "This conclusion could then be extended to the history of the past" in the middle of the paragraph I have cited. Up to that point, Kant's horizon (one not so much of expectation as of "intimation") remains future oriented. In troping his turn to the "history of the past" as an "extension" rather than a reversal of this forward-looking gaze, he seems, indeed, to wish to counter the suggestion that he has reversed field at all, to cover, or disavow, the dramatic shift of perspective that is about to ensue. And it is crucial to note that it is Kant's *perspective* which has shifted, not his method or his desire. He continues to search for "fragments," "intimations," or "signs" that will point "to the disposition and capacity of the human race to be the cause of its own advance" and to disclose its better self to itself. But now those intimations come to the present not from the future but from the past; they demonstrate "the tendency of the human race viewed in its entirety" by discovering that tendency not in a fragment of future history but in a signum rememorativum, demonstrativum, prognostikon.

Kant is not Benjamin. And I have no interest in arguing that he is. I do want to propose that his philosophy of history remains far less inimical to Benjamin's than we might think, that, most specifically, this complex Kantian signum grounds a reiterative philosophy of history (one constellated around the coincident recollection and anticipation of the demonstrative event) markedly like that Benjaminian philosophy of history (or historical materialism) grounded in the "memory as it flashes up" (as Benjamin has it in the "Theses") or the dialectical image ("that wherein what has been comes together in a flash with the now to form a constellation" [*Arcades*]) and that one way to apprehend the form of this "likeness" is through the terms these "like" philosophies define. The form of the relation of Kant and Benjamin (as regards their philosophies of history) is apprehensible, in other words, as something like "that wherein what has been [Kant] comes together in a flash with the now [Benjamin] to form a constellation"; and the names for that constellation are the signum rememorativum, demonstrativum, prognostikon, the dialectical image, and the representation a priori. Again, however, it is less important to apprehend the form of relation between Benjamin and Kant or their various signs, fragments, images, and events than to suggest that the long-durational and dialectical interplay of their engagement with such terms provide us with yet another "sign" of the extension, durability, and reiterability of our long twentieth century contemporaneity, one which precisely finds itself "extended to the history of [a] past (that . . . has always been in progress)," while providing us with an enriched vocabulary for thinking about the ways in which a given fragment, image, event, or sign both bears within itself the capacity to demonstrate a general tendency of history and the capacity to survive this demonstration by reiterating it within the coincident domains of the anticipated and the recollected.

Kant is not Benjamin. But they do seem to agree that the modern is, in one way or another, apprehensible and condensed within a field of resonant and reiterative images or signs and that condensed within such signs, modernity articulates itself not as the universalization of an homogeneous empty order of time but as a labor of repetition and recollection. What remains is to decide which type of event serves as the sign in which modernity finds itself dem-

onstrated, recollected, and anticipated. For much continental philosophy —
certainly for the philosophical tradition that traces itself to Hegel and Kant —
the French Revolution (and the Enlightenment discourses subtending and
attending that revolution) has functioned as that sign — whether happily or
unhappily so. What I have been implying, and what I want to now make clear,
is that it seems equally possible to identify the *Zong* as an alternate signum
rememorativum, demonstrativum, prognostikon or, what is almost the same
argument (but not quite), that we might transpose the image of the *Zong*, its
insurance contract, and the speculative epistemology, mode of subjectivity,
and value form that contract underwrites onto Kant's sublime revolutionary
spectacle and find in this dialectical double image a "typical" countersign in
which modernity (our long contemporaneity) finds itself demonstrated, anticipated, and recollected.

*

To grasp what might be at stake in making such a claim, however, we need to
get a slightly fuller sense of what Kant and Benjamin intend by such terms
(sign, image, event) and of how these terms, in turn, relate to some of those
other key figures of historical thinking by means of which I have been suggesting we might make sense of this "event." And the first thing to note here are
the ways in which Kant's theory of the event engages the historicist category
of the "case" and the contemporaneous practice of casuistry. Casuistry, and
the case form on which it depends, encompasses, as I have suggested following
James Chandler's lead, a bidirectional, quasi-tautological interpretive practice, one which can apply "general principles" to "individual cases" only by
first establishing a set of cases from which to deduce its general principles.
Historicism, likewise, decodes "situations" by reference to a set of determining "circumstances" which depend for their existence, coherence, and recognizability on precisely those typical situations they are understood to decode.
A fundamentally consonant set of hermeneutic protocols (those we have come
to identify, variously, with the "hermeneutic circle" and the problematics of
the "undecidable") attend Kant's definition of the "event."

In the sentences immediately prior to his recoding of the event as the
signum rememorativum, demonstrativum, prognostikon and his immediately
ensuing discovery of this sign in the sublime spectacle of the French Revolution, Kant establishes this circular methodological rule: "From a given cause
an event as an effect can be predicted [only] if the circumstances prevail which
contribute to it."[9] This is tricky, in part because the sentence seems to shift,

midway, from a general account of the nature of predictive causality ("From a given cause an event as an effect can be predicted") to an analysis of the relation of circumstance to event. The event is thus doubly predicated *from* a cause (as the predictable effect of that cause) and *by* a set of circumstances (as, ostensibly, the effect of these circumstances). The implicit syllogism would thus align circumstances with (and as) causes and so produce a general — if bare bones — historicist conception of events as the determinate "effects" of prevailing circumstances. The sentences which follow, however, complicate this. For here it seems apparent that Kant's interest is not in predicting or predicating events from prevailing circumstances (which function as these events' cause) but in predicting or predicating circumstances from determinate events (which are these circumstances' cause). The sentences in question read so: "That these conditions [circumstances] must come to pass some time or other can, of course, be predicted in general, as in the calculation of probability in games of chance; but that prediction cannot enable us to know whether what is predicted is to happen in my life and I am to have the experience of it. Therefore an event must be sought."[10] Part of the confusion here (as events seem now to precede circumstances, now to be caused by them) follows from Kant's use of the word "prediction" — by which he seems to intend something like "predication," though in such a way as to reintroduce a processual, temporal quality to the act of predication such that predication anticipates but does not yet encounter the predicated. If we assume that what Kant has in mind is some such concept of predication, then things become a little more familiar (if no less tautological). For here again Kant defines as the event that which is predicated by a set of circumstances whose (future) existence (as recognizability) it at once predicates and predicts; or, alternately put, he envisions a set of circumstances which can be understood to precede the event they are said to predicate only "after" that event has brought them to light as its set of prevailing conditions. That reformulation offers, indeed, to dissolve the tautology, as least in part. For what it suggests is that there are two competing (rather than two circular) modes of precedence in question: the precedence of the "actual" and the precedence of the "categorizable." Circumstances, thus understood, actually precede the events they predicate, but it is the event which precedes the operations of the categorizing intelligence and which enables that intelligence to retrospectively formulate (or, as Kant might have it, "demonstrate") prevailing circumstances from some singular event.

I have paused over such questions neither simply to examine the congruence between Kant's event theory and casuistic and historicist practices nor to suggest that in consequence of these several paradoxes and tautologies we should demand some alternate less vexed event theory, but, rather, because it is precisely in such terms that the *Zong* establishes itself as a event actually determined by its prevailing circumstances and as an event which makes it possible for us to recognize those circumstances in the first place. The *Zong*, in other words, can serve for the long twentieth century as a signum rememorativum, demonstrativum, prognostikon, can demonstrate those prevailing historical tendencies which preceded it, which it enables us retrospectively to apprehend and to categorize, and which, re-collecting, it also predicts, precisely to the extent that it is, in Kant's full sense, also an event, or, in the words of Alain Badiou, one of Kant's more recent interlocutors, not just an event, but a "Truth-Event."

*

Badiou, whose work is of importance to Žižek, defines the truth event in contradistinction to what he calls the "Knowledge" of the "multiplicity of Being."[11] His significance for Žižek, and also for the argument I am making here, lies at least in part in his capacity to reconcile Kant both to a tradition of French Marxist thought (preeminently, for Žižek, to an Althusserian Marxism, but also, if more agonistically, to the poststructural Marxism of Derrida's *Specters of Marx*) and, most crucially, to Benjamin.[12] The Kantian register of Badiou's thought, Žižek argues, is strong and persistent, subtends his frequent and explicit disagreements with Kant, and assumes form in his fundamental categories of analysis. "At a deeper level his distinction between the order of the positive Knowledge of Being and the wholly different Truth-Event remains Kantian: when he emphasizes how, from the [neutral] standpoint of Knowledge, there simply is no Event—how, that is, the traces of the Event can be discerned as signs only by those who are already involved in support of the Event—does he not thereby repeat Kant's notion of signs that announce the noumenal act of freedom without positively proving it (like enthusiasm for the French Revolution)."[13] The Kantian "notion of signs" Žižek has in mind is, obviously enough, that indexed to the signum rememorativum, demonstrativum, prognostikon. And indeed, by Žižek's account, Badiou's theory of the truth event is one intimately linked to Badiou's reading of Kant's discussion of the French Revolution as sublime spectacle-event and one structured by the same quasi-tautological mode of reading the relation of event and circumstance (or, in Badiou's preferred idiom, situation).

For Badiou, the truth event belongs to an epistemological domain fundamentally distinct from that encompassed by knowledge. Knowledge, he maintains, pertains to the realm of facticity and so encompasses that enormous multiplicity of phenomena by which being (as an undifferentiated totality of that which "presents itself" to experience) is constituted. Knowledge, thus, is properly the province of science, and its only true discipline, he argues, is mathematics. Truth, on the other hand, implies a fidelity to (and a "decision for") a motivated delimitation of the totality of being into concrete sets, conditions, states, or situations. Truth is thus, always, not the truth of being but the truth of a situation, the truth of a singular state of history. It includes not just the situation it names but the determination to name a situation as such (i.e., it admits the tautological protocol as integral to its operation; it acknowledges that the act of defining a situation, the act of deciding to "count a situation as One," is fundamental to and constitutive of the truth it seeks to describe).[14] And its condition of possibility is the generally sudden, generally surprising emergence of a truth event, the dramatic appearance of a disturbance (sign, image) within the field of knowledge which, precisely because it cannot be accounted for by the prevailing regimes of knowledge, precisely because it appears as an anomaly, demonstrates the repressed or previously unrecognizable truth of a historical situation. Among Badiou's premier test cases for such an event is, unsurprisingly, the French Revolution, whose appearance as a Badiouvian truth event Žižek glosses so:

> Take French society in the late eighteenth century: the state of society, its strata, economic, political, ideological conflicts, and so on, are accessible to knowledge. However, no amount of knowledge will enable us to predict or account for the properly unaccountable event called the "French Revolution." In this precise sense, the event emerges *ex nihilo*: if it cannot be accounted for in terms of the situation, this does not mean that it is simply an intervention from Outside or Beyond — it attaches itself precisely to the Void of every situation, to its inherent inconsistency and/or its excess. The Event is the Truth of the situation that makes visible/legible what the "official" situation had to "repress," but it is also always localized — that is to say, the Truth is always the Truth *of* a specific situation. The French Revolution, for example, is the Event which makes visible/legible the excesses and inconsistencies, the "lie," of the *ancien regime*, and it is the Truth of the *ancien regime* situation, localized, attached to it. An event thus involves its own series of determinations: the Event itself; its naming (the designation "French Revolution" is not an objective categorizing but part of the Event itself. . . .); its ultimate Goal (the society of fully realized emancipation, of freedom — equality — fraternity); its "operator" (the political movements struggling for the Revolution); and, last but not least,

its *subject*, the agent who, on behalf of the truth event, intervenes in the historical multiple of the situation and discerns/identifies in it signs-effects of the Event."[15]

As Žižek's comments suggest, the full scope of Badiou's conception of the truth event is entirely complex. And it is not my object here to provide a full account of his theory but, rather, as a first step to returning to the *Zong* as such a truth event, to emphasize a few of its elements: centrally what Žižek identifies as the truth event's determinations, but also its status as what we might think of as a representative anomaly and its mode of appearance as at once Kantian sign, Benjaminian image, and Derridean specter.

The spectral quality of the truth event (and the quasi-Derridean quality of Badiou's thinking), pertains to its uncanny and reiterative temporality. For the event, like the specter, is an untimely apparition: untimely in the sense that it first appears as the reapparition of itself, emerges into visibility (as an event) not at the moment of its happening but only within the retrospective purview of what Žižek calls its subjects — those who, having made a decision for the truth of the event, belatedly call the event into being (as one) by naming it as such and naming themselves as those who are faithful to the truth they have discerned in it (as Žižek has it, "we never encounter it 'now,' since it is always recognized as such retroactively, through the act of Decision").[16] Derrida, in *Specters of Marx*, proves himself, in this precise sense, a faithful subject of Marx and of a Marxian project for the emancipation of the society, much as Kant, in his essay, identifies himself as a subject of the French Revolution, subjects whose faithfulness to the event is indexed not so much to the events of the event but to their determination or decision to be faithful to the spirit of the event (whether, as in Kant's case, that spirit is attached to its spectacularly sublime quality or, in Derrida's, to its hauntological refusal to ever assume a final, empirical, ontologized form).[17] And the event is spectral in the sense that like Kant's signum rememorativum, demonstrativum, prognostikon and Derrida's revenant, it exists, for Badiou, as a promise to come again in some full, final, and absolute form.[18]

Spectral, or at least quasi-spectral, the truth event is also, in the terms I have used, a representative anomaly, in Žižek's words, a symptom: "What Truth does is to reveal that (what Knowledge misperceives as) marginal malfunctionings and points of failure are a structural necessity. . . . With regard to the *ancien regime*, what the truth event reveals is how injustices are not marginal malfunctionings but pertain to the very structure of the system which is, in its essence, as such 'corrupt.' Such an entity — which, misperceived by the system as a local 'abnormality,' effectively condenses the global 'abnormality' of the system as such, in its entirety — is what, in the Freudo-Marxian tradition, is called the *symptom*."[19] As such a "normative" abnormality within a global system, Badiou's truth event also bears comparison to the "case" form *to which and from which* Chandler, following André Jolles, suggests normative systems apply and deduce their systemic principles of operation: "The case, says Jolles, is not merely an instantiation of a general scheme or normative system; nor is it just the form in which that instantiation occurs. Rather it is the occurrence of an anomaly for such a system or scheme. . . . The case [thus] names not only the anomaly for the scheme or system, but [because it defines the limit point at which the system continues to work] the scheme or system itself."[20] As a truth event of the speculative cultural situation of finance capital, the *Zong*, I have been arguing, is just such a symptomatic case — one which identifies not a marginal malfunctioning or local abnormality within the system but the global abnormality of the system as such.

Spectral or quasi-spectral, symptomatically anomalous, the truth event is also visible as the effect of a decision, as the belated determination not merely to regard it as such but as the typical sign which brings to light the prevailing tendencies of a surrounding set of historical circumstances, as Kant's resolute determination to discern an event and his decision to see in it the truth whose existence it is his stated purpose to demonstrate. And it is with regard to this belated partisan decision for the existence and the truth of an event (this finally profoundly antideconstructive determination to reject nominalism as either an epistemology or the basis for a system of ethics) that Badiou's conception of the truth event reveals, according to Žižek, not only its Kantian but its Benjaminian character:

> Within the Marxist tradition, this notion of partiality as not only an obstacle to but a positive condition of Truth was most clearly articulated by Georg Lukács in his early work *History and Class Consciousness*, and in a more directly messianic, proto-religious mode by Walter Benjamin in "Theses on the Philosophy of History": "truth" emerges when a victim, from his present catastrophic position, gains a sudden insight into the entire past as a series of catastrophes that led to his current predicament.[21]

This seems a largely accurate reading of Benjamin, though it is worth noting that for Benjamin we are all, in the broadest sense, subjects of the catastrophes of history, and the act of decision is thus not the singular responsibility of a victim as victim but a collective responsibility of subjects as the decisive agents of history. How, we might then ask, is that agency exercised, that decision made? The "Theses" outline the perception, the *Arcades* demonstrates the method: Benjamin reveals his decision in writing *Arcades*; accumulating fragments of human history drawn not from future time but from the archives of the what-has-been; arraying and juxtaposing these fragments alongside one another in the interest of producing the resultant dialectical image — "that wherein what has been comes together in a flash with the now to form a constellation." Benjamin's dialectical images *are* his decision, his determination to discern from the multitude of what presents itself a series of truth events, his motivated, partisan resolution to seize hold of one or other of the fragments or shards of wreckage piling up at the feet of the backward-glancing angel of history and to discover in this a truth event, a demonstration of the coincidence of now-being with what-has-been, an intimation of the future agreement between "past generations and the present one,"[22] a signum rememorativum, demonstrativum, prognostikon.

Kant-Benjamin-Badiou: between these three my understanding of the form of the event as apparition and reapparition, symptomatic anomaly, sign, image, and decision is balanced, as from them (though above all from Benjamin) the compositional theory and method of this text is borrowed. What remains is to turn, once more, from the form of *the* event, *the* image, decision, sign, to what is also under discussion here: *an* image, *an* event, *a* symptomatic anomaly, *a* signum rememorativum, demonstrativum, prognostikon. What remains is what is long past overdue: a return to the *Zong*, the sign it writes into the history of the modern, the state of history it reveals. And one way to begin to read that sign is to return, at last, to the decision that Kant's contemporary Granville Sharp made in identifying not the French Revolution but the *Zong* massacre as the age's decisive truth event, the decision he made in putting pen to paper and dispatching to the Lords Commissioners of the Admiralty his account of this event and the awful truth it demonstrated.

∗

But first one more brief word on the truth event. For Badiou, as for Kant, the truth event is consistently utopic. Not so for Sharp, for Benjamin, or for this text. The event under consideration here *is* a truth event in the full sense. The truth discernible in it, however, is the truth of catastrophe.

∗

The 138-page handwritten packet of material Sharp sent to the Lords Commissioners of the Admiralty on July 2, 1783, consisted of five documents. The first, which he somewhat confusingly labeled "Voucher No. 2," comprised a transcript of the appeal of the Guildhall verdict that Lord Mansfield agreed to hear at the court of King's Bench; the second was a letter Sharp addressed to the Lords Commissioners asking that they open a murder investigation; the third was his brief account of the massacre together with his arguments against the legal case for compensation advanced by the attorneys for William Gregson et al.; the fourth was a copy of another letter he had written, this to the Duke of Portland, reviewing once more the main details of the massacre and informing him of his decision to approach the Lords Commissioners; the fifth (labeled "Voucher No. 1") was a copy of a petition the *Zong*'s insurance underwriters had sent to William Pitt in his capacity as Chancellor of the Court of Exchequer requesting that the initial verdict reached in favor of the owners be set aside and a new trial ordered.[23]

Read in its entirety, Sharp's dispatch presents itself as a formal imitation of both the events it seeks to describe and the mode of appearance of the truth event. It constructs itself, that is, via a logic of reiteration and a logic of surrogation (or, indeed, via a logic of surrogation *as* reiteration). The reiterative quality of Sharp's submission is its most obvious but perhaps also its most perplexing quality. Read from beginning to end, it presents the story of the *Zong* massacre, then re-presents that story, then re-presents it not one but seven more times: the story is heard four times in the trial transcripts (it is initially presented by the attorneys for the insurance underwriters — who Sharp thus permits the first word on the case; then by the attorneys for the Liverpool slavers; then once more by each set of lawyers in their rebuttal arguments); once in Sharp's "cover letter" to the Lord's Commissioners (which finally appears on the ninety-fifth page of the full manuscript); once more in his succeeding "Account" of the massacre; again in the copy of his letter to the Duke of Portland; and then twice more in the petition of the underwriters with which he concludes the submission and to whom he thus also offers the closing word on the case. The narrative of the massacre is thus presented nine times in 138 pages, or perhaps more than that if one also counts the testimony of the two chief witnesses read into evidence at the trial (James Kelsal, who was Collingwood's chief mate, and Governor Robert Stubbs, who was just retiring from his post at the slave fort at Anamabo and who had taken passage aboard the ship), the three separate versions of the massacre given by the three attorneys for the underwriters (each of whom felt compelled to detail the events aboard the *Zong* anew on first addressing the court), and the summarizing comments of Lord Mansfield.

Five documents, at least nine and as many as fourteen accounts: why this manner of representing "one" event (or, at least, one event which in Badiou's full sense Sharp had decided "to count as One"; one discerned event which, in Kantian fashion, he insisted "occasioned the disclosure . . . [and] brought to light" a "transaction" in which "the most obvious natural right of human nature is at stake"; one fragment of human history presented, in proto-Benjaminian mode, as a montage of texts intercut with his own observations)?[24] There is more at issue in this question than a simple matter of quantity. For Sharp's devotion to repetition is marked by more than the sheer number of representations of what Lord Mansfield, in a comment transcribed on the first page of Sharp's submission, could only bring himself to call "a very singular case."[25] The repetitions do not only accumulate in number. Accumulating so, they also disrupt any orderly principle of sequencing in Sharp's text. I have already mentioned the odd misordering of vouchers 1 and 2. The index Sharp placed as the frontispiece to his dispatch (and which, as an index, acts to assert the formal coherence and unity of the individual pieces as component elements of a single text) partially explains that misordering while proving itself, simultaneously, even more fully defiant of a straightforward chronological reading practice:

	Page
The Index	
Copy of a Letter to the Lords of the Admiralty	95
An account of the Murders of the Slaves on Board the Zong	99
Voucher No. 1	117
Voucher No. 2	1 to 91
Copy of a Letter to the Duke of Portland	113[26]

Presented by the index in an order which fails to correspond with the order of their appearance in the text it indexes (the first item listed is the second to appear in the pages which follow; the second is the third; the third is the fifth; the fourth is the first; and the fifth is the fourth), the documents not only continue to appear at the wrong time (either later or earlier than they should, but not — between them — consistently so), but the calendrical order of time under which they were written is also wildly disrupted.

Each of the documents is either dated or dateable but, as one might now predict, they are neither indexed nor actually presented in chronological order. Sharp's letters and his "Account" are all dated July 1783; Voucher No. 1 (the underwriter's petition) would have been written between March and May of that year (the dates, respectively, of the Guildhall verdict in favor of the owners and the appeal Mansfield agreed to hear as a result of the underwriter's petition); Voucher No. 2 (the transcript of the appeal), is dated May 21 and 22,

1783. In order of production, then, the underwriter's petition is the earliest document, followed, in turn by the trial transcript and Sharp's three letters. By the logic of the index, however, the sequencing would look something like this:

July 1783
July 1783
March/April 1783
May 1783
July 1783

In the order in which the texts would actually have been read, however, the reader would first have encountered the material from the May appeal trial, then Sharp's July letters to the Admiralty and the Duke of Portland and his July account of the massacre, and then, finally, what is in fact the first document and the one that set in motion both the subsequent appeal and Sharp's response to the outcome of the appeal, that is, the March/April petition. The more Sharp's text repeats its news of the massacre the more, therefore, it violates the chronological order of time in which that news was made and made known. It is not simply that Sharp both continuously repeats the news of the massacre *and* consistently disorders his presentation of the documents that testify to that news: his mode of repetition, rather, *generates* this disordering of chronological sequence as it continues to reverse the relations of before and after, effect and cause.

At the very least this would have proved deeply confusing for a reader encountering the news of this event for the first time, even were that reader to disregard Sharp's bewildering index and simply attempt to work through the material as presented, encountering first the transcript of the May appeal, then Sharp's July commentary on that appeal, then the March/April petition by the insurance underwriters protesting the verdict of an original trial (undocumented in his submission) and calling for a new hearing (which was, as it turns out, granted, and whose transcript functions as his submission's opening document). The effect of this disruption of chronology by repetition is, however, to produce more than a generic readerly confusion. It produces instead a particular form of confusion, the confusion which attends the appearance of that which appears by reappearing and reappears by appearing for the first time. Such temporal confusion attends the bringing to light of an event which we never encounter now but only in retrospect, which appears for the first time only by reappearing to the eye that has decided to discern it.

With the exception of the first account of the massacre in Sharp's submission, any given account of the event would have been read as a repetition of what has already been encountered earlier in the text. As often as not, however, that reencountered material (the narrative of the massacre provided in the underwriter's petition, for example) actually precedes (in clock and calendar time) and in part generates the account it seems to repeat (the arguments, for instance, offered by the underwriter's attorney's at the hearing that petition allowed them to secure). Even that "first" appearance of the massacre in the text (in the transcript of the appeal) recognizes itself, however, not as an original appearance or coming to light of this event but, in its turn, as a reappearance of what has already been encountered (in the first March trial in which the jury ruled in favor of the owners). Somewhat surprisingly the record of that initial trial, that first public forum in which the case was brought to light, is the *one* account of the massacre absent from Sharp's archive. Or perhaps this is not so surprising. For the cumulative effect of all these appearances and reappearances of the event as the spectral now-being of what-has-been and what-has-been-brought-to-light is the sense that some stable, "original" account is missing, unavailable for inspection, and that the event itself can thus only be made to appear (over and over again) as a reappearance of the decision to bring it to light. This is true not only as a phenomenological effect of Sharp's submission but as a legal matter at issue in the appeal trial itself (the fact that the only court transcripts Sharp provides are of an appeal of an undocumented original juridical proceeding is, in itself, a virtually complete allegory of the process I have been describing).

The *Zong's* logbook and other papers were neither presented at the original trial nor at the appeal, much to the displeasure of the lead attorney for the underwriters, Mr. Davenport ("I inquired for the Log Book, there was none; Reckoning, none; Compass [readings], none. Nothing that is common Prudence, ordinary Prudence, and requisite Prudence to Produce"), and of the underwriters themselves, who in their petition for an appeal of the Guildhall jury's first ruling insisted that the appearance in court of these documents was an absolute prerequisite to any final judgment on the case: "Your orators [the underwriters] charge that all and singular the Facts hereinbefore stated and hereinafter enquired of or a great part thereof would manifestly appear in and by the Log Book of the Said Ship Zong wherein all the Transactions of the Voyage are entered which is now in the Custody or power of the Sd. Defts [the owners] some or one of them and by sundry Journals, Books, Letters, and Papers now or lately in their or some of their Custody or power if the same respectively have not been by their or some or other Orders altered, obliterated, defaced, torn, burnt, or otherwise destroyed. . . . And the Defts the Owners well know that your Orators till they get a sight of the Sd. Log Book, Journal, Books, Letters, and Papers will be unable to make any effective defense at Law to the Actions commenced against [them]."[27] The legal demand for a full disclosure of all pertinent evidence is fairly simple and clear, as it is clear that one way to read Sharp's submission is to regard it as his surrogate version of that missing book, journal, and set of letters and papers, his constitution of a compensatory book of evidence. The absent logbook, however, is more than a missing piece of evidence. It is a present absence rhetorically invoked as the allegorical stand-in or surrogate for an absent event whose "all and singular . . . facts" it is called on to make (and in this sense does make) "manifestly appear." As something missing, that is, it functions quite precisely as the mode of appearance of the "hereinbefore" which it is asked to represent but which will never appear in its proper time, which can only become manifest in the "hereinafter" of the belated act of decision which is being made on something which is at once missing and made manifest *by* the act of decision. Calling for and calling forth that act of decision (whether as the decision of a court or as the decision of a right-minded humanity), Sharp's repetitive, anachronistic mode of documenting the "case" of the *Zong* formally demonstrates that that decision can only be made by retrospectively constructing (calling into appearance, if you will) the event whose truth that decision is meant to determine, the event which the act of juridical or ethical decision in this sense does not so much follow as constitute and precede, an event that manifests itself in the present only, and precisely, as a specter called forth by the recognizably tautological act of decision being made upon it.

If the formal design of Sharp's reiterative submission thus demonstrates its fidelity to the mode of appearance of the spectral truth event; if the event his text constructs is thus entirely like Kant's, one which appears as an event only in the future anterior of the partisan moment of decision, then his serial reiteration of the "singular" facts of the massacre also acts to imitate the particular content of the event under discussion, an event that appears not only within the domain of the reiterated but as an act of obsessive reiteration. For even if we were to assume that the intention of the text has nothing to do with its spectrological qualities, we would still be left with the question of why Sharp demands that his readers encounter the detailed horror of the massacre over and over and over again.

∗

But what are those details? We, at least, have not yet encountered them.

Whatever their inevitable differences, Sharp's nine or fourteen successive versions of the massacre agree on this basic history:

On September 6, 1781, the *Zong* weighed anchor and sailed for Jamaica from the island of St. Thomas, off the west coast of Africa. There were 440 slaves on board and a crew of 17 men.

On November 27, the ship came in sight of Jamaica, but Collingwood ordered the *Zong* back out to sea, subsequently claiming that he had mistaken Jamaica for Hispaniola. At the time over sixty of the slaves and seven of the crew had died of disease, and many of the remaining slaves were in ill health (and thus unlikely to fetch a good price on the Jamaican market).

On November 29, and no longer in sight of Jamaica, Collingwood called a meeting of his ship's officers (James Kelsal among them), informed them that the vessel's water supply was running dangerously low and that in accord with the latitude given a ship's master by the jettison and general average principles of its marine insurance contract he intended to throw overboard that portion of his cargo necessary to preserve the life of the rest. The massacre began that day. Fifty-four of the sickest slaves were singled out and thrown, handcuffed, into the ocean.

On November 30, forty-three more slaves were thrown overboard. One of these, while in the water, managed to catch hold of one of the ship's ropes and to drag himself up to a porthole, through which he climbed back into the ship. Members of the crew, finding him some hours later, either hid him or returned him to the holds. The various accounts all assume that he survived.

On December 1, rain began to fall, and the crew collected six casks of water, sufficient for eleven days drinking allowance in addition to whatever already remained on board. Collingwood ordered the murders to proceed regardless. Twenty-six more slaves were brought on deck. Sixteen were cast overboard. The last ten, as crew members were about to seize hold of them jumped overboard rather than being thrown. They also drowned.

∗

One hundred thirty-three human beings thrown or driven overboard over a period of three days. One survivor. One hundred thirty-two individual human beings methodically slaughtered, one by one by one. One killing after another. One murder after another, imitating the one that had preceded it. One slave after another brought on deck and then thrown into the fatal sea. Below deck, in his cabin, unwilling to either participate or protest sat the retiring governor of the slave fort at Anamabo, Robert Stubbs, who, by the testimony entered into evidence at the appeal, passed these three days by watching the bodies of the slaves falling past his window ("Declining to assist in the Consultation of the Officers or assisting himself in throwing the Slaves overboard [he] went down into the Cabin and amused himself with seeing them out of the Cabin Window Plunging into the Sea").[28] One hundred thirty-three window-framed moments. One hundred thirty-three appearances and reappearances of the same image. One hundred thirty-three repetitions of what even the attorney for the Liverpool owners could not avoid calling "this melancholy event."[29] One hundred thirty-two deaths. One event.

One?

The logic of his decision to testify to the catastrophic truth of what had taken place aboard the *Zong* over the three days from November 29 to December 1, 1781, obliged Sharp to count this event as one. He was not alone in this. Everyone who spoke at the appeal evinced the same determination, a determination, perhaps, to limit the manifold horror of what they were discussing by unifying it, and also, frequently, predictably, by insisting on the anomalous character of this "singular event" (Lord Mansfield), this "melancholy event" (Solicitor Lee, for the owners), this "novel and singular event" (Mr. Heywood, for the underwriters).[30] The psychology underlying such a decision may be readily parsed. The ethics, however, are far from simple or simply suspect. There is ample and good reason to refuse an easy nominalism which would refuse to recognize this as a coherent event, which would refuse to count this event as one, either as each of its moments of horror relate to one another or as this event, as an event, relates to all the other eventualities of history, capital, and knowledge which bear upon it and which it brings to light. Everything I have said to this point depends on our willingness to refuse that nominalist refusal. But equally, and correspondingly, everything that will follow in the second section of this book depends on our willingness to make another simultaneous decision; our willingness to attend to the perhaps unintended truth of the words of Lord Mansfield, Solicitor Lee, and Mr. Heywood; our willingness to recognize that this is also a singular and a melancholy event, or, perhaps more accurately, a melancholy conjunction of singular atrocities, our willingness to recognize that the number we need to find some way to comprehend is neither one hundred thirty-three nor one hundred thirty-two but one, one, one.

*

One hundred thirty-three. One. Whatever we decide, Sharp, for his part, made his decision for neither and both. One event. One hundred thirty-three singular acts of atrocity, iterated and reiterated. One hundred thirty-two murders. One event. One by one by one. Why does Sharp demand that his readers encounter the details of what transpired over and over and over again? The answer seems obvious.

*

Mr. Haywood, in presenting his evidence to Mansfield's court, paused three times to admit that he had "never felt a more violent Impression on my mind upon the introduction of any Case whatever in this Court than I do now."[31] Lord Mansfield, in summing up the case, felt himself obliged to inform his auditors that whatever the law might oblige him to rule, "it shocks one very much."[32] Solicitor Lee, for the owners, found it necessary to acknowledge that the "Act" in question "cannot be described or spoke of without exciting in any that have heard some degree of Horror."[33] At the end of the three fatal days, Kelsal apparently found himself unable to perform any further duties aboard ship and retired to his cabin. Even Luke Collingwood, testimony indicated, became "delirious" after the last slave was drowned and had to be relieved of his command.[34] Why? Why these repeated admissions? Why does Sharp force his readers to encounter and reencounter and reencounter this shock, this horror, this violent impression on the mind? For no other reason, surely, than to reproduce the shock of the event as an affect of reading, to cultivate in the minds of the belated "spectators of this event" not, as Kant would have it, "a universal yet disinterested sympathy for the players on one side against those on the other side," but a universal and *interested* sympathy, an exactly melancholy sympathy for the entirely real, entirely not abstract, entirely not "typical," entirely singular human beings thrown one by one by one into the sea.[35]

*

What if we were to regard history, Cathy Caruth asks, as the history of a trauma? What would such a decision betoken? Among other things, she argues, it would demand that we learn to submit ourselves to a reiterative practice of listening, that we learn to substitute, for a Kantian ethics whose organizing condition of possibility is a recognition in others of a capacity for the experience of the sublime, a receptivity to the voice speaking from the "wound" of another: "Trauma is always the story of a wound that cries out, that addresses us in the attempt to tell us of a reality or truth that is not otherwise available. This truth, in its delayed appearance and in its belated address, cannot be linked only to what is known, but also to what remains unknown in our very actions and our language."[36] Trauma, thus understood, speaks its "truth" not only in much the same fashion as Badiou's truth event articulates its message, it speaks also with the voice of melancholy. Caruth tends not to use the term, but trauma theory, as she develops it, is undoubtedly also a theory of melancholy, a theory devoted to the unexchangeable singularity of loss and what has been lost, a theory which in Nicolas Abraham and Maria Torok's terms incorporates its objects of loss rather than introjecting them, resolves itself to encrypt within its expressive text the exquisite corpse or corpses of its lamented dead and to guard them there.[37] Sharp's submission is such a cryptonymic text, such a traumatic text, such a text devoted both to preserving the singularity of loss and to listening to the voices speaking from the wound of this loss over and over and over again. This is true in more ways than bear discussion now (that discussion belongs, more properly, to the second section of this book). Let me then name just one way, perhaps the least certain way, in which this is so.

Melancholy, Abraham and Torok argue, abhors metaphor, wages war on it. It does so because it regards metaphor as the representational mode of that principle of exchange, that principle of substitution, that is its opposite and the precondition of that "healthy" introjective work of mourning which works by finally surrendering the object of loss and replacing it with some other affective attachment. The dilemma for melancholy, as it seeks to express itself in language, is thus its profound mistrust of representation per se. How then does melancholy refer its text to the object whose loss that text laments, but which it cannot permit itself to represent? It does so, Abraham and Torok's work suggests, through an antimetaphoric hyperrealism, through that cryptonymic mode of reference that aims to pass itself off not as a representation of the lost thing but as that lost thing itself. Hence the cryptic, frequently unparsable quality of the melancholic text. Hence its paradoxical and anxious reiterativity. Hence its attempt to reduce representation to the exclusive domain of the nominative, to the speaking, over and over again, of the secret name of the dead. Hence its attempt to strip language down to the barest, most utterly literal, and most cryptic realism.

Is Sharp's submission such a cryptic, melancholically realist text? I mentioned earlier that it runs to 138 numbered pages. That is both the case and not quite the case. Between the second and third, third and fourth, and fourth and fifth sections of the manuscript there is a blank page. One would expect the same between the first and second sections, for a total of four unwritten pages. Inexplicably, however, between the first and second sections there are three blank pages (the index tips the reader off to this, noting that Voucher

No. 2 runs from pages 1–91 while the next document, Sharp's letter to the Admiralty, begins on page 95). So, instead of four blank pages between five sections, as might be expected, there are six. Why? 138 pages in all. Six blank pages. In total: 132 handwritten pages secreted within the larger total; 132 inked pages, unless one also counts that floating, unnumbered, extra page — the index, which, if added, makes 133. One hundred thirty-two marked pages by one count. One hundred thirty-three by another. We know these numbers. They might, of course, represent no more than the greatest of coincidences. Perhaps they do. But we also know a few more things. Sharp was an obsessive copier and recopier of his correspondence. He wrote and rewrote drafts of all his letters, often leaving behind as many as five or six different versions until he was fully satisfied with the text he finally dispatched. There is something else also. The 132 or 133 marked pages of his submission are not equally filled with print. Thumbing through the entire manuscript the discrepancies from page to page are obvious. Some pages are entirely filled, some only half so, some pages are less than a quarter full. Beneath the final line of writing on each page there is a neatly ruled border. If Sharp had not set himself these borders, if he had written from the top to the bottom of each page, the manuscript would never have filled anything near its total 132 or 133 pages. Is this number deliberately arrived at? It certainly seems so. Regardless, it is there. One event. One hundred thirty-three slaves thrown overboard. One hundred thirty-two human beings drowned. Nine or fourteen reiterated accounts of this singular, melancholy event. One hundred thirty-two or 133 handwritten pages. The text guards its secrets even as it demands that we listen to them over and over and over again.

*

Sharp's reiterative submission, I have been suggesting, imitates both the form of the event it seeks not so much to describe as to surrogate and the form of appearance of this event as a quasi-Benjaminian, quasi-Kantian, quasi-Badiouvian truth event. In doing so it marks itself as the first text to situate the *Zong* within that mode of representation that I earlier indicated articulates itself in opposition to the "theoretical realism" that was the dominant mode of the age's capital, historicist, and novelistic imaginaries. It figures, in these terms, the emergence of the oppositional "melancholy realism" that dominates the representational logic of almost all the subsequent works which have attempted to offer their testimony to the truth of this event. The predominant affect of Sharp's submission and of these later texts also corresponds, not at all coincidentally, to the melancholy turn of novelistic discourse that Deidre Lynch traces to almost this exact moment, and that she argues represents a revolt, within that discourse, against its prior subscription to (and subscription of) the abstract representational and epistemological codes of a culture of speculation.[38] Contesting a novelistic imaginary at work in the court proceedings, Sharp's text also defines the contours of an emerging and alternate novelistic discourse (one that works, in part, as an analogue to the romantic historicism that I have been arguing succeeds and contests the typicalizing protocols of an earlier actuarial historicism). The question of how *this* alternative (melancholy and romantic) novelistic imaginary lends a definitive imprint to almost all the succeeding representations of the event, and of what it might mean for these texts thus to articulate themselves under the sign of a "melancholy realism," are central problems of the second portion of this book. But those are questions that need to be deferred a little longer, if only because we are not yet done with Sharp, because we have not yet come to terms either with the full nature of his understanding of this event or with the ways in which that understanding offers its testimony to the fundamental argument I have been advancing thus far.

The *Zong*, as the form of Sharp's submission indicates, may well name a trauma and an injunction, a wound and a serial obligation to listen "to the voice and the speech delivered by the other's wound."[39] That does not yet make it *either* the event in which the "moment" finds itself condensed and realized *or* an event in which our long twentieth century finds itself demonstrated, recollected, and predicted, an event that reveals our long contemporaneity's noncontemporaneousness with itself, an event that functions as a what-has-been with which our now-being is constellated. For that to become clear we need to return to Sharp's manuscript and to the event it demonstrates. And we need to recognize that what Sharp quite clearly understood was that the event in question entailed more than those three days aboard the *Zong*, more than the massacre: it entailed also, at the very least, what followed — most crucially the original trial in which a jury found for the owners and the hearing which revisited that decision. As the name for an event, in other words, the *Zong* names both a massacre *and* the set of legal decisions made upon it; both an act of atrocity and the value form on which that atrocity made its claims and which, rather than the act itself, was truly on trial.

The letter Sharp addressed to the Lords Commissioners of the Admiralty made it quite clear that though both it and its accompanying manuscripts bore witness to a single event, that event encompassed three, related, acts of injustice: the murder of the slaves aboard the *Zong*, the Guildhall jury's verdict and Lord Mansfield's insistence on treating the matter before the court not as a murder case but as a property dispute. If the slaughter itself evoked the horror of all the parties discussing it at court, then Sharp's outrage, while clearly inspired by the massacre, was redoubled by the jury's verdict and Mansfield's decision to treat this exclusively as an insurance matter, and his appeal to the Commissioners was devoted not only to demanding that they find some way to see the guilty parties punished but that they see the drowned slaves as something other than the bearers of an abstract, insured, and recuperable quantum of value: "The manuscript book (marked Voucher No. 2)," he informed the Commissioners, "contains a copy of minutes taken in short hand the last term, on the 22d and 23d May, 1783, of the proceedings in the Court of King's Bench, on a motion for a new trial of the cause of the same parties mentioned above, concerning the *value* of those murdered Negroes! Thus the contest between the owners and insurers of the ship, though a mere mercenary business amongst themselves about the *pecuniary* value, and not for the blood, of so many human persons wickedly and unjustly put to death, has, nevertheless, occasioned the disclosure of that horrible transaction, which otherwise, perhaps, might . . . have never been brought to light" (emphasis original).[40] Sharp's syntax suggests that the "horrible transaction" he has in mind is, primarily, the massacre itself. His diction, however, is precise in its ambiguity. For it suggests that what inspires horror and outrage is not only the massacre but a massacre that was, itself, solely interpretable as a financial transaction, a legal act of exchanging "goods" for their pecuniary value. If his horror is for murder as a form of fiscal transaction, then it also attends the financialization of a system of justice, the transformation of the legal system into a scene of exchange, its reinvention as a mechanism designed not to dispense justice but money, not to insure the existence of human beings as the holders of rights but to investigate their properties as the bearers of a quantum of value underwritten by the slave ship's insurance contract.

*

If mourning is the opposite of melancholy then, in the realm of capital transactions, so is insurance. Which is to say that insurance is the form that mourning takes when it equips itself for the market. For what else is mourning — upon the completion of its "work" — but the determination to exchange some lost thing for a viable substitute; and what else is insurance but that determination monetarized? Putting on trial a form of value which finds its perfect realization in the practice of insurance, the case of the *Zong* thus also puts mourning on trial. No wonder then that Sharp's outrage should have taken the form it did. No wonder that he understood that, no matter what Mansfield ruled, the terms to which he had bound his ruling had already confirmed that the law could treat slaves as no more than the bearers of an abstract measure of value. No wonder, also, that in embarrassment of this fact virtually all the parties in Mansfield's court found themselves obliged, at one moment or another, to at least pay lip service to the language of melancholy. But while the attorneys for both the owners and the underwriters may have mouthed that language, they knew that the bench was by no means inclined to enshrine it as a principle of law. Instead, as all the parties seemed to agree, the case would be decided on the technical question of "necessity." It is the most frequently spoken word in the transcript, and as Mansfield indicated in his final judgment, the sole matter at issue as a point of law. The three attorneys for the underwriters tried to put as much stress upon it as possible, largely by exaggerating its dimensions, asking the court, again and again, whether Collingwood's actions constituted, variously, "a perilous Necessity," "an absolute Necessity," "an actual Necessity," "an inviolable Necessity," "an indispensable Necessity," "an extreme Necessity," "an inevitable Necessity."[41] Solicitor Lee, in response, attempted to downgrade the intensity of the condition, repeatedly referring to Collingwood's actions simply as "a Necessity." Even Sharp, in his letter to the Duke of Portland, sought to strategically redeploy the term, opening and closing his appeal by insisting that the facts of the case demonstrated the "absolute necessity to abolish the Slave Trade."[42]

Sharp's use of the term is, however, at odds with the meaning it held in Mansfield's courtroom. For there necessity referred not to an abstract ethical obligation but to a particular stipulation within the *Zong*'s insurance contract and to the general insurance principle underlying that stipulation. As far as the court was concerned the question of necessity was circumscribed not by a code of ethics but by the terms of an insurance contract. In raising the question of necessity Mansfield did not ask whether or not it had been ethically necessary for Collingwood to sacrifice some lives to save some others. He asked instead whether his actions met the standard of necessity (for the throwing overboard of "goods") of his contract's jettison clause and whether, accordingly, the owners were or were not entitled to compensation for those lost "goods" in accord with the rules laid down by the bedrock insurance principle of the "general average." The underwriters, in their appeal for a new trial following the Guildhall jury's initial ruling in favor of the owners (and initial determination that Collingwood's actions had indeed met his contract's standard of necessity), were absolutely clear on this: "The [owners] have since pretended that the Sd. 133 slaves which were thrown alive out of the Sd. Ship Zong into the sea and perished . . . were at the rate of 30 per head and according to the Stipulation and Agreement in the Afsd. Policies of Insurance of the value of 3990 & that the loss of the Sd. Slaves was a general Average Loss which ought to be born & paid by the Underwriters."[43]

This then was the question before the court: whether or not the loss to the overall value of the *Zong*'s cargo was or was not a general average loss "according to the Stipulation and Agreement" of its insurance policy. And there were two main ways in which the underwriters' attorneys could have pursued that question: either by suggesting that that policy did not include slaves among the list of "goods" that could be treated as a general average loss or by suggesting that the policy did include slaves among that full list of "commodities that had become the subject of insurance," but that, in this case, it had not been necessary for Collingwood to destroy these "goods" and thus no compensation was owed. The first option would have entailed a fundamental engagement with the legality of slavery and the extant theory of property. The second, which is the option that the attorneys chose to pursue, depended more simply on a matter of fact.

Like any "standard" marine insurance policy of the period, the ship's insurance policy would have stipulated that:

> Whatever the master of a ship in distress, with the advice of his officers and sailors, deliberately resolves to do, for the preservation of the whole, in cutting away masts or cables, or in throwing goods overboard to lighten his vessel, which is what is meant by *jettison* or jetson, is, in all places, permitted to be brought into a general, or gross average: in which all concerned in ship, freight, and cargo, are to bear an equal or proportionable part of what was so sacrificed for the common good, and it must be made good by the insurers in such proportions as they have underwrote: *however, to make this action legal, the three following points are essentially necessary; viz — 1st. That what was so condemned to destruction, was in consequence of a deliberate and voluntary consultation, held between the master and men: — 2dly. That the ship was in distress, and the sacrificing the things they did was a necessary procedure to save the rest: — and 3dly. That the saving of the ship and the cargo was actually owing to the means used with that sole view.*[44]

"A necessary procedure to save the rest": this is the crucial condition, and the issue on which both the original trial and the subsequent appeal rested. In disputing the "absolute," "inviolable," "indispensable," or "extreme" necessity of Collingwood's actions, the attorneys for the underwriters were trying to establish, as a simple matter of fact, that the *Zong* was not in such a condition of distress that Collingwood's actions had proved necessary to save it. They granted the first condition (everyone seems to have agreed that, as required, Collingwood had called a meeting of his officers and crew to deliberate and consult with them on the alleged water shortage) and concentrated all their energies on the second, arguing that there was ample water to permit everyone aboard ship to survive, on half allowance, for upward of two weeks, that the rainfall on December 1 made up for whatever shortfall there might have been, and that the ship at any point from November 29 onward was at most a week's sail from any number of harbors in which it could have replenished its supplies. Solicitor Lee attempted to refute all these allegations of fact, and Mansfield directed virtually all his questions to resolving them. Thus the return of all arguments, again and again, to the question of necessity.

In electing to argue their case so, in choosing to engage the owners solely on the ground of necessity, the attorneys for the underwriters had, however, already conceded a fundamental point, indeed *the* fundamental point. They had admitted, by refusing to contest, the conviction that slaves were, as a matter of law, commodities just like any other, interchangeable, before the law with alabaster, beads, china, deals, glass, and so on. The attorneys for the underwriters assumed this as a given. Lord Mansfield assumed it. Solicitor Lee was, in fact, the only person to raise the issue, and then only to assert its unquestionability: "[They] are made the subject of property. . . . Your Lordship knows they are real Property. . . . not only Property but of the species Value of 30 a head. . . . This is the case of Chattels, of Goods, it is really so, it is the case of throwing over Goods — for to this purpose and the purpose of Insurance they are real goods and property."[45] This is shocking, must be shocking, even if, two centuries later, we are no longer shocked by it, no longer surprised to discover that slaves were regarded as commodities. There is nothing new in this discovery. But there is, nevertheless, something new here, something which does in fact mark this case as an event in the history of the slave trade and the modern history of property.[46] The entire proceeding in Lord Mansfield's courtroom follows on the basis of an assumption, assumes — and by assuming makes appear with stark clarity in the legal record — an a priori truth: that slaves are not only the "subjects of property," not only commodities, but commodities "which have become at some or other time the subjects of insurance." At what time? Both before the case of the *Zong* ever came to court *and* precisely at that moment, *as* Mansfield and the attorneys, assuming the truth of this proposition, mark its appearance as an event. This is the news the *Zong* trials announce; this is the truth they belatedly testify to by assuming that slaves are, like quills, rice, rosin, sedans, and silks, subject to the general average. With that assumption in place, Mansfield's ruling on the facts of the case, as Sharp understood, was largely irrelevant. He may indeed have found that the owners had not yet definitively established that the ship's water supply was so low that there had been an absolute "necessity" to drown the slaves. But by restricting his ruling to this ground, and permitting yet another trial (which seems never to have been held) for further consideration of that question alone, he had confirmed the sovereignty of insurance law over the lives of the slaves; confirmed, in other words, that there could be conditions which would render the jettisoning of slaves necessary and reaffirmed that if those conditions were met, insurance should be paid and slaves treated as objects subordinate, like soap, brass, or leather, to the law of the general average.

We have not yet, I believe, grasped the consequences of this, not yet appreciated what it means for slavery to name an extension not only of commodity capitalism into the domain of the human, but the colonization of human subjectivity by finance capital. The *Zong* trials constitute an event in the history of capital *not* because they treat slaves as commodities but because they treat slaves as commodities that have become the subject of insurance, treat them, in Žižek's terms, not as objects to be exchanged but as the "empty bearers" of an abstract, theoretical, but entirely real quantum of value, treat them as little more than promissory notes, bills-of-exchange, or some other markers of a "specie value," treat them as suppositional entities whose value is tied not to their continued, embodied, material existence but to their speculative, recuperable loss value. The *Zong* trials constitute an event not because they further subject the world to the principle of exchange but because they subject it to the hegemony of that which superordinates exchange: the general equivalents of finance capital.

Luke Collingwood's catastrophic decision signals the completion and the bringing to light of *this* financial (and financializing) revolution. His step-by-step determination to treat the slaves aboard his ship as bearers not simply of a commodified exchange value but of an utterly dematerialized, utterly speculative, and utterly transactable, enforceable, and recuperable pecuniary value represents the symptomatic manifestation of this revolution. Precisely because his act was regarded as an anomaly, precisely because his decision was treated as an exception which "a general normative schema" could nevertheless incorporate within its system of rule, it functions as the test case and truth event of the situation it brings to light (as in Žižek's terms, that "which, misperceived by the system as a local 'abnormality,' effectively condenses the global 'abnormality' of the system as such"). Precisely because the casuistic system of jurisprudence operative in Lord Mansfield's courtroom could apply its general principles to this aberrant case in which those principles find themselves most absolutely demonstrated, this case can be seen to serve as one of those "events" in which the age sees itself revealed, as a counter-signum rememorativum, demonstrativum, prognostikon by which this age of speculative revolutions is brought to light. Sharp recognized this. And it is because he recognized it that *his* act of decision, his determination to bring this event to life, demanded that he bear outraged witness not only to the slaughter aboard the *Zong* but to the horrible transaction that slaughter betokened, to the culmination of this event in a hearing not on the murder but on the value of the *Zong*'s drowned slaves.

A central problem of historical materialism that ought to be seen in the end: Must the Marxist understanding of history necessarily be acquired at the expense of the perceptibility of history? Or: in what way is it possible to conjoin a heightened graphicness to the realization of the Marxist method? The first stage in this undertaking will be to carry over the principle of montage into history. That is, to assemble large-scale constructions out of the smallest and most precisely cut components. Indeed, to discover in the analysis of the small individual moment the crystal of the total event.

Method of this project: literary montage. I needn't *say* anything. Merely show. I shall purloin no valuables, appropriate no ingenuous formulations. But the rags, the refuse—these I will not inventory but allow, in the only way possible, to come into their own: by making use of them.

— Walter Benjamin, *The Arcades Project*

CHAPTER 5

"Please decide"

THE SINGULAR AND THE SPECULATIVE

Signum demonstrativum? So much may be granted. Signum rememorativum — this perhaps also. But signum prognostikon? That, certainly, I have not yet established, nor will I establish it with anything like the detail I have attempted thus far. The late twentieth century that bookends the long twentieth century, whose emergence the *Zong* massacre and trials bring to light, represents, as I have argued, not only a repetition but an intensification of its moments of "beginning." In this case, however, intensification assumes less the form of concentrating the operations of finance capital in one or other signature event than that of distributing its modes of speculation, speculative epistemologies, and abstract value forms more fully across the global spectrum, by finding for itself, in the terms I earlier used, ever more points of application along the exchange networks of the globe. Intensification, here, manifests itself as the ever more exhaustive, ever more total, every more complex, ever more ubiquitous, and (*because* ever more ubiquitous) ever more unremarkable penetration of the world by the cultural logic of finance capital. This is, obviously enough, a Jamesonian argument, as it is Jamesonian short-hand for what we have taken to calling the postmodern. And if part of the argument of this book is that the postmodern is less original to the period with which we tend to associate it than we might think, that the postmodern is, indeed, a period concept which requires its own adjustment, then the version of the contemporary I have in mind is, nevertheless, largely Jamesonian in its understanding of this contemporaneity's dominant cultural logics (with, to repeat myself, both the Arrighian caveat that like any regime of capital this regime moves forward by moving backward at the same time, cyclically resur-recting the capital and cultural logics of a mode of accumulation that seems to have preceded it, and the Benjaminian qualification that this contemporaneity is, like any other, noncontemporary with itself, and that any adequate histori-cization of the contemporary must, consequently, address the ways in which the now-being of the postmodern constellates itself not with itself alone but with a determinate what-has-been). I do not intend, then, to offer anything like a comprehensive map of this contemporaneity which the what-has-been I have charted predicates and for which that recollected what-has-been func-tions as a demonstrative signum prognostikon. Jameson has already under-taken that labor more thoroughly than I could hope to. And indeed, the corrective that Arrighi's argument offers to Jameson's description of our con-temporaneity is itself redundant. Jameson has recently taken note of it and has incorporated Arrighi's design within his own system of analysis as the basis for a significant adjustment of his critique of the cultural logic of our contempo-raneity: a now-being that he now indicates we should examine as the habitus not simply of a generalized "late" capitalism but as the situating and the situation of a simultaneously late and reapparitional "finance capital."

Jameson makes this adjustment to the argument of his *Postmodernism, or, The Cultural Logic of Late Capitalism* in his relatively brief essay "Culture and Finance Capitalism." The essay opens with a consideration of Arrighi's *The Long Twentieth Century* and attributes to Arrighi both the framing of "a prob-lem we didn't know we had" and "a solution to it: the problem of finance capital."[1] The "problem" of finance capital that Jameson suggests Arrighi has discovered is its anachronism, its appearance not only as the dominant form of capital within capital's most recent stage of development (and thus also, by the arguments of prior models, its most "advanced" or its "final" stage), but its untimely prior appearances in both the eighteenth and the late sixteenth centuries. Arrighi's solution, Jameson approvingly notes, is to index these serial appearances of finance capital to a set of "cycles of accumulation," each of which begins and ends with a moment of finance capital, and each of which plays out, over the course of its long durée, the tripartite sequence of Marx's full formula for capital: MCM′. With this in mind, Jameson indicates that what he had previously referred to as the late capitalism of the postmodern is better understood both as its finance capitalism *and* as a mode of accumulation that marks the postmodern not as a break with what has preceded it but as the culminating moment of a long durée which repeats, by intensifying, the moment with which it began:

> Capital itself becomes free-floating. It separates from the concrete context of its productive geography. Money becomes in a second sense and to a second degree abstract (it always was abstract in the first and basic sense), as though somehow in the national moment money still had a content. . . . Now, like the butterfly stirring within the chrysalis, it separates itself from the concrete breeding ground and prepares to take flight. We know today only too well (but Arrighi shows us that this contemporary knowledge of ours only replicates the bitter experience of the dead . . .) that the term is literal. We know that there exists such a thing as capital flight: the disinvestment, the pondered or hasty moving on to the greener pastures of higher rates of investment return and cheaper labor. This free-floating capital, in its frantic search for more profitable investments . . . will begin to live its life in a new context: no longer in the factories and the spaces of extraction and production, but on the floor of the stock market, jostling for more intense profitability. But it won't be as one industry competing against another branch, nor even one productive technology against another more advanced one in the same line of manufacturing, but rather in the form of speculation itself: specters of value, as Derrida might put it, vying against each other in a vast, world-wide, disembodied phantasmagoria. This is of course, the moment of finance capital as such.[2]

Jameson is here describing the "today." As he indicates, however—and as the utter appositeness of this description not only to the "situation" in which we find ourselves today but to the eighteenth-century situation I have sketched confirms—he might equally, and indeed *is* equally, describing a yesterday this today replicates. At the heart of that yesterday-constellating-today is the separation of value from the concrete, the emergence of speculation as a hegemonic enterprise and of speculative forms as the bases for and objects of a new form of knowledge and power, and the global circulation of what, paraphrasing Derrida, he calls "specters of value." The phrase is as striking as it is apt, more resonant, even, than Jameson's usage acknowledges. For the specters of value he envisions vying with one another in a "world-wide, disembodied phantasmagoria" (which description reads like a precise analogue of "Lady Credit's" fantastical realm of speculation alternately extolled and lamented by eighteenth-century public sphere discourse) are at least doubly spectral: they are both the imaginary, disembodied value forms trading on the floor (or across the digital circuitry) of the globe's money markets and stock exchanges and the ghostly reappearances of such exchangeable abstractions, haunting reminders and revenants of this present's what-has-been.

Jameson's primary concern, however, is not with the hauntological doubleness of finance capital but, characteristically, with a dialectical reading of Arrighi's "comprehensive new theory of finance capital" that will enrich Arrighi's account by "reaching out into the expanded realm of cultural production to map its effects."[3] In the essay, Jameson restricts himself to one of these: the "effect" of finance capital on the "category of abstraction itself" particularly as abstraction assumes aesthetic life within the postmodern "fragment," which he suggests differs from both the realist and the modernist fragment precisely to the degree that it, like the spectral value forms of finance capital, has fully escaped the domain of reference, utterly detached itself from some material context, and so set itself free to wander as some narratological specter of historicity within "a world-wide disembodied phantasmagoria."[4] Jameson finds his chief instance of this process in the image fragments that saturate the films of Derek Jarman, but reminds us that he does so by way of offering what is primarily a "symptomatic" reading of the effects of finance capital in the image-fragment-dominated culture of "late-capitalist everyday life."[5]

In concluding the argument of this section of the book, I want to follow that lead, which implies, in part, also returning to the statement of method and intentions with which Kant begins his essay on "Progress" ("We desire a fragment of human history") and recognizing that, on this matter at least, Kant and Jameson are not that far apart (in either case the image fragments symptomatic of their speculative moments demonstrate the broad historical tendencies of their moments precisely to the degree that they disclose the sovereignty of abstraction over the phenomenal world of persons, events, and things), recognizing, indeed, that it is to the degree that the "fragments" central to both a postmodern culture of speculation and Kant's Enlighten-ment philosophy of history disclose their common allegiance to the category of abstraction that these two "moments" can be said to anticipate and recollect one another. Following the lead of both Kant and Jameson, however, I also want once again to borrow a cue from Benjamin: I want to attempt to demon-strate the argument I understand to emerge from the texts collected in this archive by setting the image of the *Zong* (and the specters of value that frag-ment of human history sets so catastrophically into circulation) against a dialectical counterimage, one in which (with some assistance from Gayatri Spivak) we might, in fact, come to see the what-has-been of our now-being and the now-being of our what-has-been demonstrated, anticipated, and recollected.

∗

The Nike corporation began running a new advertisement in the final months of 1999, not for their shoes or apparel or even, apparently, for that general mode of being in the world which the company has begun to refer to as Nike culture. Though, perhaps, that is in fact what the advertisement is about. For it is precisely Nike's (if not quite the Nike customer's) way of being in the world that the advertisement claims to address, Nike's way of taking on the "responsibility" of being not just an *actor* in the world but one of the *agents* of what Spivak, following Heidegger, calls the "worlding" of our world.[6] "Nike," the advertisement understands, is not just a word for an object of consump-tion, or for that libidinal affect of consuming which, when organized as the collective effect of consuming a global brand mark, is also a consumer's poli-tics of recognition, mutual identification, and global co-citizenship. It is also a word for an experience of the globe's sudden contemporaneity with and visi-bility to itself: one of the more pedestrian successor words, perhaps, to that earlier word, "Enlightenment," which, for Kant at least, was also a word for the shock of inhabiting a suddenly planetary moment. There are differences, of course, even if the affect recurs, and not just because in Niketown (or, as one of Nike's chief competitors has it, Planet Reebok), the global asserts itself through an act of sublime consumption rather than as a way of knowing, a philosophy of history, or a form of politics, but also because, if we are to believe this advertisement, our late-millennial recognitions of both the global and our worldliness within it demand a further act of recognition, a recogni-tion of something that Spivak suggests is systematically "foreclosed" by Kant and his Enlightenment fellows. Indeed it almost seems, in reading over the advertisement, that someone at Nike has been reading Spivak, and perhaps also an essay or two by Emmanuel Levinas (though perhaps not too carefully). For the advertisement would like to imply that if we are to inhabit the global with any sense of responsibility, we can do so only if we coordinate our recognition of the world-as-world with a recognition of something like a "responsibility" to the global "subaltern." In this, the advertisement is rather surprisingly "of" its philosophical moment. That it might be cynically of that moment, or willfully mistaken about what Spivak's and Levinas's arguments imply, is apparent at that moment in which the advertisement identifies the Nike corporation's understanding of how we might, in Spivak's terms, "set to work" our recognition of responsibility, the moment in which it identifies responsibility both as an obligation to set the subaltern to work and as an obligation to "suite" the subaltern for the key responsibility of global citizenship: the responsibility of borrowing.

The text of the advertisement (printed under the allusively bizarre banner headline "Good Morning Vietnam!" and typeset around the signature Nike swoosh) is as atypically straightforward as it is unusually defensive:

People have accused Nike of operating without any regard for the people in developing countries. Particularly in Vietnam, where we currently employ 43,000 people. If you're genuinely concerned about this, we've got a way for you to not only help, but to go over to Vietnam and see the results first-hand. Another token effort by a giant, multi-national corporation to help diffuse some bad press, right? Wrong. It's Nike's micro-loan program. A program that's helped thousands of people since it began over two years ago. It works like this: You make a contribution of $75 to Friendship Bridge, the group that administers the program. They, in turn, distribute the funds to people who use it to start their own businesses. With every contribution, Nike creates a matching loan for $75, giving yet another person a start on the road to prosperity. Now you might think, big deal. $75. What's that going to do? In a country where the average annual income is $260, that's some serious venture capital. (FYI: a typical worker in our Vietnamese facilities makes over double the average annual wage: $564). Micro-loan recipients don't work for us, and the businesses they start have nothing to do with making our stuff. It's simply a community based lending program for people who happen to live near one of our facilities. To date, we've issued over 3200 micro-loans, creating almost as many businesses in the process. Businesses that are growing, reinvesting and improving the lives of over 15,000 people. For less than the cost of a half dozen CDs, you can help people go from struggling to thriving. And by participating, you're eligible to visit Vietnam and see your investment in action—on us. To learn more about, or better yet, to get involved in the micro-loan program, go to www.nikebiz.com. Despite what our critics would like you to believe, Nike is doing its part to raise the standard of living for Vietnam and other developing countries. The question is, are you?[7]

There are any number of things that could be said about this but just two on which I wish to concentrate. The first, and most obvious, is the unabashedness with which the advertisement indicates that the precondition of development (and prosperity and thriving) is not labor reform but indebtedness. Indebtedness, it transpires, amounts to more than the opportunity to borrow $75. Indebtedness, as the publicity surrounding the advertisement indicates (it had its own Web site), is also a form of education. Loan recipients, all of whom are women, are obliged to take classes in, among other things, sexual hygiene, finance management, and, not so strangely enough, cosmetics. Spivak has a phrase for this. She calls it "credit-baiting": the practice by which, through just such microloans, subalternality is refitted for capital, educated, made responsible, presentable, recoded for membership within a global community of finance-capital-citizenship whose identity document is a sound credit record.[8]

The second point worth making is that for this advertisement to work it must usher into a binary theater of address, composed of corporate addressor and consumer addressee, a third term, a third figure: the former third world subject *of* address, the real subaltern-cum-finance-capitalist, the entrepreneurial Vietnamese woman, or, as Spivak has it, the "native informant." The Nike Web site for the advertisement contained a series of photographs of Vietnamese women, often accompanied by their children. Appended to those photographs are a set of testimonial statements offering witness to the benefits of the microloan program. In relative terms those benefits seem real enough. But it is not the limited financial advantage of participation in the loan program which is at issue here. Rather, what is pertinent is the presentation of these women as figures who can offer authentic validation of Nike's responsibility as a global actor: the ethnographic display of these women as the real proof of the responsible, paternal care which Nike has seen fit to invest in a woman like Mrs. Hong, of Dong Nai Province. Since she began participating in the program, the Web page informs us, Mrs. Hong has saved "over" $43. The rhetorical excess of that "over" should give us some pause, if only because it seems to admit, by acting to deny, just how embarrassing it is to have to equate global responsibility with such sums. If the advertisement is embarrassed by its claims, however, it attempts to neutralize that embarrassment by indicating that what lies over and above the $43 Mrs. Hong has saved is not just a few more nickels or dimes but something at once less measurable and more substantial. Mrs. Hong, we discover (like all the women who function here, in another term Spivak's work makes resonant, as "alibis" for multinational capital), has acquired not just a savings account and a debt burden, but a more hygienic body and home. Together with the amounts each woman has borrowed, made, and saved, the Web site discloses the steps each woman has taken to sanitize herself, her children, and her home. Mrs. Hong, we are told, has monthly meetings to learn about "hygiene and child care." Mrs. Ngoc Anh regularly visits "a family planning, health, and hygiene education program." Mrs. Lien "used to have a dirt floor."

"A little money can make a big difference," the banner headline over these women's bodies proudly announces. Apparently it can also erase it. For that, finally, seems to be the point — not just to make a big difference but to erase one; not just to credit-bait these women but, in doing so, to refashion them, to move them from alterity to likeness, to shift them from a regime of difference (coded here as a regime of filth, uneducated desire, and fiscal ignorance) to a regime of identity (coded as a corporatized biopolitics of health, regulated desire, and prudence). If this suggests that what Ann Laura Stoler, via Foucault, has identified as the normalizing project of the colonial state has been taken over, largely intact, as the civilizing mission of multinational capital, that, indeed, the unquantifiable value of what has been saved over and above Mrs. Hong's $43 is the enduring value of that not-after-all defunct project, then it also suggests that if we are to understand how global capital has come to shoulder the imperial burden of global "soul making" (as Spivak has it), that if we are to grasp how we got from there to here, then as Spivak argues so powerfully in her *Critique of Postcolonial Reason*, we must turn to the serially appearing and disappearing, disclosed and foreclosed figure of the native informant.[9] For the spectral reapparition (and disapparition) of this native informant in Nike's corner of hyperspace links the "responsibility page" (as the ad's Web site styles it) not only to the adjacent consumption pages of the World Wide Web but also to the anterior world-making pages of those Enlightenment philosophies of history, reason, and judgment in which the global subaltern was first made to perform this paradigmatic vanishing act.

*

Niketown did not figure in my earlier list of that archipelago of port cities that rim the exchange geographies of an Atlantic cycle of accumulation and function as the capitals of both this regime of accumulation and that long twentieth century whose temporal boundaries correspond with its rise. More-over, the publication of this apparently innocuous advertisement for the Nike corporation's microloan program certainly seems like a dubious successor "event" in which to see the "horrible transactions" of the *Zong* case rec-ollected. But I wish nevertheless to insist on the correspondence between the eighteenth-century financial entrepôts of the Atlantic world and late-twentieth-century Niketown implicit in my juxtaposition of these two sets of events. For it is precisely my proposition that within such an apparently in-nocuous (because now almost ubiquitous) event as that signaled by the adver-tisement, this earlier moment repeats itself in intensified (because almost ubiquitous, because unremarkable) form. This advertisement, the Spivakian native informant it stages, the theory of justice on which it is predicated, the credit-baiting imperative it articulates, and the joint imperial projects of global soul making and global financialization it illuminates, I am thus sug-gesting, belong to (and bear witness to the continued existence of) an elon-gated contemporaneity whose rise the Atlantic's eighteenth-century Capital Houses helped fashion. Despite the two hundred years that separate them, this Nike advertisement and the case of the *Zong* inhabit the same moment, exhibit the workings of a fundamentally similar cultural and capital logic, bookmark either end of our long contemporaneity, and bring to light a re-lated set of strategies for investing in a collective Anglo-American imperial and financial project: that project which, in a mild adaptation of Giovanni Arrighi's work, I have identified as the late-eighteenth- to late-twentieth-century development of an Atlantic cycle of capital accumulation.

But to make clear how the speculative protocols I have been examining enter into conversation with Nike's corporate responsibility page and Spivak's eighteenth- to twentieth-century history of the serially vanishing native infor-mant, and how the reapparition of this repeatedly disappearing subject in a Nike advertisement signals, in however minor a key, a reapparition of this long-twentieth-century's what-has-been within the now-being of its contem-poraneity, some resummarization of my arguments are in order. Like Spivak's history of the native informant, the case of the *Zong*, I have been arguing, names a vanishing event. Indeed, it names a double act of vanishing: the brutal slaughter of the slaves aboard Collingwood's ship, and their *antecedent* de-materialization as subjects of insurance. Subject to the loss-value protocols of insurance, the slaves were, in other words, regarded by the law to have van-ished (as the singular, human bearers of individualized identities, desires, purposes, and wills) *prior* to the moment of their murder, to have had, in Žižek's terms, a nonequivalent exchange forced upon them, to have been transformed from bearers of personhood into bearers of an abstract quantum of value (and thus also to have become types of that Kantian subject $ that Žižek identifies as the normative mode of modern subjectivity and that, as we shall see, Spivak, in her way, identifies with the subject-position inhabited by the native informant.)[10] The *Zong*'s insurance contract may have secured the legal existence of the slaves as no more than the empty bearers of this abstract specie value, but, as I have further argued, an insurance contract is not by itself enough to secure the existence of such imaginary, abstract, object-less value. Insurance, rather, simultaneously secures and is secured by the speculative value forms of a wider finance capitalism, underwrites and is underwritten by a more densely articulated practice of detaching the value of things from their material existence. To understand the *Zong* massacre and the legal discourses surrounding it, the "case" must therefore be situated within (and read as bringing to light the situation of) the more fundamental capital protocols of its moment. It must be placed within (and identified as typicalizing) a moment in which value is not primarily indexed to the commodity form but to the money-into-money, speculative forms of finance capital that characterize those period-shifting moments in which, Arrighi suggests, Marx's full formula for capital (MCM′: Money — Commodity — Money) learns to dispense with the commodity form and teaches itself to breed money from money — as if by a sublime trick of the imagination.

To read the case of the *Zong* so is thus both to read it as typically representative of that culture of speculation that J. G. A. Pocock reveals to have accompanied the eighteenth-century financial revolution in England (to read it, then, as contributing, like novelistic discourse, to this speculative culture's program of reifying and bearing witness to the "real" existence of speculative values and forms), *and* to read this financialized moment within the longer history of capital which Arrighi outlines. This latter argument has led me to identify the moment of the *Zong* massacre as one with which our "time" is noncontemporaneously contemporary, to read it as a moment in which a globalizing finance capital begins to develop those stock, bond, and paper-money networks, those circuits of debt and credit financing, that Pocockian world of imaginary and mobile property, which inaugurate an Atlantic cycle of capital accumulation, whose nineteenth-century midpoint enshrines commodity capitalism but whose late-eighteenth- and late-twentieth-century moments of beginning and end — as Arrighi's general model predicts — operate under the signs of finance capitalism. Thus, the long twentieth century I have had in mind stretches from the late eighteenth to the late twentieth centuries; corresponds to an Atlantic cycle of accumulation; finds its original, organizing, spaces-of-flow in the port cities of the Atlantic world; and, as it completes itself by repeating its moment of beginning in renewed, intensified form, finds itself reheadquartered in those American centers of exchange which have replaced Britain's spaces-of-flow much as *they* earlier displaced Amsterdam's financial catchment zones.[11]

To rehearse these arguments is, however, to leave somewhat unanswered the question of how we get from there to here, or of how, consequently, we should regard the form of the relation of the one (then) to the other (now). Arrighi's quasi-diffusionist, quasi-cyclical-developmental account of capital's long durées provides one way of answering the first question (provides, according to Jameson, *the* account of the way in which "the new deterritorialized postmodern contents" of a culture of "speculation" "are to an older modernist autonomization [of circulating abstract values] as global financial speculation is to an older kind of banking and credit").[12] Benjamin, and the Blochian conception of nonsynchronous time that subtends Benjamin's *Arcades Project*, provide one way of answering the second. I want now to pursue another (if related) answer, an answer which borrows from Spivak's *Critique of Postcolonial Reason* and follows her in linking the history of our extended present to the long history of the native informant and the repeated "foreclosure" of that native informant in what she calls the "great texts" of the "Atlantic tradition." In drawing on Spivak I also intend, however, to depart from her account by associating the constitutive foreclosure and disclosure of that figure not only with the imperial spread of Enlightenment judgment but with the global sprawl of that speculative, financial sublime on which Žižek has suggested the Enlightenment project depended.

If Spivak is right to trace the history of the modern as a history of the native informant, her history, I am thus suggesting, needs to be adjusted by indexing the serial appearances and disappearances of this native informant to the constitution of Žižek's subject $ and to the situating of that subject as a determinate subject-effect of the theoretical realism that accompanies and grounds the speculative cultures of the long twentieth century's oscillating, repeating, and period-bracketing regimes of finance capital. If the publication of Nike's advertisement for its microloan program can then be legitimately regarded as a reiterative late-twentieth-century demonstration of the truth the case of the *Zong* brought to light, it is because that advertisement signals the reappearance, in the guise of the native informant, of this negated subject of speculation, and the repetition, at either end of this long-durée, of a hegemonic culture of speculation.

How do we get from there to here, then to now? How does the *Zong* case predicate and predict its long twentieth century afterlife? By disclosing the appearance of this subject as the reiterative subject of modernity.

∗

A Critique of Postcolonial Reason: Toward a History of the Vanishing Present is an enormous book. The titles of its four main chapters alone indicate the audaciousness of its scope. The first chapter is entitled simply "Philosophy," and the three that follow are, equally confidently, "Literature," "History," and "Culture." There is also an appendix, which is briefer, but similarly magisterial in its ambitions, entitled "The Setting to Work of Deconstruction." The signature contribution of the text, however, is its development of Spivak's notion of the native informant, and as a first step toward tracing the movements of that native informant through the pages of Spivak's book, the worldly spaces that book maps, the oscillating period of world history whose appearances and reappearances are measured to the beat of the native informant's apparitions and disappearances, and the account of the long twentieth century I have been producing, I want to take my cue from Spivak and address what strike me as the organizing protocols and levers of her text.

The concept of the lever I borrow from this sentence from the first chapter of Spivak's *Critique*:

> It is in the spirit of such circum-spection, (ex)orbitant to the pro- and contra- of received readings, that one may ask: where in Marx is that lever to turn the text, to de-con-struct it for use, where that moment of transgression or bafflement?[13]

The notion of the protocol occurs in this sentence and accompanying footnote, also from the first chapter, also referring to Marx:

> I am making an attempt here to work at the deconstructive "new politics of reading," which involves an attempt to enter the protocols of Marx's text in order to re-inscribe it for use.
>
> [Accompanying footnote]: Protocol is not logic, but pre-comprehended procedural priority; backing out of the room in front of royalty rather than taking the quickest way; giving "the public use of reason" the priority, rather than taking the more realistic way: that the (hu)man is (not only) a rational animal; that you cannot compute the limits of reason by *rational* expectations theory.[14]

It will be apparent that protocol denominates at once a procedure and a set of assumptions governing that procedure, forming that procedure, or, indeed, lending that procedure its formal qualities. The assumption here is an assumption in favor of a certain obliquity as a mode of public reasoning, an assumption for obliquity (the indirect route) as a form of reason, where reason is comprehended both as something *in* use and *as* a use value. Obliquity thus names both a way of reasoning (in public) and a form of value. If, on the basis of this, I were to hazard a preliminary reading of Spivak's text, it would be that the text constitutes precisely such a public enactment of the (use) value of the oblique, that for Spivak critique is as much a performative as a constative mode of address. Perhaps this is another way of saying that Spivak's rhetoric ("dazzling, exasperating, unfailingly powerful," as Partha Chatterjee has it in his one-sentence puff on the book's dust jacket), *is* her argument and, somewhat tautologically, that Spivak's arguments are valuable not *despite* but *because* of their famous obliquity. One might use words other than "oblique" to characterize Spivak's argumentative protocols: "exasperating," as Chatterjee has it, "baffling," as Spivak puts it in referring to Marx, or these drawn from the text: "cryptic," "withheld," "singular." Certainly Spivak's oblique mode is singularly her own. But it registers more than style. It implies that she possesses some secret she both does and does not want to share with her readers, a secret she both advances toward and withholds from us. It implies, indeed, that the secret of this text *is* the cryptic mode with which it enacts its public performance of the value of bafflement, crypticism, and singularity as the governing rhetorical strategies of a postcolonial reason which exists to advance and withhold itself from its theaters of interrogation and address (in rhetorical imitation, perhaps, of that native informant similarly drawn into and foreclosed from the global theaters of Enlightenment reason, imperial civilizing mission, and multinational finance capital).

Let me note two more things about the protocol and the lever. I have avoided referring to obliquity, secrecy, singularity, and the like as concepts because as the organizing levers and protocols of Spivak's text they appear there less as concepts — in the sense of theoretical abstractions — than as something closer to what I would call "strategemes": the pivotal tropological units of a text whose ambition is to so lever or turn itself round a series of tropes that those turns might be directed (or, indeed, rerouted: always in something other than the most direct or reasonable fashion) not toward the production of a general theory but toward particular strategic uses. Perhaps "tropologemes" would be a more accurate term. In either case, Spivak is clear about what kind of leverage she hopes her reading protocols will generate:

Deconstructive approaches have suggested that every reading may be an upheaval parasitical to the text. Here I use the resources of deconstruction "in the service of reading" to develop a strategy (rather than a theory) of reading matching the situation of reading that might lead to a literary critique of imperialism.[15]

The distinction Spivak wishes to draw between theory and strategy is, of course, far from self-evident. It seems to amount partially to a kind of situationism (perhaps as a way of reconciling Lukács and Jameson with Derrida: though here the point is less for theory to situate its texts than to inhabit and derive its readerly protocols from its own historicized situation) and, more fully, a consideration of reading as a form, or practice, of value. Indeed the question of value raises the last general point I want to make about the protocols and levers of Spivak's text.

In the two passages I have cited, Spivak's interest in the protocol and the lever articulates itself as an interest, one might even say an investment, in "use": a desire to deconstruct "for use," to reinscribe "for use." Throughout the text she is careful to insist that this does not imply some sentimental devotion to the purity of use values. In fact she goes out of her way to denounce such sentimentalism: "Romantic anti-capitalism produces cozy axiomatics: use good, exchange bad; use concrete, exchange abstract, et cetera" (177). But the reader must wonder whether that repeated disavowal (outnumbered only by Spivak's continuous disavowals of all "nostalgias for lost origins") is sufficient to dissociate her will-to-use from such romanticism, whether, indeed, the catalogue of strategematic use values which organize her text finally mark that text and its strategemes (the cryptic, the withheld, the singular, the native informant, use itself) as a dictionary of romantic anti-capitalism updated for the global age?[16] Spivak's *Critique* contains an answer to this question (if not, perhaps, a resolution) that I would gloss as follows: The "use" which Spivak's reading protocols attempt to lever from the texts she reads does not constitute a sentimental use value (though it does accord reading a form of value) because here use is not understood to *precede* the work of abstraction but to *follow* from and on it. For Spivak, in other words, use (or the singular, the native informant, the cryptic, or the withheld) constitutes not an a priori condition but an a posteriori decision, not an essence but a strategy, not an ontic state but a setting to work: of deconstruction, of theory, of abstraction, of reading. Such, at least, is the formula. Whether the formula is as untainted by "a nostalgia for lost origins" as it hopes to be remains open to question, one Spivak herself takes up. Before seeing how she does so, and how her manner of addressing this question bears upon the usefulness of her text to the argument I am making, it is necessary however to see somewhat more precisely how Spivak sets the strategemes I have mentioned (and several others) to work.

∗

Where in Spivak is that lever to turn the text, to deconstruct it for use? There is not one such lever or strategeme, but several. Chief among these, by Spivak's account, stands the native informant, a figure (in all senses of the word) whose eighteenth- to twentieth-century career the book determines to trace. To speak of the native informant, Spivak indicates, is not to speak of a subject but of a subject position or, more accurately, a serial positionality within a range of discourses, a repeated moment within those discourses, an uncanny effect of their argumentative protocols. It is thus to speak of the systematic foreclosure and disclosure of the native informant within the philosophical, literary, historical, and cultural archive that has constituted our worldly moment, to speak of a history haunted by the traces of the native informant's vanishing, to speak of a history of vanishing points (the vanishing present in the subtitle of Spivak's text might thus be understood less as a flickering present constantly disappearing before our eyes than as a long present — perhaps one could call it a modernity — that has repeatedly attempted to constitute or solidify itself by what it abjects or causes *to* vanish). The first text in Spivak's archive of this vanishing present is Kant's *Critique of Judgment*; the most recent — a relative of the Nike advertisement — are the documents in the Bengali journal *Chinta* which report on the role of child labor in the global textile industry. Spivak fills in the itinerary from Kant's *Critique* to the *Chinta* documents with readings of Hegel, Marx, Brontë, Coetzee, Jameson, and others. Throughout this great tour, her primary concern is with the ways in which the texts in her archive foreclose the native informant both *from* and *within* discourse.

Spivak borrows the notion of foreclosure from Lacan but grafts onto his conception of foreclosure as the psychic expulsion or abjection "of an incompatible idea together with [its] affect" Abraham and Torok's notion of encrypting.[17] Foreclosure, thus understood, names a double and contradictory process of expelling from and secreting within, and becomes, for Spivak, the primary way in which the native informant is at once produced, abjected, and hidden within Kant's *Critique* and all the texts in her post-Kantian archive. How does Kant's *Critique* foreclose the native informant? The operation occurs, Spivak argues, in the analysis of the sublime, where, for Kant, a receptivity to the sublime, swiftly translated into an appreciation of that within the human which enables that receptivity, rapidly transformed into what Kant calls "a respect for the idea of humanity" (which is simultaneously a self-recognition of the humanity of the receptive subject) is denied to "man in the raw," who experiences the sublime simply as "terrible."[18] Denied the sublime, man in the raw is thus also denied the recognition of humanity in himself and others, denied the categorical imperative of recognizing and respecting humanity as an end in itself. And because for Kant this grounding aesthetic sensibility is what enables the foundational act of moral judgment, its lack, Spivak suggests, "must be corrected through culture" (14). This shift from nature—which Kant had first taken to license a receptivity to the sublime—to culture (figured as the programmatic education of aesthetic, hence, moral sensibility) marks the moment in which man in the raw, having been first foreclosed or expelled *from* Kant's system of human recognition is thereafter foreclosed *in* that system as that subject position the system exists to educate and, so, erase.

And who is this man in the raw? For Kant, Spivak indicates, he is named in a casual, almost throwaway moment in the *Critique* as the "New Hollander" or "inhabitant of Tierra Del Fuego."[19] The details of this naming virtually fail to matter, however, for what Kant names in this moment, Spivak argues, is less a particular subject than his conviction that "the subject as such . . . is geo-politically differentiated."[20] The education of aesthetic and moral sensibilities, Spivak suggests, thus licenses a geopolitical project which in turn licenses the imperial project of the civilizing mission. The point, Spivak makes clear, is not that imperialism should be blamed on Kant but that something like the power of citationality links Kant to imperialism, the *Critique of Judgement* to the civilizing mission:

> The dangerous transformative power of philosophy, however, is that its formal subtlety can be travestied in the service of the state. Such a travesty in the case of the categorical imperative can justify the imperialist project by producing the following formula: make the heathen into a human so that he can be treated as an end in himself; in the interest of admitting the raw man into the noumenon; yesterday's imperialism, today's "Development."[21]

Doubtless in condensing Spivak's argument I commit a similar travesty, but such are the lineaments of that argument and, with that argument in place, with that first disclosure of the foreclosure of the native informant by and in the "great texts" of the "Atlantic tradition," Spivak can then develop her readings of the serial repetition of this process in Hegel, Marx, Brontë, Baudelaire, the Anglo-Indian archive, multinational capital, and so on.

*

This is, in many respects, a convincing and an enormously suggestive reading, but it is also one which elides a crucial component of Kant's argument even as it opens Kant, or, more properly, Kantianism, to a worldly, postcolonial critique. For in her reading of a global Kantian civilizing mission, Spivak assumes that the sublime engine by which empire will reproduce the Enlightenment, and so normalize its subjects, is one fueled by a generalized, departicularized experience of the sublime. And that is not, in fact, Kant's position. Rather, as I have indicated, Kant suggests in the series of essays on the philosophy of history he wrote throughout the 1780s and 1790s that the prospects of what he identified as a universal history and a global cosmopolitanism (what, in Mary Louise Pratt's terms, we might call a planetary consciousness, or, in Spivak's, an imperial project of global soul making) depend on the planetary reproduction of a particular experience of the sublime, the global dissemination of a specific sublime spectacle, the universal consumption of the image of a uniquely sublime event: the French Revolution. Or almost so, as Kant takes pain to clarify and as is perhaps worth restating:

> This event consists neither in momentous deeds nor crimes committed by men whereby what was great among men is made small or what was small is made great, nor in ancient and splendid political structures which vanish as if by magic while others come forth from the depths of the earth. No, nothing of the sort. It is simply the mode of thinking of the spectators which reveals itself publicly in this game of great revolutions and manifests such a universal yet disinterested sympathy for the players on one side against those on the other, even at the risk that this partiality could become very disadvantageous for them if discovered. Owing to its universality, this mode of thinking demonstrates a character of the human race at large and all at once; owing to its disinterestedness, a moral character of humanity . . . a character which not only permits people to hope for progress toward the better, but is already itself progress. . . . That event is too important, too much interwoven with the interest of humanity, and its influence too widely propagated in all areas of the world to not be recalled on any favorable occasion by the nations which would then be roused to a repetition of new efforts of this kind.[22]

Universal history, global cosmopolitanism, a planetary consciousness, imperial soul making, are here indexed, as I have been arguing, to the universal dissemination of the spectacle of the revolution and to the moral education (the capacity to express a disinterested sympathy — however terrifying that sympathy might be — for humanity as an end in itself) that Kant feels certain must accompany that sublime spectacle. The vision of a "humanity at large and all at once," the Enlightenment project of and for modernity that imperialism assumes as its alibi, and the consequent foreclosure of Spivak's native informant as a predicate "need" of an imperial modernity thus rest, Kant implies, on the production of those subject effects and subject positions consequent on the global dissemination of this sublime revolutionary spectacle.

Kant, of course, is by no means unique in arguing so. The French Revolution, the terrifying categorical imperative it articulates (the terror-secured demand it makes that the person of individualized, particularized desires, wills, and purposes negate himself or herself under the abstract signs of "Man," the "Rights of Man," and an anonymous, collective project of freedom), and the modern subject that fashions itself by disinterestedly identifying itself with that terror, imperative, and revolution, provide, as Žižek insists, the staples of a dominant philosophical tradition of accounting for the origins of modern subjectivity. For that explanatory tradition, the shift from what Žižek designates the individualized, pre-Enlightenment subject S to the sublimely self-negated or "barred" Kantian subject $ is inevitably negotiated by the encounter with revolutionary terror and the abstract universal project of absolute freedom that terror exists to secure.

But this, as we have seen, is not the only way of accounting for that shift from S to $. Žižek and (on this issue) his surprising predecessor, Edmund Burke, suggest another. And it is this other account which I believe can profitably complicate Spivak's reading, provide us with an alternate genealogy of the vanishing subject and so alter our account of how we get from there to here, how eighteenth-century finance capital and Nike's responsibility page are trading in a common, centuries-long, economy of foreclosure, how, in Benjamin's terms, the now and the what-has-been might "come together in a flash to form a constellation." The pertinent passage is worth reciting:

> It would be of great theoretical interest to establish the conceptual link between this genesis of self-consciousness and the modern notion of paper money. . . . In order to arrive at paper money as we know it today [the] deictic promise with concrete dates and names has to be depersonalized into a promise made to the anonymous "bearer." . . . And the subject who came to recognize itself as this anonymous "bearer" is the very subject of self-consciousness . . . [a subject that] has to relate to itself, to conceive of itself, as (to) an empty "bearer" and to perceive his empirical features which constitute the positive content of his particular "person" as a contingent variable. This shift is again the very shift from S to $.[23]

I will not repeat my reading of this or of the Burkean argument with which it is in such uncanny agreement. Suffice to say that both Žižek's and Burke's analyses of the correspondence between the speculative epistemologies of the eighteenth-century financial and French revolutions and both their respective diagnoses of the origins of the modern subject in a culture of speculation that finds its reciprocal and variant forms in the ideologies of abstract reason and abstract value, permit us to bring the arguments I have been making to bear on Spivak's analysis of the long-durational and serial foreclosure or disclosure of the native informant as a predicate need of the "great texts of the Atlantic tradition" and the imperial civilizing mission. I suggested earlier that if something like a Benjaminian image of the *Zong* case were not so much substituted for the Kantian image of the French Revolution as transposed onto that image, the resultant dialectical image could function as a sign in which modernity finds itself anticipated, demonstrated, and recollected. What I had in mind was precisely such a double image of origins of the modern and the modern subject; precisely such a disclosure of the emergence of the foreclosed subject $ of modernity as a predicate effect and need of the twin-and-linked speculative revolutions these twin-and-linked events bring to light.

The problem of the modern subject, as I have further argued, is not however only one of its origin and rise but one of its spread, not only one of its emergence but one of its global reproduction. Žižek's brief comments ask us not simply to reveal how this subject $ originates but to indicate how it becomes modernity's typical mode of subjectivity, how it is universalized, how it travels from the speculative zones of an original set of eighteenth-century metropolitan spaces-of-flow and secures for itself, and for the modernity it indexes, an ever more global theater of address. Kant's answer is to link the universalization of this subject, and hence of both modernity and the promise of progress, to the recurrent spectacle of the French Revolution, the event whose extrametropolitan dissemination he insists will secure that subjective identification with a collective project of freedom on which a progressive and cosmopolitan modernity depends. Burke and Žižek imply something else, suggesting that it is not by remembering the French Revolution that humanity at large will normalize itself as a homogeneous, interchangeable, typical collectivity, but that it is through the global spread of another revolution coincident with and fundamental to that revolution, through the global reproduction of a financial revolution first headquartered in Europe's metropolitan spaces-of-flow, that the speculative subject of modernity will become the typical subject of the globe and that the modernity philosophically indexed to the existence of this subject will progressively universalize itself. On this account, a global memory of the French Revolution does not serve as a cosmopolitan modernity's precondition. Rather, the global circulation of paper money, the global implication of metropolitan and extrametropolitan subjects in the massively co-lateralizing networks of finance capital, and the global extension of *this* speculative revolution serve to secure the increasingly universal existence of a modernity coterminous with what I have been calling the long twentieth century.

Spivak's account is of course not inimical to this reading. Indeed, by the end of her text, finance capital has assumed the burden she earlier associated with the imperial dissemination of the Kantian sublime. But there is less of a shift from the culturalist project of the eighteenth- and nineteenth-century imperial civilizing mission to the financializing project of late-twentieth-century capital than Spivak implies. If the two projects both act to foreclose alterity, they do so not sequentially but simultaneously. Global finance capital does not belatedly reassume the subject-forming, modernity-distributing, Enlightenment project of empire, but licenses and is licensed by that project from the very beginning.[24] My mild Žižekian alteration to Spivak's account of the imperial foreclosure of extranormative identity is that if Spivak is correct to argue that empire licenses its civilizing mission by refitting its subjects for the consumption of the Kantian sublime, then the sublime in question is simultaneously the Jacobinical and the speculative modes of the sublime apposite to the French and financial revolutions of the eighteenth century. I do not, therefore, propose that the case of the *Zong* and Nike's microloan program are identical phenomena. They are not. Indeed, as I will suggest in concluding this section of the text, part of what is at stake in juxtaposing these events in the way I have is the need to read the singularity of systemically related phenomena. Rather, as that language of systemic relation implies, I am arguing that these late-eighteenth-century and late-twentieth-century events are subtended by and script a common and long-durational cycle of accumulation, speculation, and subjectification.

The globalization increasingly identified as the signature characteristic of our moment and regularly indexed to the spread of global finance capital is, I am thus suggesting, less of "our moment" than we often think, as "our" moment is itself less of "its" moment than we might assume. Indeed our time might, after all, best be understood in Bloch's terms as a nonsynchronous order of time, as a contemporaneity that is not contemporary with itself. If such reflections suggest that we might valuably reperiodize our present (even as we reconsider our notions of periodicity), then one way to do so is to address the ways in which we inhabit the tail end of a long twentieth century, a long contemporaneity stretching back from *this* moment to the mid– and late eighteenth century, a modernity indexed to the global production and re-production of that speculative subject of abstract reason and abstract value brought to light in the hearing held in Lord Mansfield's courtroom and re-illuminated by the reapparition of Spivak's native informant in Nike's corner of hyperspace. If the 250-year history of modern finance capital and its specu-lative epistemologies, subjectivities, and value forms provide the basis for such a reperiodization, then that same history also implies a remapping of our theaters of critical address — implies, moreover, that we need not await the advent of the late twentieth century proper to discover a set of transnational and anational territories of flow that have given and give shape to our world. The eighteenth- to late-twentieth-century Atlantic cycle of capital accumu-lation examined here is one of these; its rise and spread are what the case of the *Zong* and the announcement of Nike's microloan program in their dif-ferent but related ways bring to light; its self-reproduction through the sys-tematic foreclosure of alterity and the systematic distribution of the specula-tive epistemologies, subjectivities, and value forms of finance capital what they disclose.

*

As Spivak makes clear, however, the importance of such events cannot be restricted to what they disclose, to the broad historical trends they bring to light, to what, in one of the other terms I have used, they typify. For to regard them exclusively so is to risk reproducing, within the domain of our knowl-edge of them, an epistemological variant of that speculative violence they bring to light. Hence Spivak's profound unease with the theoretical value of her reading protocols, her desire to read, strategically or strategematically, for "use," her injunction that we learn to ground the value of our readings of such events not in the general and exchangeable value of those speculative verities we have deduced from them, but in the nonexchangeable singularity of the event. On this point, Spivak's hermeneutic of the event is explicitly anti-Kantian and suggests that the quasi-Kantianism of the event theory I have thus far adopted requires some significant qualification.

How are we to read the event, Kant asks in "An Old Question Raised Again"? Not only as a signum rememorativum, demonstrativum, prognosti-kon, he replies, but as something whose value to knowledge is governed by our determination to regard the event as something *"non singularum, sed universorum."*[25] This universality, he quickly makes clear, does not represent some radically dehistoricized, timeless truthfulness, but, quite oppositely, signifies a broadly historicist and cosmopolitan truth value: "a tendency of the human race viewed in its entirety, that is, seen not as individuals (for that would yield an interminable enumeration and computation), but rather as divided into nations and states (as it is encountered on earth)."[26] And this, in fact, is largely how I have been reading the *Zong* and also Nike's microloan advertisement: as events whose truth value is attached to a tendency of human *history* (rather than to a tendency of the human race) as that history has actually been encountered. Spivak's readerly protocols tend to read the serial appearances and disappearances of the native informant in a similar way: as events which demonstrate the operations of the conjoined projects of imperial civilizing mission and capital financialization of the globe. The appeal to the universal may have been replaced by an appeal to historicity or the episystemic, but the fundamental impulse is the same: non singularum, sed universorum. The obvious danger of this is that, constructed so, this form of event theory, precisely *as* it brings to light the subject canceling and identity negating triumphs of a culture of speculation as the catastrophic truth to which it offers its testimony, represents yet another triumph *of* such a speculative regime over this very act of bringing to light, yet another triumph of what Hegel called the "cunning of reason" — which triumphs here by subjecting not just history but the disclosure of history, not just the event but the theory of the event to a general, abstract, typicalizing standard of (knowledge) value.[27]

Thus, then, the return to the singular, the desire to reverse Kant's injunction, to read the event as one whose truth is, precisely, non universorum, sed singularum. As Spivak is aware, however, such a decision carries its own dangers, not only those Kant feared and which he might well have read Sharp's submission to the Lords Commissioner to typify (as its interminable enumeration and reenumeration of the individual horrors of the massacre threaten to break the unity and the general significance of the event down into the imperative of counting its horrors one by one by one), but what she identifies as the danger of a sentimental and romanticizing nostalgia. Troping her turn to the singular as an act that will "reopen the epistemic fracture of imperialism," Spivak repeatedly warns both herself and her reader that this must be done "without succumbing to the nostalgia for lost origins."[28] How is this to be accomplished? Spivak proposes a number of strategic solutions, perhaps the most enigmatic (but also, I believe, the most promising) being that we read for the singular by way of the archive and the example. In the literature chapter, she twice appeals to the archive as a sort of proof against nostalgia: "To reopen the fracture without succumbing to a nostalgia for lost origins, the literary critic must turn to the archives of imperial governance"; "If, as critics, we wish to reopen the epistemic fracture of imperialism without succumbing to the nostalgia for lost origins, we must turn to the archives of imperial governance."[29] In the history chapter, the archive is displaced by the example, though the formula (indeed, by this point, one might say the mantra) remains the same: "Since this essay operates on the notion that all such clear-cut nostalgias for lost origins are suspect, especially as grounds for counterhegemonic ideological production, I must proceed by way of an example."[30] Ironically, it is precisely this last move, this linking of the singular to the example, that threatens to reopen Spivak's text to that theorizing mode of value creation against whose encroachments she is equally, resolutely, on her guard. But to get some sense of how this might be and of how, despite the risks it runs, Spivak's *Critique* offers through this very move a strategic resolution to the problems the *Zong* poses to our theories of the truth it discloses (and so implies that the *Zong* must be read as at once a singular and, in the most terrible sense, an exemplary event), we need to get some fuller sense of what Spivak means by the singular.

The singular first appears in Spivak's *Critique* in a footnote on Derrida's comments on the signature: "The interest here is not merely 'speculative.' It has something to do with the fact that, reading literature, we learn to learn from the singular and the unverifiable."[31] Thereafter the term appears in a cluster of passages surrounding a reading of Coetzee's *Foe* before metastasizing, through that reading, into the variant forms of the withheld and the cryptic and then serially reappearing in its original form in the subsequent chapters of the text:

> The named marginal is as much a concealment as a disclosure of the margin, and where s/he discloses, s/he is singular. . . . To meditate on the figure of the wholly other as margin, I will look at a novel in English, *Foe*.

> Coetzee's novel figures the singular and unverifiable margin, the refracting barrier over against the wholly other that one assumes in the dark. The native informant disappears in that shelter.

> Friday . . . is the unemphatic agent of withholding in the text. For every territorial space that is value coded by colonialism *and* every command of metropolitan anticolonialism for the native to yield his "voice," there is a space

of withholding, marked by a secret that may not be a secret but cannot be unlocked. "The native," whatever that might mean, is not only a victim but also an agent. The curious guardian at the margin who will not inform.[32]

There is an enormous amount of work taking place here, work I can at best shorthand thus. While not precisely an antispeculative device ("the interest here is not merely 'speculative' "), the singular, as that first footnote suggests, is something that exists at a remove from mere speculation (read "abstraction," as at once a capital and an epistemological protocol, "speculation" as a pun on financial and theoretical forms of value creation), something like what I have called a strategeme. Reinscribing Derrida, the singular thus also reworks Deleuze, emerging as something whose value has not been coded, as, indeed, one of those decoded [that is not-yet or no-longer coded] flows which, in her Deleuzian moments, is one of Spivak's alternate terms for the native informant foreclosed within a system animated by its dread of such spaces of withholding.[33] The native informant is thus singular to the extent to which he or she discloses a space of withholding *within* the territorialized ambits of Enlightenment reason, imperial civilizing mission, and the multinational financialization of the globe; singular to the extent to which he or she marks off a cryptic, secretive space (a sort of internalized margin); singular to the extent that he or she discloses the presence of that withheld space, but guards its secret. The singular is thus, in the example at hand, the withheld secret of Friday's missing tongue, the cryptic silence that occupies that space, withholds it from coding, refuses to subject this raw man to that culturalist project of education which will not so much civilize him or render him receptive to the categorical imperative as erase him. That the singular, thus understood, is also in the terms of two of Spivak's key sources (Nicolas Abraham and Maria Torok) a species of melancholy is not an element of Spivak's stated argument, though the ghost of melancholy certainly haunts that argument.

It is not the problem of melancholy, however, but another problem that I want to consider, the problem of the singular as, also, a form of example. The example — to which Spivak appeals to guard both her text and her investment in such singularity from nostalgia — is another of those classically ambiguous deconstructive entities. For it is at once a specificity, a singleness, *and* a specification of something else. The example names itself as itself *and* it names itself as not-itself but a mere instance of what it exists to instantiate. There is another way of putting this, a less abstract formulation of the problem: What does it mean for Friday (or indeed for the *Zong*) to exemplify the singular? What becomes of Friday's strategematic usefulness when his withheld secret marks something other than itself, something other than his cryptic situation, something other than his space of withholding, something he merely represents? The interest here is precisely speculative. For such questions suggest that in its life as an example, the exemplary singular exists as two apparently opposed things: a strategeme and a concept. And it is this indirect return of the speculative, the abstract, and the theoretical (slipping backward into the protocols of the text along the path opened by Spivak's appeal to the example) that is, I believe, the source of the *Critique*'s greatest anxiety. For if the reading of the cryptic, withheld singular contains (as one of its secrets) Spivak's answer to the many critics who have denounced her dictum "the subaltern cannot speak," if what it suggests is that she really meant "the subaltern *will not* speak (in code)," then the moment in which that withheld speech licenses its abstract conceptualization is the moment in which it indeed becomes codable: for theory.

Why then the move to exemplify the singular, to render it exemplary? My sense is that Spivak makes this move, turns this lever, less from a concern that if she does not the singular will, in the end, prove too singular or too restricted to its own cryptic place of withholding to prove to be of sufficient use, than that it is by making this move that she can demonstrate (exemplify, if you will) that to speak of the singular is, once again, not to speak of a state or a condition but of an undecidability and of the imperative of decision. It is, in other words, precisely by troping the double life of the singular as strategeme and concept that Spivak can pose the singular not as a once lost but now recovered thing (a nostalgicist's treasure) but as the invitation to a decision. Spivak stages that undecidability of the singular (and the accompanying obligation of decision) in a number of ways. Sometimes she does so by dramatizing her own double life as an archivist, most notably in a remarkable series of passages in which, while literally tracing the path of the Maharani of Jaipur, she finds that "as I approached her house . . . I was miming the route of an unknowing, a progressive différance, an experience of how I could not know her"; that while gazing at the Rani's palace and the foothills of the Himalayas behind it, "I was halted by the discourse of the European sublime"; that on seeing an adjacent Kali temple, "I was halted by my own ideological formation as a child of a Kali-worshipping sect"[34] While it may be fair to say that few of us find our walks so haunted and halted by "différance," "the discourse of the European sublime," and our "own ideological formation as a child," Spivak, I believe, pauses to mark the doubleness of her archival route precisely to remind us that even such singular places exemplify conceptual geographies, that they are neither one thing nor the other but an undecidable complement of both.

Sometimes Spivak's move is in the opposite direction. When she interrupts herself to remind us that her project is a version of that Marxian project which she understands as the wish "to insert the historical narrative within philosophy, violating its form, as it were, to verify it in the strictest sense,"[35] she implies that her project duplicates Marx's by inserting or disclosing what I have been calling the strategeme within the concept, violating the form of theory to disclose its protocols of value coding.[36]

Finally, however — in the concluding paragraph of the final chapter — she stages the undecidability of the singular and the obligation of decision as a challenge: "Please decide . . . as the web of text and textile role out asymptotically, if one can stitch together Kant's *Third Critique* and documents like *Chinta* without the everyday or corrupt version of the switch from determinant to reflexive judgement — primary/secondary, data/research, fieldwork/ethnography, native-informant/master discourse — that we perform in our studies and classrooms."[37] With that challenge — that challenge not so much to suture together the strategematic and the theoretical, the global textile industry, and the great texts as to reinscribe ("for use") the knowledge of the ways in which text and textile, strategy and theory, native informant and master discourse constantly disclose and foreclose one another — we are back to the two events that I have argued cast their demonstrative, anticipatory, and retrospective light on the long contemporaneity we inhabit. We are back to that Nike advertisement, the need it expresses for the native informant, the educational project it espouses for these women in the raw, the desire it has to refit them for the responsibilities of global capital citizenship, the 250-year-old project of financialization it codes onto their bodies even as it discloses and forecloses the singular images of these women from and within hyperspace. And we are back to the case of the *Zong*, back to that set of horrible transactions it brings to light, to that both novel *and* long-durational speculative epistemology, mode of subjectivity, and value form it demonstrates, to the great historical trends it exemplifies by bringing these tendencies of history to bear on the bodies of the utterly singular human beings thrown one by one by one into the sea. *And* we are thus also back to the undecidable and the obligation that accompanies it, back to the obligation disclosed in Spivak's cryptic challenge: Please, decide.

*

For each of these two events we are thus asked to make not one decision, but two. Above all, for my concerns here, the *Zong* demands that we determine to regard it, in the full sense, as a truth event. That is the first decision. It is the second, however, that Spivak's work reminds us is so pressing and so vexed. For the question of deciding what sort of truth the *Zong* names remains unresolved and returns us, in Spivak's deconstructive terminology, to the problematics of the undecidable. Kant's way of framing and resolving this dilemma is to demand that we view such an event as something non singularum, sed universorum. Spivak offers a series of reformulations and suggests that the problem is one of deciding whether we should incline to a theoretical or a strategic (or strategematic) reading of such a truth event, of determining whether it speaks to the episystemic truth of a global, worldly, situation, or whether it declines to speak in such code, withholding itself from our critical recoding, maintaining a cryptic silence. Most everything I have said in this first section inclines to the former set of choices, proceeds on the determination that the *Zong* speaks to and of a situated and episystemic set of catastrophic worldly truths, and assumes, in Benjamin's terms, that it is possible "to assemble large-scale constructions out of the smallest and most precisely cut components . . . to discover in the analysis of the small individual moment the crystal of the total event."

Read thus, the *Zong* constitutes an event only and exactly as the example names itself as the crystallization of something more general, more abstract, more total than itself. Read as a catastrophically exemplary event, the *Zong* manifests itself as the individual moment in which a total event becomes retrospectively and proleptically visible. What total event? The arrival, I have been arguing, of the contemporary. It brings its light to bear on the inauguration of a long twentieth century underwritten by the development of an Atlantic cycle of capital accumulation: a cycle of capital dominated at either end of its 250-year history by the stock, credit, insurance, and other money forms of finance capital; headquartered in the spaces-of-flow of an archipelago of circum-Atlantic port cities; enabled by and productive of a set of speculative revolutions and a culture of speculation whose dominant aesthetic modes, epistemological innovations, subject effects, and value forms are governed by a theoretical realism.

The list of features goes on, and I will not again rehearse all the details of this argument. For my point here is not to repeat that argument but, in concluding this first section of the book, to note something of what is at stake in deriving this *type* of argument from this event. To do so, as I have argued throughout, is to adopt that quasi-tautological mode of reading characteristic of both historicist critique and casuist reason: to read this event as one coded by its historical circumstances and governed by the general norms of the system in which it is situated *and* as an event which serves as a representative type or case from which those circumstances and norms are deduced in the first place. In Žižek's terms this implies not an error of reasoning but a determination to read the case or event symptomatically, to discover in an entity "misperceived by the system as a local 'abnormality,' . . . the global 'abnormality' of the system as such."[38] It is thus, as he further argues, to read the event as Kant reads it, and as Badiou does, and as Benjamin determines to read the fragments, shards, wreckage, and small individual moments of history: perpetually on the lookout for the large scale constructions latent within them. That is how I have been reading, how I have, to this point, decided to read this event.

As Spivak reminds us, however, this is a decision, not a necessity. And it is a decision which in this instance is particularly troubled. For to read so, to read the *Zong* as symptomatic, exemplary, typical of something larger, more abstract, and more total, to read it, in the phrase I used in my opening pages, as something *worth* reading, *worth* uncovering, *worthwhile*, because the utterly singular history it assembles can be seen to find its general equivalent in a reassembled history of the modern, is to risk grounding the value of such a way of reading in the very value form whose speculative and catastrophic triumphs this event brings to light. This then is the second decision that the case of the *Zong* asks us to make, as it asks us not simply to determine that it does in fact name a modern truth but to decide whether this is, in Spivak's terms, a singular or an exemplary truth. As I have suggested, the virtue of Spivak's *Critique* is to undo that opposition a little, to imply that it is possible to make a decision for neither by deciding for both. This is what undecidability looks like when it names not a retreat from judgment but an appreciation of the constructedness of both the choices available to judgment, a recognition that the singular is itself not an a priori state but the product of a decision. The imperative remains however. The need to make one or other of those decisions survives this recognition. What sort of truth does the *Zong* name? A small individual moment that crystallizes in its precisely cut and horrific components a total event (the arrival of the contemporary)? Or something that withholds itself from such large-scale reassembly, something that maintains its cryptic silence, something singular and unverifiable?

∗

Please, decide, Spivak enjoins her readers. Please, decide, I have echoed, and echo again. The pages that precede this request have indicated what one response to that request might resemble. The pages that follow ask what the decision for the cryptic and the singular might imply. But first one more thing must be noted. Whatever form such a decision takes, it can neither presume its own decisiveness nor its own originality. Like the event itself, the decisions made on it appear as the reappearances of what has come before. Even as we make them, decisions have already been made. Many of them. Granville Sharp, I have indicated, found himself obliged to decide, though only after Olaudah Equiano, catching wind of the case in the newspaper coverage of the original trial, decided to urge Sharp to make a matter of it. Equiano's determination, in its turn, followed on the Guildhall jury's initial decision on the case, while Lord Mansfield, for his part, found himself unable to depart from the financial system of reasoning that had inspired Luke Collingwood's original actions. Collingwood, Mansfield, Equiano, Sharp: They stand as the first interpreters of this case, the first to decide what it might signify. Or almost so, and not at all. There is another cohort, another group of eighteenth-century ghosts who made their decision and whose determination haunts anything we might have to say about the meaning of this event. That final ten of the one hundred thirty-three: the ten slaves, who as they were about to be thrown overboard, decided instead to throw themselves into the sea. What was the meaning of that decision? On this matter, Spivak's language seems best. It withholds itself from speculation.

*

Not just metaphorically. When he was informed of their action, Lord Mansfield swiftly ruled that whatever else the court might decide, these ten slaves were no longer subject to the insurance contract written on them. Destroying themselves, they destroyed the value invested in them. They withdrew themselves from speculation.

*

And then there is this. On April 21, 1807, the year the slave trade was abolished, the year the bank he had founded with his father went bankrupt, John Gregson, former mayor of Liverpool, made his last decision. The son of a former rope maker, he took a rope and hanged himself in the house he had inherited from his father.[39] Unless he chose to turn his back against the windows, his last sight, as the consequences of this decision tightened around his neck, would have been of the nonconformist cemetery across the road, the burial ground on a corner of whose space his family's magnificent house had been built.

History's ironies are, as ever, the most brutal, the most exacting, and the most precise.

Part Two

SPECTERS OF THE ATLANTIC:

SLAVERY AND THE WITNESS

the truth was

the ship sailed

the rains came

the loss arose

the truth is

the ship sailed

the rains came

the loss arose

the negroes are

the truth is

— M. NourbeSe Philip, *Zong! # 14*[1]

CHAPTER 6

Frontispiece

TESTIMONY, RIGHTS, AND THE STATE OF EXCEPTION

Granville Sharp's counterhistory of the *Zong* massacre, the testament he submitted to the Lords Commissioners of the Admiralty as the missing log's
surrogate book of evidence, stands as a frontispiece to the volume of melancholy the event has inspired over the past two centuries. Or almost so. To call
it a frontispiece to the assortment of images and texts that serve as the quasi-
Benjaminian "convolute" which the remaining portions of this text seeks to
assemble ("convolute," as Benjamin's editors indicate, translates the German
Konvolut, "a larger or smaller assemblage — literally a bundle — of manuscripts
or printed materials that belong together") is, of course, to ignore its own
entirely convoluted character and form while both allying it to *and* holding it
apart from that bundle of material it prefaces and introduces.[2] As a frontispiece to those *Zong*-haunted works which have succeeded his act of writing,
assembling, and bundling, Sharp's submission certainly upholds its responsibility partially to advertise, partially to miniaturize what is to come. If in the
ideal frontispiece each component element of the work that is to ensue finds
itself advertised in miniature, then the frontispiece is, for this reason, also
something very much like the Benjaminian fragment, the small "precisely cut

component" that "assemble[s] [a] large-scale construction" within itself.[3] Or, to put things in Spivak's terms, the frontispiece is an artifact that exhibits an exemplary relation to the ensuing work it at once depicts and promises. It is as such an exemplary fragment that Sharp's submission stands as the frontispiece to what (in the double sense) is to come. Or, as I have said, almost so.

Why "almost so"?

In part because as an exemplary fragment of the melancholy bundle to come, Sharp's submission also serves as a *testament* to what has been (or what has been brought to light) and as a *testament* to what follows, as thus not only a Benjaminian fragment and a Spivakian example but also a Kantian *signum rememorativum, demonstrativum, prognostikon.* Frontispiece and testament at once, the submission bears witness to both its future and its past, delivers its word both to what is to be and to what has been. There is of course nothing unusual in this. Any frontispiece to a book of history or book of evidence bears witness in this way, offers its testimony to the truth, the argument, or the lesson of the as-yet-unread book *and* to the shape, nature, or meaning of the historical past to which that text offers its own belated act of argumentation or witness. History's frontispieces identify themselves, like those who testify, as occupying a hinge between times, as neither utterly within the past time they argue (or to which they attest) nor utterly within the future time in which the work of argumentation or testimony is complete. Neither completely proper to nor dispossessed by the work it opens, neither completely something that belongs to the anterior time of the written or the posterior time of writing, neither completely of one or the other, the frontispiece defines for itself a third space, a third scene, a third time. And in this sense, at least, the frontispiece is not just contingently but (by at least one etymological account) definitionally testamentary.

"Testament," according to the *Oxford English Dictionary*, derives from the Latin *testari* ("to be a witness, attest, make a will, etc.") and signifies "a formal declaration, usually in writing, of a person's wishes as to the disposal of his property after his death, properly applied to a disposal of personal as opposed to real property," or alternately, "the writing by which a person nominates an executor to administer his personal or moveable estate after his decease." Read as an act of testament, Sharp's submission thus parses not only as a work of attesting or witnessing, nor simply as one designed to survive its compiler's demise, but as one that exists to call into being an executor or body of executors engaged to dispose of the property it names. What property? Not the *Zong*'s drowned slaves, certainly. For if this is a testament it is one written, quite precisely, to protest the conversion of these slaves into so much mobile property. Rather, the property this testament names and whose future it seeks to secure is something closer to the affective property Sharp's melancholy has permitted him to take in the dead. It is this melancholy interest Sharp has taken in the slaves that his testament seeks to transmit to future generations by calling into life the body of executors charged with the task of passing on this very property (of being interested). Orchestrating the future history of its melancholy investment in the event, the testament thus bears witness to its dream of the property a just future will take in (and from) the past. Binding the future to this vision of just transmission, the testament thus weds the possibility of the continued existence of justice to the future being of one, or some, who will bear witness to the claims it has made on what is to come, someone who will act as history's third party, engaged to execute the claims the past and the dead make on the present and its futures.

And it is on this point that a second philological tradition begins to close the gap between the testament and the frontispiece. For testament, as Jacques Derrida has noted in his essay " 'A Self-Unsealing Poetic Text': Poetics and the Politics of Witnessing," derives not only from the witness-bearing and witness-engaging of *testari* but from a "Latin etymology [in which] the witness (*testis*) is someone who is present as a third person (*terstis*)."[4] To this testis/terstis/testari cluster Derrida adds a cognate culled from Emile Benveniste's *Dictionary of European Institutions*: "superstes" which, in Derrida's gloss, means " 'witness' in the sense of survivor: someone who, having been present then having survived, plays the role of witness" or, by Benveniste's more expansive definition, "describes the 'witness' either as the one who 'subsists beyond,' witness at the same time as survivor, or as 'the one who holds himself to the thing.' "[5]

In drawing attention to the dual identity of the witness (testis) as either (or both) terstis (a third) and superstes (one who survives), Derrida's immediate interest is to cast some light on an enigmatic sequence of lines in Paul Celan's "Aschenglorie":

Aschenglorie . . .
No one
bears witness for the
witness.[6]

What, Derrida asks, can this mean? What, in a poem bearing this enigmatic neologism as its title, can Celan mean when he attests that no one (can, will, does, should) bear witness for the witness — without ever telling us what that witness has witnessed (other, perhaps, than an unsettling epiphany of ash)? Whatever the lines mean, Derrida argues, we can only begin to make sense of them if we attend to the etymological substrate of Celan's text and so consider his witness as one who "having been present . . . survived" *and* as one who presents himself not as the survivor of some incinerating event but as that event's observer; as some one (some "third") who "holds himself to the thing" he has not experienced. To witness, to speak of witnessing, Derrida thus suggests, is at the very least to speak of this apparent opposition between the witness (testis) conceived as terstis and the witness conceived as superstes, to speak of that third who, holding himself to the thing, takes a melancholy property in it, *and* to speak of the one who having survived the event "subsists beyond it." To speak of witnessing, of the work of testament, is thus to speak of the witness as *either/or and both* "terstis/superstes," as third or survivor or third and survivor at once. We know enough of Derrida to predict that this detour through the etymological thickets must have as its object some or other "unworking" of the dichotomies these etymologies seem designed to produce. And though the details of that unworking defy reworking here, that is what it effects. For by the terms of Derrida's reading, the survivor or observer opposition cannot but announce its failure to hold as the meaning of one term so bleeds into *and* blanches the semantic field of the other that the belated observing third re-emerges simultaneously as a survivor of the event (one who subsists beyond it) and one who (by holding himself to the thingness of the event) has not yet survived it; while the survivor (by subsisting beyond the incinerating event) re-appears as one who has not yet experienced it, *except* as one who, *holding* himself to it, experiences it by not yet surviving it, not yet exchanging a melancholy property in this event-thing for some other property of experience.

Thus Derrida's witness as terstis/superstes. And the witness testari? The witness who calls into being a body of executors charged with the task of assuming and transmitting the property she has taken in the event as its observer/survivor? The witness who, in the terms I have been using, figures his words *of* witness as a frontispiece to the volume of testimony to come? Derrida adduces this function also, indeed weds it to his most suggestive reading of Celan's lines. "No one bears witness for the witness," by which, Derrida indicates, Celan manages to indicate not only that no one bears witness in favor of the witness, and that no one can bear witness in place of the witness, but that when witness *is* borne, when testimony *is* offered, when historical testaments *are* written, witness is not borne, offered, or produced for those who have themselves witnessed. Which means that witness exists for the nonwitness, that testimony is offered to those who have neither survived or held themselves to the event or thing. Or almost so and not at all. For even in a court of law, or especially in a court of law, Derrida continues, while "the judge, arbiter or addressee of the testimony thus is not a witness . . . cannot and must not be," nevertheless "at the end of the day the judge, the arbiter or the addressee do have to be *also* witnesses; they do have to be able to testify, in their turn, before their consciences or before others, to what they have attended, to what they have been present at, to what they happened to be in the presence of: the testimony of the witness in the witness box. . . . The judge, the arbiter, the historian [thus] also remains a witness, a witness of a witness when he receives, evaluates, criticizes, interprets the testimony of a survivor, for instance a survivor of Auschwitz."[7] To bear witness, Derrida thus suggests, is not only simultaneously to observe, hold to, survive, and subsist beyond the event but to transmit to another this property of observing, holding, surviving. It is, therefore, to serialize the event and its affect and also to elongate its temporality, to stretch its time along the line of an unfolding series of moments of bearing witness.

It is in this sense that each iteration of witness articulates itself not only as a testament to what has been but as a frontispiece to what follows. More particularly, it is in this sense that Sharp's submission assumes its place as both testament to the *Zong* massacre and frontispiece to the melancholy bundle to come. At once observing, holding itself to, surviving, and subsisting beyond the event to which it bears witness; making its decision for, and so, in part, belatedly calling into existence the catastrophic truth event it brings to light while also calling into being a body of judges, arbiters, addressees it desires to bear witness to the witness it has born; setting itself the impossible task of bearing witness *for* the witness and asking its readers to inhabit the same experience of the impossible; simultaneously testifying to the unjust past it names and serving as the frontispiece to the just future it hopes to fashion by passing on to that future the melancholy property it has taken in the past, Sharp's submission to the Lords Commissioners thus makes its lie of the truth Celan's lines also so intimately travesty.

*

But to what does Sharp's submission stand as such a frontispiece? To what past does it bear witness and what future does it urge into life? The question demands a variety of answers. To what does Sharp bear witness? The coming of the contemporary; the institution and reign of a long-twentieth-century culture of speculation and its abstracting, subject-canceling protocols; the rise and spread of a globalizing finance capital. But what does he urge into life? Himself, or one or some such as him, one or some who will bear witness, testify, judge the injustices of this hypercapitalized contemporaneity. Calling himself into being as a witness, Sharp thus also calls into being the *figure* of the witness. And in this he is by no means alone, either in invoking those who will testify to this event or those who will testify as such, either in his time or in ours. Indeed, as the second section of this book argues, if the *Zong* trials can be seen to exemplify the advent and triumph of an abstract, speculative, hyper-capitalized modernity, Sharp's book of evidence also bears witness to the emergence, internal to the speculative culture of our long contemporaneity, of the figure of the interested historical witness *and* so testifies to the emergence, internal to Euromodernity, of a testamentary counterdiscourse on and of modernity: a recognizably romantic counterdiscourse; a melancholy but cosmopolitan romanticism that sets itself, in Michael Lowy and Robert Sayre's evocative phrase, "against the tide of modernity"; a cosmopolitan melancholy that, like Lowy and Sayre's anticapital and antimodern romanticism, is thus less proper to a period than expressive of a worldview.[8] Or, if it implies a period, it implies one that, like their romanticism, defines itself as a "world-view [that] is coextensive with capitalism itself," as a long-durational counter-current within the tide of Euromodernity.[9] Subject to (if set against) this Euromodernity, the type of witness Sharp calls into life, the type of witness whose most recent incarnations include Derrida's third, the type of romantic, interested, melancholy, *and* cosmopolitan witness whose long-twentieth-century career I intend now to trace, is, however, more than contingently or analogically related to the particular witness Sharp determines to be. Rather, this witness (figured as a type of modern historical observer, actor, and judge, and recently conceived by Derrida and others as *the* type of the ethical actor in history) is if not exclusively then crucially Atlantic in its provenance; crucially, if not exclusively, haunted by the specter of the trans-Atlantic slave trade.

But to say that is already to assume too much regarding the nature of that witness I understand Derrida and others partially to inherit from the Atlantic eighteenth and nineteenth centuries. So before returning to this Atlantic scene let me briefly return to the more recent incarnations of this figure.

∗

Derrida is not alone in adducing his witness, his third, from Celan and from the holocaust camp. Giorgio Agamben has also linked the emergence of this figure to Celan's poetry and to the fact and example of Auschwitz. Agamben, to be sure, routes that reading of poet and camp through a reading of one of the camp's exemplary witnesses: Primo Levi, whose own reading of Celan's poetry ("This darkness that grows from page to page until the last inarticulate babble fills one with consternation like the gasps of a dying man . . . It enthralls us as whirlpools enthrall us, but at the same time it robs us of what was supposed to be said but was not said") and whose meditations on the camp as an experience of drowning experienced and drowning observed ("Those who saw the Gorgon, have not returned to tell about it or have returned mute, but they are the Muslims, the submerged, the complete witnesses . . . We who were favored by fate tried, with more or less wisdom, to recount not only our fate but also that of the others, indeed of the drowned"), establish a link — at least rhetorically — between the witness who survives, beholds, and holds melancholy property in the holocaust camp and the witness who stands as third to the terrors of the trans-Atlantic slave trade.[10]

I do not, however, want to make too much of that rhetorical link, either as it emerges from a text such as Levi's *The Drowned and the Saved* or from that far broader interchange of diaspora language central to Jewish and black histories. Rather, my interests here are more formally genealogical, more properly directed toward tracing a genealogy of Agamben and Derrida's third that takes as its horrific historical examples the witnesses to both the holocaust camp and the trans-Atlantic slave trade. Agamben's work suggests the contours of that genealogy, particularly that portion of his *Homo Sacer* project devoted to an exploration of the state of exception whose prime twentieth-century example is the camp. As many of his readers have noted, however, Agamben remains largely silent on the matter of slavery, on *that* state of exception. While this greater absence of slavery from Agamben's account constitutes a significant weakness in his work, and while much of what ensues might be read as an attempt to reroute his and other recent discourses on the witness through the history of the trans-Atlantic slave trade (or, more particularly still, that history of the slave trade whose test case and singular example is the *Zong* massacre), I nevertheless believe that Agamben's work can help illuminate the enduring, repeating object and form of that politics of witnessing which has not only become one of the signature features of our late-twentieth-century moment but which recurs over the course of occidental modernity as the characteristic politics of a melancholy counterdiscourse on and of the modern.

*

What form does that politics assume? How does it articulate itself? It takes shape as a politics of ascriptive melancholy, of unsurrenderable attachment. It fashions itself, in Badiou's terms, as a politics of persistent interest, or, as I will put it, as a politics of cosmopolitan interestedness. And what is its object? To what does it attach its melancholy ferocity and singlemindedness? In what is it interested? The human, or, indeed, humanity — which implies (as we shall see) that over the course of its long-twentieth-century career, the politics of witnessing has not in fact been single-minded but double-minded, even schizophrenic. For the humanity to which the Euromodern witness or third has attached itself over the course of the past 250 years is, in fact, dual. It is both a singular and historically particular humanity in extremis, a humanity apprehensible to its aggrieved observers as what I will be calling a melancholy fact of history, and a humanity apprehensible as a speculative idea and a speculative (and regulatory) ideal, a humanity grounded in natural law and natural right, an abstract humanity called into existence by the discourses of the rights of man and of human rights. The singular humanity to which the third attaches itself, the humanity an eighteenth- and nineteenth-century circum-Atlantic politics of witnessing found paradigmatically exemplified (through its brutalization) in slavery and which a twentieth-century discourse of the witness has found constitutively exemplified (through its brutalization) in the camp, thus alternates with (and sometimes exchanges itself for) the humanity which Enlightenment, liberalism, and neoliberalism have adduced from a discourse of rights. To the cosmopolitan interestedness that I will be indicating characterizes the politics of witnessing, there is then a second political form the Atlantic and Euromodern witness (in its reappearance as a disinterested or impartial spectator) has recurrently called into being: the politics of a liberal cosmopolitanism. Or perhaps there is one other way to put this. To speak of the witness as Agamben and Derrida in their separate but overlapping ways do is not in fact to speak of *a* third, but of two: two thirds who circle the atrocious, exceptional, sovereign scenes of an enduring Atlantic and occidental modernity alternately (and sometimes interchangeably) in melancholy and impartial, interested and disinterested, romantic and liberal guise. An Atlantic and occidental modernity, I am thus arguing, proves itself haunted by these two thirds, these two incarnations of the witness (and arbiter and judge). The case of the *Zong*, I wish further to insist, illuminates the rise and vacillating return of these two thirds just as fully as it brings to light the vacillations and rise of those speculative discourses and practices I have examined thus far.

*

The three volumes of Agamben's *Homo Sacer* (particularly the first and the third) provide some of the key terms by which to begin to render a genealogy of this split or doubled figure legible. As its title suggests, volume three, *Remnants of Auschwitz: The Witness and the Archive*, takes as its object the witness itself and does so in ways that at times lead Agamben very much to resemble Derrida. Here, too, the witness emerges from the philological record as both an external observer and wounded survivor. "In Latin there are two words for 'witness.' The first word, *testis*, from which our word 'testimony' derives, etymologically signifies the person who, in a trial or lawsuit between two rival parties, is in the position of a third party (*terstis*). The second word, *superstes*, designates a person who has lived through something, who has experienced an event from beginning to end and can therefore bear witness to it."[11] Here, too, witness is not only an act of the survivor but often the very thing which renders survival possible. "In the camp, one of the reasons that can drive a prisoner to survive is the idea of becoming a witness."[12] Here, too, witness (as the inaccessibly true) simultaneously grounds the very possibility of the juridical exercise of law and names that thing which a juridical enforcement of the law must put outside itself. "The ultimate aim of law is the production of a *res judicata*, in which the sentence becomes the substitute for the true and the just, being held as true despite its falsity and injustice. . . . It has taken almost half a century to understand that law did not exhaust the problem [of Auschwitz], but rather that the very problem was so enormous as to call into question law itself, dragging it to its own ruin."[13] Here, too, the key to the language of witness is the cryptonymic, antirepresentational, antimetaphoric language of melancholy. "The language of testimony is a language that no longer signifies and that, in not signifying, advances into what is without language, to the point of taking on a different insignificance — that of complete witness, that of he who by definition cannot bear witness. To bear witness, it is therefore not enough to bring language to its own nonsense . . . It is necessary that this senseless sound be, in turn, the voice of something or someone that, for entirely other reasons, cannot bear witness."[14] And here, too, as the foregoing statement suggests, witness is haunted by the perpetual knowledge of its own impossibility. "The value of testimony lies essentially in what it lacks; at its center it contains something that cannot be borne witness to. . . . The 'true' witnesses, the 'complete witnesses,' are those who did not bear witness and cannot bear witness. They are those who 'touched bottom': the Muslims, the drowned. The survivors speak in their stead. . . . [And yet] whoever assumes the charge of bearing witness in their name knows that he or she must bear witness in the name of the impossibility of bearing witness."[15]

To what then does this witness bear witness? As with Derrida, so for

Agamben: witness testifies to its own impossibility, its own cryptonymic opacity, and its serial persistence. On that last score, to be sure, Agamben bears comparison not only to Derrida but to Badiou, for whom persistence, in the mode of perseverance, consistency, or unrelenting interestedness, renders at all possible that ethical determination which permits the subject of a truth to testify and commit to the appearance of a historical truth event.[16] Badiou clarifies this point in his brief work *Ethics: An Essay on the Understanding of Evil* where he provides the following definition of "the ethics of a truth": "What I will call, in general, the 'ethic of a truth' is the principle that enables the continuation of a truth-process — or, to be more precise and complex, *that which lends consistency to the presence of some-one in the composition of the subject induced by the process of this truth*."[17] He then explicates that "formula" thus:

> What is to be understood by "some-one"? "Some-one" is an animal of the human species. . . . It is *this* body, and everything that it is capable of, which enters into the composition of a "point of truth" — always assuming that an event has occurred, along with an *immanent* break taking the *sustained* form of a *faithful* process. "Some-one" can be *this* spectator whose thinking has been set in motion, who has been seized and bewildered by a burst of theatrical fire. . . . (emphasis original)

> What should we now understand by "consistency"? . . . When all is said and done, consistency is the engagement of one's singularity (the animal "some-one") in the continuation of a subject of truth. Or again: it is to submit the perseverance of what is known to a duration peculiar to the not-known. Lacan touched on this point when he proposed his ethical maxim: "do not give up on your desire" . . . If "do not give up" is the maxim of consistency — and thus of an ethic of truth — we might well say that it is a matter, for the "some-one," of *being faithful to a fidelity*. And he can manage this only by adhering to his own principle of continuity, the perseverance in being what he is. By *linking* (for such, precisely, is consistency) the known by the not-known.[18] (emphasis original)

Against the figure of the impartial spectator which a liberal and neoliberal ethical tradition (traceable, somewhat counterintuitively, to both Kant and Adam Smith) will pose as the measured, disinterested alternative to the melancholy witness of a more recognizably romantic and neo-romantic ethical and moral philosophy (itself indebted to Smith and the Scottish Enlightenment), Badiou thus posits the consistent, persistent, or seized spectator (a figure, in its turn, both traceable to Longinus and to Smith's occasional sympathetic variations on the Longinian sublime). But if Badiou's subject of a truth (his some-one of a truth process) sometimes masquerades as the consistent *spectator* of a truth, what does he in fact intend by consistency? And how does the attitude of consistency ally his some-one with Agamben's witness?

Consistency, as Badiou indicates, comprises two key elements: a relation to the not-known and a commitment to interestedness. The not-known in which Badiou's subject perseveres is the unknowable within the truth event, the immanent gap in knowledge the belated subject of a truth can never entirely grasp, a gap that corresponds to the lacuna both Agamben and Derrida situate at the heart of testimony. To persevere in a truth, to refuse to give up on it, is thus not only to continue but to endure *with and in* precisely what cannot be known, only affirmed: by testimony, by bearing witness, by the public example of perseverance. The word Derrida and Agamben prefer for this commitment to the not-known is "responsibility." Badiou's alternate word (other than "consistency") is "linking." The subject of a truth (the responsible witness) does not, he suggests, merely stand as a spectator to the not-known of the event but, finding himself or herself seized by it, determines to link himself or herself to it. Mark Sanders suggests that such a decision (a decision, in more standard deconstructive terminology, at once in favor of and despite a pervasive epistemological undecidablity) might also be understood, particularly in reference to Derrida, as a type of acknowledged complicity: a complicity that "takes place on behalf of another"; a complicity in the fate of another that "at least tacitly . . . accept[s] and affirm[s] a larger complicity — etymologically, a folded-togetherness (*com-plic-ity*) — in human being (or the being of being human)."[19] Derrida might well dispute that final contention. But the rhetorical figure Sanders deduces from the etymology of complicity seems apt. Responsible to, linked with, persevering in the not-known of the fate of another (or the not-known of being human), witness and the ethics of a truth both seem to entail a persistent folding together of some-one and some other. Badiou's final word for this is "interest."

> If we define interest as 'perseverance in being' . . . then we can see that ethical
> consistency manifests itself as *disinterested interest*. It concerns interest, in the
> sense that it engages the motivating forces of perseverance . . . But it is dis-
> interested in a radical sense, since it aims to link these traits in a fidelity, which
> in its turn is addressed to a primary fidelity, the one that concerns the truth-
> process. . . . I am altogether present there, linking my component elements via
> that *excess beyond myself* induced by the passing through me of a truth. But as a
> result, I am also suspended, broken, annulled; dis-interested. For I cannot,

within the fidelity to fidelity that defines ethical consistency, take an interest in myself, and thus pursue my own interests. All my capacity for interest, which is my own perseverance in being, has *poured out.* . . .[20] (emphasis original)

Poured out from the self, dislocated from the self, interest (or, more precisely, interestedness) thus engages, links itself to, folds itself within the outside with which the self discovers itself complicit. The disinterested interest of some-one, the persistent interestedness of witness, thereby, in Spivak's terms, worlds the self, or, as I will be putting it, commits the self to a persistent habit of worldly, cosmopolitan interestedness. Such interestedness is not necessarily singular. But it is directed toward, linked with, folded into a range of historical singularities — an array of singular instances of the unfolding of history in the fate of a potentially limitless range of others whom interest need not know in order to address.

While Agamben, Derrida, and Badiou can be seen to agree in these re-spects, their projects are in other fashions meaningfully distinct. Badiou's latent Kantianism, his overt commitment to the universal, and his resolution that truth, while only emergent from singular situations, must be a truth of the same, a truth that is the same for all, certainly distinguishes him from Agamben and Derrida, even if the formal characteristics of his subject of a truth so nearly corresponds to Agamben and Derrida's anatomy of the wit-ness. Agamben and Derrida, while more alike in their mutual difference from Badiou, also part company in a number of ways, the chief of which, for my purposes, relates to the varying grounds from which their two versions of the witness arise. To simplify matters drastically, where for Derrida the witness emerges as a virtually inevitable if primary actor in a critique of metaphysics and, in consequence, risks taking on the characteristics of a transhistorical deconstructive abstraction (entering the stage as a recognizable figure — of and within — a neoskeptical nominalist philological method), for Agamben the witness emerges from within a distinctive (if equally philological) political philosophy and bears witness to an essentially political — and geopolitical — history of state and parastate power. This is perhaps less a way of saying that Agamben is as epistemologically indebted to Foucault as he is rhetorically *like* Derrida than it is a way of recollecting that *Remnants of Auschwitz: The Witness and the Archive* is the third in a series of volumes whose first text, *Homo Sacer: Sovereign Power and Bare Life*, mixes its Foucauldianism with a sustained en-gagement with Carl Schmitt and his ruminations on the operations of sov-ereignty. And it is with regard to the problem and history of modern forms of state and parastate sovereignty that slavery emerges alongside the camp as organizational to a circum-Atlantic genealogy of the occidental witness whose contours, as I have indicated, Agamben suggests without quite developing.

∗

"Originally conceived," as Agamben notes, "as a response to the bloody mystification of a new planetary order," *Homo Sacer: Sovereign Power and Bare Life* ultimately resolves itself as an investigation of the holocaust camp, the state of exception it exemplifies, the structure of abandonment it instances, the bare life it reveals.[21] Structured as a quasi-teleological reading of modernity with the camp as its atrocious terminus, *Homo Sacer* thus leaves its intended hermeneutic of the planetary no more than implicit. But though it remains undeveloped, that hermeneutic is at least implied by *Homo Sacer*: as a planetary order is implied by the camp; as the general class or set is implied by, but does not coincide with, the example that names it: "What the example shows," as Agamben notes, "is its belonging to a class, but for this very reason the example steps out of its class in the very moment it exhibits and delimits it . . . The example is truly a *paradigm* in the etymological sense: it is what is 'shown beside,' and a class can contain everything except its own paradigm."[22] But if the camp, in this very precise sense, exemplifies the planetary order it exhibits and steps out of, then for Agamben, the camp implies the planetary not as the class to which it belongs but as an additional term in a common set. The planetary, that is, belongs to this set but does not define it; it is a term better understood in parallel with the camp as the member of a class that Agamben suggests is now becoming the global rule, and that class, that set, is "the state of exception." This, he argues, is what the camp exemplifies, and this is what trans-Atlantic slavery may also be understood to instance or front.

Agamben has many interlocuters in *Homo Sacer* (Walter Benjamin, Antonio Negri, Hannah Arendt, and Michel Foucault among them). As I have indicated, however, his chief intellectual correspondent is Carl Schmitt, from whose *Political Theology* he derives his notion of the state of exception and the theory of sovereignty it licenses. In Schmitt, as Agamben indicates, the state of exception names a legal prerogative, invested in a sovereign power (and ultimately constitutive of sovereign power), to suspend the law. The state of exception thus demarcates a zone of law within the law in which the law legally fails to operate. When the apartheid government of South Africa imposed a quasi-permanent state of emergency during its final decade in power, or, to take a still more recent example, when the United States government asserted a legal right to suspend international law in the Middle East, both invoked this sovereign power: the South African government to juridically encamp the mass democratic movement, and civil society more generally, within the sphere of the lawless operation of the law; the United States to constitute Iraq less as a hostile (or even a rogue) state than as a state of exception whose mere existence confirms U.S. global sovereignty and its planetary constituting power. As both of these examples indicate, the state of exception classically entangles justice and violence, suspending the peacetime application of the rule of law and setting in its place a form of sovereignly sanctioned state violence. As they further suggest, the state of exception is not incidental to sovereignty (not a sort of reserved entailment to which a sovereign power has occasional recourse) but the outer limit and first principle of sovereignty, even when the state of exception exists only in potential, only as something that might or might not be invoked.

Constituting Iraq as a state of exception in international law, the United States, thus understood, has invoked a claim to global sovereignty even over those spaces in which it has no expressed intention of suspending the rule of law but where it might potentially do so. "Potentiality (in its double appearance as potentiality to and potentiality not to)," Agamben notes in this regard, "is that through which Being expresses itself *sovereignly*, which is to say, without anything preceding or determining it . . . an act is sovereign when it realizes itself by simply taking away its own potentiality not to be, letting itself be, giving itself to itself"[23] In the conjunction of a global war on terrorism without end and a new security doctrine of preemptive attack, the United States seems to have mixed together, absolutely formulaically, this sovereign potential *to* and potential *not to*, to hold the globe subject to the knowledge that it might, henceforth, at any moment or place of its choosing, take away its potential not to be sovereign, might let itself be, might give itself to itself.[24] From this perspective once more, Iraq functions both as a war zone and as an example the United States has made of its globally sovereign power to let itself actually be.

If, as Agamben's discussion of potentiality indicates, the state of exception thus precedes and survives its moment of actual imposition at a time of emergency, then it also extends itself as more than this perpetually latent potential to be. Rather, the state of exception exceeds those moments of crisis in which it is called from virtual into actual existence by providing the state with an ongoing mechanism of population management and territorial control. Agamben's state of exception, in other words, constitutes more than an emergency power or a mode of geopolitics: it constitutes a fundamental demographic and topographic principle of sovereignty. Topography, here, is both figurative and literal, both a way of identifying the legal conceit that codes the state of exception as a power within the law to operate without the law, and a way of addressing the literal division of sovereign territories into normal and exceptional juridical terrains. All sovereign domains, Agamben argues, are thus split. At the near end of the long history of occidental modernity, he suggests, the camp operates as the paradigm of the topographic state of exception extrinsically within the boundaries of a sovereign power. For Carl Schmitt, early occidental modernity's exemplary *space* of exception is the New World: a zone "exempted from the law," "a free and juridically empty space . . . beyond the line."[25] Though aware of this current within Schmitt's thought, Agamben does not choose to pursue it. Disregarding the New World in favor of the old, he thus leaves absent from his account not only the territories of the Caribbean and the Americas but the history of New World slavery and that vast number of persons subjected, through slavery, to the mode of sovereignty whose planetary history he had originally intended to write. Whatever the reasons for this omission, slavery simply fails to appear as one of Agamben's subjects or, in his very precise sense, as one of his examples. His concern, particularly as he turns to the question of sovereignty and population control, is instead with the classical figure of *homo sacer* (the one who under Roman law could be killed but not sacrificed; the one, that is, given over to death without thereby being devoted by a sovereign power to an ennobling sacrificial cause) and with the subjects whom he understands to be that figure's twentieth-century counterparts: the refugee (whom he introduces to consideration via Arendt's essay on "The Decline of the Nation State and the Ends of the Rights of Man" in *The Origins of Totalitarianism)* and the Jew.[26]

These two figures are held together, Agamben argues, not only by their twin twentieth-century encounters with the totalitarian state but by a demographic code deeply internal to the daily rule of the state of exception, a code he formulates (not entirely surprisingly) with the help of Badiou. Following Badiou's lead, Agamben suggests that the individual subjects of any given state (or other sovereign power) are grouped and identified according to the two different codes of membership and inclusion.[27] Badiou calls membership "presentation" and uses that term to designate all those present before and subject to a body of law. Inclusion Badiou calls "representation," which figure names for him all those who find themselves represented in and by the formal institutions of the law. Crucially, if obviously, the two terms fail to coincide. Membership (or presentation) always exceeds inclusion (or representation), and those members of a polity who find themselves present before the law but not included or represented by it (like those whom the law includes but who are not among a community's extant members), find themselves living in a permanent state of exception. Among the latter (those the law includes but who are, nevertheless, not among its living community) we might find the beloved dead of nationalist discourse: the Founding Fathers, for example, superenfranchised by American constitutional law. Among the former, those who are members of a community but not included in its formal, legal structures of representation, Badiou finds the refugee and the Jew but, to be sure, does not indicate that with them the set is closed.

And indeed, it seems more than possible to suggest that over the course of its modern history, the state has also exclusively included a vast array of others, among them: children, women, immigrants, convicts, colonial subjects, and, I am arguing, slaves. To which list it seems equally possible to add that alongside the camp, occidental modernity's classical spaces of exception (those physical territories, internal to the sovereign exercise of the law, in which the law legally suspends itself) include the prison; the torture room; the asylum; the riot zone; the colony, protectorate and reservation; the plantation, the barracoon, and, most pertinently here, the slave ship.[28] Considered in this light, the massacre aboard the *Zong* reemerges once more — by the terms of Žižek's gloss on the Badiouvian truth event — as an entirely symptomatic anomaly: an event "misperceived by the system as a local 'abnormality,' [which] effectively condenses the global 'abnormality' of the system as such."[29] Now, however, the massacre can be seen to condense not only the operation of speculative reason but the exceptional constitution of a sovereign power over the lives of the slaves. Invoking the jettison clause of the vessel's insurance contract, following its outlined procedures step by fatal step, formulaically upholding all the contract's emergency stipulations, Collingwood legally suspends the law, reconstitutes the ship as a space of exception within the law, renders what has long been potential actual, gives the sovereign law of slavery over to itself, realizes that sovereignty by simply taking away its own potential not to be, and lets it be. And in doing so, Collingwood did something that was both entirely eventful and entirely symptomatic, something singular and something whose singularity was exemplary of the global system as such, something particular to this case and something that through this case brought to light the planetary rule of slavery as such. What is that rule? It is the rule of living in a permanent state of exception, a rule of permanently awaiting and so already living within, that moment in which the sovereign law of death fundamental to modern

Atlantic slavery, the law that permitted the slave to be killed without thereby being sacrificed, realizes itself by simply taking away its own potentiality not to be.

Orlando Patterson's word for this condition is "social death."[30] Agamben, more paradoxically, and with the condition of the camp inmate rather than the slave in mind, calls it "bare life." This, indeed, is what he understands the state of exception daily to produce, or what he understands it to produce as the obverse of the coin of sovereignty. Constituting sovereignty, the state of exception also constitutes (for the subjects of such sovereignty) a life stripped bare of all but its biological characteristics, a life denuded of any individuality or signature features, a life given over to an absolute state of abandonment, a life put outside the law and put under its banner and its ban. But if this bare life, this zoe, this life in and of abandonment, is the condition of life under the state of exception, then such bare life is, itself, productive of more than the sovereignty dependent on it (in Agamben's implicit version of the master-slave dialectic). Rather, Agamben suggests, over the course of modern political history such bare life has been constitutive of two other political forms: the politics of witness and the politics of human rights.

*

To what does the witness bear witness? To bare life, abandoned.[31] But the politics of witness, as Agamben makes clear, is not alone in attending to bare life. It is joined (has been joined over the past two centuries) by the politics of human rights. And what is immediately crucial to understand is that for Agamben these two modes of politics — the politics of witness and the politics of human rights — are not complementary, they are opposed (on which point Agamben rejoins not only Derrida and Badiou, but also Hardt and Negri, for whom the contemporary manifestations of empire are indissociably bound to a global militarization of the politics of human rights). Certainly for Agamben, a global politics of human rights not only fails to oppose the sovereign production of bare life in the camp but must be grasped as one of the very things which links the state to and establishes its sovereignty over life itself, life stripped bare, life in its abandoned appearance as zoe:

> It is time to stop regarding declarations of rights as proclamations of eternal, metajuridical values binding the legislator (in fact, without much success) to respect eternal ethical principles, and to begin to consider them according to their real historical function in the modern nation-state. Declarations of rights represent the originary figure of the inscription of natural life in the juridico-

political order of the nation-state. The same bare life that in the *ancien regime* was politically neutral and belonged to God as creaturely life and in the classical world was (at least apparently) clearly distinguished as *zoe* from political life (*bios*) now fully enters into the structure of the state and even becomes the earthly foundation of the state's legitimacy and sovereignty. A simple examination of the text of the Declaration of 1789 shows that it is precisely bare natural life — which is to say, the pure fact of birth — that appears here as the source and bearer of rights.[32]

The eighteenth- through twenty-first century discourse on rights (whether on the "rights of man" or on human rights), Agamben thus contends, does not so much function to limit state power or restrict the operations of sovereignty as it massively expands the boundaries of state control and sovereign power. Reconstrued as a right, "life" does not name the state or space that sovereign power is restricted from regulating or entering. Life does not dwell outside sovereignty. Rather, it constitutes the definitionally *exceptional* outside modern sovereign power takes within itself, the bare condition modern sovereignty constitutes in order to constitute itself. The argument is not that declarations of right and the camp are the same thing, but, instead, that they belong to a common set; that both know the human by knowing humanity as bare life and both arrogate to a sovereign power juridical authority over such abandoned life.

Read alongside the examination of rights discourse in Hardt's and Negri's *Empire*, *Homo Sacer* suggests that over the course of the past several centuries, rights discourse has constituted bare life and the sovereign regulation of bare life in two primary ways: via an internal (or biopolitical) regime of sovereign power and via an external (or geopolitical) regime of sovereignty.[33] For Agamben, the internal or biopolitical operation of rights-based sovereignty is primarily characteristic of the domestic functioning of the modern nation-state and arises the moment a state accords to itself what Foucault called the "care" of life.[34] Taking the care of life (as life) into its own hands, the state thus potentially (and actually) affords itself the power to regulate, evaluate, normalize, produce, or end the life of both its citizens and its resident aliens, that is, both those it nominally represents and all those others present before (or within) it. The external or geopolitical corollary to this constitutional power arises the moment a state or extrastate body gives itself the responsibility to care, globally, for bare human life and so potentially (and actually) affords itself the legal prerogative to exceed its domestic boundaries and suspend the normal operation of international law in the name of defending such abandoned life (which the state or extrastate body thus renders legally present to itself but takes on no corresponding obligation to represent).

For Agamben (now following Arendt's lead as much as Foucault's), such internal and external exercises of sovereignty have repeatedly revealed the grimmer side of rights-based discourse whenever a state body has linked the possession of rights to the figure of the citizen. This is not only because by linking rights to the citizen the state thereby also strips the noncitizen of rights (hence the haunting figure of the refugee) or awards itself the power to strip a subject of rights by stripping him or her of citizenship (hence the paradigmatic figure of the German Jews), but because by linking bare life to rights to citizenship, the state (or other sovereign body) causes even those who are citizens, even those both present before the law and represented by it, to stand before the law as a type of bare life (zoe) only accidentally imbued with signature political characteristics (bios) which the state might at any moment no longer oblige itself to recognize. The more fully it is globalized and the more fully it is linked to a global humanity, therefore, the more fully a discourse of rights renders everyone, citizen and noncitizen alike, bare life — whether actually or potentially so. But if this is the case, then once again, Agamben's history (of sovereignty, bare life, rights, and the witness) remains crucially incomplete. The problem of citizenship may well reveal much regarding the inner workings and perils of rights-based discourse, and a genealogy of modern sovereignty that runs from the French Revolution to the Holocaust may be essential, but it is also partial. While the latter fails to recognize that for the bulk of its modern history the Western state has been not only national but imperial, the former fails to acknowledge that over that same time period the haunting opposite (and double) of the citizen has been both the domestic interloper (the refugee, the Jew) and the extradomestic alien captured by the imperial state (the colonial subject, the slave).

There has been a great deal of work in recent decades on European colonialism and modern state power that valuably complicates and expands the sort of analysis Agamben provides.[35] My interest here is with the other history Agamben neglects but without which his account, however productive, also remains excessively partial. I do not mean to suggest that slavery is uniquely original to a modern discourse on rights and a Euromodern politics of witnessing, *the* genealogical source of modern sovereignty, or modernity's first scene of bare life abandoned, but, instead, that all of these things (above all that practice of witness that is my chief subject here) have taken on much of their dominant modern form (that is, their imperio-occidental form) in relation to slavery. Which also means that like the figure of the colonial subject, the refugee, or the Jew, the figure of the slave (as an embodied *type* of bare life) has also recurrently produced and splintered the politics of witness and the politics of human rights, and that that figure has been — crucially if not exclusively — organizational to the two major political forms whose long-twentieth-century history I am attempting to outline: the cosmopolitan inter-estedness I associate with witnessing and the liberal cosmopolitanism that characterizes the politics of human rights. To take only the example of the Anglo-Atlantic world (as I do here), it seems clear that an archive of melancholy witness of the sort exemplified by Granville Sharp's testament and the other texts I will be discussing serially contests not only the legitimacy of slavery itself but recurrently competes for an oppositional property in the fate of the slave (and hence, by its own terms, in the fate of humanity) with a liberal, cosmopolitan, and rights-based discourse on slavery and humanity whose eighteenth- and nineteenth-century paradigm was the trans-Atlantic abolitionist movement, and whose late-twentieth- and twenty-first-century incarnations are manifest in the range of global human rights movements of the sort exemplified by the 2001 Durban World Conference against Racism.

Let me be clear. I am not thereby indicating that slavery and abolition (or contemporary human rights movements) are the same thing. Offered a choice between the two the choice is clear. What I am suggesting is that the choice itself is meaningfully false, that it both obscures the fact that this is not the only choice available to us (suggesting, as it does, that liberalism is the only alternative to the grim alliance of race terror, global capital, and modern state and parastate power) and conceals the twin epistemological grounding of rights discourse and sovereign reason in a speculative idealization and regulation of humanity as bare life. The trouble with human rights discourse is not that it fails to indict sovereign violence but that its language of indictment, its grammar of human understanding, is borrowed from (and implies the universal unquestionability of) the epistemological register and human understanding on which both democratic and totalitarian forms of sovereignty draw. Indeed, as Hardt and Negri argue, and as the recent justification of the conquest of Iraq as a human rights war would seem to indicate, we appear to be inhabiting a moment in which humanity (channeled through the language of human rights) is on the point of becoming *the* articulated principle for the constitution of an entirely global sovereign power. I part company with Hardt and Negri (and join Agamben, while also offering my revisions to his account) in arguing, however, that this moment is not in fact recent but long, repeating, and intensifying (formally commensurate, that is, with the repeating, intensifying, long twentieth century whose nonsynchronous period contours I have sketched). By my reckoning, this moment dates back over two centuries. And one of its moments of beginning is in the late-eighteenth- and early-nineteenth-century history of circum-Atlantic slavery, which both saw the still most massive ever constitution of an entire class of raced persons as exceptional subjects of the law and revealed, in the name of an opposition to slavery, a militarization of human rights discourse whose effect was to demonstrate and expand the global sovereignty of a hegemonic world state. I am speaking, now, of the British state, whose post-1819 determination to blockade the West African slave factories of its European rivals and to interdict their slave ships seamlessly linked Enlightenment human rights discourse to the project of securing the British navy's maritime sovereignty and the British economy's global hegemony.

It may well be the case that in creating its Royal Navy anti-slave-trade squadron, the imperial British state was co-opting and refitting to its own purposes the sympathy rhetoric of that Atlantic alliance of abolitionists who had christened themselves the friends of the world's slaves (and of humanity), much as the American government may be understood to have co-opted the language of contemporary human rights discourse.[36] But that does not mean that both the abolitionists and the British state (or, for that matter, both current human rights activists and the Bush administration) were not and are not speaking the same language. It also does not mean, as I have indicated, that that is the only language available to us. There are and have been other languages. More than one, of course, but one in which I am primarily interested: the language of testimony, the language, in Lowy and Sayre's terms, of a romanticism set "against the tide of modernity," the language of what I earlier called a melancholy realism, the language of cosmopolitan interestedness.

That language, too, is not recent, but long in the making, as it is repeating, and intensifying. If, in the past few decades, it has primarily been spoken and theorized as the language of witness, then in the late eighteenth century and early nineteenth it was most frequently spoken and theorized as a language of sympathy and of sentiment. Those are now broadly discredited terms, terms to which Agamben, Badiou, and Derrida would be disinclined to acknowledge a debt. And in much of what follows I share a broad skepticism regarding their political possibility. But even as I share that skepticism, I also want to argue that sympathy and sentiment are not necessarily or exclusively the property of a liberal theory of global responsibility and cosmopolitan linkage. Indeed — as

I intend to suggest by following these terms in and out of abolitionist history, the moral philosophy, Scottish Enlightenment historiography, human rights discourse, novel theory, and romantic poetry with which abolition was in conversation, and the appearances, disappearances, and reappearances of the *Zong* massacre throughout this archive — sympathy, its regular correlate sentiment, and its sometimes spokesperson the friend, name that exact condition of ambivalence I believe to characterize Agamben, Badiou, and Derrida's contributions to a more than 200-year-old history of testimonial reason and cosmopolitan thought. This does not mean that these recent theories of the witness merely duplicate eighteenth- and nineteenth-century sympathy discourse but that, now as then, both find themselves entangled in a cosmopolitanism that is sometimes interested, sometimes disinterested, and frequently both: a cosmopolitanism that finds in the figures of the spectator and the witness, in these two thirds, both an alternate set of political imperatives and an abiding indistinction of political roles and responsibilities. As I sketch out in the pages that follow an alternate, long, Atlantic genealogy of the witness, sympathy and sentiment thus frequently name what I alongside Agamben, Derrida, and Badiou attempt to hold apart — as they name what they and I cannot finally separate from the figure of the witness. Now, as then, in other words, sympathy, sentiment, and the witness name not so much a pure state as a state of undecidability: an ethical dilemma in the absent presence of suffering and the rights discourse that offers itself as that suffering's solution and alibi; a radical impulse always on the verge of moderating itself and a liberal impulse always haunted by the ghost of melancholy.

evidence is

        sustenance is

        support is

        the law is

        the ship is

        the captain is

        the crew is

        peril is

        the trial is

        the rain is

        the seas is

        currents is

        jamaica is

        tobago is

        islands is

        the case is

        murder is

        justice is

        the ground is

        africa is

            negroes

        was

—M. NourbeSe Philip, from *Zong!* # 24

CHAPTER 7

The View from the Window

SYMPATHY, MELANCHOLY, AND THE PROBLEM OF "HUMANITY"

At the second of the *Zong* trials, the attorneys for the underwriters concentrated their arguments on the alleged "necessity" of Captain Collingwood's actions. For the ship's insurance contract to be in effect, they argued, its stipulations had to be met. As the key stipulation of the contract's jettison clause was the necessity of any act of throwing "goods" overboard, they sought to deny the necessity of Collingwood's actions, knowing that if they were successful in this they would have established that Collingwood had violated the contract and, hence, that compensation was not owed. By devoting the bulk of their attention to this matter of necessity, however, they implicitly recognized that the primary matter before the court was contractual rather than criminal. The necessity debate thus established a narrative of contract as the trial's dominant plot. In both their written appeal of the Guildhall jury's original ruling in favor of the owners and in their arguments before Mansfield's bench at the appeal trial, however, the underwriters' attorneys (who were appearing in court not only as counsel for the insurers but at the behest of Sharp, Equiano, and other abolitionists who had helped organize the appeal) sporadically introduced a counterargument: one whose key term was not necessity but humanity.

This, to be sure, is somewhat unsurprising. It would have been almost unimaginable for them not to have asserted, if only intermittently, the humanity of the slaves. And, from time to time, they did. For the most part, though, they accepted the shipowners' contention that the slaves had become "the subjects of property" and made relatively little of their humanness. What is perhaps at least a little surprising is that when "humanity" was invoked in the court, when the underwriters' attorneys intermittently suggested that this was not a contract dispute but a case in which humanity itself was on trial, it was the humanity of virtually everyone but the slaves that became a point of contention. Only flickeringly attached to the drowned slaves, humanity generally entered the trial (and established itself as the key term of a narrative of contract's counterplot) either as an abstract idea or as a property denied to or claimed for those surviving witnesses who could testify to what had taken place aboard the ship (Governor Stubbs and the *Zong*'s chief mate, James Kelsall) *and* as a property that the words, actions, and dispositions of the litigants, the attorneys, and the judge of the case might disqualify them from claiming for themselves.[1] Recognizing the shipowners' contractual property in the lives of the slaves throughout most of their arguments, the attorneys for Sharp and the underwriters occasionally sought to affect the outcome of the trial by indexing the court's knowledge and decisions to another kind of property, by linking the attitude taken by any witness to what had transpired aboard the ship (*and* the attitude of any witness of such a witness) to the property they could claim to take in humanity. Two discourses of property (one overt, one covert) thus emerge from the trial transcripts: two discourses of property that effectively permitted the attorneys to fight their case on two fronts at once (as, respectively, spokesmen for the island's insurance industry and for its abolitionists). Whatever its motivation, the rhetorical implications of the attorneys' strategy was clear: by introducing a second discourse of property to the trial, they sought to render any affirmation of the shipowners' unbroken contractual property in the slaves one that would oblige the owners, their attorneys, and the court's chief and subordinate justices to alienate themselves from any property they might claim to hold in humanity.

How was this effected? The seeds for the attorneys' strategy were sown in the final pages of their appeals brief, scattered among a series of questions they insisted the court must address. The vast majority of those questions, unsurprisingly, bore upon the question of necessity. But in the closing sections of the brief a new set of queries suddenly emerges:

> [Did the slaves] not pray or earnestly request and with tears in their Eyes or how otherwise or some sign or gesture signs or gestures express or signify a desire that he or she might not be thrown overboard or did not they or some and how many of them in some and what manner and in some and what Language or by some and what Gestures or Signs Gesture or Sign respectively express or signify some desire that they he or she might be permitted to live? . . . *And what effect on the said defendant Mr Kelsall and the other Officers and Crew and which of them [did this] produce? . . . [Did it] produce any Remonstrances Expostulations and Expressions from them?*

> [Did] James Kelsall or who else being shocked by the Inhumanity of the said Luke Collingwood's proposal or for what other reason not at first object and say there was no occasion for such a measure? . . . [Did] Kelsall or some other person and who not remonstrate against the said Luke Collingwood's proposal in some such humane Terms and Language or in Terms and Language to the like or something like the foregoing purport and effect and in what other Terms and Language or to what other purport or effect did he they or any of which of them expostulate with the said Luke Collingwood?

> And [do] all the said defendants [the shipowners] not in their Respective Consciences deem the throwing the said Slaves alive into the Sea to have been an unnecessary and inhuman Act . . . *and if not why not?*[2]

Did the slaves make some sign, gesture, or otherwise signify a desire to live? What "effect" did this produce on Kelsall or the other witnesses of the massacre? Did it call forth the "humane language" of "remonstrance and expostulation"? Can the owners testify to their ability to speak that language, if not publicly then before their "consciences"?

Visible sign, external effect, internal conscience: an entirely novel theory and vocabulary of character is collapsed within this linked set of questions, as is an alternate theory of juridical decision. The question before the court, now, is not whether Collingwood's actions were "necessary" but whether the *Zong's* officers, owners, and crew can demonstrate themselves to possess a humane character, a humanity signified here by a capacity for sympathy, the ability to convert the external pleadings of the senses into the internal testimony of conscience, demonstrable possession of a fund of that romantic inwardness that Deidre Lynch suggests had begun to replace credibility and perspicuity as the hallmark of novelistic "character" at almost exactly this moment and that Pierre Barberis argues had been in the process of establishing itself as the touchstone of an emergent romantic theory of character over the course of the previous century.[3] As Barberis comments of Jean de la Bruyère's appropriately titled *Characters* (which was translated into English and published in London in 1700):

> Whereas the bourgeoisie had already taken possession of broad zones of social life and ruled it with an iron hand, in the eyes of a feeling person starved for justice, what is the weight of its claims to offer a better explanation of the physical universe? The demands of what could already be called *sentiment* entail the condemnation of all harshness, all inhumanity. Here we have the seeds of both the return to religion that will be affirmed by Rousseau and the condemnation of "progress" that has not brought about the reign of greater love, but only new forms of force and extortion. In *Character*, sentiment is already rising up against certain claims to a "modernism" that is more technical than human.[4]

La Bruyère's popular text was of course not a unique representative of this emergent sensibility. Aphra Behn's *Oroonoko*, one of the earliest examples of that literary form (the historical romance) through which romantic discourse would give fullest expression to this model of "sentimental" and "humane" character, had detailed its plot of humane character in terms that align with the general sentimental model of La Bruyère's text and the rhetoric adopted by Haywood and his colleagues. Trefry, the sole European character other than the narrator to demonstrate a humane response to Oroonoko's suffer-ings, the character who, in this sense, most fully models the ideal reader's appropriately sentimental and aggrieved reaction to Behn's romance of the suffering slave, demonstrates his humanity to Oroonoko by vehemently "re-senting all the Injuries [that] were done to him" and so demonstrates to Oroonoko and the reader the credibility of his character: "As Oroonoko afterwards said, he had little Reason to credit the Words of a Backearary [a white person], yet he knew not why; but he saw a kind of Sincerity, and awful Truth in the Face of Trefry; he saw an Honesty in his Eyes, and he found him wise and witty enough to understand Honour."[5]

Whatever the rhetorical source of the attorneys' strategy (and it is at least a little instructive in this regard that at one point Solicitor Lee accused his opponents of presenting their argument as if it were one of a series of "Cases from Romance"), their questions sought, most crucially, to establish that humanity expresses itself (finds its "language") in the practice of "remonstrance and expostulation" — that form of speech which means not only "to demand" and "to demand the reason for a person's conduct" but also "to complain of injury," or, as the *Oxford English Dictionary* further has it, "to argue or debate as an aggrieved person."[6] The character of the *Zong*'s owners, of the witnesses to the massacre, and, also, by implication, of all the parties at court, was thus not simply put on trial but attached to their ability to show that a knowledge of Collingwood's actions had produced its grievous "effect" in them, had converted them from mere bystanders or belated observers of the event into a party of those who found themselves injured by it, a company of those who, in Benveniste's terms, had resolved to "hold themselves to it" and to speak as ones "aggrieved by it." Only in this way, only by expostulating against the slaughter, only by bearing witness to the damage they had suffered by suffering themselves to bear witness to it, could they demonstrate their humanity and the credibility of their characters. And also, such arguments implied, only by ruling against the owners, only by demonstrating its own fund of romantic inwardness, could the court claim to hold possession of its humanity.

Lest the link between humanity, credibility, character, witness, and decision was too loosely established by the questions of the brief, the underwriter's attorneys made the connections quite clear in the few moments at trial in which they returned to this line of argument. Now, however, it was neither the owners' nor Kelsall's humanity and character that they put to the question but that of the other surviving witness to the massacre, Governor Stubbs. In an effort to rebut Stubb's testimony in support of Collingwood, Solicitor Haywood reminded the court that the governor had passed the three days of the massacre in his cabin counting the bodies falling past his window. Haywood then drew this conclusion: "It makes an Impression upon my Mind that the man that could calmly and cooly commit such an Act as that and not remonstrate and endeavour to prevent it is not deserving of much Credit here or in any other Court of Justice."[7] To seek to discredit a witness is, of course, no uncommon thing. It is a generic legal practice. The code by which Haywood discredits Stubbs, however, is not generic. Rather, Haywood deploys precisely those "terms" of the "language of humanity" that the brief had floated as a potential counterdiscourse to the trial's dominant discourse of contract. Credibility (and by implication, character) is here attached neither to a generalized perspicuity or to any particular knowledge of the facts of the case. It is, instead, a function of an affective capacity; a product, indeed, of the capacity to be affected by events and to testify (expostulate, remonstrate) as one aggrieved by them; a capacity Haywood demonstrates himself to possess ("It makes an Impression upon my Mind") and one which Stubb's evident coolness of character disqualifies him from possessing.

If in a culture of speculation the linked concepts of credit and credibility testify to the financialization of character, here an exactly opposite process reveals itself to be at work. Character is definancialized as the credit individuals earn no longer finds itself indexed to the "real" or abstract property they possess, or to their canniness as readers of social and financial transactions, or to their demonstrable or theoretical knowledge of persons or events, but is instead generated as the social profit earned on what I earlier called the melancholy property individuals take in other persons and events. A man of character, a man deserving of much credit, is, by the terms of this counterdiscourse, one who invests himself in the language of humanity, one who can remonstrate or expostulate, one who can speak as if aggrieved by something he has not suffered *except by witnessing it*, one who, precisely in Agamben's and Derrida's terms, can testify as third or survivor or, ideally, as third and survivor at once. Recoded as the capacity to remonstrate or expostulate, the ability to testify ("in such Humane Terms and Language") is thus implicity redefined as the ability to claim possession of humanity by bearing witness to the affective melancholy property one has taken in it.

If Haywood and his colleagues were attempting to supplement the trial's dominant narrative of contract with this counternarrative of humanity and, thus, also to alter the terms of the dispute by asking the court to rule not on the contractual property the shipowners could or could not be said to hold in the slaves, but to rule on the melancholy property the massacre's witnesses and the court itself held or refused to hold in the event, then their counterparts on the owners' side were quick to prove themselves, their clients, and their witnesses no strangers to a "like or something like" language of humanity. Solicitor Lee, responding to Haywood's attack on Stubbs, acknowledged that he too found this to be "a melancholy event," as did his witness, "a Gentleman who knows the sea," and, he averred, a man quite unlike what Haywood had painted him to be. Indeed, Lee insisted, "This Gentleman [Stubbs] gave his evidence with as much apparent Sympathy and as great a tenderness as I ever saw in my life and he must have been a Brute if he had not then shown it."[8] Lee's impulse to defend his witness is, again, understandable. But it was a tactical mistake. For, the moment Stubb's sympathy for the slaves rather than the necessity of Collingwood's actions became the matter of contention (the moment, as Haywood later put it, that this turned from being an insurance matter to one investigating "men who had forgot the feelings of men") was the moment that a humanity narrative could begin to displace rather than merely to interrupt the trial's contract plot.[9]

Haywood and his partners recognized this and sought to press their advantage by extrapolating from the question of Stubb's sympathy or brutal disinterest a world-historical claim. "That in point of importance," Haywood ventured, "this is the greatest [case] that ever came before this court cannot be disputed. We are not now before your Lordships merely defending the Underwriters . . . [but] on this occasion appear as Council for Millions of Mankind and the Cause of Humanity in General."[10] This is the boldest claim Haywood and his colleagues made for their counternarrative. If it were to have worked, if it could have successfully announced itself as self-evident (if, indeed, "it [could not have been] disputed"), it would have been because that dramatic final assertion, that sudden unveiling not simply of "Millions of Mankind" but of "Humanity in general," had been so carefully stage managed. Spectrally present as a ghostly company of witnesses in Mansfield's court, humanity in general could be made to appear there as nevertheless self-evident because humanity had already been made to appear at Governor Stubb's window, peering over his shoulder with him at the bodies falling into the sea, calling itself into being as the capacity to be aggrieved by what it saw through that melancholy porthole on history, invoking itself by teaching itself to speak in its own tongue, by learning to expostulate, by training itself to speak as if injured by what that view afforded, by what it had been in the presence of, what it had attended to: the slaves falling one by one by one; their witness coolly tallying the count; an English court resolving that each falling body signified a fall into the currency of finance capital.

The view from the window is, by the sporadic logic of the trial's counterplot, the view of humanity on the *Zong* massacre, the viewpoint that, indeed, *produces* humanity *as* a testamentary effect of bearing witness to the massacre, *as* a determination to take some melancholy property in it, to hold to it, to subsist beyond it by not yet surviving it, by not yet surrendering a melancholy investment in this event for some other property of experience, by not yet consenting to acknowledge that this melancholy "past" event leaves no burden of debt as the compound "interest" the what-has-been accumulates within now-being. The view from the window, more immediately, is the view Haywood and his colleagues intermittently tried to fashion as the appeal court's view on this case, the view they insisted Mansfield's court now shared, the view from which it could catch a glimpse of itself as disinterested brute or custodian of humanity. No wonder then that almost the moment he had shown himself familiar with the language of sympathy, tenderness, and feeling, Solicitor Lee sought to switch the language of the court back to the reasoned terminology of contract, denouncing his opponents for their "declamations addressed to the Passion and not to the judgment of those that were to decide the question."[11]

Finally, as Lee knew, as his appeal to the court's "judgment" sought to remind the bench itself, it was neither he nor Haywood who would decide the case but Mansfield and his subordinate justices. And even before the attorneys for either side could begin their oral arguments, Mansfield revealed the terms by which the court would ultimately choose to view the case. Summarizing the outcome of the initial trial and verdict in favor of the owners and the various issues the appeals briefs had asked the court to raise or revisit, Mansfield began by asserting himself, too, to be no stranger to the language of humanity. "It is a very singular Case," he allowed, "a very Shocking Case." But though Mansfield could thus, however briefly, prove himself capable of speaking as one aggrieved by the massacre, the matter at stake, he announced, was not the interest he might take in it, the sympathy he might find himself capable of expressing, the melancholy property he might demonstrate himself to hold in the event, and so, also, in humanity in general. Rather, as his very next sentence insists, "The Question [is] whether there was not an Absolute Necessity for throwing them overboard. . . . [The court] was of the opinion there was — We granted a rule [appeal] to show Cause from the *necessity* of the Case."[12]

∗

Necessity or humanity; the language of contract or the language of melancholy; the view from Exchange Alley or the view from the window: these are the choices the trial's plot and counterplot afford. In this instance the former set of terms prevailed. Necessity trumped humanity. Contract triumphed over melancholy. Loss value won its victory over the value of bearing witness to loss. The speculator trumped the witness. The attorney's counterplot, however, was not utterly lost to history. The terms it established for a counterknowledge of this event survived Haywood's framing. The view of the massacre he asked the court to take exemplifies the regard subsequent generations have learned to cast on this event, educating not only Sharp's investment in the massacre but the interest Sharp's successors have taken in it. They are not alone, nor is the melancholy interest they have taken in this event unique. For such, also, as I have begun to suggest, is the *form* of interest our late twentieth century now has been learning to take in its what-has-beens. Such is the property an ever more self-consciously disjointed contemporaneity has been learning to take in modernity's foundational, violent, moments of beginning. Such is the melancholy, traumatic, hauntological possession our nonsynchronous (and hyperspeculative) present has begun to take of its pasts. Such, increasingly, is our moment's knowledge of the state of the debt the present owes the past and of the long-deferred, long-ignored, long-accumulating payment of interest the living owe on the lives of the dead.

Which, of course, brings us back if not precisely to Agamben then to Derrida, to his hauntology, his state(ment) of the debt, his work of mourning, his poetics of witnessing, his claim to some property in the what-has-been. But before returning to Derrida, a fuller genealogy of how we get from then to now is necessary, as, more immediately, are a few brief words of elaboration on some of the terms I have been using: centrally "property" and "humanity."

∗

To speak of property as I have done, to pun on it in the ways I have, is of course to take advantage of the definitional variousness of the term, to speak of property not only as "the condition of being owned by or belonging to some person or persons," or as "that which one owns," but also as "an attribute or quality belonging to a thing or person."[13] To suggest that the underwriter's attorneys asked the court to take some affective *property* in the event of the massacre and, by so doing, to claim some property in humanity is thus not only to indicate that they wished to demonstrate the claims sentiment can make as a collector of possessions but also to suggest that they wanted to demonstrate as an intrinsic *attribute* of sentimental personhood (or, what Haywood claimed was the same, as a defining attribute of humanity) the determination to take possession of grievous experience, to "hold" loss. To hold property in what has been lost (the very opposite of insurance, which determines to hold property in what can be exchanged for what has been lost) is by such modes of argumentation and such etymological license, the very property (attribute, quality) of humanity. Etymology alone, however, is an inadequate justification for the use I have made of the word. The greater authority I would claim for that use is, in fact, usage itself: the use of the term in both the trial's primary and counterdiscourses.

Whatever the two forms of property circulating in the courtroom (contractual property in the slaves, affective property in the event), all sides seemed to have shared something between a Lockean and a proto-Hegelian theory of property. To both Locke and Hegel, of course, property is not primarily a thing but the outcome of an investment or expenditure, something which, by virtue of that expenditure, acquires value by detaching itself from the thingliness of the object. For Locke, as he made clear in his *Second Treatise of Civil Government*, property is the result of an investment or an expenditure of "labour": "It is allowed to be his goods who hath bestowed his labour upon it"; it is that which some individual "has mixed his labour with."[14] A century and a quarter later, Hegel was essentially to duplicate Locke's formula while altering its key term. Property, as the long section Hegel devotes to the matter in *The Philosophy of Right* establishes, is not that on which one has expended "labour" but that in which one has invested the "will": "A person has as his substantive end the right of putting his will into any and every thing and thereby making it his, because it has no such end in itself and derives its destiny and soul from his will"; "The reason I can alienate my property is that it is mine only in so far as I have put my will into it."[15]

Addressing the court a century after Locke's writings had assumed a foundational position in British thought and a few decades before Hegel was to formalize his theory of property, the attorneys on both sides of the *Zong* case demonstrate not so much an entrenched fidelity to Locke or an anticipatory fidelity to Hegel as a faithfulness to the formula common to both. For either side, that is, the slaves ground a property claim (whether contractual or affective) not as things but as something in which an investment has been made. For the owners and their attorneys what has been invested in the slaves is not so much labor as agreement. They function, by the terms of the contract narrative, as that novel, speculative, immaterial, and indestructible form of property that can exist (and, more importantly, bear value) because two parties have agreed that it exists and have agreed to credit the fiction of its value. For their opponents this was generally also the case. The problem, they tended to suggest, was simply that the terms of that agreement (the contract) had been violated, and with that violation of contract the slaves' value had been annulled. We should, once more, not be surprised by this. As legal counsel for Britain's insurance industry, what other form of property could the attorneys have defended?

Their brief, however, was dual: appearing before Lord Mansfield on behalf of the underwriters, they also addressed him as representatives of Sharp, Equiano, and the island's community of abolitionists. And as the spokesmen for this group, the attorneys offered an alternate claim or, rather, one that altered terms while preserving the general formula. From this perspective the slaves functioned as tokens for or signs of property by virtue not of the agreement but of the sentiment that had been invested in them. If sentiment, or the degree of intensity of sentiment, is thus something like the money form by which melancholy measures the level of its interest in humanity, much as the bill of exchange, the stock coupon, and the credit agreement are the money forms in which finance capital measures the value of its parallel investments, it is because for both value is not perishable with the life of the thing but depends only on the durability of the investment made in it. In either case property exists solely as the outcome of an imaginary expenditure. And if this indicates that another matter at stake in the *Zong* trials was the status of the *imagination* itself, if it indicates that the trials were staging a contest between the speculative imagination of finance capital and the sentimental, romantic imagination of melancholy (and so perhaps also dramatizing romantic discourse's anxious fascination with the power of the imagination to create both speculative and melancholy objects of value), it also perhaps accounts for why a *formulaic* melancholy (one which can say, as Derrida in the essay I have been citing says, "for instance, Auschwitz," or as I have been careful not to say but have certainly implied, "for instance, the *Zong*") and a formalized finance capitalism can sometimes operate not only as antagonists but as secret sharers in the philosophical discourse of modernity. This last point, needless to say, will require some greater elaboration. For the moment, however, I merely want to indicate that it is possible to speak of melancholy property just as fully as contractual property because both assume property not as an object but as an investment, whether of agreement or sentiment, and that it is in this sense that both the trial's plot and counterplot can be understood to entail narratives of property as they ask Mansfield either to acknowledge the contractual property the *Zong's* owners hold in the slaves as a result of the agreement they had made with the underwriters, or to assert the property the court could claim to hold in humanity as a result of its willingness to invest its (aggrieved) sentiment in the spectacle of this melancholy event.

This last formulation of the choices the attorneys laid before the court, this formulated opposition between the claims of contract and finance capital on the one hand and melancholy and humanity on the other, draws attention to the second of the terms on which I have been laying some stress. If the contractual narrative of finance capital finds its opposite in a testamentary narrative of humanity, and an investment in the category of humanity (under the guises of "man" and "the rights of man") is, in its turn, one of the hallmark characteristics of continental Enlightenment discourse, how does such an alliance of the continental Enlightenment with the cause (or at least the concept) of humanity align with my earlier contention that Enlightenment philosophical discourse does not oppose the subject-canceling speculations of finance capital but functions as the very discourse foundational to such speculative practice? If, in other words, the notion of humanity in general, or, as Kant has it, "the human race at large and all at once" is one of the Enlightenment's signature contributions to the philosophical discourse of modernity, and if this humanity in general or at large is the very figure to which Haywood and his colleagues appealed in asking the court to set aside its earlier verdict in favor of the shipowners, how can an Enlightenment theory of humanity be said to endorse rather than to refuse the negation of the slaves as anything other than the bearers of an abstract, theoretical, recuperable quantum of value?[16] Is Enlightenment philosophical discourse not the very thing that produces the terms by which Haywood, Sharp, and their successors can assert the humanity of the slaves?

No.

Certainly not if we assume Kant's image of humanity at large and all at once as paradigmatic of an Enlightenment investment in humanity. Indeed, despite all the apparent similarities between Kant's humanity at large and Haywood's humanity in general, it is their different modes of *investing* in the spectacle of humanity, their respective determinations to make a *speculative* and a *melancholy* investment in humanity, that separate Kant's Enlightenment discourse from the recognizably romantic discourse of the trial's counterplot and so can help resolve this apparent paradox in which the category of humanity seems to, and in fact does, operate as the discursive property of both a speculative and a testamentary epistemology. For just as there are two forms of property at stake in the *Zong* trials, so are there two competing knowledges of humanity.

How does Kant arrive at his humanity at large and all at once? Like Haywood, he does so through an act of spectation. But the view on humanity Kant fashions is not the view from the window. It is, instead, the view of the belated spectator who derives from an observation of historical events a "mode of thinking" that "manifests" itself as "a universal yet disinterested sympathy."[17] It is precisely this disinterest that accounts for the difference between a speculative, Enlightenment image of humanity at large and Haywood's aggrieved, sentimental, romantic image of humanity in general. Enlightenment philosophical discourse invests itself speculatively in the concept of humanity; it abstracts the concept of humanity from the observed turn of human events, contracts itself and its audience to agree disinterestedly to recognize a transcendent category relieved from its entanglement in all brute particulars, and binds itself to honor that agreement (regardless of the singularity of any given case).[18] A melancholy counterdiscourse of humanity, by contrast, assumes the singular conditions of its occasion of address as its foundations, it invests its interest in the event, but invests, precisely, in the ontological fabric of the observed event, in the deeds and crimes that Kant says are the one thing the event is not ("This event consists neither in momentous deeds nor crimes committed by men . . . No, nothing of the sort. It is simply the mode of thinking . . ."etc.).[19] Mixing its sentiment with the grievous substance of what it has thus observed, melancholy assumes an affective property in the image of the thing it holds itself to and derives from this determination to hold to the injured and injurious image-thing and from the willingness to speak as if injured by what it holds in unrelenting observation, the fundamental property of humanity. Melancholy thereby adduces humanity not by invoking the disinterested spectator but by invoking the aggrieved witness, not by contracting itself to the speculative recognition of a category (at large) but by investing itself in "what it has attended to, what it has been present at, what it has happened to be in the presence of," even if what it has attended to is the *disinterested* testimony of a survivor of grievous loss, for instance, a survivor of the *Zong*.[20]

∗

Melancholy may make this claim, may assert this aggrieved interest in humanity, may even, as Haywood's trial strategy suggests, attempt to hold a court of law accountable to such a practice of sympathetic witness. But neither melancholy, sympathy, nor humanity has standing before the law, at least not in Lord Mansfield's 1783 courtroom. Sixty years later, however, the successors to Granville Sharp and the other abolitionists who had paid Haywood's bill gathered in London to reassert not only the moral authority and argumentative legitimacy of this claim but to insist on its legal validity, to insist, that is, that both humanity and sympathy be enshrined as principles of international law: the one (humanity) as a principle of legal sovereignty superordinate to the sovereignty of the nation-state; the other (sympathy) as a principle of legal standing that might permit any justly aggrieved person to appear before the law not as the legally elected or appointed representative or delegate of a sovereign state but as a "friend of humanity." The event was the 1840 inaugural World Anti-Slavery Convention, to my knowledge the first ever international human rights gathering.

The convention, which had been organized by the British and Foreign Anti-Slavery Committee, convened in Freemason's Hall, Great Queen Street, London, on June 12, 1840. The hundreds of delegates collected in the hall, representing abolitionist and emancipist organizations from around the Atlantic (there were delegates from Britain, France, the United States, Spain, Switzerland, Haiti, Jamaica, Trinidad, the Bahamas, British Guiana, Sierra Leone, Canada, and numerous other countries and territories) had gathered not only in opposition to slavery but as the self-appointed ambassadors of a cosmopolitan ideal.[21] Devoted simultaneously to decrying slavery and, as Dr. Greville, one of the delegates, somewhat exorbitantly put it, to constituting themselves as a body "representing no nation in particular, but all nations," the conventioneers came to London, in the words of the summons the committee had prepared, as both "friends of the slaves" and as "friends of humanity."[22] That self-identification as "friends" (both of the slaves and of humanity) was, it becomes clear from the convention transcripts, crucial to the conventioneers' sense of their own legitimacy, not only because it allowed them to articulate a double claim of identification (with a particular set of human beings subject to a specific form of historical oppression *and* with the idea of a humanity in general) but also because it provided them with the figure by which to assert their right to represent those in whose name they had gathered. As advocates not only for a popular denunciation of slavery but for a reform of international law that would outlaw slavery, the conventioneers understood that they needed some title, some legal standing, to speak on behalf of their dual chosen constituency (humanity and the slaves).[23] Precisely because they found themselves assembled neither as electoral representatives nor as legal ambassadors, either of the slaves, their respective nations, or the human race, but yet wished to claim some right to speak on behalf of a worldwide body of (absent) others, they required — understood themselves to require and accepted that the operational procedure of international law required of them — some alternate form of representational legitimacy. And that form was the form of the friend.

But if a friend is neither appointed nor elected (to speak on behalf of another), how is friendship fashioned? How is the friend (of the slave, of all nations, of humanity) made? By remonstrance, expostulation, and sympathy, as the summons to the convention and the subsequent transcript of the convention proceedings made quite clear. "More than half a century has elapsed since the horrors, the cruelty, and crime of the African slave trade awakened the sympathies of Britons," the summons noted in its opening sentence before briefly describing the travails and eventual triumph of the British abolitionist movement ("the sympathies of the British nation were aroused, and, under the blessing of the Most High, the efforts of the friends of justice and humanity were finally crowned with success").[24] Globally, however, the summons admitted, slavery continued ("to an unprecedented extent, and with aggravated horrors").[25] It was this melancholy fact that had "induced the friends of justice and humanity again to assemble," and that generated the organizers' overtly sentimental call to gather: "Degraded and forlorn as is the condition of the slave, the members of the British and Foreign Anti-Slavery Society cannot but feel persuaded, that there is no country in which there will not be found those who commiserate his condition, and who would desire to prove themselves the friends and protectors of the oppressed. To these, in EVERY LAND, the Society offers the right hand of fellowship, and earnestly solicits their co-operation. . . . [The Society] is thus announcing itself to the friends of the slave of every nation. . . . To this Conference they earnestly invite the friends of every nation and every clime."[26]

This is a summons, but it is also a manifesto, a theory of political representation, and a doctrine of legal personality that introduces a new (sympathetic, cosmopolitan) figure to the stage of international politics and international law, a figure self-appointed to contest the monopoly the nation-state had in asserting its exclusive sovereignty as agent of international law and its sole standing before the law. Who are the delegates? They are friends (of the slaves, of humanity). And who is a friend? One who commiserates or sympathizes. For the "human rights" activist (the phrase was employed at the convention), sympathy, rather than the ballot, thus becomes the principle of political representation, while humanity, rather than the nation, holds sovereignty over the law. You are not, by this doctrine, elected to speak on behalf of the other and for humanity. You commiserate with others and by commiserating with them come to represent both them and the humanity made manifest by and in your capacity to sympathize. What is true of the theater of the mind (where sympathy causes us first to become or stand in for another and then to recognize in our own capacity for sympathy, our title to humanity) thus becomes true of the political and legal arena also. But, if sympathy produces friendship and friendship delegates and legitimates the antislavery activist and human rights spokesman, how is sympathy produced?[27]

How, in particular, the delegates asked themselves, might sympathy be stirred where the law had not yet abolished slavery (in India, Ceylon, and, above all, the United States)?[28] To which question, after much debate, the convention provided a remarkably consistent response. How is sympathy produced? By literature, above all, by sentimental literature. As Henry B. Stanton (the president of the American Anti-Slavery Society) put the matter in offering a resolution calling for a world literature, antislavery in its principles and sentimental in its address:

> The civilized world must erect a wall of fire around America, which may melt down the hard heart of the slave-holder. The abolitionists are feeble in number but strong in moral power . . . Therefore is it that we fall back for assistance upon the enlightened sentiments of the civilized world. One influence which we desire to bring to bear for this purpose is the literature of the world. We are in America a reading people. . . . We come to England and say give us an anti-slave literature. You have heard that the Americans are a combative nation. True, they are a brave, courageous people, they can resist tyranny and oppression, but moral power they cannot resist; and they will not be able to resist the combined influence of the literature and religion of this country. This is our last hope. I speak as one who has stood up against slavery amidst strife and opposition, in company with brave men who have bared their bosoms to the storm in defense of their principles. We fall back for assistance upon British sentiment, upon English literature, and our common Christianity. . . . Send us a purified, a vivifying literature; a literature instinct with the principles of freedom. . . . Thus shall we reach the ears of men whom the voice of the American abolitionist cannot reach. Thus shall we convince their judgements, until they shall acknowledge the truth of our principles, and unite with us in their dissemination, and then slavery shall cease.[29]

Stanton was not alone in discovering this power in literature. Rising to address the convention in support of the resolution Stanton had offered, Wendell Phillips, a Massachusetts delegate, also called for a literature to put before the slaveholders of the world, one which would cause the cold and the indifferent to find "their feelings . . . harrowed up."[30] George Bradburn, also of Massachusetts, echoed the point: "We call on Englishmen to 'come over and help us.' . . . We do not urge you to come in person, but come to us in the columns of your daily press, in the pages of your books, of your novels and romances."[31] The next day Stanton's plea was met with the demanded offer of assistance. The resolution carried. A sentimental literature was promised; the pledge of friendship was given.

The promise, of course, was redundant. A vast, sentimental, abolitionist literature already existed.[32] The American abolitionists already had their friends, sending word. Sympathy already possessed its trans-Atlantic lending library, its circulating archive of "impossible witness," as Dwight A. McBride has put it in his study of abolition and romanticism.[33] But though the resolution was largely superfluous, it was also entirely revealing. For it demonstrated the delegates' conviction that if a global abolitionist movement was, indeed, to have any "hope" of altering international law, of enshrining humanity as a principle of law superordinate to the nation-state, of opening the legislative chambers and courtrooms of the world to Solicitor Haywood's melancholy porthole on history, the gathered "friends of humanity" would need the world's jurists and lawmakers to enter their courtrooms, congresses, and parliaments not merely as politicians or justices but as readers — and not just any type of readers, but readers trained in a habit of sympathetic, even melancholy, knowledge. The hard facts of slavery, the brutal knowledge that slavery continued "to an unprecedented extent, and with aggravated horrors," were not alone sufficient. If those facts were to have any impact they would need to be viewed, as it were, from the window, from the purchase the sentimental novel and other forms of sympathetic literature gave on the world, from the melancholy perspective of the witness that, in Derrida's terms, "the judge, the arbiter, or the addressee" must also come to be.[34]

To so render the judges and legislators whose sentiments they hoped to address a fellow company of interested witnesses (rather than a body of impartial spectators), the delegates would thus need more than the rhetorical figure of humanity; they would require a means of rendering the unseen visible, the unexperienced grievous, sympathy communicable, melancholy actionable. What they would not need, at least at the time the convention met, was a fresh aesthetics of melancholy attachment or an as-yet-unformed epistemology of sympathetic identification. For by 1840 all these things existed, and had, indeed, been drawn on by the abolitionist movement for the preceding half century or more. If Stanton did not realize that, he need only have read *the* contemporaneous classic of the abolitionist movement, Thomas Clarkson's 1785 *Essay on the Slavery and Commerce of the Human Species, Particularly the African* which perfectly blends history, polemic, and romance melancholy, or, barring that, he might simply have walked a few blocks across the city to the Royal Academy where he would have encountered just the sort of work he was demanding, a remarkable, harrowing by-product of British abolition, British sentiment, and British literature: not a novel, to be sure, but a Romance certainly, or a scene from a romance, designed to give its observers "an idea of the sufferings of the Africans"[35] and of the observer's own suffering before such suffering: *Slavers Throwing Overboard the Dead and Dying, Typhoon Coming On*, J. M. W. Turner's painting of the *Zong* massacre, the work that together with Clarkson's *Essay* would become the single most famous period meditation on the trans-Atlantic slave trade and a global abolitionist movement's work of sympathetic witness.[36]

```
                              lives own their facts

                                  of spent lives

                                  murder

                                  market

                                  misfortunes

                                              &

                                  policy

                    lying dead

                    under seas

                                  facts own their lives
```

— M. NourbeSe Philip, from *Zong! # 22*

CHAPTER 8

The Fact of History

ON COSMOPOLITAN INTERESTEDNESS

"The foregoing scene, though it may be said to be imaginary, is strictly consistent with fact. It is a scene to which the reader himself may have been a witness, if he has ever visited the place where it is supposed to lie; as no circumstance has been inserted in it, for which the fullest and most undeniable evidence cannot be produced."[1] The "scene" Thomas Clarkson had in mind in this passage from his 1785 *Essay on the Slavery and Commerce of the Human Species, Particularly the African*, was not the scene of the *Zong* massacre, the window-framed view on history to which Solicitor Haywood and his colleagues had called the court's (and humanity's) attention two summers before, the scene their sentimental rhetoric so framed that it appeared in court not just as a view on history but (as their opponent, Solicitor Lee, dryly observed) as if it were a scene drawn from a case of romance. Rather, Clarkson is referring to a fictional vignette he has just sketched detailing the manner in which slaves are acquired on the west coast of Africa. It is not until the paragraph that immediately follows these sentences that the case of the *Zong* makes its appearance in his text as one of those pieces of "evidence" that will allow him to describe, "in general terms," the treatment of slaves embarked on the middle passage.[2] And though the *Zong* massacre thus enters the text whose publication is often identified as the crucial publishing event in the formative years of the British abolitionist movement (and so, too, in a modern Atlantic discourse of human rights) not as something whose factual nature Clarkson explicitly obliges himself to defend, it does appear as an "instance" (the word Clarkson prefers to "event") whose facticity is haunted by the rhetorical license the author has just afforded himself. The case of the *Zong* — or, indeed, any case, instance, or event identified in the remainder of the *Essay* — appears, that is, in the testamentary shadow of that earlier "scene" whose "factual" character, Clarkson insists, is no less absolute for being imaginary, and whose quality as "evidence" is no less reliable for needing to be attested to by the very reader whose skepticism Clarkson is trying to counter. How does Clarkson counter that skepticism? By asking the reader to stand "witness" to the truth of a scene he or she "may have" seen, or, if that proves impossible, by agreeing experimentally to posit the existence of another reader who might have witnessed such scenes on behalf of the stay-at-home reading public. If this begins to sound like an increasingly tautological theory of historiography (as the "factual" truth of an "imaginary" scene comes to rest on the suppositional existence of an imaginary other who, at best, may have seen the truth of what has been "supposed'), that, however, is not the point I want to stress. My point is that this is all beginning to sound increasingly fictive, or even *fanciful*.

For as *readers*, Clarkson's readers have "in fact," *witnessed* the scene he is describing, though they have done so neither by visiting "the place where it is supposed to lie" nor by having been taken through a tour of the historian's archive, but by encountering that scene in a testamentary space which contemporaneous poetic and novelistic discourse sought to make available to the mind, an imaginary space whose experimental fidelity to historical truth it was the greater burden of both the late-eighteenth-century novel of sympathy and British romantic poetry to assert while simultaneously acknowledging that readerly territory's evident, and *fanciful*, "fictionality." To accept an "imaginary" "scene" (of enslavement, in this case) as nevertheless an encounter with historical "fact" (and so, also, with the obligations of humanity), Clarkson maintains (together with an influential fraction of his era's novelists and romantic poets), is to encounter fancy as reality, fact as fiction, and fiction as fact, or, as Lennard Davis has put it in his study of the eighteenth-century novel, to encounter history as a "factual fiction."[3] Clarkson's initially puzzling determination to set an imaginary scene at the midpoint of what is otherwise a conventionally scholarly historical essay, and so also to install fiction as a not-so-secret sharer of the evidentiary protocols of what was to become one of abolition's canonical texts is thus not so surprising as it might at first seem. Appealing to the conscience and the sentiment of a body of readers who in all likelihood could not literally have witnessed the scenes he demands they see but who, he could reasonably assume, had some knowledge of contemporary poetry or some experience of novel reading, Clarkson explicitly fictionalizes his text to assert for his *Essay* not only the humanitarian but also the historical truth claims that the novel had spent the greater part of the century consolidating for its "factual fictions" and that romantic poetry was simultaneously claiming for its flights of fancy.

*

I will have more to say regarding the testamentary poetics of fancy below. For the moment, however, a brief word of clarification on the epistemology of the eighteenth-century novel is in order. In the first section of this book, following the lead of Catherine Gallagher, Deidre Lynch, and Michael McKeon, I drew some attention to the early English novel's discovery of fiction as an epistemological category somewhere between truth and lies. The seventeenth- and early-to-mid-eighteenth-century English realist novel, all these scholars in their various ways suggest, can be understood, in part, as that form of narrative willing to break the monopoly that history, philosophy, and theology had long been understood to hold on truth by advancing a set of moral, characterological, or social truth claims consistent with the *fictional* representation of reality. Davis's argument, as the title of his book suggests, is similar. The novel, he argues, is not merely an innovative prose form, it is a revolution in epistemology, an ongoing attempt to collapse the truth and lies binary by presenting fiction as fact. As such, obviously enough, the history of the English novel comprises not only a history of the rise of fiction but a continuing history of the vicissitudes of what constitutes and counts as a fact. Through the middle of the eighteenth century, I have further suggested, the novelistic labor of constituting fictional facts is broadly consistent with what I have been calling the theoretical realism of speculative culture. Which means that to the extent that the preromantic novel advertises and articulates itself as capable of a form of historical (and historicizing) knowledge, the facts its fictions generate are not only compatible with but foundational to what I have also called an actuarial historicism, a historicism whose key figure is the average, aggregate, and abstract type. Such types operate by abstracting, from the manifold of observed, recorded or categorizable persons, events, or things, average representations of those persons, events, or things. The actuarial type, then, in terms that will become crucial not only to the English and British novel but to post-Kantian German idealist thought (particularly Hegel's theory of right and his philosophy of history), is the type of someone or something that does not exist as *this* or *that*, but only as *such*, only in the aggregate or the abstract. To the extent, therefore, that the preromantic English and British novel licenses a revolution in epistemology, that revolution is generally consistent with the other historical, financial, and cultural revolutions of modern European speculative discourse. Fielding's fictional character Tom Jones (and the example here, as we shall see, is anything but contingent) is factually true to the type of "new social person" J. G. A. Pocock discerns at the heart of England's postrepublican commercial society precisely to the extent that he represents an aggregate, averagely "truthful" embodiment of the type of the dispossessed son which McKeon suggests had become central to the plots of the novels of the time. (Like the social truth attached to the images of a porter, a debtor, a highwayman, and a politician on display at the 1784 Liverpool dissertation upon faces, Tom Jones's truth, as the full title of Fielding's novel suggests (*The History of Tom Jones, A Foundling*), is the truth and the factual fiction one might derive from the history of "*a* foundling").

The type of factual fiction and fictional (or fanciful) fact with which I am now concerned is, however, of an altogether different type. It is the type of truth generated not by an actuarial but by a sentimental (in Chandler's terms, a romantic) historicism, not by speculation but by melancholy, not by a Fieldingesque depiction of character, society, and history but, rather, by the representational protocols of a novel such as Sir Walter Scott's *Waverley; Or, 'Tis Sixty Years Since* (which, like *Tom Jones*, takes the 1745 Jacobite insurrection as its historical scene of departure but "knows" the truth of that historical event in an altogether different way). The truth claims of a romantic or sentimental historicism are, then, not claims foreign to the realm of eighteenth-century novelistic discourse or a novelistic construction of a factually fictional knowledge of history. Rather, by the late eighteenth century and early nineteenth, novelistic discourse splits in two while continuing to orbit a common epistemological center. The novel, in Davis's terms, continues to revolve around its own capacity to spin factual fictions, its ability to create imaginary scenes strictly consistent with fact, but now the type of knowledge it induces are both abstract and melancholy, speculative and romantic. The romantic novel, particularly in the form of the historical romance, emerges alongside the canonically realist novel to secure for its readers a factual knowledge of persons, events, things, and scenes that exist not in the abstract or aggregate but in a sort of ghostly, fictional afterlife. It insists on its ability to return the lost or absent scene, person, or thing imaginatively, fancifully, but also, crucially, *truthfully* to life. That the romantic novel begins to insist on its ability to construct *this* type of factual fiction is in part a function of its return to and re-creation of that narrative form which Davis insists is not original to the prior emergence of Defoe, Richardson, and Fielding's novelistic practice: the romance.

For these three writers, and that tradition of "formal realism" they are commonly held to represent, Davis argues, the novel's precursor genre is not romance but the news, that other modern challenger to history's monopoly on the truth. On this score Davis's argument is entirely convincing. It is not, after all, a mere coincidence, as he points out, that both Defoe and Fielding were not only novelists but journalists, or even that the play whose suppression by Walpole turned Fielding from drama to the novel was entitled "The Historical Register." As he further indicates, this preromantic strain of realist novelism secures its conditions of arrival by rejecting the chivalric romance and its conventions of *vraisemblance*, or likeliness, and *bienseance*, or moral desirability (together with the romance's thematic obsessions with distant history and its ideological commitments to tradition, authority, and stability) in order to affirm for the novel a more *plausibly* factual knowledge of contemporary history. But while Fielding and his predecessor's obligation, as Davis argues, is not to a *vraisemblance* tempered by *bienseance* but, like the contemporaneously emergent actuarial sciences — though Davis does not make this connection — to "probability," then for a romantic counterstrain of novelistic practice it is the news itself, rather than the fate of legendary heroes, which becomes the subject of historical romance.[4] The romantic novel, that is, also exists under the sign of the fact or fiction nexus, but the factual fictions it delivers to its readers are facts it cultivates by romancing the news. The difference is that for the romantic novel there is one primary sort of news, the news of loss, and one key variant on this sort (a variant that will prove central to abolitionist discourses' adoption of the conventions of both the romantic novel and the romantic history lyric): lost news. Indeed, if there is a paradigmatic type of historical "case" with which both the romantic novel and a fictionalizing abolitionist treatment of the facts of history concern themselves it is this — the lost news of the news of loss.

Why?

For a romantic abolitionism, at least, as Clarkson's example makes clear, the answer is obvious enough. *The* problem for abolition (as for all subsequent cosmopolitan humanitarian discourse) is the problem of the unseen, the problem of nonappearance, the problem of blocked vision. If the general task of what I am calling the testamentary, melancholy realist counterdiscourse of modernity is to recover the lost, to acknowledge and take some affective property in the ruinous "past" continuously, if nonsynchronously, present within now-being, then the particular task for a interested cosmopolitanism, for eighteenth-century abolitionist discourse, and, certainly, for all the displaced "witnesses" to the horror of the *Zong* massacre is not merely to make the past present but to render the unseen visible, to bear witness to the truth of what has not been (and what cannot have been) witnessed. Melancholy may constitute an inability to forget what cannot be remembered, but it also comprises the obligation to see what has not been seen. This is not just a psychic or an epistemological dilemma, it is also the consequence of a geopolitical impasse. For what is lost is not only lost in damaged or unrecorded time, it is also, frequently, lost in space, unseen not merely because time, measured chronologically, continues its implacable, imperturbable march but because the extent of geographic space and the constraints of politically organized sightlines on history intervene between the witness and the unforgettable spectacle of what has not been witnessed. This is Clarkson's problem — as it is the problem for any afterimage image of the *Zong* massacre or any other such obscure (or obscured) historical catastrophe — as the distance of passing time or the obstacles of geographic space separates the witness from the scene of witnessing.

A melancholy romanticism, resolutely set against the tide of modernity, may contribute to a crucial reinvention of the human (as a type of sympathetic observer, determined to invest in and remonstrate against the sufferings of another). But if that interested observer is to exist, it must first find some vantage on history, some view from the window by which to witness the melancholy facts of history. And if these facts are lost? inaccessible to inspection? blocked from view? What then? The witness (and, by implication, humanity) then requires some theory of knowledge by which to render the invisible visible, some technology of displaced knowledge by which to make the work of witness possible, some way of authenticating the credibility of the melancholy facts it brings imaginatively into view. The witness requires what late-eighteenth- and early-nineteenth-century epistemology, moral discourse, and novelistic and poetic practice was in the process of providing: a truth theory of lost but nevertheless present knowledge, of imaginary but credible facts, of absent but inescapable, haunting events and scenes. It requires the historical romance, the romantic history lyric, a developed theory of identification, and a remodeled account of what might constitute and be recognized as historical fact. Without all these, humanity, as Solicitor Haywood construed it, could not have survived. Without all these, his window view on the *Zong* massacre could not have remained open.

∗

In the course of the 1806 parliamentary debate that finally resulted in the abolition of British participation in the trans-Atlantic slave trade, William Wilberforce addressed exactly the same problem that had plagued Thomas Clarkson twenty years earlier, immediately before he too recounted the story of the *Zong* massacre as one of the facts of the trade.

> If the Members of this House could actually *see* one thousandth part of the evils of that practice which they have, for so many years, under one pretense or other, been prevailed on to suffer to be continued; I do in my conscience verily believe, they would not suffer the Slave Trade to exist for another year, if they would for another hour. But it is *because they do not see*; because some among us, receive the profits, *and do not see*, the sufferings of their fellow creatures; *because the objects, as they actually exist, are not allowed to obtrude upon their vision*, and interpose the reality of things between these Gentlemen's consciences and their calculations: — It is for these reasons that arguments such as we constantly hear, in favour of the continuance of the Slave Trade, are heard at all. *If one thousandth part of the real horrors of this Traffick (I repeat it) were to be the subject of actual vision with these its defenders, none of their arguments, I am confident, would be urged again.*[5]

But of course, comfortably seated in Westminster, Wilberforce's auditors could not literally see what he was attempting to describe. So Wilberforce did the next best thing — or, indeed, he did what the romantic novel had begun to insist amounted to the same thing: he told, in his own words, a story, the story of the *Zong* massacre, a story in which his audience could see the real horror of the trade and the enslaved objects of that trade as they actually exist and actually suffer. To see the slaves in such a story of suffering was not only, as the sentimental discourse of Solicitor Haywood and his colleagues had earlier suggested, to take on or assume some property in that suffering (though, as Wilberforce's canny use of "suffer," "suffering," and "to suffer" indicates, it is that too). It was also, Wilberforce insisted, just as Clarkson had earlier asserted, to discover in such sentimental narrative the factual objects of the historical world as they actually exist; or, as the full title of William Godwin's contemporaneous and paradigmatically sentimental novel *Caleb Williams* had it, to encounter, sentimentally and imaginatively, *Things as They Are*.

Clarkson and Wilberforce were not alone, either in evincing a general determination to adopt fictional protocols for abolitionist discourse or, more specifically, in discovering in the conventions of contemporaneous romantic discourse the secret of how to cause those who could not have witnessed the *Zong* massacre to nevertheless "see" that event and to see it as fact. In the twenty-three years that separated the hearing in Lord Mansfield's courtroom from Parliament's 1806 decision to abolish the slave trade, the story of the *Zong* was told and retold by a score of abolitionist speakers, editorialists, essayists, pamphleteers, and politicians as one of the key facts of the trade. The scene Haywood and his colleagues had made to appear at the court of King's Bench, the melancholy porthole on history they had opened, was levered ajar again and again as the outrage it inspired and continued to inspire proved morbidly invaluable to the abolitionist cause. David Brion Davis and a number of other historians of the abolitionist movement have identified the publicization of this event as something like a founding moment in the rise of abolition as a political cause in Britain. But if the abolitionist movement (and the transnational politics of human rights which abolition helped to establish) was, at least in part, founded on the story of the *Zong* massacre, then it also found in the massacre not just a stable if horrifying point of beginning but something like a portable tableaux, a romantic scene of horror perfectly fitted for serial reframing, an indisputably sentimental fact that could be endlessly reintroduced into evidence.

Sharp's 1783 submission to the Lords Commissioners of the Admiralty is the first text to effect this reworking of history into sentimental fact and sentimental fact into melancholy evidence. And as I have indicated, that text makes abundantly evident the narratological character of its presentation of this fact, the fictionalized quality of this evidence as it both gestures to the more general historical truth which the event brings to light and appeals to the aggrieved imagination of the historical observer who agrees to take some property in it. If the relation of evidence to truth (whether melancholy or disinterested) may be understood to approximate the fact and value binary, then, we might say, from the moment of Sharp's letter to the occasion of Wilberforce's parliamentary address (and after), the *Zong* serially enters abolitionist and humanitarian discourse as a valued fact made to speak a dual fictional truth — one politicohistorical and one affective. One brings to light the general historical reality of the trade as it actually exists in, and can be induced from, the particular instance. The other bears witness to the capacity of humanity in general to extrapolate itself from the sublime determination to take some melancholy property in the suffering that such facts bring before the eyes of those who have been made to see what they do not see. In either case, however, the shift from fact to value represents an investment not simply in inductive reason or the sympathetically sublime imagination but in the (factual) fiction that truth (whether epistemological or affective) resides in evidence; resides, moreover, in the sort of testamentary evidence it had increasingly become the business of the historical novel and the romantic history lyric to provide.

If this is true of Sharp's, Clarkson's, and Wilberforce's representations of the *Zong*, then it is also the case for other works such as Ottobah Cuguano's *Thoughts and Sentiments on the Evil and Wicked Traffic of the Slavery and Commerce of the Human Species* (1787), which cites "among the many instances of [British] barbarity [in the trade] *only one*," the "melancholy instance" of the *Zong* massacre[6]; and Thomas Cooper's *Considerations on the Slave Trade* (1791) which "extracts" an account of the massacre from a compendium of texts (including volumes by Gregory and Ramsay which also recount the atrocity) as a "singular" "anecdote" of the trade.[7] And then, of course, there is the canonical visual representation of the event, the most famous attempt to make it "the subject of actual vision" in order that the belated or displaced historical spectator might indeed witness (and bear witness to) what he or she had not witnessed: Turner's *Slavers Throwing Overboard the Dead and Dying, Typhoon Coming On*, the canvas Turner painted to coincide with the opening of the first World Anti-Slavery Convention as his singular visual anecdote of the horrors of slavery at the same time that he was completing a series of assignments as an illustrator to Sir Walter Scott.

*

By the time Turner painted his canvas, the massacre — repeatedly extracted from the historical archive, serially reproduced as an anecdote, instance, or unit of evidence, multiply reprocessed by the sentimental machinery of a melancholy purview on history — had, in other words, become what in Clarkson's text it had only begun to be. It had survived the moment of its happening not simply as a catastrophic and melancholy truth event but as a sentimental fact, a factual fiction, a romantic tableaux, and a novelistic scene. As such, now firmly enlisted within a melancholy discourse on value, property, and humanity, it had also been made to figure a novel type of romantic knowledge claim. And it is precisely as such a fact, fiction, and scene that the event animates and more fully brings to light that long-durational melancholy counterdiscourse of the witness traced in the second part of this book. Stated another way, it is exactly to the extent that the scene of the massacre can be represented as simultaneously imaginary *and* strictly consistent with fact that the sentimental imagination of melancholy not only can take some affective property in this event but can also discern in such a romantic or romance investment in history the sublimely melancholy truth of a globalizing modernity as it actually exists before its impossible witnesses. To reproduce the event *as*, or to find the truth of history *in*, such a melancholy scene, in other words, is not to disassociate affect or imagination from epistemology. It is, rather, to identify an affective, interested, and imaginary investment in the traumas of history as a truthful form of knowledge. Affect, here, is epistemology; imagination, sentiment, and melancholy *the* keys to a factual knowledge of an increasingly planetary (and hence increasingly invisible) European ordering of modern history. If for Solicitor Lee such a conviction denoted a "romance" attitude to history; and if for Lowy and Sayre it implies a romantic counterdiscourse of the modern, then the overarching epistemological genre organizing such a conception of history (one which encompasses both romance and romantic epistemologies without limiting itself to either) is that apposite to what I have been calling melancholy realism. But if the mode of this melancholy counterdiscourse of modernity is thus realist, then unlike the theoretical realism I earlier allied with the speculative epistemologies and practices of the modern, the knowledge grammar of this melancholy realism, as I have begun to indicate, is composed not of actuarial types strictly consistent with the average character of persons and things but of imaginary scenes strictly consistent with fact. Or, to put it this way: it is a realism whose key unit is neither the type nor the average but the sentimental, romantic, or melancholy case, scene, or fact.

For instance, the fact of the *Zong* massacre.

*

To speak of the romantic or melancholy fact, or to speak of such a sentimentally factual knowledge of the global and of humanity, is to speak not only of the emergence of an alternate mode of novelistic practice, an alternate type of (melancholy) realism foundational to both the historical romance and the romantic history lyric, and an alternate historical observer (the witness) to that sublimely disinterested historical spectator posited by Kant. It is also to speak of a zone of trouble within one of the more recent and magisterial histories of modern European epistemology: Mary Poovey's *A History of the Modern Fact*. This does not mean that the melancholy or sentimental fact is entirely absent from Poovey's text. She does record traces of its presence (though she does not name it as such) as a troubling counterunit to those disinterested facts she identifies as central to European modernity's core inductive epistemology. She discerns the existence of such facts (or counterfacts) primarily in three territories of thought: the experimental moral philosophy and conjectural historiography of the Scottish Enlightenment (particularly the work of Adam Smith); British romantic poetry; and a variety of postmodern knowledge projects. Poovey, however, does not fully elaborate how romanticism, the Scottish Enlightenment, and the antifoundational, counteruniversalizing, and local rationality variants of the postmodern are related or how their common reliance on what I am calling the melancholy fact or scene might open the epistemological domain of a Euro-centered modernity to an affective and imaginary countervision and counterknowledge of the modern, the human, and the facts on which they are posited. What Poovey offers instead is a genealogy of the modern European discourses commonly reliant on what might be called the speculative fact or, as she indicates, a history of modern European epistemology as a history of abstract reason. It is, indeed, the will to abstraction, the will to derive systematic knowledges, general theories, or any number of the other "versions of abstraction: universals, generalizations, aggregates" from observed particulars that, for Poovey, characterizes the history of the modern European fact, while also setting the problem of inductive reason at the center of European modernity's knowledge projects and unifying all the political, economic, and natural scientific knowledge practices she studies as coparticipants in a long-durational history of abstraction coterminous with the history of European modernity itself.[8] As she notes in the introduction to her text: "All [these] practices reveal that one effect of efforts to generate systematic knowledge was the production of a set of abstractions, which rapidly became the objects of these sciences. These abstractions, which include "society," "the market system" (then "the economy") . . . now constitute the characteristic objects of the modern social sciences."[9]

Poovey argues that what distinguishes European modernity's knowledge projects (scientific, governmental, and aesthetic) from classical Aristotelian models of epistemology — which had bred abstractions from abstractions (universals from a priori truths) — is that for European modernity abstraction predicates itself on observed particulars, assemblages of fact from which abstract reason can never entirely detach itself, and whose relation to the abstracting impulse's systematic or universal truth claims, Europe's modern philosophical, social, and political discourses continuously oblige themselves to theorize. It is this ongoing effort to theorize the relation of the observed particular to the systemic that Poovey traces throughout her text, as it is the characteristically anxious self-knowledge of modern European theoretical thought that accounts for the fundamentally paradoxical character of facts that have been privileged as "*both* observed particulars and evidence of some theory" (9). If this begins to sound as if the history of the modern European fact (or at least Poovey's *History of the Modern Fact*) is as much a history of dialectical reason (a history, that is, of the ways in which thought effects the shift between and comprehends the synthesis of phenomenal contents and ideal concepts) as it is a history of the fact and value binary, then that is, to a certain extent, an accurate reading.[10]

But there is a difference. Where for Hegel the transition from brute particulars to the Idea and back again is effected by reason, one of Poovey's major arguments is that throughout Europe's modern period what has connected and, perhaps more importantly, *what has repeatedly been understood to connect* observed particulars to theories, aggregates, universals, ideas, or any other type of abstraction is not reason but fiction or the imagination. The guilty and continuously worrisome secret of the modern European fact, in other words, is that the relation of facts to values, particulars to theories, phenomena to universals, is not rational but fictional or imaginary. As Poovey, to cite a single example, notes of Hume's understanding of his own abstractions ("society," "the state of nature," etc.):

> We can see that Hume is *implying* that society is the historian's trope: what he actually *says* is that the "state of nature," which supposedly preceded society, is "a mere philosophical fiction, which never had, and never cou'd have any reality." Even though it is a fiction, however, the idea of a state of nature is necessary, for "nothing can more evidently show the origin of those virtues, which are the subjects of our present inquiry." . . . Indeed, Hume's initial representation of man "only in himself" (that is, before society; that is, as an incarnation of "human nature") is also a fiction, although it too is necessary to his demonstration about the origins of property and justice. Thus, by an intricate series of displacements, deferrals, and self-corrections, Hume has installed fiction-making . . . at the heart of both the idea of society and theorizing about society (and, by extension, human nature). This fiction-making affects deduc-

tion because, in Hume's account, deduction reasons from a fictive premise; and it affects induction because, by this account, induction proceeds by subsuming the individual (human being, detail) into the (social, theoretical) whole.[11]

The point here is not that the facts from which Euromodernity abstracts its theories, ideas, and general knowledges are false but that in order to move from one register to the other, in order to move from the details it has collected to the theories it wishes to propound, a knowledge practice (and not just that apposite to novelistic discourse) must fictionalize its archive of facts. If epistemology can thus be understood to depend, as Poovey has it, on a type of fiction making, the question then arises: what *type(s)* of fiction does Euromodernity fashion for its knowledge projects? Or indeed, from what type(s) of fiction do Europe's modern knowledge projects makes themselves? Here the question of genre or mode has to be reintroduced to the history of epistemology. For if epistemology is displaced, deferred, or masked fiction making, then fiction making is not all of a kind but various in its genres and modes. The fiction, in other words, that relates a detail to a theory is as likely to be elegiac as epic, novelistic as lyric.

Having just made that point I would abide by it, and so would suggest that a fully developed genre critique has a valuable role to play in fleshing out a fuller history of modern knowledge. But I also want to argue, somewhat in line with Northrop Frye's contention that all genres are ultimately a subset of allegory, that there are nevertheless two dominant modes of epistemological fiction making (and fictional epistemology making) that have subtended the many variant forms of modern European epistemology: the allegorical and the counterallegorical, the modes, respectively, of what I have been calling the speculative and the melancholy discourse and counterdiscourse of modernity. At a base level, that is, abstraction, theory, systemic thought — call it what you will — seems to demonstrate either an allegorical or a counterallegorical relationship to observed particulars, singular instances, assemblages of detail. The fiction making of speculative discourse allegorizes the facts it values by emptying them of local significance and conferring a superordinate meaning and conceptual exchange value on them (this is what Jameson calls transcoding and Bruno Latour calls rerepresentation). The counterallegorical fiction making of melancholy discourse, on the other hand, sentimentalizes, romanticizes, or encrypts the facts that wound and haunt it (and which it thus finds invaluable, beyond all value because outside all possibility of substitution, surrender, or exchange). But if this is true, if Europe's modern fiction making knowledge projects are alternately allegorical or counterallegorical, speculative or melancholy, actuarially or romantically typicalizing, then, to belabor a tautology, so too are the types of facts such projects fictionalize. Which returns us to the problem of the sentimental, romantic, or melancholy fact, the very type of fact the *Zong* massacre was in the process of becoming to its observers over the last quarter of the eighteenth century and the first half of the nineteenth.

How then does such a fact differ from and trouble the sovereignty of the modern European speculative fact and its fictional abstractions and modes of fiction making (by my terms, its theoretical realism)? How indeed does the melancholy fact emerge from and within the interstices of modern European reason and modern European aesthetic practice? As I have suggested, and as we shall see, it emerges in the romantic and romance domains of fiction, imagination, and fancy — not only in the historical novel and romantic poetry but in a set of surrounding discourses on which both these forms drew, most crucially the experimental moral philosophy of Adam Smith and his Scottish Enlightenment contemporaries. And it emerges in response to the circum-Atlantic projection of modern European political and economic power and the yet more expansive globalizing project eighteenth-century Europe set for its speculative knowledge, value, and civilizing projects.

The melancholy fact (and the various sentimental, romantic, and romance politics, epistemologies, aesthetics, and practices of witness it grounds), in other words, emerges in the late eighteenth century and early nineteenth not merely as the logical or aesthetic counterunit to the speculative fact (and its politics, economics, aesthetics, and epistemology) but as a political imperative and as an alternative unit of geopolitical knowledge. At either end of the long twentieth century, when the possibilities of progressive politics seem to be dominated by universalizing end-of-history narratives, triumph-of-the-market rationalities, speculative epistemologies, and the twin ideals of consensual disinterestedness and liberal cosmopolitanism, the melancholy fact of history and its dominant genres of articulation (now as then) offer the promise of an alternative vision, knowledge, and politics of the global, one which can predicate itself on a frank avowal of interestedness: in the subaltern, in the hauntological, in the multitudinous scenes of global injustice, in an entire planetary array of melancholy facts, scenes, images, *and* fictions of history.

While I will not here attempt a catalog of those such scenes of history in which our haunted present has invested its interest, I do want to note that the three that most demanded the attention of late-eighteenth-century British and continental thought (the French Revolution; the subjugation of England's

Gaelic peripheries, particularly the Scottish Highlands; and the trans-Atlantic slave trade) collectively define a circum-Atlantic theater of modernity and a circum-Atlantic arena of modern sentimental discourse. It is a fact of our profound intellectual impoverishment that the Scottish and trans-Atlantic cases have largely been reserved for the academic specialist, while the case of the French Revolution has been allowed to figure a more universal engagement with the problem and the unfolding drama of modernity. It is now well past time for anyone wishing to speak of the European discourses on and of modernity to have done with this monomania of historical vision. Occidental modernity *is* of and in the French Revolution. It is also, minimally, of and in the pacification of the Highlands and of and in trans-Atlantic slavery (to provide only two coordinates of only an Atlantic frame for a renovated geographics or geo-optics of the modern).[12] Late-eighteenth-century Britons knew this. Hegel and any of the other myriad continental figures eagerly following, discussing, and debating the Haitian Revolution knew it.[13] The circum-Atlantic alliance of Americans, Europeans, and enslaved or manumitted Africans for whom emancipation and abolition were the crucial political issues of the time knew it. Adam Smith, Dugald Stewart, and the other architects of the Scottish Enlightenment knew it. The British, American, Caribbean, and African sailors and port-city radicals who collectively compose the "many-headed hydra" of Peter Linebaugh and Marcus Rediker's eponymously titled history of modern Atlantic revolutionary movements knew it.[14] The century's romantic poets and novelists certainly knew it.

*

To repeat: the late-eighteenth-century and early-nineteenth-century European discourse of modernity was not an exclusively Francocentric affair. It was also, minimally, Scottish and trans-Atlantic. Indeed, the trans-Atlantic, French, and Scottish facts of modernity constitute more than three paratactic instances of the modern. Rather, they assume the form of a historical circum-Atlantic conjuncture: both *systematically*, by way of France and Scotland's social, political, and commercial incorporation within the Atlantic world system, and *discursively*, most appositely, for the purposes of this text, in late-eighteenth-century moral philosophy, contemporaneous sentiment and sensibility discourse, the historical romance, and the romantic history lyric. As I will be arguing, Turner's slave ship canvas, which overlays a Scott- and Smith-inspired habit of viewing the tragedies of modern imperial history and a romantic mode of lyrically encrypting the greater traumas of the French

Revolution onto a sentimental testament to the horrors of the slave trade, brings that set of conjunctures to light just as fully as Sharp's submission to the Lords Commissioners of the Admiralty illuminates the conjuncture of speculative systems and discourses I discussed in the first section of this book. As Scott's novels are more than a romance fictionalization of an episode in Scottish history (they are also, simultaneously, narratives of the advent of a Europeanizing modernity), so too is Turner's painting more than a romance and romantic fictionalization of the melancholy fact of the *Zong* massacre. It is simultaneously a highly overdetermined site of affective and epistemological conjuncture; the scene where a range of abstract knowledges and sublimely melancholy counterknowledges of the circum-Atlantic theater of the modern meet. But before turning to the painting (via Smith's, Scott's, and Turner's other romantic interlocuters), a further set of terms needs to be introduced.

The difference between the speculative and the melancholy fact (the difference coded by the gap separating the view from Exchange Alley and the view from the window) is further analogous, on first glance, to a distinction Peter Dear, one of Poovey's sources, allows her to draw between evidence and the evident:

> As the kind of experience the natural philosophers consulted changed, so did the epistemological significance of the singular event: "the singular experience could not be *evident*," Dear explains, "but it could be *evidence*." The singular experiences or observed particulars that natural philosophers began to value in the seventeenth century were not *evident*, because they were neither signifiers of anything nor self-evidently valuable; only when such particulars were interpreted as evidence did they seem valuable enough to collect, because only then did they acquire meaning or even, I contend, identity as facts. . . . [This] distinction between an evident particular and a particular that constitutes evidence helps us understand what I am calling the peculiarity of the modern fact. On the one hand facts seem (and can be interpreted as being) simply the kind of deracinated particulars that Bacon claimed to value; on the other hand, facts seem (and can be said) to exist as identifiable units only when they constitute evidence for some theory — only, that is, when there is a theoretical reason to notice these particulars and name them as facts.[15]

It is clear from this passage that to the extent that it is operative in the modern European period (and Poovey argues convincingly that from the time of Bacon on it has operated as one of the constitutive binaries, perhaps *the* binary, of the West's natural scientific, moral, and governmental discourses), the evident/evidence binary articulates both a distinction and a dialectics. Indeed, it is precisely in its ability to *overcome* this distinction while still preserving it, in its capacity to frame some cognitive operation (some mode of epistemological fiction making) that will allow the fact to exist as both "deracinated particular" and "evidence for some theory" (both "in itself" and "for itself"), that the inductive rationality of modern European natural science, political economy, and conjectural historiography clears the ground for the subsequent emergence of the dialectic as the signature operation of Idealist thought. And so too, one might further suggest, is it the countervailing desire to reassert the distinction by working through the dialectic *to* a mode of thought in which the particular, the singular, and the evident reemerge as something of (invaluable) value precisely because they thus block the continuing operation of theoretical reason that clears the ground for what, following Adorno, we have come to call negative dialectics, what, in deconstructive terminology, animates the imperative undecidability/decision, what, as we shall see, informs the dyad relation/exception in Edouard Glissant's meditations on the traumas of Atlantic and Caribbean history.

But if the project of Adorno's negative dialectics, Glissant's exceptional poetics of relation, or a Spivakian setting-to-work of deconstruction (like the project of an earlier romantic and a more encompassingly melancholy habit of meditating on the singular fact[s] of history) is to recover that distinction, to recover, that is, the negative, the singular, the exceptional, or the evident not as a sort of lost foundation but as something that emerges on the far side, and in consequence of, the dialectical operation, a relational poetics, or the act of setting to work (as something, that is, like Adorno's wound, Spivak's example, or even Badiou's truth event, all of which do not precede but succeed the dialectical operation or act of decision that permits us to recognize them *belatedly and in the first place*), then even if that distinction is recovered, it is recovered in such a way as to ground another. This distinction, however, is postural or spectatorial rather than ontological and reminds us that as far as epistemology is concerned, ontology succeeds rather than precedes observation. Which, in this case, means that the difference between evidence and the evident is both analogous to and a function of the prior determination of the historical, aesthetic, or scientific observer to express a partial or an impartial posture to the evident, a melancholy or a speculative knowledge of the singular, an *interested* or a *disinterested* attitude to facts. Indeed, as Poovey makes clear, the history of the modern (European) fact might as accurately be reformulated as a history of disinterest as it can be reframed as a history of abstraction. For it is the refusal of interestedness, and the cultivation of a posture of scientific and cosmopolitan disinterestedness in the ontological singularity of the evident, that function as the absolute preconditions for the conversion of the evident into a species of evidence (and so also for the birth of any speculative system or abstract theory of knowledge).

I use the phrase "scientific and cosmopolitan disinterestedness" in the above sentence advisedly. For while we are not always accustomed to holding these two paradigmatically modern attitudes to nature and politics together (though even a stray knowledge of the consistency with which scientific method was read as a challenge to prescriptive political ideologies and organizations of state power in the early modern and modern European periods should remind us of the longstanding links between the two), Poovey's work makes clear that they are not just rhetorically related but intimately connected by means of their dual investment in the ideal of observational or spectatorial disinterest. As she notes in summarizing one of the major arguments of her text: "The first theme that recurs in *A History of the Modern Fact* centers on the vicissitudes of the concepts of 'interests,' 'interestedness,' and 'disinterestedness.' . . . By connecting this cluster of concerns to both reason-of-state arguments about government and theoretical defenses of liberalism and . . . what we think of as (scientific) impartiality . . . I have given interestedness and disinterestedness the prominent place I think these concepts deserve: at the intersection of political concerns about government and the epistemological stance we now call objectivity."[16] On all these points, Poovey seems right on the mark. What I want to add to her account, however, is that to refuse disinterestedness (to cultivate a posture of interestedness in the evident, to attend to the exceptional, to render a decision for the melancholy fact of history), is not necessarily to refuse either epistemology or cosmopolitanism (though it certainly is to refuse a liberal cosmopolitanism). Rather, it is to adopt an alternative mode of epistemological fiction making and to adopt a countercosmopolitanism, an alternate mode of inhabiting the planetary, a cosmopolitan interestedness.

On this point Julie Ellison's recent history of seventeenth- and eighteenth-century sensibility (*Cato's Tears and the Making of Anglo-American Emotion*) functions as an invaluable countertext to Poovey's history of the modern European fact.[17] For sensibility, sentiment, and melancholy, as Ellison makes clear, emerge in this period neither as a flight from knowledge or the cosmopolitan but as a self-consciously *interested*, while self-consciously *fanciful*, knowledge of the facts of modern European geopolitics. Interest, fancy, knowledge, geopolitics: These are the key words of Ellison's text. Or they are if we add one other which modifies each of these four: circum-Atlantic. Thus, circum-Atlantic interest, circum-Atlantic fancy, circum-Atlantic knowledge, and circum-Atlantic geopolitics: *the* crucial terms of what might be identified, thanks to Ellison, as the affective, aesthetic, epistemological, and political unconscious of the late-eighteenth-century "age of sensibility."

Whatever else it is, sensibility, as Ellison fairly conventionally argues, is interested. But, as she demonstrates, it is situationally and not just psychologically interested (as most standard accounts have it). As an experimental discourse on the other, that is, sensibility positions the interested subject in a not entirely solipsistic world, even when the act of imagining the (sufferings of an) other can be said primarily to shore up and enrich the imaginative self. In Spivak's terms, sensibility constitutes a supplementary worlding of the self. It supplements the self by investing the subject's interest in the world. But what world? By Ellison's account there are two worlds in which sensibility invests its interest: one world of noble equals (coterminous, though she does not make this point, with what Hegel identifies as the defenders of the properly premodern world of aristocratic right), whose sentimental investment in the restrained grandeur of one another's sorrows dominates British sensibility discourse through the duration of Pocock's republican period (which culminates somewhere between the Exclusion Crisis of 1679–81, the Glorious Revolution of 1688, and the signing of the Treaty of Utrecht in 1713), and a bourgeois world, one in which the newly powerful mercantile and financial classes that rose to dominance in British society in the decades following the Glorious Revolution assert their ethical superiority to their aristocratic rivals by demonstrating their capacity to share in (or, at least, remonstrate against) the sufferings of their unequal, lower-rank, fellows.

The post-1713 shift Ellison detects in sensibility discourse, a shift aesthetically marked by the difference between the stoic Roman plays of the late seventeenth century and early eighteenth—Nathaniel Lee's *Lucius Junius Brutus* (1680) and Addison's *Cato* (1713) are two of her key examples—and the late-eighteenth-century abolitionist verse of Anna Letitia Barbauld, Robert Southey, and William Cowper, thus constitutes more than the internal realignment of an aesthetic or affective mode. By plotting the transition from a political order predicated on the hegemony of aristocratic equals (whose individual members, in properly Hegelian fashion, recognize one another's equality, and thus the ontological coherence of their common class rank, by shedding tears, onstage and off, for the stoic suffering of their noble counterparts, friend or foe) to the hegemony of a world political system predicated on the enfranchisement of the bourgeoisie and, hence, on the recognition and the contractual management of inequality (between nobles, the bourgeoisie, and the lower orders), a renovated sensibility discourse also mirrors and helps to effect a transition in theories of governance from a neo-Machiavellian republicanism to a Lockean and Smithian version of liberalism. The bourgeoisie, by this account, not only usurp the aristocracy's political privileges over this crucial period in British history, they also seize control of the aristocracy's political theater of emotion.

In the process, however, the bourgeoisie refashion the ideology and the subject-object relations of that sentimental theater. No longer something traded between equals, and no longer an essentially conservative, aristocratic, and quasi-republican means of demonstrating virtue, sensibility now grounds a protoliberal politics of recognition. It becomes a way of recognizing that the very economic processes which permitted the bourgeoisie to displace the aristocracy have rendered the middle classes complicit with a system that extracts class privilege from the sufferings of a vast order of nonenfranchised others ("Seiz'd in thought, / On fancy's wild and roving wing I sail, / From the green borders of the peopled earth, / . . . To the dim verge, the suburbs of the system," Barbauld announces in "A Summer Evening's Meditation"[18]). To imagine, sympathize with, or invest interest in the sufferings of these dimly known ex-urban others thus constitutes both a recognition of systematicity per se ("sensibility is bound up with notions of interdependent structures and economies, the circulatory systems that no liberal author feels able to escape," Ellison notes, and thus it constitutes, one might say, an almost Marxian recognition that the individual is nothing but the sum total of his or her system of unequal relationships) and a means of imaginatively (representationally) enfranchising these others the system both exploits and leaves out.[19]

But if the world of liberal bourgeois sensibility is founded on (and repeatedly obliges itself to demonstrate its interest *in*) systematic inequality, it does not invest that interest at random. Rather, as Ellison demonstrates, later eighteenth- and nineteenth-century British sensibility most commonly expresses its sympathy for a determinate array of suffering others: chief among them the rural peasantry, the Celtic-fringe subjects of imperial rule, the Native American, and, above all, the slave. As sensibility becomes a means of recognizing (and guiltily worrying about) systemic inequality, in other words, some unequals turn out to be more (un)equal than others as some aspects (and *some* of the geopolitical extent and reach) of the system by which the bourgeoisie seized power return more regularly than others to haunt the political imaginary of the progressive middle class. Ellison contends that the primary boundaries of this real and imagined geopolitical system are circum-Atlantic, that eighteenth- and nineteenth-century British sensibility, no less than the financial, mercantile, and other capital revolutions that brought the British middle classes to power over the same period of time, are a product of the Atlantic world system, that, indeed, sensibility generates the discursive forms in which for many or even most Britons that Atlantic system makes itself and its effects rhetorically visible.

∗

Speculation and melancholy, the view from Exchange Alley and the view from the window: the plot and counterplot, I have been suggesting, of the long twentieth century. Ellison's argument is more historically confined and more generically specific. Nevertheless, it assumes a common dialectic. In the figures of the slave, the Highlander, the dispossessed rural peasantry, and the Native American, the melancholy realism of eighteenth- and early-nineteenth-century sensibility discourse discovers the traumatic geopolitical facts of a hypercapitalized, circum-Atlantic modernity; in the sympathy it invests in these figures, it expresses its sometimes melancholy, sometimes liberal, sometimes interested, sometimes disinterested, but always cosmopolitan objection.[20] In the image of the *Zong*'s massacre, I am suggesting, it intermittently finds a sort of negative apogee: a "black star of melancholy," a defining center of testamentary *interest*. But if the circum-Atlantic political unconscious of sensibility is thus interested and worldly (geopolitical), how does it also produce a type of knowledge rather than just an affective experience or mode of recognition? How, in other words, does sensibility convert its recognition of the world (system)—particularly the Atlantic world system—into a knowledge of that world? How does it assert for sympathy or melancholy not just an ethical but an epistemological claim? How does it derive from the traumatic fictions and scenes its assembles a knowledgeable arrangement of historical fact?

How does sensibility convert the melancholy scenes and images it assembles into a factual system of political knowledge? It does so, Ellison contends, by "fancy": a gendered and frequently perjorative emblem of the imagination, but also a figure, as she argues, granted specific and notable powers in romantic-era theories of poetic discourse.

Definitions of fancy catalog verbs for operations performed on images and ideas: associating, collecting, combining, embellishing, mixing. . . . Fancy enjoys mimicry, the exotic, nomadism, displacement, strangeness. . . . As a form of motion, fancy's spatial or geographical dimension connects it to the poetics of the prospect. The view from mental heights induces fancy to stage "the magnitude of prospect a rising empire displays" and then to entertain visions of imperial time ranging from elegy to celebration, from apocalypse to panegyric. In these historical or geographical prospects, fancy meets politics. The mental trajectory of the fanciful poet dramatizes an engagement with historical process. Situated in retirement but ascending to survey international or even cosmic change, these speakers often rely on the conventions of the poetry of rural retreat in order to launch a more inclusive perspective. Panoramas of the progress of empire and of poetry . . . bring into fancy's view vignettes of the national or racial other. And with the appearance of a stereotypical sufferer, fancy modulates into sensibility.[21]

How does this work? How does fancy seize a worldly vignette of (suffering) alterity and convert it into evidence for a systematically melancholy or sympathetic knowledge of the geopolitical? How, by the terms I earlier used, does fancy become sensibility's privileged mode of epistemological fiction making? How does it, sometimes, generate the melancholy fact(s) of history? To begin with, fancy must render the nonevident evident. Fancy, that is, must address the problem that plagued both Clarkson and Wilberforce; the problem that organizes the aesthetic protocols of the historical romance's politics of justice; the problem to which Adam Smith, in the more stoic passages of his *Theory of Moral Sentiments*, refused to attend. It must resolve the problem of a long-distance sympathy so extreme that the sufferings in which the observing self might invest its interest are not just unfamiliar but invisible ("miseries," as Smith put it, "which we never saw, which we never heard of, but which we may be assured are at all times infesting such numbers of our fellow-creatures"). And it must address this problem of historical witness bearing even if, or precisely if, to do so, to redefine sensibility not simply as "a [stoic] bond between elite males deeply but reticently involved in one another's humiliations and triumphs" but as a "downwardly directed" type of imaginative action-at-a-distance is, as Smith feared, "to render a certain melancholy dejection habitual to all men."[22]

Fancy, as Ellison suggests (and as the brief passage from Clarkson's *Essay* cited above indicates), resolves both this affective and this spectatorial dilemma through a perspectival conceit. It fashions for the mind of the observer a hypothetical space of poetic or fictional retreat from within which panoptically to survey the world. Barbauld's antislavery verse provides Ellison with her chief examples of this strategy. And a poem such as "A Summer Evening's Meditation," with its appeal ("Seiz'd in thought") to "fancy's wild and roving wing" on which the poet sails and which discloses to her eye not just the metropolitan center but "the dim verge, the suburbs of the system," certainly fits the bill.[23] As does, to an even more striking extent, her masterful history lyric, "Eighteen Hundred and Eleven," the melancholy apocalyptic lament on the state of England's turn of the century contemporaneity that James Chandler has identified as one of the singularly paradigmatic instances of a romantic historicism, and a poem which, as Ellison points out, "combines the tense connection between sensibility . . . system . . . [and] the power of fancy . . . through an explicitly trans-Atlantic vision."[24] "Where wanders Fancy down the lapse of years, / Shedding o'er imaged woes untimely tears?" Barbauld's poetic narrator demands. Panoptically in, over, and around the Napoleonic continent, the text replies, and then across the Atlantic ocean to the Americas where the "imaged woes" of the Napoleonic wars are intensified by fancy's long-distance apprehension of the fate of plantation slaves and Native Americans, whose "imaged" vignettes of suffering generate a systematic knowledge of empire: "Arts, arms, and wealth destroy the fruits they bring / . . . / With grandeur's growth the mass of misery grows."[25]

Barbauld, however, was by no means alone as a romantic poet of fancy, sensibility, and systematic, cosmopolitan, geopolitical knowledge and vision. Wordsworth, as Ellison again indicates, converted his interested reading of Samuel Hearne's *Journey from Prince of Wale's Fort in Hudson Bay to the Northern Ocean* (1795) into the fancifully sympathetic lyric "The Complaint of a Forsaken Indian Woman," whose melancholy exploration of imperial abandonment and humanity abandoned ("I should not feel the pain of dying, / Could I with thee a message send; / Too soon, my friends, ye went away; / For I had many things to say") adheres to the deathbed lyric formula that is also one of sensibility's paradigms.[26] More canonical Wordsworthian verses such as "The Ruined Cottage," as Alan Liu has shown, also link a "knowledge of humanity" and an informed, interested, "sense of history," to the ability to cultivate the "strange discipline" (as Wordsworth called it in the "Reconciling Addendum" to the poem) of reading a melancholy, local scene of ruin or suffering (in this case, Margaret's descent into absolute poverty following her abandonment by her husband) as evidence of a more systematic, if causally invisible, circum-Atlantic catastrophe.[27] The eminent bluestocking and educational reformer Hannah More revealed herself, too, no stranger to the fanciful world of sympathetic and circum-Atlantic interestedness in her influential abolitionist lyric "Slavery, A Poem" (1788), a text strongly reminiscent of, and quite possibly indebted to, Clarkson's "imaginary [but for all that, *factual*] scene" of West African enslavement:

> When'er to Afric's shores I turn my eye,
> Horrors of deepest, deadliest guilt arise;
> I see, by more than Fancy's mirror shown,
> The burning village and the blazing town:
> See the dire victim torn from social life,
> The shrieking babe, the agonizing wife!
> She, wretch forlorn! is dragg'd by hostile hands,
> To distant tyrants sold, in distant lands.[28]

Fancy, interest, witness, and the problem of long-distance suffering are here conjoined in an almost formulaic manner to a systematic knowledge of what, in Althusserian terms, we might think of as the otherwise absent (or invisible) cause of imperial wealth and the otherwise absent or invisible effects (facts) of that insular enrichment.

And then there is William Cowper, a poet Ellison does not discuss, perhaps because his antislavery verse, though celebrated in his lifetime (Cowper's 1793 poem "The Negro's Complaint," subsequently set to music and multiply reproduced in pamphlet form, soon became the virtual ballad of the abolition movement in England), comprises a distinctly minor part of his oeuvre. But even in his more canonical writings Cowper proved himself an entirely geopolitical poet of fancy, perhaps even the foremost romantic poet for whom fancy licensed a worldly observation of global history from within a melancholy hideout of retreat. As Kevis Goodman has recently argued, two of the most celebrated lines from Cowper's "The Task" ("T'is pleasant through the loophole of retreat / To peep at such a world")[29] have historically been misinterpreted, and not only because the pleasure Cowper here admits is a distinctly melancholy pleasure but also because "the ambiguous genitive 'of' [has been] understood as a designation of description rather than possession, so that the poet's 'loophole' out of the turbulent world becomes his Olney retreat . . . and cultivation of a self."[30] As Goodman points out, however, the loophole of retreat is equally susceptible to being read as naming an "aperture, channel, or passageway" cut out of the space of retreat, and virtually demands that reading when we recall that the line exists as a gloss on an extended meditation (a "brown study" as Cowper called it) on the poet's own paralyzing melancholy and a subsequent rumination (which Coleridge was to adopt virtually wholesale in "Frost at Midnight") on the compensatory profit to thought of such a condition of melancholy and cognitive indolence:

> . . . such a gloom
> Suits well the thoughtful or unthinking mind.
> . . . I am conscious and confess
> Fearless, a soul that does not always think.
> Me oft has fancy ludicrous and wild
> Sooth'd with a waking dream of houses, tow'rs,
> Trees, churches, and strange visages express'd
> In the red cinders . . .
> Nor less amus'd have I quiescent watch'd
> The sooty films that play upon the bars,
> Pendulous and foreboding, in the view
> Of superstition prophesying still
> Though still deceiv'd, some stranger's near approach.
> 'Tis thus the understanding takes repose
> In indolent vacuity of thought . . .[31]

Turned by gloom in upon itself, the poet's mind encounters both its own "indolent vacuity of thought," its "unthinking" thoughtfulness, *and*, as Goodman stresses, a world outside that presses in on the "bars," window, or "loophole" of this retreat in the form of a "stranger's near approach." Turning in upon itself, in other words, the "indolent" mind of romanticism here finds a space from within which fancifully to open itself out onto the world, not just any world but a world of approaching strangers, a nonfamiliar, noninsular, nonsolipsistic world of others at the window.

But what strangers? For Cowper, Goodman argues, these fancied strangers are the subjects of empire brought to the poet's attention by the newspapers he obsessively read and from which he produced his own sustained variation on modern melancholy's otherwise typically novelistic tendency to romance the news. She suggests that in the passage I have just cited, Cowper was quite likely thinking of Omai, the Tahitian islander brought to England in 1774 and then returned to the South Seas in 1776: "Methinks I see thee straying on the beach," Cowper had earlier apostrophized Omai,

> I see thee weep, and thine are honest tears,
> A patriot's for his country. Thou art sad
> At thought of her forlorn and abject state,
> From which no power of thine can raise her up.

Thus fancy paints thee, and though apt to err,
Perhaps errs little when she paints thee thus.[32]

If Cowper was again thinking of Omai in the brown study, and thus again pondering the degree to which fancy could be said to ground a truth claim (if fancy can depict ["paint"] truth even when erring, these passages from "The Task," together with the fuller romantic history of fanciful discourse imply, it is because to err is perhaps not so much to be in error as to be errant, in flight, in movement across the world),[33] then it is nevertheless significant that here Cowper paints the imperial subaltern under the more general guise of the stranger. For it is that generic (systematized) stranger whose near approach to the world-consuming eye of fancy — like the near approach of the contemporaneous scientific observer to the revealed facts of the natural world — allows Cowper to effect the epistemological transition from the perception of an evident and melancholy singular to a more systematic knowledge of worldly things as they are. Retreating to the gloomy abode of melancholy, fancy, in absolutely paradigmatic fashion, here carves out for the thoughtful mind a place from within which to regard the world, to countenance its near approach, to interest itself in that world's forlorn and abject state, to invest the melancholy observer's sympathy in the world's imaged woes, and so to paint into sight and into knowledge the sufferings "which we never saw . . . but which we may be assured are at all times infesting such numbers of our fellow creatures."[34]

*

To conclude this pastiche of sensibility discourse with Adam Smith's words may seem a little unfair, or even inaccurate, but perhaps only partially so. For even though for Smith, as Ellison argues, sentiment is ultimately stoic rather than melancholy, ultimately constitutive of an ideal spectatorial type (the quasi-republican, quasi-Roman type of the disinterested spectator to history) rather than productive of a historically incorporative melancholy without limit and without end, it is also, at times, dejected, immiserated, and fanciful. And what else could it be, at least occasionally, for one of the founding figures of modern liberal thought? What else, if Ellison's schema is correct, could sympathy at least intermittently induce in the great theorist of modern political economy but a melancholy and dejected habit of mind as that mind sets as *its* great task the panoptic and global mapping of the system of capital? But *is* liberalism (even of a limited, Smithian, sort; even for such an influential celebrant of the market) melancholy? Or, at the very least, is it inevitably haunted by the unquiet ghost of melancholy? Certainly liberalism is constitutively guilty in conscience. And by identifying sentiment as a sufficient internal governing constraint on the greater excesses of the market and the systemic suffering it breeds, Smith's *Theory of Moral Sentiments* might well be read as an attempt to sketch out, in advance, a systematic rejoinder to conscience's guilty moral objections to the ode to system he was to pen in *The Wealth of Nations*. Which does not mean that Smith is willing to risk Barbauld's or Cowper's systematic perspective. For as a theorist of sentiment, at least, Smith insists that systemic thought must rein itself in, must refuse the vision of "the miseries we never saw," must limit itself countersystematically to the immediate, local, and immediately visible effects of an imperializing capitalism if the mind of capital is not to find itself paralyzed by a global knowledge and vision of capital's systematically produced social effects, and so thrown into a gloomy and habitual state of melancholy dejection. The more he commands a global knowledge of capital, in other words, the more Smith demands a parochial territory of moral vision and knowledge, and the more he recommends to the agents of capital a restrained, stoic habit of sympathizing with a limited set of others and to the subjects of capital, a stoic response to the fact of their own suffering.

Which does not mean that a Smithian knowledge of capital does not, *in fact*, know the suffering capital effects. *That* is the fantasy. As Smith's insistence that only a direct experience of vision can ground a knowledge of suffering is his eminently contradictory way of keeping that fantasy in place (why contradictory? because here, on the question of human suffering, Smith admits the existence only of the palpably, visually evident, where otherwise, on the question of the market, Smith makes clear that political economy's descriptive and explanatory power depends for *its* existence on the existence of the nonvisible, the abstract, the hidden-handedly imaginary). But as Smith is obliged to admit, even the "miseries we never saw" are miseries we nevertheless know to be; miseries we "may be assured" are "infesting such numbers of our fellow creatures." The mind of capital may refuse to see, may refuse to admit into evidence what imagination forces it to know; or, barring that, it may choose to neutralize the ethical burden of such knowledge by collapsing all the system's imaged miseries into a dispassionate, disinterested, actuarial science of aggregates, averages, and such numbers. ("Take the whole world at an average," Smith's *Theory* advises those inclined to take a global "interest in the fortune" of others: "for one man who suffers pain or misery, you will find twenty in prosperity and joy, or at least in tolerable circumstances. No reason can be assigned why we should rather weep with the one than rejoice with the twenty. . . . All men, even those at the greatest distance, are no doubt entitled to our good wishes. . . . But if, notwithstanding, they should be unfortunate, to give ourselves any anxiety upon that account, seems to be no part of our duty.")[35] But however systematically such an actuarializing discourse of stoic disinterestedness averages the world (the only law operative in the *Zong* trials, it hardly bears repeating, was not a law of melancholy property but the law of the average), Smith cannot wholly avoid revealing that such (speculative) numbers do not precede but succeed and constitutively repress the melancholy facts (the knowledge of the "one") they cannot afford to recognize; that such disinterest (such an actuarial rather than a melancholy realism) covers, and is a way of abjecting, a prior, dejected, systematic (that is, by the terms of romantic discourse, a fanciful) knowledge and vision of history.

Take as initial evidence of this claim a crucial passage in the early chapters of *The Theory of Moral Sentiments* in which Smith clarifies his conception of the imagination: "It is by changing places in fancy with the sufferer that we come to conceive or be affected by what he feels."[36] This, as we cannot now avoid recognizing, is anything but a throwaway line. Smith here not only admits fancy, he enshrines it at the heart of European modernity's sympathetic imagination. The five hundred pages of *The Theory of Moral Sentiments* that follow read, in part, as an elaborate attempt to disavow that disabling first admission. The romantic discourse of sympathy (both poetic and novelistic) that flourished in the half century following the text's publication might be read, oppositely, as an effort to make good on this dejected promise. Both attempts succeeded after their own fashion. Smith, certainly, is not included in Ellison's list of the rhetoricians of sympathetic fancy, and on balance he doesn't seem to belong there. But if Smith attempted to close the door on melancholy fancy, if he tried to paper over that loophole in the sentimental retreat with his science of averages, aggregates, and numbers, he had also opened it. And it is to that door he opened into the melancholy dark, that door on the miseries we never saw but which we know to exist, that I now wish to turn. For it is this opening on suffering, this aperture on history, that I believe frames Solicitor Haywood's view from the window, as it frames the view of the historical romance and the romantic history lyric, informs Clarkson's imaginary scenes strictly consistent with fact, illuminates Wilberforce's actual visions of the "real horrors of the Traffick," and ultimately limns Turner's dark vision of the gloomy facts of Atlantic history and all those subsequent works (abolitionist and postabolitionist) which have come to know the *Zong* (and by knowing the *Zong* to know, or claim to know, the melancholy truth of modernity as it actually exists) by bearing a simultaneously, impossibly, interested, and disinterested witness to the horrors made visible on the surface of Turner's canvas. Which is perhaps simply another way of saying that if we are to discover how what I have been provisionally holding together as the melancholy *or* sentimental fact actually incorporates two types of fact and implies two ways of being in the world, two types of cosmopolitanism, it is to Smith's *Theory of Moral Sentiments* and the schizophrenic spectator who is the odd hero of that text that we must turn.

this is

not was

or

should be

this be

not

should be

this

should

not

be

is

—M. NourbeSe Philip, from *Zong! #4*

CHAPTER 9

The Imaginary Resentment of the Dead

A THEORY OF MELANCHOLY SENTIMENT

The above title, as one might now expect, is drawn from Smith's 1759 *Theory of Moral Sentiments*.[1] Quoted thus, Smith's text expresses its more than passing interest in the sentimental affections of the dead. But it is not the dead in whom Smith, in this work, is primarily interested. Rather, it is the living — who, in the full passage from which this citation is drawn, displace the dead as the primary object of Smith's attention by taking upon themselves the resentment of the slain as if it were their own (that is, by imagining it) — with whom he is principally concerned. Or, to be more precise, it is not the living as *living* in whom he is interested but the living as watching, observing; the living as "spectators" of the suffering of the dead. Indeed, as much as it is a theory of the operations of sentiment, Smith's text is also, perhaps even preeminently, a theory of what it means to be a historical spectator. And it is primarily as a theory of the spectator that I am interested in Smith's work, in large part because it is as a problem and through a practice of spectation that what I have been calling the melancholy fact of history exerts its claim on a late-eighteenth- and early-nineteenth-century romantic counterknowledge of the modern, and that the larger melancholy circum-Atlantic counterdiscourse of modernity and the witness with which I am concerned seeks to articulate its oppositionality to finance capital's discourse of speculation.

As Kant's writings on the philosophy of history make clear, however, Enlightenment speculation is equally invested in the figure of the spectator. Perhaps a better way to put things, then, is to suggest that just as modernity's speculative and melancholy discourses jointly invest in the category of the imagination and its cognates (what "imaginary value" and "evidence" are to such speculative discourse so equally and oppositely, I am suggesting, "imaginative sympathy" and the "evident" are to melancholy), they also find as one of their sites of antagonistic conjunction the figure of the spectator. As Spivak's serially foreclosed and disclosed "native informant" is to her long-durational history of the vanishing present and the "master texts of the Atlantic tradition," so, indeed, is this figure (in both its "disinterested," speculative, Enlightenment guise and in its haunted, witness-bearing, melancholy incarnation) to my account of an internally fissured, doubly self-conscious, simultaneously and antagonistically speculative and melancholy Atlantic modernity.

As anatomized by Smith in his *Theory of Moral Sentiments*, this doubly capable "spectator" is the genealogical progenitor of more than Solicitor Haywood's twin and opposite models of the observer (the "cool brute," and the aggrieved expostulator of "the language of humanity") or even of the wavering protagonists of Scott's historical romances. This spectator is also the source of a speculative and a melancholy modernity's two versions of the historical witness, the precursor to the two versions of the "judge" before whom occidental modernity understands itself to appear and in whom it invests the right to evaluate the consequences of its own unfolding. In its "disinterested" form (as the objective collector and judge of an abstract assemblage of historical facts) Smith's spectator functions as the late-eighteenth-century ancestor of the impartial juridical "third" Alexander Kojève will derive from Hegel's Scottish Enlightenment inspired *Phenomenology of Spirit* and *Philosophy of Right*: the neutral historical third party on whose existence, Kojève argues, the ultimate appearance of Hegel's "end of history," "homogeneous and universal state" depends.[2] In its melancholy-sentimental form (as an injured property holder in the traumatic facts of modernity) this sympathetic spectator prefigures, oppositely, the disclosure, at one end of the long twentieth century, of the witness Solicitor Haywood hoped to introduce to Lord Mansfield's courtroom, and, at the other, of Derrida's third, his counter-Kojèvean witness "terstis/superestes" whose task it is to offer a statement of the debt the living owe to the dead and, in so doing, to bear witness to the ethical imperative of holding *to* and taking some melancholy property *in* the historical traumas by which occidental modernity has repeatedly secured its conditions of arrival.

But that is the end of the story I want to tell, and we are still at one of the points of beginning, still back with Smith and his as-yet-unopened *Theory of Moral Sentiments*. Smith may seem like an unlikely candidate for the role I am assigning him, and certainly, as I have indicated, in his more famous role as an observer of political economy, the historical spectator Smith imagines seems to hold out little hope of grounding both a theory *and* a critique of capitalized modernity, both an account of a speculative and a melancholy apperception of the constitutive facts of modern European and circum-Atlantic history. But it is precisely because Smith holds the historical spectator he posits in *The Theory of Moral Sentiments* (however briefly and provisionally) to the dual demands of interest and disinterestedness, of melancholy and abstract judgment, of a speculative and a melancholy cosmopolitanism, that Smith's work must be reckoned with. In the 1759 text of *The Theory of Moral Sentiments* the spectator portrays in miniature the dual path of its future career: it appears, that is, in all its supplementary splendor, in the fullness of its self-relating difference as both the melancholy and the disinterested judge of humanity, as both a creature of interest and a model of detachment, as both the spokesperson of a romantic language of humanity and as the cool brute of a Kantian system of judgment.

*

The spectator does not appear, as such, in the opening pages of *The Theory of Moral Sentiments*. But though Smith's man of "principles" briefly awaits a definitional reappearance as the historical "spectator," it is as a beholder, witness, observer, onlooker, and judge of the "sorrows" of "others" that Smith's ethical subject appears from the first pages of his text.[3] Smith is not Levinas, but from the opening pages of this text, ethics (if ethics is construed as an attending to the fact, fate, and presence of an other) certainly ranks as first philosophy for this founding figure of the Scottish Enlightenment. By which I do not mean to imply that Smith explicitly identifies the text's interests as ethical. Rather, *The Theory of Moral Sentiments* postulates itself as a discourse alternately (and, ultimately, interchangeably) on propriety and justice. Indeed, sentiment is of interest to Smith not only because it binds us to the affairs of an other but because in being so bound we develop a concern for the just treatment of others. Law may regulate the dispensation of justice but, for Smith, it is sentiment that inspires a passion *for* justice. Sentiment is thus for him a "social passion,"[4] one on which both the cohesion and the ethical self-relating of society depends. Sentiment at first glance then represents the very opposite of the self-interest on which, in *The Wealth of Nations*, Smith would subsequently argue the economic well-being of society is grounded. Indeed, in a concluding section of *The Theory of Moral Sentiments* on systems of approbation (approbation and disapprobation are, in Smith's terms, the forms of reward and punishment by which social justice is meted out), he offers a brief but spirited reading of Mandeville's *Fable of the Bees* to explicitly reject the possibility that a system of justice can be "deduced" from the principle of "self-love." As a "social" rather than a merely personal passion (as, that is, an ethical construct), Smithian sentiment, as I earlier suggested, can thus be seen as something like an antidote, countermeasure, or restraining influence woven into the social fabric of an otherwise necessarily self-interested society; a means of limiting the untrammeled self-interest of those social agents who otherwise appear in Smith's work as actors in the market; an analogue to, or perhaps a substitute for, those minimal regulatory procedures by which classical liberal political philosophy will attempt to constrain the operations of laissez-faire capital.[5]

If sentiment inspires a passion for justice, sentiment also has its own internal economy, an internal system of measuring, valuing, and distributing the social passions. This is what Smith calls "propriety," and if sentiment can be said to represent something like the humanization of capital, then propriety certainly represents the capitalization of sentiment. By Smith's terms propriety is that which regulates the system of justice sentiment inspires by first determining the value or magnitude of some or other experience of unjust suffering and then fixing the appropriate magnitude of society's response to that injustice. It ensures that a system of justice's compensatory response to injustice be strictly equal to the value or magnitude of the injustice that has been observed. In this sense, Smith's propriety (and it is revealing that the entire first section of *The Theory of Moral Sentiments* is framed as a discourse on propriety) operates as something like justice's price mechanism. And it is because Smith is ultimately most interested in the equitable economic functioning of this ethical price mechanism, or, to borrow another set of terms from his more famous lexicon, because he is primarily interested in the "nominal" as opposed to the "real" value of the suffering of others, that his *Theory* is ultimately conducive to rather than critical of the general operations of capital and to the ever-greater epistemological expansion of capitalism's market of abstract and equivalent values.[6]

Before sentiment can be regulated, however, it must be generated. And it is on this point that Smith provisionally strays into melancholy and romantic territory. For while the sentiments of approbation and disapprobation are ultimately to find themselves regulated by propriety's price mechanism, neither sentiment can first exist without the free play of the imagination. How do we relate ourselves to the sufferings of an other? How, in Smith's terms, do we "place ourselves in his situation . . . and become in some measure the same person with him?" Through "the imagination only."[7] I commented in the first section of this book on the ways in which the network of co-lateral social identifications through which a credit economy expresses itself depend on the imaginary coidentification of subjects with one another by means of their mutual confirmation of the real existence of imaginary objects and values. Where finance capital thus depends on the power of the imagination to affirm the real existence of imaginary values and imaginary social relations, and, like commodity capital, thus manages, as Lukács has it, to reify social consciousness (though here it does so by redefining the relations between subjects as a set of relationships not to commodified objects but to imaginary values),[8] in the opening pages of his text, Smith expresses his interest in an alternative, melancholy, protoromantic mode of imaginary coidentification. But where finance capital invests the social body in imaginary values (such as the insurance or stock average), such romantic sentimentalism trades in imaginative sympathy. In either case, however, it is not only the affections of the social body which are at stake but, as a way of securing those affections, the fate and disposition of the imagination. If the speculative and the melancholy operate as antagonistic secret sharers of modernity not by articulating radically unlike discourses on and of modernity but by competing with one another for control of the same discursive territory, then Smith's text allows us more specifically to see that speculation and melancholy stage their struggle for the soul of occidental modernity, at least in part, by wrestling for possession of the imagination.

*

And it is because the case of the *Zong* not only exemplifies but so repeatedly occupies that scene of struggle that I am continuing to hold it out as one of an Atlantic and occidental modernity's truth events and test cases. Appealing to the Lords Commissioners of the Admiralty to cast their eye on the events of this case, Sharp demanded that it be considered exactly thus. What will the verdict be? Imaginary value or imaginative sympathy? Disinterested propriety or aggrieved sentiment? The view from Exchange Alley or the view from the window?

*

Smith, obviously enough, was not thinking of the *Zong* massacre in 1759, but he was, as Robert Mitchell has convincingly argued, thinking of another historical event: the 1745 rebellion of the Stuart Pretender against the English throne and the subsequent subjugation of the Highlands and round of public executions which followed on this failed revolt.[9] This is worth noting not only because the still-fresh material consequences and psychical wounds of "the forty five" lend a historical urgency to Smith's text while also helping to explain the work's recurrent fascination with scenes of torture and death, but also because as a work written simultaneously as a response to a specific historical event, as a general theory of how to respond to the spectacle of historical events, and as a treatise on the relation between the historical event and the human imagination, Smith's *Theory* codes deeply within its conception of the imagination and passes on to its inheritor texts the unresolved contradiction of its own dual relation to a singular historical occasion of address and a universalizing dehistoricized grammar of thought. Among these texts is Hegel's *Phenomenology of Spirit*, a work haunted by a crowd of historical events it proves itself reluctant to name (among them, as Susan Buck-Morss has argued, not only the French but the Haitian revolutions), as are Scott's novels and Turner's slave-ship canvas — a painting, as I have noted, which Turner produced after a long collaboration with Scott. If it is, as we shall thus later see, ultimately unsurprising that Turner came to depict the *Zong* massacre as if it were a scene from one of Scott's historical novels, then it is also unsurprising that, like Scott, Turner came to see (and to invite his audience to see) such an event from the twin spectatorial positions outlined in Smith's *Theory*. Which is another way of saying that if Turner (and those who have come to know the *Zong* massacre primarily through the mediating surface of his canvas) saw that event *as* Scott and Smith had seen the Pretender's revolt and the subsequent subjugation of the Highlands, then like Smith's *Theory* and Scott's historical novels, Turner's history painting strongly suggests that whatever ability the belated reader or spectator might have to sympathize with the sufferings of such rebels and victims of empire (and so to come into sympathetic solidarity with all those others equally affected by such visions of suffering) ultimately depends on the simultaneously interested and disinterested operations of the sentimental imagination.

*

That sentiment and a sentimental knowledge of the facts of history are, for Smith, a function of the imagination is apparent from the first page of his text:

> Though our brother is upon the rack, as long as we ourselves are at our ease, our senses will never inform us of what he suffers. They never did, and never can, carry us beyond our own person, and it is by the imagination only that we can form any conception of what are his sensations.

> By the imagination we place ourselves in his situation, we enter as it were into his body, and become in some measure the same person with him.[10]

The import of these passages seems fairly clear, and though they do not yet introduce the figure of the spectator by name (that will happen on the next page), they contain in outline the basic structure of Smith's *Theory*: "We" (or, as Smith has it on the following page, the "attentive spectator") are carried beyond ourselves into the "place" or "situation" of another by the "imagination" and come thus to sympathize with that suffering other, with all those others equally affected by the witness of such suffering, and (as the subsequent chapters indicate) to desire a just (that is, and crucially so, an *equitable*) response to his suffering. But, of course, it is not as simple as that, not only because it is not yet clear what Smith means by the "imagination" but also, to pause over a not insignificant trifle, because of Smith's odd but revealing use of the preposition in the concluding clause of the final sentence I have cited.

What model of the imagination does Smith have in mind? What does he intend by arguing that the imagination allows us to "become in some measure the same person *with*" (rather than the more grammatically predictable "the same person *as*") the suffering other we observe? The second question contains the beginning of an answer to the first. Whatever the imagination is, however dramatically it permits us to displace ourselves from ourselves and to enter into or to place ourselves in the situation of another, the imagination is not that which threatens to erase or annul the self. Smith's imagination is instead less a switching than a multiplying mechanism, less that which exchanges than that which quantitatively expands the self. It does not cause us to reconceive ourselves (even momentarily) *as* another but, rather, permits us to exist in solidarity *with* another and, more importantly still, with all the other witnesses to this other's suffering. And if this is one way of allying the imagination with the fundamental philosophical project of political liberalism, if, in fact, this begins to sound rather exactly like an anticipatory version of a neo-liberal, Rortian conception of solidarity, then, perhaps unsurprisingly, it also sounds rather like the fundamental formula for capitalism. For though the economy of the imagination appears at first glance to be devoted less to an act of exchange than to the generation of surplus, it is in fact quite precisely *through* the mechanism of exchange that the imagination generates its subjective surplus. Were we to substitute the notations s (self), ɪ (imagination), s′ (the self plus) for Marx's ᴍᴄᴍ′, we would have a pretty accurate description of Smith's formula — sɪs′: the self, through the operations of the imagination, generates the self "plus."

Or, to put things another way: where the ethical demand the sentimental imagination appears to make on us is that we place ourselves at risk, that we risk the "self" in changing places with another, sentimental risk (as in Smith's own later theories of capital risk) is in fact not so much that which endangers the self as the necessary precondition to the self's enrichment. And unlike prior theories of ethical action, unlike, for instance, the Christian imperative to bodily take on the suffering of another that Smith appears to be subtly reformulating, the risk here is wholly imaginary even while the reward (the promise of a better, enriched, communitarian self) remains the same. The imagination, indeed, simultaneously short circuits and safeguards the entire process: it permits the self, that is, to make a purely speculative investment in the suffering of another without ever having to abandon the safety of its purely spectatorial position. Enriched rather than endangered by the imaginative stock it takes in the fate of another, Smith's Scottish Enlightenment spectator is thus not so unlike the "sophisters, oeconomists, and calculators" Edmund Burke discerned governing the affairs of the continental Enlightenment. In either case, as Burke had it, "at the end of every visto, you see nothing but a gallows." The difference, of course, is that for Smith's sentimental spectator the sight of the gallows is the source of the self's speculative enrichment and not the fate to which it is unwittingly handing itself over.[11]

But is the difference in fact that marked? Perhaps not, for while Smith's enriched, surplus subject s′ appears to be the very opposite of the cancelled Enlightenment subject $ that Slavoj Žižek, in one of his more Burkean moments, derives from his reading of Kant and Hegel, the path from the one to the other, from the surplus to the cancelled self, or, indeed, from Smith's attentive to Kant's disinterested spectator is not that great. This is so for at least three reasons, each of which has to do with the ways the imagination operates in Smith's *Theory*, where it appears not only as a mechanism for subjective enrichment but as a mode of abstraction and typification and as a means of access to the sublime. In the formula I used above (sIS'), the imagination mediates the self's relation to itself and generates what I have been calling the subjective surplus of sympathy. But the imagination clearly mediates more than this: it not only relates the self to its own enrichment, it also mediates the self's relation to the historical event and to a type of social existence. The social actors in Smith's text—his "men of principle," the fellowship of moral agents who make up the community of his "we"—seem to be clearly embedded in history, seem indeed to inhabit a historical moment of a particular sort, to dwell within a world of suffering bodies, of "brothers upon the rack," of men "oppressed and injured by another." Theirs is a world of "the injured [who have] perish[ed] in the struggle," and of the "deformed and mangled carcas[ses] of the slain."[12] It is, in short, the Scottish world savaged by the English crown in its response to the 1745 insurrection. Or that, at least, appears to be the historical correlate of the universe of suffering and death Smith's "melancholy" subjects inhabit. But if this is the historical landscape in which both Smith and the brotherhood of readers he invokes dwell, then that landscape, the injured and moribund bodies that fill it, and the historical event that produced it, are available to the reader of Smith's text not immediately but imaginatively, not materially but (by means of an imaginative allegoresis) abstractly.

The historical, Smith's text implies, can be accessed only at a spectatorial remove that the imagination does not so much bridge as create. It can be apprehended solely as a speculative allegory the imagination does not so much decode as fabricate. The sIS' formula I have been using might thus be reunderstood as one that elaborates a second function for the imagination, one that identifies the imagination not only as the source of the self's enrichment but as the mechanism by which history is reproduced as allegorical spectacle (Self–Imagination–Spectacle). For it is through that very process by which the imagination enriches the observing self that the imagination also produces the immaterial spectacle of history: *as* the substance of the self's enrichment, *as* the allegorical dividend the imagination returns on the self's willingness to "risk" an affective investment in history. If the imagination allows us to enter into the historical world and to demonstrate some sympathy toward those who have suffered its violence, then it is also the imagination that, for Smith, abstracts that world, strips it of its historical specificity, allegorizes it. And it is this that accounts for the strange fact that the '45 is both everywhere and nowhere in Smith's *Theory*: behind every scene of torture, every glimpse of anguish, every sight of the body injured and the body slain, *and* admitted by none of these traumatic images, named by none of them, *singularly* nonexistent, evident, at best, as a piece of speculative evidence. Like the *Zong* massacre in Turner's sentimental canvas (or, as Buck-Morss has argued, the Haitian Revolution in Hegel's *Phenomenology*),[13] the melancholy "fact" of the '45 survives its imaginative reconstitution in Smith's *Theory* as the merest and most entire abstraction of itself, as an allegory of the event, as a Jamesonian "specter of historicity." Mediating our grasp of the historical event, Smith's sentimental imagination thus delivers history to us only at the expense of stripping it of all that is specific to it; of exchanging its real for its nominal value and mode of appearance; of transforming a singular melancholy fact or event within the history of empire into an occasion for the production of theoretical discourse and those speculative, surplus, and exchangeable abstractions (sympathy, sentiment, the imagination) that are eighteenth-century theoretical discourse's stock-in-trade.

Smith's imagination may abstract the speculative (in this case, the speculations that constitute his *Theory*) from the allegorized spectacle of the historical event, but the process does not stop there. For as the imagination relates an observing self to the spectacle of history, it also doubles back to reconstitute that observing self as a social type. The imagination, that is, both abstracts the spectacle and the speculative from the event and typicalizes the subject as an interchangeable consumer of that spectacle. And it is on this score that Smith's enriched and Žižek's cancelled subjects begin most to resemble one another. The sis′ formula I have been using functions, in other words, as shorthand for the self's enrichment by means of its imaginary investment in event history; as a way of noting the imagination's allegorical reconstitution of event history as historical spectacle; and as a code for the imagination's ultimate reconstitution of the unique observing self as a representative and reproducible social type: the type of the spectator. The self, thus, does ultimately find itself imaginatively negated by its investment of sympathy. It finds its singularity annulled as it is reconstituted in the form of the typical (bourgeois, "disinterested") spectator.[14] If Žižek's $ is made to denote that unique self cancelled and refashioned as the abstract spectator, we then have a final restating of the sis′ formula with which I began: si$ = Self–Imagination–Spectator.

While the self I have extrapolated from Smith's theory of sentiment is simultaneously reconstituted by the imagination as ethically enriched, abstractly speculative, and typically spectatorial, it is also, by virtue of being all three of these things at once, at least one other. It is sublime, and sublime in an almost exact, proleptically uncanny, Kantian sense. Indeed, the subject of the Kantian sublime (or at least that "disinterested" subject of the historical sublime that emerges from a cross-reading of Kant's *Critique of Judgment* and his "Conflict of the Faculties" essays of the 1780s and 1790s), is, formally at least, a virtual analogue — counterintuitive as this may seem — of the sympathetic subject of Smith's *Theory of Moral Sentiments*. For what else is Kant's historical sublime than a way of describing that putatively risky but ultimately rewarding experience by which the self, exposed to the terrifying spectacle of historical events, "deeds," and "crimes," survives the shocking appearance of such historical traumas by discovering that the secret of such events is not material to their particularity but to the mode of thought of the spectator who becomes aware of them and who, becoming thus aware, comes to recognize in itself the capacity to invest a disinterested sympathy in the idea of humanity at large, and so to emerge ethically enriched by its speculative consumption of the spectacle of abstract historicity? Read thus, it is no surprise that Kant's theory of the historical event ultimately reformulates itself, like Smith's *Theory*, as a discourse on the thoughtlife of the spectator and the desirability of effecting a global dissemination not of the specific actions or events of the French Revolution but of its imagistic spectacle and of its properly disinterested spectators, or that, by the closing chapters of his text, Smith's attentive spectator has been replaced by the still more proprietous (and no less sublime) figure of the impartial and the indifferent spectator.[15]

*

I have come a long way from my original suggestion that Smith's *Theory* details the emergence of a historical spectator equally foundational to a speculative *and* a melancholy discourse on and of modernity, equally attuned, in my shorthand, to the view from Exchange Alley *and* the view from the window, equally foundational to the emergence of the speculative *and* the melancholy "facts" of history. The imaginary investments of the Smithian spectator I have thus far sketched are all in the epistemological domain of the speculative, in its unbroken sovereignty over the thoughtworlds and affective dispositions of the modern. It is my sense that this is finally where Smith's sympathies lead him, that he is, at the last, a theorist of the speculative far more than he is an apologist of the melancholy. In Ellison's terms, Smith's spectator is finally of the party of Cato rather than, say, Antigone, far more a neorepublican emblem of restrained civic virtue than a representative of an emergent habit of romantic melancholy. But, as I have also mentioned, his *Theory of Moral Sentiments* is nothing if not a schizophrenic text. For if his spectator is ultimately modeled on a stoic Roman original, then there is also the shadow of a less temperate Greek progenitor lurking in the background of his text. If not Sophocles, then Longinus. And where Cato signifies that posture of heroic restraint in the face of historical suffering and political injustice that Smith ultimately wished to inculcate in his readers, the ghost of Longinus, or at least the ghost of a type of Longinian exploration of the passions, is important to Smith because it provides him with the classical rhetorical cover from within which to investigate the experimental moral states that were also central to his work and to the larger project of Scottish Enlightenment moral philosophy.

This is nowhere more evident than in the dual versions of the sublime to which Smith's text demonstrates its loyalties and the two versions of the spectator it adduces from these two versions of the sublime. Anticipatorily like Kant, Smith's *Theory* is no less (if, therefore, entirely contradictorily) indebted to Longinus and that Longinian version of the sublime which, at the time of Smith's writing, was experiencing a pronounced critical, pedagogical, and publishing revival. By the mid–eighteenth century, spurred by Nicolas Boileau's 1674 French translation of Longinus's treatise, there were at least three English translations and a significantly greater number of editions of "On the Sublime" in circulation in Britain. As Ian Simpson Ross indicates in his biography of Smith, Smith's knowledge of Longinus (to whom he refers in his lectures on rhetoric of both 1762 and 1763) would have been supplemented by the movement in Edinburgh to produce within Scotland's universities a "New Rhetoric" similar to that "based on the finest precepts of Aristotle, Cicero, Quintilian, Lucian, Longinus and other famous authors" which Fenelon had established in France (William Stevenson had translated Fenelon's *Dialogues concerning Eloquence* in 1722).[16] By the beginning of the next century both Coleridge and Wordsworth were heatedly addressing Longinus's treatise in both published essays and personal correspondence.

Critical orthodoxy has long taken as the heart of Longinus's conception of the sublime that experience of transport which the Greek philosopher argued defined the reader's or auditor's response to sublime poetry and speech ("As if instinctively, our soul is uplifted by the true sublime; it takes a proud flight, and is filled with joy or vaunting, as though it had itself produced what it has heard").[17] But it is the epistemological conceit subsequent to the moment of transport — the conceit that permits the reader or auditor to believe that what they have come to know through the aesthetic labors of another is, in fact, something they have caused to be, the conceit that allows the subject of the sublime to come to knowledge of itself as one who has "itself produced what it has heard" — that has the greatest resonance for Smith's conception of sympathy, while also aligning both Longinus's sublime and Smith's sympathy with what, since Freud, we have come to understand as trauma. At the heart of all three experiences — the traumatic, the sympathetic, and the sublime — there is a cross between something like that blocked encounter Cathy Caruth finds in the heart of trauma and what we might think of as a form of affective theft or, as W. Rhys Roberts's English translation of Longinus has it, a type of imaginative "plagiarism."[18] It may be ultimately unsurprising that the blocked encounter Caruth discovers at the unrepresentable center of the Freudian scene of trauma, the inaccessible traumatic occurrence that fails to present itself to consciousness because it happens too fast and too soon, catching the subject unaware and positioning the subject subsequently as a perpetual latecomer or screened spectator to *the* event of his or her own life, might find its sublime double in the lightning flash of the Longinian sublime, in the apprehension of having come into surprising contact with something we ourselves have produced while failing to possess any knowledge of having done so (so that we find ourselves in the position of being perpetual latecomers or screened spectators to the generative scene of our own vaunting passion). Twentieth- and twenty-first-century understandings of trauma have long dwelt in the province of the sublime. It might be a little more surprising that the traumatic sublime owes as much to Longinus as to Kant, Burke, or Wordsworth, that trauma, witness, and the sublime overlap with Smith's Scottish Enlightenment conception of sympathy, and that all three might be reunderstood as forms of affective theft (as, that is, intimately connected with problems of intellectual and psychic property).

Longinus's eviction from the modern canon of the sublime — an eviction which, as J. Jennifer Jones argues, Wordsworth and Coleridge were eager to foster even if they were consequently, perhaps predictably, unable to entirely abject the imprint of Longinus's *Peri Hypsous* from their reformulations of the sublime — was effected largely on idealistic grounds.[19] Longinian sublimity, that is, falls out of the standard modern canon because rather than contenting itself with describing a mode of apprehension or thought, it insists on the manifestation of the sublime as a form of bodily imitation also. That transport, which Wordsworth, Coleridge, and Kant could all, in one or other way, celebrate as a mode of thinking, they resisted when it manifested itself as what eighteenth-century medical discourse spoke of as a type of nervous or corporeal sympathy: an imaginative transfer into the body of the auditor, reader, or spectator of those expressions of physical passion Longinus discovered in Sapho's paradigmatically sublime verse:

Yea, my tongue is broken, and through and through me
'Neath the flesh impalpable fire runs tingling;
Nothing see mine eyes, and a noise or roaring
    Waves in my ear sounds;

Sweat runs down in rivers, a tremor seizes
All my limbs, and paler than grass in autumn,
Caught by pains of menacing death, I falter,
    Lost in the love-trance.[20]

This, Longinus insists, is sublime, the very essence of the sublime, and not only because, in producing this verse, Sapho assumes as the property of her poetic persona the bodily passion she describes, but because the audience of such poetry must assume as their own (must, one might say, take some affective property in) the corporeal passion to which they have only, in fact, born witness. Sapho's poetry provides Longinus with his most famous examples of this version of the sublime, this coding of transport which Longinus admits is akin to a form of somato-affective plagiarism even as he insists that it is not ("This proceeding is not plagiarism; it is like taking an impression from beautiful forms or figures or other works of art").[21] But Sapho, he argues, is by no means unique. To experience the sublime, Longinus repeatedly argues, is to put yourself in the place of another, to assume another's passion as if it were your own property. Discovering the same process at work in Euripides's account of Phaethon's wild chariot ride ("He lashed the flanks of that wing-wafted team; / Loosed rein; and they through folds of cloudland soared. / Hard after on a fiery star his sire / Rode, counselling his son—'Ho! thither drive! / Hither thy car turn—hither!'"), Longinus insists: "Would you not say that the soul of the writer enters the chariot at the same moment as Phaethon and shares in his dangers and in the rapid flight of his steeds?"[22] Turning his attention to Homer's description of Hector's rout of the Greek ships in book 15 of the *Iliad*, he strikes the same notes: "This is . . . the case in which a writer, when relating something about a person, suddenly breaks off and converts himself into that selfsame person."[23]

∗

To suddenly break yourself off from yourself and become the person of another, and to assume as your own the passion (particularly the physical passion) to which you have borne witness — this, for Longinus, is the very essence of the sublime. But it also apprehensible under another name, apprehensible, to Adam Smith, as the very essence of sympathy. Sympathy, for Smith, *is* sublime, and not only in a propleptically Kantian, but also in a residually Longinian sense. What is more, sympathy, for Smith, is never more sublime than when it is tremblingly physical, and Smith is never more Longinian than when he is addressing that traumatic imaginative transport which causes the spectator to regard his or her own body as the sublime and phantom double of another: "When we see a stroke aimed and just ready to fall upon the leg or arm of another person, we naturally shrink and draw back our own leg or our own arm; and when it does fall, we feel it in some measure, and are hurt by it as well as the sufferer. . . . The horror which they [the spectators] conceive at the misery of those wretches affects that particular part in themselves more than any other; because that horror arises from conceiving what they themselves would suffer, if they really were the wretches whom they were looking upon."[24] As these passages indicate, Smith is certainly more interested in the horror of the body in pain (and the sympathetic transfer of that pain and horror) than in the joyful physical pleasures that preoccupy Longinus. But the form of experience the two writers identify under the names of sympathy and the sublime are fundamentally the same. And not coincidentally so, for while Smith never explicitly defines sympathy as analogous to the sublime, he does share with Longinus the conviction that to speak of either sympathetic identification or sublime transport is, ultimately, to speak of the imagination.

Longinus's theory of the imagination is more rudimentary than elaborate but it is nevertheless central to his conception of the sublime: "In a general way the name of *image* or *imagination* is applied to every idea of the mind, in whichever form it presents itself, which gives birth to speech. But at the present day the word is predominantly used in cases where, carried away by enthusiasm and passion, you think you see what you describe, and you place it before the eyes of your hearers."[25] This is not quite yet Smith's insistence that "it is by the imagination only that we can form any conception of what are his [another's] sensations," or that "by the imagination we place ourselves in his situation, we conceive ourselves enduring all the same torments, we enter as it were into his body . . . and thence form some idea of his sensations, and even feel something which, though weaker in degree, is not altogether like them,"[26] but it is close. However, as Smith's *Theory of Moral Sentiments* comes to articulate itself as a fully double-minded discourse on the sympathetic sublime, as simultaneously proto-Kantian and neo-Longinian, in its more Longinian moments (in its Longinian formula, that is, if not, therefore, in the adoption of a Longinian thematics) it also begins to formulate itself as a treatise on what we might think of as the melancholy sublime.

Melancholy, as I have previously discussed, is canonically distinguished from mourning by its refusal to abandon the suffering, degraded, ruined object of loss, by refusing, in Abraham's and Torok's terms, to introject loss, and determining, instead, to incorporate loss, to encrypt the lost, damaged, ruined object within the secretive, museological or, indeed, mausoleumological architecture of the self. To reduce matters to a formula: mourning exchanges, melancholy encrypts. The question that then presents itself is whether traumatic sympathy and the traumatic sublime are more properly mournful or melancholic. In its stoic, disinterested, Kantian register, Smith's version of sympathy is recognizably, even narcissistically, mournful: devoted to rewarding the subject's investment of sympathy by means of an act of imaginative exchange which allows the historical mourner to substitute an enhanced, enriched, "surplus" version of *itself* for the lost other. In his experimental Longinian moments, however, Smith construes sympathy as more properly melancholic, more primarily devoted to encrypting the dead and the passions (the imaginary resentments) of the slain in the body of the sympathetic spectator.

Or, as ever, almost so. For, and this is what strikes me as the most astonishing and original aspect of his *Theory*, Smith's sympathetic spectator takes a melancholy, affective property in the passions of another *not*, as every standard account of melancholy has it, by encrypting that other within itself *but by encrypting itself within that other*:

> We sympathize even with the dead. . . . It is miserable, we think, to be deprived of the light of the sun; to be shut out from life and conversation, to be laid in the cold grave, a pray to corruption and the reptiles of the earth; to be no more thought of in this world, but to be obliterated, in a little time, from the affections, and almost from the memory, of their dearest friends and relations. Surely, we imagine, we can never feel too much for those who have suffered so dreadful a calamity. The tribute of our fellow-feeling seems doubly due to them now, when they are in danger of being forgot by every body; and by the vain honours which we pay to their memory, we endeavour, for our own misery, artificially to keep alive our melancholy remembrance of their misfortune. . . . *The idea of that dreary and endless melancholy, which the fancy naturally ascribes to their condition, arises altogether from our joining to the change which has been produced upon them, our own consciousness of that change; from our putting*

ourselves in their situation, and from lodging, if I may be allowed to say so, our own living souls in their inanimated bodies. . . . It is from this very illusion of the imagination, that the foresight of our own dissolution is so terrible to us, and that the idea of those circumstances, which undoubtedly can give us no pain when we are dead, makes us miserable while we are alive.[27]

"The shadow of the object," Freud indicates in one of his briefest descriptions of melancholy, "has fallen on the subject."[28] For Smith's experimentally melancholy spectator (that is his Longinian rather than his Kantian spectator) the reverse is true. Longinus's Phaeton does not cast his shadow on the one who witnesses his doomed chariot ride; the spectator, rather, enters the chariot, occupies Phaeton's soaring body, and dies with him. Smith's dead do not haunt us by sending their shades to take up residence within us. Rather, they compel our "melancholy remembrance" by inviting us to reside within their entombment, to lay ourselves "in the cold grave" with them. And with this fundamental reversal of melancholy's subject-object relations, with this reverse encryption of the melancholic *within* the mangled carcass of the slain rather than the encryption of the slain within the animate body of the living, Smith effects a fundamental redefinition of the nature of melancholy.

∗

The fantasy of both Freudian and post-Freudian accounts of melancholy (and of those theories of testimony and witness they inspire) is that melancholy (Derrida's mourning without limit) is a fundamentally pastoral practice, that it serves to preserve, safeguard, or protect the dead by offering them an unsurrenderable, interminable, commemorative lodging within the social, political, and psychical imagination of the living.[29] For Smith, however (at least at moments such as the one cited above), melancholy does not so much imply the pastoral or the curatorial as the cultivation of an alarming, even a suicidal, vulnerability. It is as if he has temporarily eschewed Rome for Greece, or, indeed, set aside that classical version of melancholy derived from the opening scenes of Sophocles's *Antigone* to associate the heroine's melancholy with her ultimate fate, substituting Antigone's living entombment in "death's stone bridal chamber" for her refusal to abandon the dead as the true secret of her melancholy. Thus construed, experimental (or what we might call ascriptive) melancholy is not a practice of survival (a way of securing the afterlife of the dead and of testifying to our own continued existence).[30] It is, instead, a way of living in death. It is not the dead that the elective melancholic keeps alive, Smith insists, it is instead their own melancholy that his melancholy subjects seek to sustain, their way of "lodging . . . [their] own living souls in . . . [the] in-animated bodies" of the dead that his sublimely melancholy spectators "en-deavor . . . artificially to keep alive."

And though this plagiaristic sentimentality (this act of assuming as one's own property another's experience of suffering) might seem to imply not only a form of affective theft but, moreover, an abandonment of melancholy's political project, though it might seem to suggest a turn away from what we have come to regard as the political possibilities of a testimonial melancholy, that is not at all the case. Because to regard melancholy as Smith does here, to identify it with the experiment of "putting ourselves in . . . [the] situation" of the dead, is to recover for melancholy that degree of intentionality, that im-perative of a project to be pursued (if, perhaps, never completed) which is the minimal prerequisite of a politics. For Smith (at least in such moments), experimental melancholy names less a condition than a determination, less something we suffer than something we choose, less a way of being wounded by the world than a way of entering into it. And precisely to the degree that melancholy manifests itself not as the result of the traumas that have hap-pened to us but as a way of making ourselves happen within the space of the traumatic, not as a way of lodging the past within the present but as a way of lodging the present (and ourselves) in the deathly afterlife of past historical situations, not as a way of describing effects but as a way of identifying causes, it manifests itself as a politics — the politics of cosmopolitan interestedness.

And, of course, it manifests itself as something else also — a type of roman-tic historicism. As Smith makes clear, his melancholy spectator (as opposed to his disinterested spectator) not only invests in the dead, not only lays down in the grave with them, but also seeks to enter into the historical situation that led to their death. The passage I have just cited makes this reasonably clear, the one that follows is more explicit still:

> Even our sympathy with the grief or joy of another, before we are informed of the cause of either, is always extremely imperfect. General lamentations, which express nothing but the anguish of the sufferer, create rather a curiosity to enquire into his situation. . . . The first question we ask is, What has befallen you? Till this be answered, though we are uneasy both from the vague idea of his misfortune, and still more from torturing ourselves with conjectures about what it may be, yet our fellow-feeling is not very considerable. *Sympathy, therefore, does not arise so much from the view of the passion, as that from the situation that excites it. . . . When we put ourselves in his case, [then] that passion arises in our breast from the imagination.*[31]

Contrary to virtually everything I have observed regarding Smith's proto-Kantian, disinterested historical spectator, Smith here explicitly allies the melancholy sympathy of the spectator with a radically historicizing sensibility. It is not just the dead, or the passions of the dead, that the sympathetic spectator holds in view. It is, more fundamentally, a view on the historical situation, an inspection of the determinate case of the suffering other, that renders sympathy possible and so allies it with that sort of pluri-interested melancholy cosmopolitanism, that systematic geopolitical determination to know and inhabit the world's endless scenes of injustice that we have also seen to be the signature characteristic of a romantic discourse of aggrieved fancy. If sympathetic melancholy is political, it thus entails a politics with a particular and recognizable epistemology and method. It articulates itself as a systematically historicist and historicizing politics, and not in the sense in which, in the first section of this book, I allied early- to mid-eighteenth-century historicism with an abstract epistemology and an actuarial method, but in such a way as to ally melancholy with the worldly *case-driven* obsessions of what James Chandler calls romantic historicism, or indeed, with that more recent, late-twentieth-century Marxist historicism which, as Fredric Jameson argues, identifies as *its* political project the determination to "give us an adequate [and systematic] account of the essential *mystery* of the past, which, like Tiresias drinking the blood, is momentarily returned to life and warmth and allowed once more to speak, and deliver its long-forgotten message in surroundings utterly alien to it."[32]

I do not, by this, intend that Jameson's version of historicism, or Marxism itself, is irreducibly melancholy, but I do wish to suggest that, as Chandler has argued, late-twentieth-century historicist thought is haunted by the ghost of an earlier romantic historicism, that *this* is the specter our various "new" and Marxist historicisms have momentarily returned to life and allowed once more to speak. This is entirely noncoincidental. Because, if the general historical model I have been outlining is at all valid, that is precisely what we would predict as our neo- and hyperspeculative moment both recuperates within itself the antecedent speculative practices it repeats and intensifies *and* re-stages, in more elaborate and globally pervasive forms, the romantic, historicist, testimonial sensibilities of a prior melancholy European counterdiscourse on and of modernity. Historicism, for Stephen Greenblatt, "begins" with the "desire to speak with the dead."[33] For Jameson, historicism is a cruder or subtler elaboration of that originary desire to encounter the shade of Tiresias, to drink the mysterious blood of the past, and return it, momentarily, to life. These are gothic tropes. They are also the sustaining fantasies of the melancholic and the obsessions of Smith's experimental (Longinian) historical spectator. However named — as melancholic, historicist, or sympathetic — the fundamental attitude under consideration is the same, both as regards its phenomenology, which, in Derrida's terms, is recognizably hauntological, and as concerns its fundamental consciousness of historical time as fractured, sedimented, nonsynchronous.

∗

This, however, is not the moment to consider in detail what it might mean to adduce this set of structural correspondences between melancholy, sympathy, witness, and historicism. Rather, my quite restricted point is that both the melancholy sensibility and the historicist critical practice readily identified as characteristic features of our postmodern contemporaneity again locate this contemporaneity in a noncontemporaneous relation to itself, and that they do so not only by typing the postmodern as a sort of neo- or belated romanticism (as Jim Chandler, Walter Benn Michaels, David Simpson, and Alan Liu, in their various ways have argued), but by aligning the core affect and method of postmodern historical thought with the affective investments and method-ological conceits of late-eighteenth-century sympathy discourse.[34] We are only now beginning (thanks to Chandler and other scholars) to come to terms with what it means for much contemporary critical thought to trace itself, via a Jamesonian reception of Lukács's reception of Sir Walter Scott, to the Scottish Enlightenment (rather than exclusively to the continental Enlighten-ment). But we have not yet begun to grasp what it means to read Jameson (and Derrida) as the very strange bedfellows of Adam Smith, as, indeed, those who have made their beds in the graves Smith opens and in which he episodically urges his readers to lay themselves.

In a still more restricted fashion, I want to ask what it might mean, politi-cally, for the belated historical actor to imagine himself or herself experimen-tally laid in such a grave. And on this point, at least, Smith is remarkably clear:

> When we see one man oppressed or injured by another, the sympathy which we feel with the distress of the sufferer seems only to serve to animate our fellow-feeling with his resentment against the offender. We are rejoiced to see him attack his adversary in his turn, and are eager and ready to assist him whenever he exerts himself for defense, or even for vengeance, within a certain degree. If the injured should perish in the quarrel we not only sympathize with the real resentment of his friends and relations, but with the imaginary resent-

ment which *in fancy* we lend to the dead. . . . [As] we put ourselves in his situation, as we enter, as it were, into his body, and in our imaginations, in some measure, animate anew the deformed and mangled carcase of the slain, when we bring home in this manner his case to our own bosoms, we feel upon this, as upon many other occasions, an emotion which the person principally involved is incapable of feeling and which yet we feel by an illusive sympathy with him. The sympathetic tears which we shed . . . seem but a small part of the duty which we owe him. . . . His blood, we think, calls aloud for vengeance. The very ashes of the dead seem disturbed at the thought that his injuries are to pass unrevenged. The horrors which are supposed to haunt the bed of the murderer, the ghosts which, superstition imagines, rise from the grave to demand vengeance upon those who brought them to an untimely end, all take their origin from this natural sympathy with the imaginary resentment of the slain. And with regard, at least, to this most dreadful of all crimes, nature, antecedent to all reflections upon the utility of punishment, has in this manner stamped in the human heart, in the strongest and most indelible of characters, an immediate and instinctive approbation of the sacred and necessary law of retaliation.[35]

It is hard to read this as anything other than a prescription for a rebel politics, a politics of insubordination, a resentful, aggrieved, melancholy politics of the living on behalf of the slain. But of course that is not, finally, what Adam Smith was preaching, even if 250 years later we can hear echoes of this swiftly tempered burst of expostulatory speech in the necropolitics that Achille Mbembe argues has become one of our moment's dominant political forms.[36] Or perhaps we elect not to hear those echoes at all, or, when we hear them, do little more than respond to them with the anxious liberal commonplaces of degree, measure, and restraint with which Smith so rapidly responds to his own voicing of such speech. And that is perhaps because we do, after all, inhabit a moment deeply indebted to Smith, one not only beholden to *The Wealth of Nations*, but to a liberal and neoliberal theory of sentiment that, the very moment it risks even an imaginary sympathy with such exorbitant passions, such illiberal sentiments, draws back, reasserts the sovereignty of a practice of judgment that confines itself to the immediate and the near-at-hand, the moderate and even-handed calibration of degrees (of loss, of violence, of suffering, of injustice), and reminds us that if sympathy is original to a concern for justice, then justice must elect a parochial and not a global territory of address, and even then must subordinate itself to the demands of propriety, measure suffering according to its nominal rather than its real value, and commit the liberal historical spectator to an attitude that is more properly disinterested than melancholy. And perhaps *this* is because now, as then, a formal and proper discourse on justice is finally more concerned with us than with them, more a means of cultivating a type of subject whose ultimate goal is not to acknowledge some responsibility for the unpaid debt of global suffering or to assume some property in the global suffering of the world's dimly lit ex-urban others but to enter into a liberal, cosmopolitan community of those like-minded progressive souls who recognize in one another's ability to be affected by such vision of global suffering the grounds of their own common humanity and the (pleasurably guilty) title to their own political sovereignty.

And yet, the words are there, as, perhaps more importantly, are the melancholy theory of knowledge they express, the habit of historical observation they demand, the practice of witness they command, the experiment of cosmopolitan interestedness they urge, and the act of decision they invite. Smith may have turned the page on such sentiments, but that does not mean the book was closed. Contemporaneous and subsequent history has kept it open. The melancholy facts of empire and the slave trade, among so many others, are written on its pages. The scene of the *Zong* massacre illuminates it.

*

Appearing before Lord Mansfield both as representatives of the island's insurance industry and its fledgling assortment of abolitionists, the attorneys for the *Zong*'s underwriters appeared before the bench also as the members of a late-eighteenth-century discursive community beholden to Adam Smith's *Theory of Moral Sentiments*. With every appeal to the court's sympathy, with every request that the bench exert the power of its sentimental imagination, they brought the hearing into closer conversation with Smith's ruminations on the nature of ethics and justice. The question, of course, is with *which* Smith did they thus put the court in conversation? Which advocate of sentiment did they thus return to life? The theorist of melancholy or of the speculative? The advocate of an aggrieved or a disinterested sympathy with the imaginary resentments of the slain? The answer, of course, is both. For if Solicitor Haywood and his colleagues were relying on something like a Smithian theory of sentiment to convince the court of its obligation to take some melancholy property in the massacre, then Smith's work also provided the late eighteenth century with the arguments by which to refuse that obligation as it dictated that it is never the real suffering of those whom we observe (or, even, fancy) bruised and battered on the rack of history with which a system of justice must ultimately concern itself, but the just and ethical spectator's own propriety in the face of such suffering, the historical judge's own disinterested equipoise, the nominal rather than the real value of the ruined, lost, or degraded thing. And the source of *such* value, of course, is not the romantic imagination but the stipulations of contract (social, institutional, or financial) and the equally (but incommensurably) imaginary investments contract makes, and allows itself to recover, in the objects it nominates.

And if the question were changed? If we were to ask, instead, what it meant for Solicitor Lee to accuse his opponents of presenting their case not simply as Smith's interlocuters but as if they were asking the court to exchange its critical judgment for that form of historical decision invited by the literary form that breathed renewed, novelistic life into the mangled carcass of Smith's schizophrenic historical spectator? If we were instead asked what it might mean, after all, to represent or view the *Zong* massacre as if it were a case drawn from historical romance? What then? What perspective would such a view afford? What type of historical knowledge and practice of justice would it command?

By way of answer it is time, at last, to address Turner and Scott.

a sea of negroes

drowned

live

in the thirst

— M. NourbeSe Philip, from *Zong! # 20*

CHAPTER 10

"To Tumble into It, and Gasp for Breath as We Go Down"

THE IDEA OF SUFFERING AND THE CASE OF LIBERAL COSMOPOLITANISM

"The committee also in this interval brought out their famous print of the plan and section of a slave-ship; which was designed to give the spectator an idea of the sufferings of the Africans in the Middle Passage, and this so familiarly, that he might instantly pronounce upon the miseries experienced there. . . . [The] print seemed to make an instantaneous impression of horror upon all who saw it, and . . . it was therefore very instrumental, in consequence of the wide circulation given it, in serving the cause of the injured Africans."[1] Thus, again, Thomas Clarkson, now from his two-volume *History of the Rise, Progress, and Accomplishment of the Abolition of the African Slave-Trade by the British Parliament* which he published in 1808, twenty-three years after the appearance of his *Essay on the Slavery and Commerce of the Human Species.* The print Clarkson has in mind is the London Committee for the Abolition of the Slave Trade's indeed-famous cross-sectional sketch of the slave ship *Brookes* jammed with the bodies of 450 prone, chained African slaves, an image disseminated throughout England and the continent in the early 1790s and essential to the spread of the abolitionist movement (Figure 1).[2] Circulated in

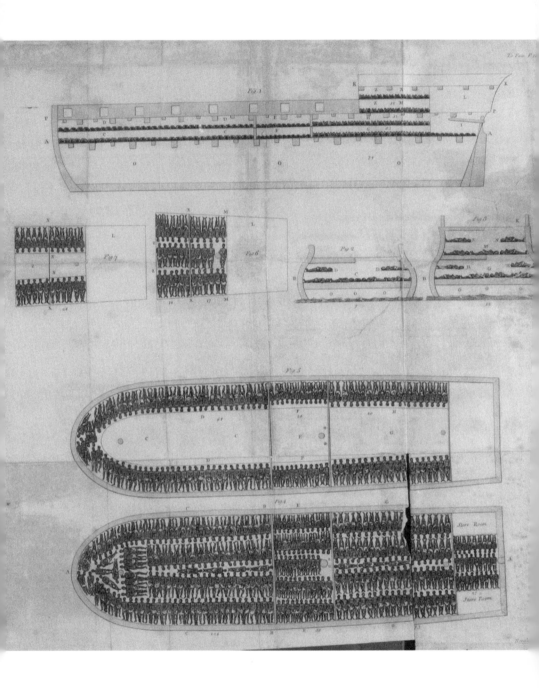

Figure 1: "The Slave Ship" in Thomas Clarkson, *History of the Rise, Progress, and Accomplishment of the Abolition of the Slave Trade*, 1808. Courtesy of the Rare Book, Manuscript, and Special Collections Library, Duke University.

France during Clarkson's 1790 visit to the continent, the print proved crucial to the success of his embassy: "This distribution had not been long begun," he subsequently noted, "before I witnessed its effects. The virtuous Abbe Gregoire, and several members of the National Assembly, called upon me. The section of the slave-ship, it appeared, had been the means of drawing them towards me . . . it made its impression upon all who saw it. . . . The Bishop of Chartres . . . had not given credit to all the tales which had been related of the Slave-trade, till he had seen this plate. . . . The Archbishop of Aix, when I first showed him the same plate, was so struck with horror that he could scarcely speak."[3] In England, Clarkson maintains, the image had no less powerful an effect: "Though we felt a considerable degree of pain, in finding [an] adverse disposition among so many members of the Lower House [of Parliament], the people . . . were still warmly with us. Indeed their hatred for the trade had greatly increased. Many circumstances had occurred in this year to promote it. The committee, during my absence in France, had circulated the plate of the slave-ship throughout all England. No one saw it but he was impressed. It spoke to him in a language, which was at once intelligible and irresistible. It brought forth tears of sympathy in behalf of the sufferers, and it fixed their sufferings in his heart."[4]

Clarkson may tend toward the hyperbolic at these moments, but the substance of his claim certainly withstands scrutiny. Together with Josiah Wedgwood's enormously popular cameo of a kneeling, pleading slave (subsequently adopted as the emblem of the London Committee) and the pamphlet version of Thomas Cowper's "The Negro's Complaint," the committee's slave-ship plate furnished late-eighteenth- and early-nineteenth-century British and continental mass culture with one of the most influential images of the slave trade and survives into the twenty-first century as one of the fundamental icons of the trans-Atlantic trade. But if this image was thus "instrumental" to the rise and spread of the abolitionist movement, how did it prove so irresistible, making so "instantaneous" an "impression of horror upon all who saw it"? What was it that "all who saw" could not avoid seeing? What "language" did it in fact speak?

It spoke the language of sympathy through a fanciful language of fact. And in speaking that language the image was not alone, not only because this language ("at once intelligible and irresistible") is also the language of romantic melancholy and romance sympathy, the language of sentimental and cosmopolitan interestedness, the language (as Clarkson himself indicates) of moral philosophy, the Scottish Enlightenment, and Adam Smith, but also because fifty years later, when J. M. W. Turner was searching for a subject for a painting to exhibit in parallel with the 1840 opening of the inaugural World

Anti-Slavery Convention, it was to Clarkson's 1808 *History* of abolition that he turned. Reading that book (which had been republished in 1839), Turner would have found in it not only Clarkson's account of the *Zong* massacre (on which art historians agree Turner then based *Slavers Throwing Overboard the Dead and Dying, Typhoon Coming On*) but also a reproduction of the committee's slave-ship plate, Clarkson's repeated discussions of the affective power and sympathetic grammar of that image, his ventriloquization of a Humean language of sentiments, ideas, and impressions, his more explicit analysis of the importance of Smithian sentiment theory (and the Scottish Enlightenment more generally) to abolitionist discourse and the abolitionist cause, and his detailed exploration of how one might so exhibit the facts of the trade as to closely interest an otherwise disinterested spectator in the sufferings of an actually unseen other.[5]

In addition to Clarkson's description of the *Zong* massacre, Turner scholars have identified a number of artworks on which *Slavers'* aesthetic vocabulary draws, central among them Gericault's *Raft of the Medusa* (1819) and the continental tradition of romantic history painting that canvas exemplifies.[6] The Gericault comparison certainly seems apt. But the more immediate influence on the visual language and affective design of Turner's painting, I believe, is the committee's slave-ship print, not only in its realized form but in its mode of construction and principle of historical typification, which blends, in utterly paradigmatic fashion, the knowledge grammars of what I have been calling an actuarial and a melancholy historicism. The committee's print, in other words, speaks the melancholy facts of the trans-Atlantic slave trade by fashioning an image designed to transform an actuarial knowledge of modern global history into a fanciful investment in history, a speculative field of evidence into the horrifically evident, a disinterested (sublimely "cool" and proto-Kantian) historical spectator into an interested (sublimely melancholy and neo-Longinian) cosmopolitan. And so too does Turner's canvas. Which is not to say that Clarkson's print exerts a solitary influence on Turner's painting. The pressure of Gericault's hand is evident too, as, still more crucially, are David Hume's, Adam Smith's, and Walter Scott's impress. But the canvas whose subject Turner found in Clarkson's *History* also finds its sentimental theory of historical representation in the central image of that book, and so it is with a slightly more extensive look at this image that I want to begin my approach to the painting that for the past two centuries has been to the *Zong* massacre what the committee's plate has been to the slave trade more generally (Figure 2).

*

Figure 2: J. M. W. Turner, *Slavers Throwing Overboard the Dead and Dying, Typhoon Coming On*, 1840. Courtesy of the Museum of Fine Arts, Boston.

Clarkson's *History* may be divided into three primary sections: a brief intro-duction on the evil of the slave trade and the sufferings of enslaved Africans, a survey of the committee's various forerunners in the abolitionist movement and of the events leading up to the committee's founding in 1787, and an account of the committee's work from 1787 to Parliament's passage of an abolition bill in 1807. This last section assumes something of the form of a sentimental picaresque or historical romance with Clarkson cast as its wan-dering, melancholy, fortune-buffeted but ultimately triumphant protagonist. I will have more to say regarding the narrative form of this portion of the *History* below. For the moment however it is Clarkson's introductory overview that demands attention. That the trade is evil and the history of abolition a history of a struggle with evil are Clarkson's chief framing assumptions for the book. His problem in writing this text, however, remains the central problem of his earlier *Essay on the Slavery and Commerce of the Human Species, Par-ticularly the African*: that evil, he understands, remains unseen to most Britons and remaining unseen it cannot interest them. (Interest — or, more accurately, interestedness — it is worth noting, emerges as a type of good in its own right in the *History*: an ethical disposition valued apart from any discrete attach-ment. The primary justification Clarkson provides for writing his book after the successful passage of an anti-slave-trade bill is that his *History* might serve to keep alive the habit of worldly and sentimental interestedness the commit-tee had successfully cultivated in the British mind in the years leading up to the bill. As he somewhat coyly makes the case for his right to write: "An individual, for example, begins; he communicates his sentiments to others. Thus while alive he enlightens, when dead, he leaves his work behind him. Thus, though departed, he yet speaks and his influence is not lost. . . . Let us consider, too, that this is the cause of mercy, justice, and religion; that as such, it will always afford renewed means of rallying; and that the dead will always be heard with interest, and the living with enthusiasm upon it.")[7] But how then to promote (or sustain) such interest and such interestedness?

Now, as earlier, Clarkson invests his readers in the sufferings of the slave through a fictional conceit predicated on a trick of vision:

> A few pages will do all that is necessary! A glance only into such a subject as this will be sufficient to affect the heart — to arouse our indignation and our pity — and to teach us the importance of the victory obtained. . . . Let us suppose our-selves on the [African] Continent . . . what object is that, which first obtrudes upon our sight? Who is that wretched woman, whom we discover under that noble tree, wringing her hands, and beating her breast. . . . Three days she has

been there . . . and no tidings of her children yet. . . . But let us leave the cries of this unfortunate woman, and hasten into another district; — And what do we first see here? Who is he, that just now started across the narrow pathway, as if afraid of a human face? . . . Behold, as we get into the plain, a deserted village! . . . The old have been butchered, because unfit for slavery, and the young have been carried off. . . . But let us hasten from this cruel scene, which gives rise to so many melancholy reflections. Let us cross yon distant river and enter some new domain. But are we relieved even here from some afflicting spectacle? Behold, the inhabitants are all alarmed! . . . The neighboring village is on fire . . . The Prince, unfaithful to the sacred duty of the protection of his subjects, has surrounded them. He is now burning their habitations, and seizing, as saleable booty, the fugitives from the flames. Such, then, are some of the scenes that have been passing in Africa.[8]

Such are Clarkson's suppositional scenes. Such are the afflicting scenes which, by the logic of the earlier *Essay*, while "imaginary" nevertheless remain "strictly consistent with fact." Such are the sorts of scenes with which Clarkson would have been familiar from his reading of Smith's *Theory of Moral Sentiments* (whose virtues he praises immediately prior to providing his account of the *Zong* massacre), from the conjectural historiography he rightly associates with the mid- and late-century faculty of the University of Edinburgh (whom he approvingly numbers as central among the forerunners of the abolitionist movement), and from the more general "Moral philosophy . . . adopted . . . by some of the colleges in our universities" whose "sentiments," he argues, "may be supposed to have produced an extensive effect . . . [and] must be considered as having been a considerable coadjutor in interesting the mind of the public in favour of the oppressed Africans."[9] Such, in a word, are the *type* of fanciful, affecting, conjectural scenes the abolitionist movement borrowed from the Scottish Enlightenment, Clarkson borrowed from Hume and Smith, and his *History* of abolition borrowed from, among other sources, Smith's *Theory of Moral Sentiment*.

But while Clarkson's *History* evidently draws from Scottish Enlightenment moral philosophy and conjectural historiography, his conjectural method fails when he turns from his imaginary catalogue of scenes "passing in Africa" to attempt the horrors of the middle passage:

Here I must observe at once, that, as far as this part of the evil is concerned, I am at a loss to describe it. Where shall I find words to express properly their sorrow . . . ? Where shall I find language to paint in appropriate colours the horror of mind brought on by thoughts of their future . . . ? How shall I make known their situation, while labouring under painful disease, or while struggling in the suffocating holds of their prisons, like animals enclosed in an exhausted receiver? How shall I describe their feelings . . . ? How shall I exhibit their sufferings . . . ? Indeed every part of this subject defies my powers, and I must therefore satisfy myself and the reader with a general representation, or in the words of a celebrated member of Parliament, that "Never was so much human suffering condensed in so small a space."[10]

"How shall I describe their feelings?" "How shall I exhibit their sufferings?" "Where shall I find language?" "Where shall I find words?" These are extraordinary questions, extraordinary for all their idiomatic banality, extraordinary for the very predictability of their rhetoric of the unspeakable, extraordinary precisely because as he had so consistently shown over his quarter-century career as an abolitionist activist and writer, Clarkson had an enormously refined grammar and vocabulary available to him designed for this very task: a grammar of absent feeling communicated, a vocabulary of unseen suffering exhibited.

To say that the middle passage cannot be spoken in this tongue, to say that sentiment cannot exhibit it, that sympathy cannot paint it, that fancy cannot grasp it, that imagination cannot color it, is tantamount to saying that the great abolitionist project of historical interestedness is blocked at its very witness-bearing core, that it cannot do what it understands itself utterly obliged to do: make us see, and see as fact, what we do not in fact see, and not only see, but feel — "and this so familiarly, that [we] might instantly pronounce upon the miseries experienced there." It is tantamount to saying this, but it is not identical. For Clarkson manages to imply that there is a category of human suffering so intense, an experience of horror so absolute, that the descriptive precision of the conventionally fictional is inadequate to it, that if we are indeed to find ourselves rightly afflicted by such a scene of human suffering, instantaneously impressed by the evil of it, it will be the image of what we do not see rather than the fiction of seeing that will affect us. In the passage I have cited, Clarkson calls this image of what we do not see a general representation; promises his readers that he will make that general representation available to them in lieu of the descriptive scenes to which they are otherwise accustomed; promptly fails to provide any such general representation; and, by failing to provide it, confirms that in this case representation is the representation of what we do not see.

There are, however, several qualifying points that need to be made here. The first is that Clarkson does eventually make that general representation of the middle passage available to his readers, though only 600 pages and one volume of his *History* later when he finally comes to describe and reprint the committee's "famous print of the plan and section of a slave-ship; which was designed to give the spectator an idea of the sufferings of the Africans in the Middle Passage." The second is that by offering that print as this general representation, by offering a meticulously scaled cross section of a typical slave ship as the image of what we do not see (as the emblem of the middle-passage unseen), Clarkson here manages, counterintuitively, to yoke the language of sympathy to the method of political economy and actuarial reason, which in Marx's terms make us see what we do not see (canonically, labor: whether wage labor or slave labor, whether on a typical factory floor or hidden beneath the holds of a typical slave ship) as a simple abstraction, and, by Poovey's argument, allow us to encounter the invisible or the theoretical as fact. In fashioning a general representation of the unseen horrors of the middle passage, in other words, Clarkson and his fellow committee members provisionally abandon the *overtly* romantic and fictional facts that elsewhere serve them so well to produce a more hegemonically modern and abstract set of facts—the facts graphically depicted in their slave-ship plate and annotated in Clarkson's *History*. If Clarkson cannot make us see the horror of the middle passage, he will instead make us measure it, count it, and find, in the very disinterestedness of number, the very coolness of the mathematical facts of suffering, the obligation to interestedness.

How did the committee produce these facts, manufacture this general representation of what we do not and cannot see? They did so in utterly paradigmatic fashion, by seizing on an *evident* particular and converting it into a simple abstraction, theoretical *evidence* of the facts of the trade. Clarkson describes the process thus:

> It must be obvious that it became the committee to select some one ship, which had been engaged in the Slave-trade, with her real dimensions, if they meant to make a fair representation of the manner of the transportation. . . . The committee therefore, in choosing a vessel on this occasion, made use of the ship Brookes. . . . The vessel then in the plate is the vessel now mentioned, and the following is her admeasurement as given in by Captain Perry.

	Ft.	In.
Length of the lower deck gratings and bulk heads . . . AA	100	0
Breadth of beam on the lower deck inside, BB	25	4
Depth of hold ooo, from ceiling to ceiling	10	0
Length of the men's room, CC, on the lower deck	46	0
[Etc. . . . .]		

The committee, having proceeded thus far, thought they should now allow certain dimensions for every man, woman, and child; and then see how many persons, upon such dimensions and upon the admeasurements just given, could be stowed in this vessel. They allowed, accordingly, to every man slave six feet by one foot four inches for room, to every woman five feet by one foot four, to every boy five feet by one foot two, and to every girl four feet six by one foot. They then stowed them, and found them as in the annexed plate, that is, they found [that] . . . four hundred and fifty could be stowed in her.[11]

"They then stowed them" — by which Clarkson intends that the *Committee* then "stowed" 450 imaginary slaves in the hold of this now mathematically typical ship and then produced the plate that bore theoretical witness to the abstract facts of the trade. The plate, no less than Clarkson's fictional vignettes in both the *Essay* and the *History*, thus represents an imaginary scene nevertheless consistent with fact, but it does so by substituting the accountant's or the political economist's imaginary for the melancholic's, an actuarial for a romantic historicism, a theoretical for a traumatic realism, an aggregate for a spectral type of type. If Clarkson's "scenes that have been passing in Africa" come painted in the melancholy hues of the *Theory of Moral Sentiments*, then this general representation of the middle passage certainly owes more of its method to the author of *The Wealth of Nations*.

Or partially so. For having solicited an evident particular (the slave ship *Brookes*) as evidence for its general statistical representation of the conduct of the trade, the print seeks simultaneously, dialectically, to turn the empire's disinterested modern science of wealth sentimentally against itself by fashioning a visible abstraction (an image of what we cannot see) designed not merely to account for the trade but "to give the spectator an idea of the sufferings of the Africans in the Middle Passage, and this so familiarly, that he might instantly pronounce upon the miseries experienced there." And this, to arrive finally at my fundamental point, is also what Turner's *Slavers* canvas effects as it too stages this complex dialectical movement from an evident particular (the massacre aboard the slave ship *Zong*) to a general representation (generic "slavers" throwing overboard the anonymously dead and dying) designed nevertheless to elicit the sympathy and invest the interest of the historical spectator in what is abstractly evident on the surface of the canvas.

Why *abstractly* evident?

Because in depicting the *Zong* massacre as an allegory of the middle passage, Turner fashioned his canvas entirely as Clarkson and his fellows on the committee constructed their general representation of this (or rather "such"

a) scene of horror, that is, less as a singular image of things as they are than as a representative image of what we do not see (or, perhaps, as a typical image of a global modernity whose most essential, most urgently *interesting* things *are* what we do not see). In Turner's case, to be sure, we are made aware of the image of what we do not see not as a horrifically simple abstraction (so many imaginary slaves theoretically allocated to so many square feet of cargo hold on deck M; so many imaginary slaves theoretically allocated to so many square feet of cargo hold on deck N, etc.) or as a melancholically actuarial type (the dismal but mathematically typical slave ship). Rather, that image of the unseen reveals itself here as a type of brushstroke. Turner, that is, applies a smear of paint where the committee applies statistics. But though they differ in representational kind, the statistic and Turner's romantic brushstroke are consonant in phenomenological type: both *evidently* abstract the reality of what they claim to represent, *evidently* cover it, *evidently* body forth an image of what we do not see. How does Clarkson "exhibit the sufferings" of the middle passage? Where does Turner "find language to paint in appropriate colours [that] horror"? For one, in the evident banality of actuarial reason, in the graphic inadequacy of a language of fact made to call forth the language of sympathy. For the other, in the blurry impression of the romantic brushstroke, in a language of color that like the language of statistics makes us see what we cannot see even as it creates an image of what, seeing, we yet cannot see (beneath the banality of number, beneath the smear of paint, beneath the deck, beneath the water).

*

Reading through Clarkson's *History* in search of a subject for a painting, how could Turner have resisted the challenge Clarkson's admission of failure makes to the imagination of any sympathetic reader ("I am at a loss to describe it. Where shall I find words?") or avoided the lesson his compensatory representation of a "typical" slave ship offers the romantic historian of the unseen? Turner's melancholy canvas and Clarkson's economical print may seem to occupy diametrically opposite poles of the historical imagination, but the truth of the matter is that they speak an identical language, a language of sympathy spoken through an abstracted language of fact. That both works understand sympathy to follow rather than to precede the general representation; that both precede dialectically from a phenomenal content to the general idea and then, sympathetically, back again; that both men, like Kant, ultimately attach the sympathy of the historical witness to an image *non sin-*

gulorum sed universorum implies, however, that neither is as melancholy or unabashedly interested as they might at first appear. Like Adam Smith, even when Clarkson and Turner solicit the spectator's sympathy and demand our interest in their acts of witness, it is not, finally, to an evident, singular instance of human suffering that they testify but to a method (statistical abstraction in one case, a romantic painting style in another) and to an idea: the idea of sympathy itself, the idea, after all, of a (their) interested disinterestedness.

The paragraphs with which Clarkson introduces his readers (and Turner) to the facts of the *Zong* massacre reveal no less than this paradigmatically liberal ambivalence of sentimental interest. Immediately after praising moral philosophy for the role it has played as "a considerable coadjutor *in interesting the minds* of the public in favour of the oppressed Africans," Clarkson has this to say about Granville Sharp, a "case" in which Sharp "took part" (the *Zong* massacre, as the ensuing paragraphs make clear), and what strikes me as the eighteenth- and nineteenth-century version of the ethical dilemma late-twentieth-century thought has baptized the experience of the impossible: "In the year 1783, we find Mr. Sharp coming again into notice. We find him at this time taking a part in a case, the knowledge of which, in proportion as it was disseminated, produced an earnest desire among all disinterested persons for the abolition of the slave-trade."[12] A desire among the disinterested *for*. A disinterested desire to take a part in a case. An interesting of the minds of the disinterested in favor of the oppressed. An interested disinterestedness. An experience of the impossible. As Clarkson describes it, so, as we shall see, Turner pictures it. Which implies also that on the far side of this experience, as Clarkson encounters the dual obligation that Spivak, following Derrida, calls "undecidability/decision," so Turner too will stage his undecidability even as he decides: interest or disinterest, melancholy or impartiality, the singular or the universal.

But of course we don't need Spivak, Derrida, or Badiou to make that evident. We need only look at another of the writers Turner was reading as he set to work on his canvas: Sir Walter Scott, in whose pages Adam Smith and Thomas Clarkson's melancholy *and* impartial, interested *and* disinterested spectator emerges as the very type (in Lukács's terms, the "typical representative") of the age.

*

As Scott is to Turner, so William Hogarth is to Henry Fielding. If to say this is to register a shift in aesthetic precedence from the middle of the eighteenth to the middle of the nineteenth century (to note, in other words, that while in 1749 it was the fate of the English novel to follow where English painting led, by 1840 the situation was so thoroughly reversed that England's premier painter found himself pursuing the formal and stylistic innovations of the novel form), it should also be understood to imply that if we are fully to understand Turner's slave-ship canvas, we must gain a slightly clearer sense than I have thus far provided of what happens to the novel in the movement from *Tom Jones* to *Waverley*. And one way of doing so is by looking once again at the distinct types of *type* from which the mid-eighteenth-century realist and the early-nineteenth-century romantic novel construct their factual fictions. Fielding's types, the types of character from which he constructs his narratives, the types apposite to a theoretical realism are like the character types made famous by Hogarth's various didactic series and his popular catalogues of typical faces: the aggregate, abstract representatives of one or other actually existing social person—a rake, a harlot, a foundling (as the subtitle of *Tom Jones* unabashedly declares). Indeed, by Fielding's own protestation, his character types are not just "like" Hogarth's, sometimes they *are* Hogarth's, as is the case with Tom Jones's "aunt" Bridget Allworthy, whom Fielding acknowledges he has not so much created as taken on loan from the painter.

> I would attempt to draw her picture, but that is done already by a more able master, Mr. Hogarth himself, to whom she sat many years ago, and hath lately been exhibited by that gentleman in his print of a winter's morning, of which she was no improper emblem, and may be seen walking (for walk she does in the print) to Covent-Garden church, with a starved foot-boy behind, carrying her prayer-book.[13]

This, as so much else in Fielding, is almost too self-knowingly playful to bear commentary, but it is perhaps worth noting that even as he pretends to reverse temporal sequence by having Hogarth take his "emblem" of censorious, wintry age (the print Fielding mentions is of "Morning," the initial image in Hogarth's *The Four Times of Day* (1738) which depicts an aged woman spying on a pair of young lovers) from his own, later, novel, Fielding acknowledges that whoever came first (the painter or the novelist), the characters both drawn are drawn less to a found than to an emblematic scale. It is, in other words, immaterial whether Fielding borrowed Miss Allworthy from Hogarth or Hogarth drew her from Fielding. In either case she is no more than the image of the type of the moralistic old woman who is herself merely the emblem of an elemental (wintry) disposition. Bridget Allworthy, in a word, is less entirely a person than she is a theory of a mode of personhood, an abstract emblem of a *real* human type, a composite drawn not from nature but from an aggregated variety of sources.

Scott's types, I have intimated at various moments, are of another sort entirely, and not accidentally but quite deliberately, even antithetically so. It is no accident after all that *Waverley*, like *Tom Jones*, is a novel of the '45. Replotting the insurrection, Scott attempts to effect more than a retelling of a historical event. He redeploys that shared event to replot the history and future of the English-language novel, rewrites this Highlands incursion into sovereign English space to stage his own raid on the narrative territory Fielding had earlier staked out. And he effects (or, at least, undertakes) that revolution in genre in large part by reinventing the form of the type at the heart of the novelistic representation of history. The factually fictional type of person fundamental to Scott's haunted historical romances, in other words, is not the type of the census, actuarial table, dissertation on faces, or history of a foundling, but the type of a person rediscovered, as the subtitle of *Waverley* has it, "sixty years since": the type of one who once existed and now recurs; the type of the unquiet ghost; the type of the dead. This is how Chandler puts it in his explication of Scott's invention of what he (Chandler) calls the "romantic type."

> In those opening paragraphs of *The Eighteenth Brumaire* which have provided such sanction for recent cultural history, Marx made much of the slogan: "Let the dead bury the dead." Scott, in effect, produces the converse injunction — to let the living revive the dead. Thus, in extending his rehearsal of the prior exchange with Dryasdust [in the "Dedicatory Epistle" to *Ivanhoe*], Templeton recalls an elaborate and macabre conceit: "The Scottish magician, you say, was, like Lucan's witch, at liberty to walk over the recent field of battle, and to select for the subject of resuscitation by his sorceries, a body whose limbs had recently quivered with existence, and whose throat had but just uttered the last note of agony" . . . Writing within short weeks of Scott's composition of the Epistle, at the end of 1819, Shelley had figured the "glorious phantom" of the spirit of the age arising from the "graves" of contemporary conditions understood as passed away. Here Scott imagines the bodies themselves as requiring the life-breath of the historical necromancer."[14]

Where the theoretical realism of speculative discourse abstracts its aggregate types from the tables of social life, Scott's experimentally melancholy realism here resuscitates the romantic type from the fields of history. Resuscitation thus becomes the historical novel's privileged mode of historical representation, displacing a Fieldingesque commitment to aggregate or plausible *representativity*, and rendering the romantic type (the subject of resuscitation) one that the novel disinters from a buried past rather than contracting to imagine as presently real.

What the historical novel disinters, however, it does not leave inert. Rather, as the resuscitative conceit demands, the necromantic text breathes life into the types it pulls from the grave. How? In part, to be sure, merely by depicting them; more crucially, however, by soliciting our readerly sympathy, by inviting us not merely to encounter the dead but to identify with them, to put ourselves in their place, to take on their agonies as if they were our own. Reviving the dead, one might say, Scott's novels simultaneously entomb the living, or invite the living, in Adam Smith's terms, to lay themselves down within the graves of the still quivering dead and their restless political quarrels. Certainly that is the invitation *Waverley* makes to its readers as it presents precisely this choice to the reader's proxy in the text, Edward Waverley, who is asked to assume as his own the historically untimely and doomed political struggles and vanishing folk culture of the Highland insurrectionists who appear to him, in Saree Makdisi's words, as nothing so much as "a horde of ghosts issuing forth from the past" (both the cultural "past" of a bardic Gaelic nationalism and the political past of an anterior monarchical crisis (un)resolved by the Glorious Revolution of 1688–89).[15]

If the narrative "field" Scott shares with Fielding is thus the battlefield of the '45, then, I am suggesting, Scott wrests novelistic possession of that field from Fielding by electing to share it, instead, with the insurrection's other great mid-eighteenth-century chronicler: Adam Smith. Surveying that field Scott determines to represent what he finds not as a journalist depicts the historical terrain (as backdrop for one or another in an essentially interchangeable and formulaic series of events: a battle, a campaign, an insurrection, a rout) but as the theorist of moral sentiment knows the field of history — as a territory littered with the "mangled carcass[es] of the slain"; bodies "whose limbs had recently quivered with existence, and whose throat had but just uttered the last note of agony"; and corpses, each of which speak an obligation to sympathize with the dead and dying, to effect an act of sublimely melancholy identification with them.[16] The narrative form that had appeared to Fielding, in one of his more memorable formulations, as "a newspaper of many volumes" thus finds *itself* resuscitated in a novelistic practice resolved, as I earlier suggested, not merely to "romance the news" but to romance the news of loss, or more particularly still, to romance the now ("sixty years since") lost news of the news of loss.[17]

There is another, more precise way to put this. Scott's genius, Lukács concludes (in part from a reading of the "Dedicatory Epistle" Chandler cites above), resided "in his novelistic capacity to give living human embodiment to historical-social types" representative of "the historical peculiarity of their age."[18] The type Lukács has in mind, however, is not so much the type of the dead as the Edward Waverley type, the "mediocre, prosaic hero" Scott set at the heart of so many of his novels, the indecisive, middling representative of an incipient bourgeois sensibility, the lukewarm, even regretful, and faintly guilty, liberal standard-bearer of a post-Union political accommodation and progressive philosophy of history.[19] But as Ian Duncan has argued, Waverley and his like protagonists are typical not just of an average person caught in the midst of competing historical forces and social orders. Rather, the Waverley hero is typical of a historical figure whose social personality is produced by an act of sympathetic spectation that dallies with melancholy (and with an economy of feeling in which the past, briefly resuscitated or disinterred, is not past but present) but which eventually exchanges a melancholy sympathy with the dying and the dead for the idea of the impartial spectator's capacity to be moved (and moved into a liberal future) by the spectacle of its own display of sympathy.

What Chandler calls the romantic type — the "type" foundational to the romantic historicism he understands Scott's novels virtually to invent — is, in other words, but one actor in a dialectical interaction of *two* types of type: the type of the dying and the dead (whether personified in a figure such as *Waverley*'s Fergus or associated with an entire waning cultural ensemble) and the type of the spectator (Waverley himself), who, in properly Smithian fashion, first interests himself in a spectacle of human suffering, experimentally lays down in the grave of a dying people or folk culture, and then exchanges the melancholy sublimity of this experiment in interestedness for a more properly liberal habit of historical disinterestedness that, by virtue of the reader's own sympathetic identification with the romance protagonist, is also the posture the reader learns to adopt. What might appear at first glance as an invitation to melancholy, or even to a politics of resentment or revenge (on behalf of the slain), thus converts itself, as in Smith's *Theory of Moral Sentiments*, into the exact opposite. To revise an earlier formula then: where melancholy classically encrypts what mourning proves willing to exchange, here it is melancholy (or at least the experiment of melancholy) that generates exchange, melancholy that permits the historical outsider or historical latecomer (that is, the reader/spectator) to assume some interest or property in an event — an interest he or she will subsequently exchange for a more proprietous and liberal disinterestedness. Refashioned as a romance convention, melancholy emerges not as liberalism's negation but as liberalism's transitory precondition.

For Scott, such arguments imply, the ultimate task of the novel is to convince the reader to substitute a provisional experience of reading (sympathetically) — to substitute, that is, the *experiment* of interestedness — for any vengeful, resentful, relentlessly melancholy politics of justice the experience of reading might have seemed to demand. Reading (whether that sort of mournful ethnographic reading of vanishing Highlands difference Waverley undertakes, or the reading performed from the greater comfort of the armchair) thus figures itself as a type of suffering, while the suffering of the reader/spectator offers itself as an adequate substitute for what we observe to be lost or dying. Spectatorially sympathizing with the spectator who sympathizes, the reader finds himself or herself invited to sympathize with the idea of sympathy itself or, alternately put, to exchange the possibility of an obsessive, melancholy *sympathy for this* (*this* singular experience of suffering, *this* experience of the Highlanders, *this* slave-trade massacre) for the idea of *sympathy as such*. A narrative experiment in interestedness thereby autoreferentially satisfies any demand for justice the reader or protagonist might otherwise be inclined to articulate and so permits the reader/spectator to abandon the damaged past (and the melancholy it induces) and claim full liberal citizenship in the present (and its futures to come).

Rewriting the ethical script of Scottish moral philosophy in novelistic form, Scott thus also confirms the essential predicates of a Scottish Enlightenment philosophy of history. Central to that philosophy of history (as exemplified by the stadial theory of history outlined in a text such as John Millar's 1771 *The Origin of the Distinction of Ranks*) was the sense that the experience of modernity was not, as the continental Enlightenment suggested, an experience of the synchronization of experience, the reduction of historical time to a single, dominant base time, a homogenizing, leveling, everywhere-available time of modernity, but the experience of a contemporaneity noncontemporaneous with itself, an experience of time as fractured, broken, constellated by a heterogeneous array of local regimes of time. Scott's novels work by tracing the wanderings of a character across just such an uneven geography of time — typically the Highlands and the Lowlands, territories which he treats, in Raymond Williams' terms, as the geographies of the residual and the emergent, the customary and the cosmopolitan — and obliging that character to make a choice for one order of time or another.[20] That choice, however, is always predetermined, as Scott figures any time but the time of cosmopolitan capital as wounded and dying, worthy, finally, of no more than a passing expression of sympathy and an honorable burial. The typical posture of Scott's protagonists, as Duncan suggests, is thus the posture of one who "looks on" at scenes of suffering and death, sympathizes less with the dying and the dead than with the idea of his own display of sympathy, and then moves on to inhabit a liberal modernity cleansed of the "ghosts issuing forth" from the past.[21]

And with its own depiction of the dying and the dead, its own mute appeal for the spectator's sympathy, Turner's painting captures this paradigmatic romance scene exactly; not least because opposite the canvas in the Royal Academy, Turner hung another, *Rockets and Blue Light*, an image of the coming of steam power, of the mechanization of the sea, of the modernization of Britain's imperium. With that painting in place opposite Turner's "Tis sixty years since" canvas, the image of the *Zong* massacre as a scene in a historical novel is complete. Indeed, it is not only complete but completed. For by locating the *Zong* massacre within these generic conventions, Turner, as we shall see, manages both to acknowledge the unevenness of time, to admit the uncanny, repetitive presentness of the past within the present, *and* to smooth time out, to contain the massacre within "past" time by appearing to enjoin a choice between the past and an emergent, modernized, present while indicating that there really is no choice, only an occasion for disinterested sympathy and a decent burial (of the dead, of the slave trade) that the living might live on unhaunted by these specters of the Atlantic.

*

Turner's first contact with Scott came in 1818, when the writer asked him to become one of the illustrators for his *Provincial Antiquities and Picturesque Scenery of Scotland* (1819–26).[22] Turner agreed and for the next twenty years he continued to accept commissions, either directly from Scott or from Scott's publisher Robert Cadell. Turner's designs for the *Provincial Antiquities* were followed by his illustrations for the *Poetical Works* (1833–34), the *Prose Works* (1834–36) (including a good number of etchings for the *Life of Napoleon*), and a commission to illustrate Cadell's luxurious new edition of the *Waverley* novels. In 1840, after having worked on and off since 1834 preparing sketches for the *Waverley* novels project (particularly for *Old Mortality* and *Waverley* itself), Turner declined, however, to continue. Cadell had decided that unlike the earlier illustrated editions of Scott he had published, the *Waverley* novels would be embellished with woodcuts rather than copperplate. Turner, who had spent decades perfecting his copper- and steel-plate technique, disdained wood engraving, which struck him as insufficiently "delicate."[23] Nevertheless, in the decades between accepting the first and withdrawing from the final commission, Turner had become intimate with Scott's work and with Scott himself, whom he visited while on sketching tours in Scotland and with whom he stayed on a number of occasions from the early 1830s onward. The period in which he found himself employed as Scott's illustrator (from 1818 to 1840) also coincided with the major shift Turner scholars see in his work from his descriptive to his expressive stage and with the emergence of an ever more pronounced literary tendency in his art. As Gerald Finley has it:

> By the time of his "expressive" phase . . . Turner had become convinced that a more intimate relationship between poetry and painting was possible and that his illustrations, if adapted, could participate more directly in the poet's vision. . . . This change ultimately led Turner closer to an abstraction which invested his landscapes with a new geometry and a new tautness of design; it also allowed him to invest his illustrations with a wider range of emotions and ideas than they had previously possessed. . . . That the most decidedly abstract designs prepared during this second phase were those done to embellish literature, and especially poetry, may not be entirely fortuitous. For, in a number of these, Turner employed devices equivalent to those found in poetry by which to strengthen the emotional content. Now, the artist, like the poet, is concerned not only with the objects of nature but also with his knowledge of, and responses to, them, and the fusion of these provides the basis for his creative experience. In poetry, metaphor is a means of giving expression to this experience, and of this Turner seems to have been well aware. It was for this reason that he appears to have imposed elements of a literary structure on his art, notably in the 1830s and often in his illustrations.[24]

Finley's appraisal of the transition in Turner's style during the years he worked as an illustrator to Scott echoes the evaluation of what remains the canonical study of Turner's art, John Ruskin's *Modern Painters*, volume 1. This is particularly true of the link Finley traces between the increasing emotional "intensity" of Turner's mature work, its ever greater tendency to abstraction, its heightened "literariness," and what he calls Turner's "knowledge" of the "objects of nature," which echoes the relationship Ruskin discerns between these same three characteristics of Turner's late painting style and what he identifies as the artist's "idea of truth." In either case, whether associated with knowledge or with truth, Turner's developed epistemological method, both critics agree, is abstract, literary, and (in Hume's sense) sentimental.[25] Which is another way of saying — as Ruskin's extended discussion of the dialectic of "thought" and "fact" in Turner's art will indicate — that Turner's method (on Poovey's terms, his knowledge project) is the method of what one might call the *sympathetic fact*: a fact ultimately closer to the abstract fact or the speculative fact than to the melancholy fact I earlier discussed.

This is how Ruskin begins to establish the terms for that rather complicated point in the first subsection of the first section on "Truth" in *Modern Painters*. The subsection falls under a header ("The two great ends of landscape painting are the representation of facts and thoughts") and advances the following argument:

> It cannot but be evident from the above division of the ideas conveyable by art, that the landscape painter must always have two great and distinct ends; the first to induce in the spectator's mind the faithful conception of any natural objects whatsoever; the second to guide the spectator's mind to those objects most worthy of its contemplation, and to inform him of the thoughts and feelings with which these were regarded by the artist himself. In attaining the first end, the painter only places the spectator where he stands himself; he sets him before the landscape and leaves him. The spectator is alone . . . But in attaining the second end, the artist not only *places* the spectator, but *talks* to him; makes him a sharer in his own strong feelings and quick thoughts, hurries him away in all his own enthusiasm; guides him to all that is beautiful; snatches him from all that is base, and leaves him more than delighted, — ennobled and instructed, under the sense of having not only beheld a new scene, but of having held communion with a new mind.[26]

To paint fact or to paint thought — that, Ruskin argues, is the choice the landscape artist must confront. In framing that choice (though really, he suggests, there is no choice, only the painting of thought is worthy, delightful, ennobling) Ruskin restates, almost exactly, the principles Adam Smith had established as fundamental to a proper historiographic method and "stile." Smith's argument in his lectures on *Rhetoric* was that historical truth is to be found not so much in the truth of the event (or fact) as in the truthful representation of the historian's affective response to a fact or event, or, as he puts it, in that "stile" whose "perfection" "consists in Express[ing] in the most concise, proper, and precise manner the thought of the author, and that in the manner which best conveys the sentiment, passion or affection with which it affects or he pretends it does affect him and which he designs to communicate to his reader."[27] "Truth" is thus not only thought, passion, sentiment, and feeling, but *style*: the style through which passionate, sentimental thought expresses itself. For the romantic epistemology and method that Ruskin shares with Smith and perceives in Turner, the path from object to thought, from fact to truth, is paved by style. Style abstracts the object, fact, or event, "ennobles" it, turns it into a thought, a feeling, a sentiment, or as Hume, Ruskin's other philosophical source for this argument would say, an idea.

Ruskin's debts to Hume are evident from the opening pages of *Modern Painters*, both in his discussion of "taste" in the early chapter on "Ideas of Beauty" and by virtue of his decision to dedicate the entire first section of the volume to an entirely Humean theory of ideas (in this case, a theory "Of the Nature of the Ideas Conveyable by Art" — the ideas in question are the ideas of power, imitation, truth, beauty, and relation). As Chandler, along with countless other commentators has noted, Hume's theory of ideas is intimately related to his theory of sentiments and to a cluster of key concepts, central among them the concept of the "impression" which, as both Solicitor Haywood's rhetoric in the *Zong* trials ("It makes an Impression upon my Mind") and Clarkson's *History* suggest, also played such a central role in a romantic abolitionist theory of historical representation and sentimental spectation (Clarkson's slave-ship print we recall, "was designed to give the spectator an idea of the sufferings of the Africans in the Middle Passage . . . to make an instantaneous impression of horror upon all who saw it"). This is how Chandler parses the relation of Humean "impression" and Humean "idea":

> To state the crux of the matter briefly, an impression on this account is something that we feel, and an idea is an afterimage of the impression. . . . The image that is the idea might therefore not inaptly be termed the specter or afterlife of the impression. What becomes crucial in the theory of sentiments that grows out of the theory of ideas, however, is that our minds work in such a way that the idea or image-of-the-impression has the capacity to return to us in a reflective modality. Such a return of the idea, itself cognitive in character, occasions a new affective event in our experience. Hume's name for this new reflective event is an "impression of reflection." . . . This basic scheme . . . became the framework of the so-called Romantic revolutions in poetry, especially the one led by Wordsworth and Coleridge in the *Lyrical Ballads* collaboration of 1798–1800. The Preface that Wordsworth wrote for the volume in 1800 . . . announced its epistemological premises in terms that deviated from the Humean

exposition only trivially. Describing the act of meditation that he felt entitled him to the authority of the poet, Wordsworth explained its operations in terms of his disciplined attention to "thoughts" (what Hume calls "ideas") that are the "representatives of past feelings" (what Hume calls impressions). . . . And in a versified passage written at about this same time for *The Prelude*, Wordsworth reproduced the schema in much the same form when he spoke of how "objects and appearances" were "impressed" on the mind. . . . This practice, grounded in what he punningly calls an "impressive discipline," was itself the basis of his great art of memory.[28]

Chandler is of course right to point to Wordsworth and Coleridge as among Hume's primary romantic inheritors, but, as the discourse on facts and thoughts in *Modern Painters* suggests, so too is Ruskin; and, Ruskin's argument implies, so too is Turner, the premiere artist, Ruskin maintains, among all landscape painters, the only painter wholly capable of conveying to the spectator not merely the facts of the world but the feelings, sentiments, and affections the impression of those facts induce as ideas in the mind.

As the historian or landscape painter's style conveys truth by transforming fact into affect, a romantic discourse of thoughts, sentiments, and feelings thus participates in the abstraction of the thingly world, fostering that world's idealized negation, its despecification. This somewhat unlikely emergence of idealist from romantic thought not only explains Finley's contention that the greater the emotional intensity of Turner's work the more abstract it becomes, but accounts for (or at least partially makes sense of) Poovey's broader claim that a hyperspeculative and autoreferential postmodern knowledge practice, itself a form of neoidealism ("whether it takes the form of Ferdinand de Saussure's claim that signs are arbitrary, Jacques Lacan's definition of the ego as lack, Jean Baudrillard's fascination with simulation's ability to end all original reference, or Slavoj Žižek's celebration of the 'meaningless traces' that thrust meaning production onto analysis itself"), finds its unlikely historical antecedent in "the romantic poets' turn away from phenomenal particulars and toward the mind that contemplates those things."[29] In turning the mind away from the things of the world toward the spectacle of a mind contemplating those things, this variant of romantic epistemology, no less than the speculative epistemology that I have been suggesting romanticism initially invokes itself to oppose, thus resituates the spectator at the center of the theater of "truth." Or, as Ruskin puts it, in rendering "truth" "the artist not only *places* the spectator, but *talks* to him; makes him a sharer in his own strong feelings and quick thoughts, hurries him away in all his own enthusiasm; guides him to all that is beautiful; snatches him from all that is base, and leaves him more than delighted, — ennobled and instructed, under the sense of having not only beheld a new scene, but of having held communion with a new mind."[30]

Ruskin's claim that the spectator of true art does not so much enter into visual conversation with the represented world as hold communion with the thoughts, sentiments, feelings, and ideas of another mind looking at the world, places him not only close to Smith (for whom sentimental identification is finally always with another sentimental spectator rather than with the scene, object, or event that occasions sympathy) but close to Scott, whose romantic types, I have argued, exist to call into being the type of the liberal spectator with whose sympathies the reader is invited to sympathize. It is equally evident for Ruskin that this is how Turner too commands sympathy, that in his art, also, the circuit of sympathy links the mind of the spectator to the ideas of the artist rather than to the facts of the world, that, for Turner, sympathy abstracts us from history instead of attaching us to its brute terrain. "The highest art, being based on sensations of peculiar minds . . . and being expressive of thoughts which could only rise out of a mass of the most extended knowledge. . . . can only be met and understood by persons having some sort of sympathy with the high and solitary minds which produced it — sympathy only to be felt by minds in some degree high and solitary themselves."[31]

But though sympathy associates minds with truth by associating them with one another rather than with the matter of nature or history, it remains the case, Ruskin insists, that some facts, some objects or events, some sorts of spectacle, are more conducive than others to such high, solitary, detached thought. And chief among these (for Ruskin as for Scott — as for Turner, the painter who inspired the former and imitated the latter) are the facts, objects, and spectacles of death: "There are few things so great as death; and there is perhaps nothing which banishes all littleness of thought and feeling in an equal degree with its contemplation. . . . But it is not the fear, observe, but the contemplation of death. . . . There is no sublimity in the agony of terror. . . . But the simple conception or idea of greatness or suffering or extent of destruction is sublime, whether there be any connection of that idea with ourselves or not. If we were placed beyond the reach of all peril or pain, the perception of these agencies in their influence on others would not be less sublime, not because peril or pain are sublime in their own nature, but because their contemplation, exciting compassion or fortitude, elevates the mind, and renders meanness of thought impossible."[32] It is hard to tell whether Ruskin is here describing Turner, Scott, or Adam Smith or merely glossing a generalized, deradicalized theory of the sentimental sublime that a century after the publication of Smith's *Theory of Moral Sentiments* had become the virtual common sense of what I am inclined to call romantic liberalism.

And that is precisely my point, precisely what underlies my argument that when, some sixty years after the event occurred, and finding himself beyond all reach of pain or peril, Turner cast his eye on the scene of the *Zong* massacre to paint that scene of dying and death, what he saw and caused his audience to see in *this particular event* was what such a romantic liberalism, detaching itself from its prior melancholy commitments, had learned to see, and to cause its communicants to see, in all *such events*: a fact rendered sentiment and thought by style; a sentimental thought to be exchanged between the high solitary mind of the artist and the mind of the spectator sympathetically bonded to that spectacle of the idea; an opportunity not only to place the spectator before the facts of history but to make "him" a sharer in strong feelings and quick thoughts, to leave him "under the sense of having not only beheld a new scene, but of having held communion with a new mind." Which is another way of saying that what *Slavers Throwing Overboard the Dead and Dying* renders visible is not the *Zong* massacre, not this atrocious thing, but—like Smith's *Theory* and Scott's novels—the very mind of romantic liberalism, contemplating such things.

Slavers, moreover, not only exemplifies the working of such thought in a mid-nineteenth-century moment discursively continuous with its mid-eighteenth-century moment of beginning, it is the very paradigm of a deradicalized mode of sentimental thought which over the past two and a half centuries has continued to inform (and liberalize) a Euromodern knowledge of the facts and truth of this and such atrocious events: events from which the idea of a rights-bearing, globally human subject is born as occidental modernity's dominant response to the spectacle of humanity in extremis, of life stripped bare. Modern human rights discourse, as I have discussed, owes much of its emergence to the circum-Atlantic abolitionist movement. The abolitionist movement, in its turn, emerged as a response to the unseen (but "fancied") horrors of the slave trade. The miseries abolition never saw in the slave trade but which it knew must exist were, above all, the miseries its unseeing eye saw in the middle passage. And the indescribable, unrepresentable middle passage rendered itself susceptible to representation in two iconic forms: the London Committee's cross section of a slave ship and Turner's painting of the *Zong* massacre. *Slavers Throwing Overboard the Dead and Dying* may not have created the modern subject of human rights and mournful liberal cosmopolitanism, but it certainly stands at the center of the history of both. For as I have said, what that painting ultimately makes visible is not the *Zong* massacre, not that "fact," but the sentimental mind of a romantic liberalism, the mind through which, for the past 150 years, liberal cosmopolitanism has continued to "know" the "truth" of the world and all its unseen miseries and so not to know the melancholy facts of history it has "thought" to represent.

Ruskin, of course, could not see that future of his present way of seeing (though he would have known its past) but he could see in *Slavers* the apogee of Turner's art, and, by virtue of the value he accorded Turner's artistry, the perfect achievement of high art and the perfection of a late, moderated romantic habit and method of converting fact to thought, impression to idea. That perfection, for Ruskin, was long latent in Turner's work, but it expressed itself fully only late in his career. When it came, however, it came quite completely and at a clear and definable moment: "[Turner's] powers did not attain their highest results till towards the year 1840, about which period they did so suddenly, and with a vigor and concentration which rendered his pictures at that time almost incomparable with those that had preceded them."[33] Readers familiar with the narrative structure and argumentative design of *Modern Painters* will find nothing surprising in this statement or in the date Ruskin ascribes to the perfection of Turner's art (whose "great characteristic," Ruskin asserts, was not simply "its power, beauty, and majesty of color" but its final "abandonment of all littleness and division of thought to a single impression."[34] For it was in 1840 that Turner produced the work that, for Ruskin, represented the apotheosis of his genius; and it is, in many respects, as a vast introduction to his reading of that single canvas that Ruskin wrote the preceding five sections of *Modern Painters*.

The painting, of course, is *Slavers Throwing Overboard the Dead and Dying*: the canvas that for Ruskin is easily Turner's "noblest work"; one whose "united excellences and perfection as a whole" *Modern Painters* exists to demonstrate; one to whose "power" and "truth" Ruskin's study offers its unqualified testimony as it finds that canvas ("dedicated to the most sublime of objects and impressions") "completing thus the perfect system of all truth which we have shown to be formed by Turner's works."[35] If, for Granville Sharp, the *Zong* massacre and the insurance trials on that slaughter functioned as one of the truth events toward which the great abolitionist subsequently devoted himself, then for Ruskin that truth event was not so much the massacre but the painting Turner made of it: the "impression" he took from it, the quick "feeling" and "thought" he derived from that "sublime object" and communicated to the mind of the spectator. What did Turner paint? Not the melancholy "fact" of the massacre, but the thought, feeling, and sentiment it inspired. And if *this* begins to sound entirely like Kant on the French Revolution ("This event consists neither in momentous deeds nor crimes committed by men . . . No, nothing of the sort. It is simply the mode of thinking of the spectators which reveals itself in this game of great revolutions, and manifests such a universal yet disinterested sympathy"),[36] then we should perhaps be entirely unsurprised to find a second-generation British romanticism dallying in the courts of idealism and speaking the thought of liberalism.[37]

Nor should we be surprised if this also begins to resemble, rather exactly, Sir Walter Scott and the scenes he brought before his spectators' eyes. For, as I previously noted, 1840 was not only the year in which Turner painted *Slavers*, it was also the year in which he completed his work for (and painterly apprenticeship to) Scott; the year he elected to discontinue his preparations for an illustrated edition to the *Waverley* novels and elected, instead, to paint his own historical romance. What had Turner drawn from Scott over the course of the preceding decades? The type, I have argued, of the *mournfully* liberal romantic spectator; and the type, Finley suggests, of a "literary structure" that "superimposed" on his paintings a late aesthetic theory of the romantic habitus, a theory which, even as it dictated "that landscape was [to be] considered more than mere topography: it was the silent witness to the events of human nature," simultaneously insisted that the "mood of 'historic presence'" in landscape be "commemorated through a recognition that what has passed must be irredeemably lost to the present."[38] Where Scott managed that recognition through the orchestration of his plots, Turner, as Finley subtly demonstrates, achieves it by the arrangement of figures (particularly the figure of the tourist, observer, or spectator) in the visual field:

> Turner is able to strengthen and amplify this historic presence by the particular relationships which he establishes between the tiny figures which populate these landscapes and ancient architecture. His architectural remains tend to be placed either in the deep middle ground or in distance, while figures, on the other hand, usually occupy the foreground or near-middle ground. By locating architecture in a position somewhat remote from the figures, Turner perhaps intuitively illustrates Racine's observation, in his Preface to *Bazajet*, that "people do not distinguish between that which is . . . a thousand years, and that which is a thousand miles away from them." In other words, by creating a physical gulf between figures and architecture, Turner is instilling a sense of temporal distance."[39]

Finley's argument might be rephrased this way: in Turner's landscapes the sequence of pictorial planes (foreground, middle ground, and distance) visually recapitulates a stadial, Scottish Enlightenment philosophy of history that cuts time into a series of distinct historical stages. Those diverse stages might coexist in a given moment, or in a given historical landscape, but their coexistence is more segmented than mutually constitutive. What is visible in the far distance or deep middle ground (architectural remains in the cases Finley discusses; the slave ship itself in *Slavers*; the Highlands, as I have argued, in Scott's novels) belongs more properly to a past that the present (visually associated with the watching figure in the foreground) *may* perceive but which it has, in effect, already left behind.

Slavers both conforms to this model and departs from or qualifies it. The ship occupies a visual field temporally removed from the present, but this marine landscape is inhabited by no watching figures. There are, to be sure, human figures in the painting, or portions of figures — the outstretched limbs of the drowning slaves. And their menace to the orderly arrangement of the painting's visual fields and subtending philosophy of history is evident: though drowning, though destined to disappear beneath the water, they do not remain in their assigned place, in the distant plane reserved for ruins and remnants, but spill out, water borne, into the foreground of the canvas, into the space reserved for the watchful eye of the present. Or almost so. For though the forward press of these bodies threatens to break the sentimental contract that Turner (with the assistance of Scott, Smith, Hume, and others) seems to make with his audience, that displacement of the bodies of the dying and the dead into the zone of the present, that contamination of now-being by what has been, that invitation to lay ourselves down in the watery grave with them, is effectively contained or quarantined by the border Turner draws around the scene. While *Slavers* seems to violate Turner's standard principles of composition by drawing the deep and middle ground (the past) into the foreground (the present) on the wave-borne bodies of the drowning slaves, the lower horizontal of the painting so markedly cuts across the death-filled expanse of water as to insist that in this painting there is no foreground, no stable point of observation within the painting itself. That foreground, rather, lies outside the painting. It coincides with the space in which the viewer stands. There is no figure of the spectator *in Slavers* because that spectator is, instead, invoked *by Slavers*, summoned to stand in front of the painting, safely sealed off from its fatal indeterminancy of time and ground by the canvas's frame. The distinction (between near and far, now and then) erased in the painting itself is, in other words, firmly reestablished by the border of the work. We stand as spectators before it, not as witnesses in it. Indeed, that seems to be its overriding visual imperative. There is no place for the witness in this historical scene, no place to stand, aggrievedly, within it. We must, instead, stand outside it. As with all of Turner's water scenes, "we are not," Ruskin insists, "allowed to tumble into it, and gasp for breath as we go down."[40]

Summoned to stand watchfully outside the painting (to occupy an observational position that thus becomes *Slavers'* true foreground, its space of presentness in which we both bear disinterested "witness to the events of human nature" *and*, in properly Scottian fashion, recognize "that what has passed must be irredeemably lost to the present"), the painting's spectator thus takes on the persona of the watching figure more typically present within but affectively unpossessed by Turner's Scottian "landscapes of memory." Finley's comments are again useful here: "Temporal separation becomes more pronounced when an emotional gulf exists as well. Figures in many of these illustrations [Turner's illustrations of Scott] appear unaware of or indifferent to the architectural fragments that surround them. . . . The figures in these views appear to be passing through the landscape . . . and the implied brevity of their presence enhances their temporal isolation."[41] The paradigmatic posture of Scott's protagonists, as Ian Duncan suggests, is that of the impartially sympathetic spectator who looks on and then moves on. Reappearing in 1840 in the guise of a visitor to the Royal Academy, that spectator, finding himself or herself pitched up before Turner's slave-ship canvas, would have found Turner's "noblest work" asking him or her to play the same role, to stand sympathetically outside this historical scene, to attend not to the melancholy facts it paints but to the thoughts and feelings it invites us to share, and then to pass on, the implied brevity of our presence before the scene enhancing our temporal isolation from it. Where Scott's readers learn to move on by turning the page to find Waverley and his ilk exchanging the damaged past of imperial history for the happy future of its liberal present, Turner's spectators would have found that same lesson confirmed by turning their eyes to the second painting that, as I have mentioned, Turner hung at the 1840 exhibition: *Rockets and Blue Light*, a painting of the steam age, of the new imperialism, of the current majesty of British naval power, of a present and future global order firmly *after* the age of sail, the age of slavery, and the age of interest.

*

Turning his eye to the awful sufferings of the slaves embarked on the middle passage, Thomas Clarkson found himself asking "How shall I describe their feelings?" "How shall I exhibit their sufferings?" "Where shall I find language?" Throughout his career, when attending to the horrors of slavery in Africa or on the Caribbean and American plantations, his answer to such questions had been quite clear: Where shall I find the language? In fancy, in fiction, in a realm of the imagination nevertheless "consistent with fact." But when it came to the middle passage, fancy, as I have argued, failed him, or, more accurately, lengthily abandoned his manuscript before eventually reappearing in statistical guise. Where before Clarkson had given his readers imaginary scenes "strictly consistent with fact," he now gave them an abstract, general representation, the committee's plate of a slave ship, and demanded that they discover in this "evidence" both an obligation to interestedness and an image of what they did not, could not, see. Turner's painting, *his* image of a slave ship, offers its audience exactly the same thing: evidence, the occasion for sympathy, and an evident depiction of what remains unseen. But as the form of Clarkson's queries makes quite clear, both Clarkson and Turner offer their audiences one more thing: the observing "I," the bruised spectator in search of a language of "feeling." The committee's slave-ship plate, Clarkson indicates, was "designed to give the spectator an idea of the sufferings of the Africans." That may be so. But like Turner's painting it could only make that gift, only hand that idea over, if it first gave the observer the idea of *himself* or *herself* as historical spectator. The idea of the sufferings of the Africans comes after this idea, and then, crucially, precedes another: the idea of the self as a historical spectator impressed by the idea of its own sympathy for the suffering.

In saying this I have been relying not only on my sense of the general economy of sympathetic identification that Clarkson and Turner derived from Smith, Hume, and Scott but on the particular meaning the terms "idea" and "impression" had acquired by the late eighteenth century and early nineteenth. To restate Chandler's formulation: "An impression on this account is something that we feel, and an idea is an afterimage of the impression.... The image that is the idea might therefore not inaptly be termed the specter or afterlife of the impression."

As the idea is to the impression in this general scheme (a less vibrant double, phantom, afterimage, or specter of an original feeling), so the "idea of the sufferings of the Africans" is to the "instantaneous impression of horror" the image of the slave ship affords. The "idea" of suffering, the one thing the image was designed to create, constitutes, in other words, an untimely affective event in the experience *of the spectator*. The spectator belatedly suffers the idea of the slave's suffering and so sentimentally secures the "past feelings" of the slave (or, at least, a representation, image, or "memory" of the past feelings of the slave) *as* the experience of his or her own spectral haunting by the idea of an observed moment (an "impression") of suffering. While the "idea" of suffering thus manifests itself as something like the intellectual property the spectator takes in the pains and sorrows of another, the suffering itself, the historical "real" that idea copyrights, virtually drops out of the picture or appears in the picture only as a spur, an impression, designed to invest the mind of the observer in the idea of his or her own agonized spectation.

And it is on this point, I have further indicated, that Clarkson and Turner, while clearly sharing a language of impressions, feelings, and ideas with Wordsworth (and Hume) reveal a debt not only to the romantic lyric but to the historical romance, not merely to the Lake poets but also to Scott and the suffering spectators who people his historical romances. I suggested earlier that Clarkson's *History* frequently reads like a sentimental picaresque or historical romance. What I meant by that is that once Clarkson appears on the scene as the central character of the text (after his initial description of abolitionist forerunners is complete), his *History* modulates its generic form, shifts from the recognizably historical to the protonovelistic or, indeed, if Chandler's larger argument regarding the revolution romantic thought provoked in historical consciousness, historiographic method, and historicist sensibility is correct, begins, in properly late-romantic fashion, to tell its history as if the past *were* a novel, and a novel of a specific sort plotted in relation to the adventures and sentimental journey of a particular type of protagonist. That sort of novel is, of course, the historical romance and that type of protagonist the Waverley type, the romance hero whose "elemental posture" as Ian Duncan has it, is "the posture of a *stranger who looks*": "In the role of liberal subject [he] arrives, watches, sympathetically suffers——and departs . . . [he plays] the spectator's part as that of a mourner, composing his sensibility upon the prospect of others' loss and death."[42]

I do not by this intend that either Clarkson or Turner were merely playing at mourning, simply counterfeiting sympathy as the price of admission to moral liberal subjectivity, but that their respective modes of bearing witness to the *idea* of historical suffering, death, and loss are utterly typical both of the spirit of the age and of the romance protagonists through whose novelized wanderings late-romantic-period Britons were learning to observe, make sense of, and screen themselves off from the greater violence of history. "The perfect historian," Macaulay observed in an essay on historiographic method published in the *Edinburgh Review* in 1828, "is he in whose work the character and spirit of the age is exhibited in miniature . . . by judicious selection, rejection, and arrangement, he gives to truth those attractions which have been usurped by fiction."[43] That Macaulay accords to the historian the precise task Lukács understands the period's historical novelists (above all others, Scott) to have assumed and mastered, that, indeed, Macaulay understands history to stand methodologically in debt to a fictionalizing practice that has "usurped" the historian's monopoly on historical truth, perhaps goes some way to explaining why in exhibiting the character and spirit of the abolitionist age as a portrait of his own sympathetic adventures, Clarkson's *History* might not only adopt fictional protocols in selecting and arranging its material but might stage the character of the historian himself in romance guise, or why Turner, coming to his subject matter by way of Clarkson's romance *History* and his own work as Scott's illustrator staged the *Zong* massacre as if it were indeed (as Solicitor Lee had facetiously complained some sixty years earlier) a scene from a historical romance: a scene of death to which the spectator (in the role of liberal subject) is invited — to watch, sympathetically suffer, and then depart.

To be so invited is of course also — at least potentially — to receive an invitation to melancholy as well as to liberalism, an invitation to lay down in the grave of the dying and the dead, an invitation to effect *that* sublime act of identification (and identity theft). Adam Smith understood this — his *Theory of Moral Sentiments* was written both to explore the experimental pleasures of just such an act of melancholy identification and to warn his readers of its dangers. In response to that danger his *Theory* gave us the "impartial spectator": the great hero (simultaneously sympathetic and disinterested) of worldly liberalism. In response to Smith and as a greater elaboration of his liberal protagonist, Walter Scott gave us Edward Waverley and all his novels' other spectators of suffering and death, all those middling protagonists whose romanticism is ultimately prior to and constitutive of a liberalism compounded, in equal measure, of the twin postures of looking on and moving on. In response to Smith, Scott, and the historical romance, Clarkson gave us his *History*, his print of a slave ship, and, most crucially, his portrait of his own worldly sympathy. And in response to Smith, Clarkson, and Scott, Turner gave us *Slavers Throwing Overboard the Dead and Dying* and so gave us the *Zong* massacre as, once more, at least potentially, an invitation to a decision. For at first glance the painting does invite us to assume some property in the event; to hold to it; to discern in the image of the miseries we never saw the melancholy "facts" of history, a worldly knowledge of things "as they are," and an obligation to act on that knowledge — to persist in it as it persists in the world.

This is what I mean by cosmopolitan interestedness. But, simultaneously, Turner invites us to watch, sympathize, and then move on, to compose ourselves (and our liberal virtue, worldly virtuosity, and virtuoso disinterestedness) as an effect of the *idea* of our witness to the sufferings of another. And this is what I understand by liberal cosmopolitanism.

there was

the this

the that

the frenzy

leaky seas &

casks

negroes of no belonging

on board

no rest

came the rains

came the negroes

came the perils

came the owners

master and mariner

the this

the that

the frenzy

— M. NourbeSe Philip, from *Zong! # 17*

CHAPTER 11

This / Such, for Instance

THE WITNESS AGAINST "HISTORY"

The Hegelian "end of history," "universal and homogenous state," or, as Alexandre Kojève, Hegel's primary twentieth-century interpreter sometimes more simply put it, "Empire," will come, Kojève reads Hegel to suggest, when a three-stage evolution in the history of right (or "droit") completes itself. As Kojève indicates in his *Outline of a Phenomenology of Right*, a magisterial synthesis (as its title suggests) of Hegel's *Outline of a Phenomenology of Spirit* and *Philosophy of Right*, Hegel's tripartite history of right corresponds to his three-stage anthropology of culture. In a first stage, right is aristocratic and its key procedure is to recognize and assure the formal equality of aristocratic actors in their relation to one another. In this moment right devotes itself to problems of "status" and derives its concept of status (and its obligation to preserve equality in status) from property — specifically landed, inherited, nonalienable property. In a second stage, right is bourgeois and its key procedure is to regulate and assure the formal equivalence of exchanges and relations between bourgeois actors. In this moment right devotes itself to the management of transactions and derives its theory of equivalent transactions from the realm of contract — particularly contracts for exchangeable property in the marketplace. In the third and final stage (the moment of Empire, or the universal and homogenous state), right is statist and its key procedure is to establish conditions of equity between the citizens of the state by balancing the often competing claims of equality and equivalence. In this moment right devotes itself to equivalently redressing the practical inequalities between citizens abstractly conceived as equal to one another, and it derives it procedures from jurisprudence. Aristocratic right, grounded in a concept of status equality and the fact of landed property; bourgeois right, grounded in a concept of equivalent value and the facts of contract; and citizenship right, grounded in a concept of equity among actors and the fact of juridical decision: these, then, are Hegel's three stages of history and of right.

It is perhaps worth noting that Hegel first conceived this theory while reading deeply in Scottish Enlightenment philosophical history (features of an Edinburgh "stadial" philosophy of history certainly find themselves refashioned here) and political economy (he began reading James Steuart and Adam Smith in the Steiger family library in Berne in 1796 and continued to be strongly influenced by Smith, in particular, throughout his life).[1] It may be further worth remarking that the transition from his first to his second stages (from aristocratic to bourgeois right, from landed property to contract, from status equality to transaction equivalence) duplicates both the "drama of property" Alexander Welsh understands Scott's novels to sketch (in their narrativization of the transition from a feudal order grounded in landed property and aristocratic virtue to a bourgeois order grounded in imperial market society) and the social revolution Pocock attributes to the contemporaneous replacement of feudal, heritable, propertied models of virtue by the credible virtue of the market's "new social personalities."[2] But there is one other feature of this theory of right, history, and the coming of the universal homogenous state that I want to stress, a feature that I am inclined to think Hegel was more likely to have drawn from the Scottish Enlightenment's moral philosophy than from its philosophy of history or political economy.

In all three stages of his history, Hegel's principles of right (equality, equivalence, equity) depend for their existence on the actions of someone able to enforce right's claims. And that someone, in Kojève's gloss on Hegel, is the "third":

> [The] *Droit* which realizes Justice is embodied in the person of the "impartial and disinterested third," in his three avatars as the juridical Legislator, Arbiter or Judge, and the judicial Police. It is he who applies the idea of Justice to a given social interaction, transforming it by this application into a juridical situation, into a relation of *droit* between two subjects of *droit*. And *Droit*, as the effective application of the idea of Justice to real interactions, is the realization of this idea. Therefore, if the idea of Justice is born in and from the anthropogenic Struggle between *two* adversaries, it is realized and exists as actual reality thanks to its application to bipartite interactions by a *third* who — by his impartial and disinterested intervention — makes the interactions in question conform to the idea or ideal of Justice, or at the very least, notices their conformity or non-conformity to this ideal. As for this ideal itself, it can be based upon either the aristocratic principle of equality or the bourgeois principle of equivalence, or finally upon a certain synthesis of these two primordial principles carried out by the Citizen, and that one could call the principle of equity.[3]

For Hegel, or at least for that Hegel Kojève has taught his readers to know, both the history of justice and "History" itself are thus tied to the history of the "third," to the "impartial, disinterested" "arbiter" or "judge," whose long-twentieth-century career (together with that of the "witness," this figure's counterpart and opposite) I have been tracing. I note this coincidence of interest in the figure of the third, not, however, to suggest that Hegel's *Philosophy of Right*, *Phenomenology of Spirit*, or theory of history is in some simple way reducible to Smith and the Scottish Enlightenment or indebted, in ways we have not yet appreciated, to Walter Scott (whom Hegel certainly read, though, at least in the case of Scott's *Life of Napoleon*, with some displeasure).[4] Rather, in concluding this section of my text, I want to look to what succeeds Hegel rather than to what precedes him. It is, in other words, the Kojève connection in which I am interested, the connection Kojève establishes between Hegel and Derrida, one of a generation of French philosophers whose understanding of Hegel Kojève intimately shaped.

If we read Derrida with this connection in mind, it will become apparent that Derrida's poetics of witnessing, *his* discourse on the third, the arbiter, and the judge, is entirely in conversation, via Kojève, with Hegel and so also with that entire Hegelian philosophy of history that has dominated much occidental thought for the past two centuries. It is no accident, I am thus suggesting, that Derrida's alternate name for the witness is the third. More significant, in figuring his witness so, Derrida can be seen both to accept Hegel's argument that this figure is not incidental to modern history but central to its unfolding *and* to reverse the force of that argument by reversing our conception of this third's obligation and character. For Derrida, that is, the third must be understood as neither impartial nor disinterested but aggrieved, wounded, damaged by the history he or she has both observed and not yet survived, the history in which, as witness, the third holds some melancholy property. As we have seen, there are other ways of naming such aggrieved interest, such melancholy property (in "humanity"), as there are figures other and earlier than Derrida (or Agamben or Badiou) who have helped shape that discourse of cosmopolitan interestedness I associate with this witness, this third. Where I want, however, to reconnect Derrida to the history I have traced (a history, to be sure, both of interested witness and of the disinterest that stands as its constant temptation) is at this point of Hegelian intersection. For what this conjuncture suggests is that to speak of the witness, to speak, for instance, of the witness to Auschwitz or the witness to the *Zong* massacre, is not to speak of an ethical practice esoteric to the history of the modern, but to speak of a practice of interest fundamentally at odds with the disinterested practices central to the emergence of occidental modernity, its universal philosophy of history, its theory of justice, its practices of empire, and its dreams of a universal and homogenous state of history.

To what, I earlier asked, does Granville Sharp's testament bear witness? What does his testimony front? This practice. This melancholy refusal of empire from within. This alternate, interested philosophy of history that invests itself in the property it holds in the what-has-been which it finds now-being has not yet survived. This does not mean that I understand the practice of witnessing to be somehow immune from the contaminations of history or to exist as some kind of pure and absolute mode of ethical and historical critique. In its eighteenth- and nineteenth-century incarnations as a romantic sympathy discourse, as I have indicated, witness is as apt to take its melancholy as an invitation to sympathize with the abstract spectacle of its own suffering as it is to hold itself to the singular instances of historical injustice in which it invests its interest. And indeed Derrida's writing is prone to a similar abstraction (or conceptualization) of its interest, not only at a general level of argumentation but even in apparently innocuous rhetorical moments, moments such as that in his " 'A Self-Unsealing Poetic Text': Poetics and Politics of Witnessing" in which Derrida appends a "for instance" to his revision of the Hegelian-Kojèvean figure of the third as arbiter or judge: "The judge, the arbiter, the historian also remains a witness, a witness of a witness when he receives, evaluates, criticizes, interprets the testimony of a survivor, for instance a survivor of Auschwitz."[5]

"For instance a survivor of Auschwitz." It seems impossible to imagine that a writer so attuned to the finest valence and pitch of language would permit himself an unconsidered use of such a formulation; one which, though it stops short of "for instance, the Holocaust," is no less troubled by the relationship it seeks to establish between surviving *this* and surviving *as such*, between bearing witness to *this* and bearing witness *as such*, between Auschwitz as a singular, named, and catastrophic truth event and Auschwitz as a rhetorical and conceptual example. My point in noting this is ultimately less to query Derrida's text than to call attention to the paradoxes of my own. For though I have tried to avoid the parallel phrase "for instance, the *Zong*" (or even, "for example, the *Zong*"), that formulation has been implicit to much that I have said. Indeed if there has been an organizing set of questions animating this second section of the book, they are questions that address the status and meaning of exactly this and such formulations; questions that ask again what the *Zong* might be exemplary of; questions of what it means to formulate it as such an instance, case, example, or type; questions of how precisely *this* mode of formulation (one which can say "for instance Auschwitz" or "for example, the *Zong*," one which, more formally, predicates itself on the ability to read "this" as "such") is fundamental to a modern labor of witness *as such* and in being thus central to a politics of witnessing threatens to undo the counter-Hegelian enterprise that I understand to be crucial to Derrida's project and that is certainly vital to my own.

To get some sense of how such formulations ("for instance," "as such") potentially destabilize Derrida's (and my own) poetics of witnessing and also, consequently, whatever politics of melancholy might attend any "like" act of bearing witness *to*, or holding interest *in*, an event "such" as the *Zong* massacre, it is worth returning to the text Derrida selects as the rhetorical centerpiece of his essay on witnessing and to the relation Derrida seeks to establish between the singular witness of Celan's poem and the exemplary witnessing of his, Derrida's, poetics. As witness is to witnessing, and as a poem is to a poetics, so, indeed, is the singular to the exemplary. The conceit of Derrida's essay (in fact a master conceit of deconstructive method) is, however, that neither poem nor poetics, neither witness nor witnessing, is ever simply one or the other, ever solely singular or exemplary, in-itself or for-itself, but always already both at once. To apprehend the dyads poem/poetics, witness/witnessing, in-itself/for-itself in this way (which is to say, in *such* a way) is, by the language of deconstruction, to engage the experience of the impossible. In epistemological terms, this experience of the impossible manifests itself as the undecidable; ethically it articulates itself as an obligation to decision. That this experience of the impossible is also another way of describing, without naming, the dialectic is one of deconstruction's imperfectly kept secrets. Which does not mean that deconstruction is merely the most recent instance of German idealist philosophy.[6] But it does imply that a Derridean deconstruction is as fully haunted as is Derrida's Marx: haunted by the specter of the dialectic, haunted by Hegel. And it is this Hegelian specter that Derrida's "Poetics and Politics of Witnessing" seems both most willing to exorcise and most prone to calling back into life as he engages Celan's poem and its undecidably singular and exemplary text of witness/ing.

Celan's poem, or at least those portions of it that Derrida cites, is, it emerges, a virtually ideal document from which Derrida can derive his poetics, primarily because of the tension it sustains between the nominative particularity of its title ("Aschenglorie") and the departicularized abstractions of the lines that fall under that title and move it ever further from its apparent occasion of naming and address. A poem that seems simultaneously to demand and to refuse a discrete referent, "Aschenglorie" contains within itself the twin and contradictory (and "impossible" and "dialectical") imperatives of the in-itself and the for-itself, the particular and the conceptual, the singular and the exemplary. Derrida's essay reproduces that undecidablity — at least theoretically — as it adduces from Celan's text a poetics of witnessing dually, impossibly, undecidably, and dialectically obligated both to the singularity of what Celan's witness has witnessed and to the exemplarity of that act of bearing witness. Throughout the essay, Derrida stages this undecidability in precisely such terms, speaking from the opening paragraph on of his poetics of witnessing as "a poetics which must also, as if *across* its generality, *become, invent, institute, offer* for reading, in an exemplary way, signing it, both sealing and unsealing it, the possibility of the poem. This would come about in the event itself, in the verbal body of its singularity."[7] The essay's indecision is however only apparent. And it is Derrida's "for instance" which reveals this: that "for instance" which, like the singular/exemplary dyad, also repeats across the essay, springing not only the phrase "for instance a survivor of Auschwitz," but also, later, this:

One cannot and (in addition or moreover or above all) one should not bear witness for the witness, in all the senses of 'for.' One cannot and should not (claim to) replace the witness of his own death, for instance someone who perished in the hell of Auschwitz (but that does not mean that this poem is a poem on Auschwitz—and for the very reason that I am in the process of pointing out again, namely that no one bears witness for the witness). One neither can nor should replace (thus bear witness *for*) the witness of his or her own death, or the witness of others' deaths, the one who was present and survived, for instance at the hell of Auschwitz."[8]

Ironically, as the second of these sentences indicates, it is precisely by positing a referent for the poem, by provisionally decoding its title and attaching it ("for instance") to a named historical event ("the hell of Auschwitz"), that Derrida reveals his decision *not* for the singular, *not* for the obligation of bearing witness to *this* hell, but for the exemplary, for the obligation of bearing witnessing *as such*. That reformulation of the decision "Aschenglorie" seems to demand, that restatement of its twin ethical imperative of bearing witness to "this" and bearing witness "as such," is, indeed, one of Derrida's own reformulations of his impossible poetics. And, to be sure, he seem at moments to be more than willing to privilege the former over the latter, to choose, as the final sentences of the essay indicate, to read this as a poem that "speaks about witnessing in general, but first of all about the poem that it is, about itself in its singularity, and about the witnessing to which any poem bears witness. Left here to itself, in its essential solitude, in its performance or in its happening, the poetic act of the work perhaps no longer derives from the presentation of the self *as such*."[9] But whenever the underlying logic of this decision obliges Derrida to in fact indicate what "this" might be, whenever it constrains him to cease, for the moment, to speak of witnessing "as such," whenever it binds him to speak of "a survivor of Auschwitz," or "someone who perished in the hell of Auschwitz," or simply "the hell of Auschwitz," that decision is immediately withdrawn. Indeed it is reversed, either straightforwardly ("but that does not mean that this poem is a poem on Auschwitz") or, more generally, by virtue of that qualifying "for instance" which guarantees that any naming of "this" will immediately withdraw itself, immediately insist on its mere exemplarity, immediately reconceive *this* "as such." Perpetually substituting witnessing for witness, witnessing *as such* for witnessing *this*, an exemplary poetics for a poetry of the singular by repeatedly exchanging the "for instance" for *the* instance, Derrida consistently makes the very opposite decision to that he appears to enjoin, consistently recalls the Hegelian ghost at the very moment he seems to exorcise it.

Why? And to what effect?

Slavoj Žižek, in a broader critique of the political ideology of deconstructive method that reveals his frankly partisan preference for Badiou over Derrida, has suggested that such moments are emblematic of an aversion to, indeed a dread of, "ontologization" pervasive in post-1968 left French thought:

> Perhaps the gap separating Badiou from the standard postmodern deconstruc-
> tionist political theorists is ultimately created by the fact that the latter remain
> within the confines of the pessimistic wisdom of the failed encounter: is not the
> ultimate deconstructionist lesson that every enthusiastic encounter with the
> Real Thing, every pathetic identification of a positive empirical Event with it,
> is delusive semblance sustained by the short circuit between a contingent posi-
> tive element and the preceding universal Void. In it, we momentarily succumb
> to the illusion that the promise of impossible fullness is actually realized — that,
> to paraphrase Derrida, democracy is no longer merely *à venir* but has actually
> arrived; from this, deconstructionists draw the conclusion that the principal
> ethico-political duty is to maintain the gap between the Void of the central
> impossibility and every positive content giving body to it — that is, never fully
> to succumb to the enthusiasm of hasty identification of a positive Event with
> the redemptive Promise that is always "to come."[10]

If, to paraphrase Žižek, the self-assigned ethicopolitical duty of deconstruction has thus been to insist that we are finally always "before" the event, to
maintain, even when — or especially when — the revolutionary event seems to
be taking place, that it is in fact yet to come, then it must also be an obligation
of deconstruction to withhold the same ontological authority from the catastrophes of the past which, because in this sense they have also not absolutely
come, we are also in no real sense "after."

Regardless of the virtues of Žižek's answer, I do not intend to indicate that
this refusal to ontologize somehow disqualifies the oppositionality of Derrida's politics. To the contrary, Derrida here, and in his other, more well-
known writings, has helped to produce the very terms and language of that
politics of melancholy and that theory of the enduring (because unfinished)
event in which I have invested my own interest. I do however want to suggest
that even as Derrida has helped fashion the key terms of this counterpolitics of
the modern, he regularly demonstrates (and, I believe, understands himself to
demonstrate) the danger of committing to these terms as concepts. For reconstituted by that "for instance" as yet another concept, witness (or, more precisely, witnessing) runs the risk, the moment it enters this Hegelian domain of

the conceptual, of finding itself outwitted by the cunning of dialectical reason. Derrida's gambit, as I understand it, is that this is a risk not just worth taking but necessary to take, that absolutely stripped of any conceptual possibility, witness (witnessing) might indeed both seek to pass itself off as some pure, absolutely uncontaminated thing and wholly fail to contest the general, imperial authority of the disinterested, impartial, Hegelian third and the narrative of historical time that third abstractly personifies.

To bear witness to the singular is, therefore, *not* the opposite of an exemplary act of witnessing. Rather, it is by bearing witness to *this* that witness simultaneously offers its testamentary opposition to the coming of the disinterested, liberal, imperial, universal, and homogenous state *as such*. And among the most crucial things that such an act of witness testifies against are not only the manifold and singular injustices of imperial history but the very concept of historical time fundamental to Hegel's philosophy of history itself. If the universal, homogenous state is to be denied, if an imperial "end of history" is to be outwitted, it must be countered, *such* a conception of witness and the third understands, not only by recalling to memory the violence of the imperial past but by refusing that Hegelian and post-Hegelian model of historical time which views this past and its violence as, in fact, *past* and, so, no longer pertinent to a present practice of justice or philosophy or right. In the conclusion of this book, I want therefore to briefly consider a series of recent representations of the *Zong* massacre (or of *such* an event) whose acts of witness (and poetics of witnessing) collectively articulate an entirely counter-Hegelian, antiprogressive, and testamentary philosophy of history. In doing so, however, I also want to examine the ways in which these works, while certainly investing their energy in the figure of the witness, nevertheless displace this figure (whether in its Derridean incarnation as the third or in the form of the Benjaminian historical materialist) as the redemptive, ethical agent of anti-imperial history and turn our attention instead to the very nature of an order of historical time they do not so much urge us to produce as enjoin us to inhabit: an order of time that does not pass but accumulates.

Part Three

"THE SEA IS HISTORY"

Where are your monuments, your battles, martyrs?

Where is your tribal memory? Sirs,

in that grey vault. The sea. The sea

has locked them up. The sea is History.

First, there was the heaving oil,

heavy as chaos. . . .

Then there were the packed cries,

the shit, the moaning:

Exodus.

Bones soldered by coral to bone,

mosaics

mantled by the benediction of the shark's shadow

— Derek Walcott, "The Sea Is History"

CHAPTER 12

"The Sea is History"

On Temporal Accumulation

An image has been haunting the Martinican novelist and philosopher Edouard Glissant, an image of slaves drowning. First present in his *Caribbean Discourse* as something called to his mind by a phrase in one of Edward Braithwaite's works ("the unity is submarine"), that image not only repeats itself in the first section of the later *Poetics of Relation* but recurs in the epigraphs framing the book as a suggestion of what has been seen and what is about to be seen again. Here, in the earlier work, *Caribbean Discourse*, is the atrocious image Brathwaite's comment conjures: "To my mind this expression ["the unity is submarine"] can only evoke all those Africans weighed down with ball and chain and thrown overboard whenever a slave ship was pursued by enemy vessels and felt too weak to put up a fight. *They sowed in the depths the seeds of an invisible presence*. And so transversality, and not the universal transcendence of the sublime, has come to light. It took us a long time to learn this. We are the roots of a cross-cultural relationship. . . . We thereby live, we have the good fortune of living, this shared process of cultural mutation, this convergence that frees us from uniformity."[1] And here, some years later, is the reapparition of that image (a reapparition that is staged on the second page of *Poetics of Relation* but which, in a sense, does not wait until that page is turned to present itself again, encroaching, instead, on the reader's eye as an intimation of the *déjà vu* the moment the eye, scanning the book's epigraphs, sees there, again, the line by Brathwaite ("the unity is submarine,") alongside another by Walcott ("the sea is history") and sees in anticipation, and in memory, what Glissant himself is about to see again:

> The next abyss was the depths of the sea. Whenever a fleet of ships gave chase to slave ships, it was easiest just to lighten the boat by throwing cargo overboard, weighing it down with balls and chains. These underwater signposts mark the course between the Gold Coast and the Leeward Islands. Navigating the green splendor of the seas . . . still brings to mind, coming to light like seaweed, these lowest depths, these deeps. . . . In actual fact the abyss is a tautology: the entire ocean, the entire sea gently collapsing in the end into the pleasures of sand, makes one vast beginning, but a beginning whose time is marked by these balls and chains gone green. . . . For though this experience made you, original victim floating toward the sea's abysses, an exception, it became something shared and made us, the descendants, one people among others. Peoples do not live on exception. Relation is not made up of things that are foreign but of shared knowledge. This experience of the abyss can now be said to be the best element of exchange."[2]

The reversal that structures Glissant's first image of this scene, the reversal that replaces an image of terror with an image of promise, a knowledge of endings with a knowledge of beginnings, is once again present here, though now that reversal manifests itself not only as an essentially performative act (in Austin's sense of the word) but as a tropological argument, as a "poetics" whose organizing figures ("exception," "exchange," "errancy," "endurance," "accumulation," "relation") name Glissant's attempt to grasp and make sense of the reversal he had earlier merely insisted upon.

Indeed, this passage from exception to relation, this passage from a vision of exceptional suffering and of those violently excepted from history, to the vision of a unity, a solidarity, functions as a shorthand code for, or condensation of, Glissant's entire poetics of relation. Crucially, however, what enables this passage (from endings to beginnings, from terror to promise, from exception to relation) is a second, implied reversal: a reversal of what, with reference to the slave trade, we must understand exchange to entail. For if, in this context, "exchange" continues to suggest not only a generically formal logic of dematerialization (a stripping away of the exceptional quality of things in their transit from use values to exchange values), but also a historically particular absolutization of such dedifferentiating protocols (an apocalyptic stripping away of the exceptional quality of persons in their speculative transit from humanness to money), then, however counterintuitive this might seem, Glissant suggests that exchange must be apprehended, in precisely such moments, not only as a word for loss but as a word for gain. Exchange, in this sense, once more names a form of substitution, though here what replaces exceptionality is not fungibility but relation, where relation is a word for what I have been calling an interested politics of the abysmal event (an antitranscendent and recognizably counter-Kantian habit of holding to "the deeds and crimes" from which Kant's sublimely disinterested theory of the event seeks to detach itself), *and* a word for those new "transverse" forms of culture, identity, and solidarity that emerge from the act of holding to, enduring, relating, and avowing our (present's) relational complicity with modernity's most violent scenes of exchange.

The *Zong* massacre never enters Glissant' *Poetics of Relation* by name. But there can be little doubt that just "such" an event has been haunting his writing and (150 years after Turner completed his slave-ship canvas) thus once again, if far more systematically and far more radically, hurt an understanding of our global "folded-togetherness" (what Glissant calls our "giving on and with" the fate of one another), into articulation. But if the sentimental scenography of Turner's canvas might be seen to ghost Glissant's image of the drowning slave, then in re-appearing as an abiding and haunting spirit of Glissant's poetics of "relation," this image certainly disrupts the sympathetic protocols of what I have been calling the politics of liberal cosmopolitanism — not least because of the ways in which, for Glissant, this image of the Atlantic "abyss" folds together an ethics of global interestedness, a theory of cultural production, and an interested philosophy of history.

Time, I earlier indicated, does not pass, it accumulates. For Glissant, as for a range of other writers who in recent years have demanded that we regard the Atlantic slave trade as a (perhaps *the*) foundational event in the history of modernity, to speak of the testamentary, interested politics of the cosmopolitan is to avow precisely such a conception of time and so to break not only with the mournful sensibilities of political liberalism but to abandon the temporal schemes of its progressive philosophy of history. In concluding this book

I want to examine some of the ways in which for both Glissant and a collection of other writers invested in the task of elaborating a black-Atlantic genealogy and counterculture of modernity, an interested Atlantic cosmopolitanism has thus come to imply not only a way of being, presently, in the world but a way of conceiving a world which is resolutely "after" the "present," a world in which, in a not-entirely-Benjaminian fashion, now-being accumulates within itself a vast global array of what-has-beens. While it is not the case that for all these writers the *Zong* massacre is that determinate, singular what-has-been in which our long modernity finds itself anticipated, demonstrated, and recollected, it is nevertheless true that for many of them the work of elaborating a responsible politics of the modern has rendered itself coterminous with the testamentary obligation to bear witness to just such an event and the challenge it puts to a post-Enlightenment understanding of the unfolding of historical time.

*

Glissant's *Poetics of Relation* is no less magisterial, various, or ambitious a text than Spivak's *Critique of Postcolonial Reason*. Indeed, Glissant shares with Spivak a will to a near-total accounting of the modern. But where Spivak situates at the center of this account an abjectly worldly figure (the "native informant") and a set of deconstructive "protocols" for interpreting the world (the cryptic, the singular, the experience of the impossible), Glissant's text discovers itself as the elaboration of a posture toward the world and a grammar of geopoetical forms of being in the world. That posture is the posture of errancy (which, by the terms I have been using, may be recognizably "fanciful" and thus, even, romantic, but immediately distinguishes itself from the late, neoliberal romanticism of both Turner and Ruskin by its profound antipathy to romantic liberalism's worldly attitude of sympathetic guilt). What I am calling the geopoetical forms of this disposition to the world (this way of giving "on and with" it), concatenate around a set of tropes which organize the composition of the text: endurance, exchange, exception, accumulation, and, above all, relation. I will return to these organizational lexical units of Glissant's *Poetics*, but first a word on the fundamental posture they detail.

To be errant, I earlier suggested, is not so much to be mistaken, as to be in transit, to be in imaginative flight across the world. Errancy, for Anna Letitia Barbauld, is the prerogative of fancy, and fancy's obligation is to navigate the globe, to bring to light the far reaches and dim suburbs of the world system. So too for Glissant, who begins the *Poetics of Relation* with a claim upon the imagination, a demand that we see what we have not, in fact, seen: "Imagine," he insists in the first paragraph of the text, "two hundred human beings crammed into a space barely capable of containing a third of them. Imagine vomit, naked flesh, swarming lice, the dead slumped, the dying crouched. Imagine, if you can, the swirling red of mounting to the deck, the ramp they climbed, the black sun on the horizon, vertigo, this dizzying sun plastered to the waves."[3] Imagine, he asks once again, the slave ship. For him also, that is where we must begin. But unlike his abolitionist interlocutors, unlike Clarkson or Turner, for whom the capacity to *imagine* just such an atrocious resolution to the career of a human life is the *end* (the point, the purpose, the object) of the ethical imperative, and unlike Hegel (or his partial source, Adam Smith) for whom the capacity to stand as a neutral, impartial, equitable judge before such a scene is to help bring about the completion and end of history, this is not where Glissant's poetics of relation ends. Not only because the slave trade refuses to detach itself from slavery itself, nor the slave ship from the plantation, nor the plantation from the ghetto and the shantytown, but because this brutal passage of world history is not, he argues, terminal but originary, or, rather, a middle-passage into an experience of global modernity and a type of global responsibility whose errant, wandering, political tangent is not "vectoral" but "circular," not equitable but relational.

Errancy (the interested questioning of modernity and the world, interested acknowledgment of our multiple entanglements in the world of modernity, and interested engagement with an inveterately worldly modernity's multiple networks of relation) should not, Glissant insists, be confused with a one-way ("vectoral") movement of thought or connection. It implies neither a simple moving out into the world nor a mere extension of interest from one of modernity's fixed poles (or metropoles) to one of its zones of agony. For conceived thus, errancy would amount to little more than a unilinear trade in affect, a centripetal market of feeling headquartered in the world's "centers" of political sympathy as they radiate their spokes of concern to the global "peripheries" of modern experience, a renovated liberal cosmopolitanism which could only serve to confirm the global centrality of those metropolitan elites whose profit on the knowledge of suffering they import is the disinterested sympathy they warehouse or put on display. In David Armitage's terms the problem with this sort of politics (the problem, one might say, of British abolitionism) is that it remains resolutely "cis-Atlantic," liberally directed out and back from one privileged point in the Atlantic archipelago, rather than rendering itself grievously "circum-Atlantic," resolutely in transit via a set of circular trajectories of interest around, across, and through the Atlantic world system.[4] And it is just such a circular "exchange" of interest and interestedness that for Glissant characterizes the thought and politics of a global errancy which "leads from periphery to periphery, makes every periphery into a center . . . abolishes the very notion of center and periphery."[5]

This does not mean that Glissant utterly dismisses the eighteenth- and nineteenth-century project of sympathy I have traced. Though the relational politics of errancy may seek to put an end to such a liberal project, Glissant discovers in precisely such a dead end of political attachment the first stirring of a more promising beginning: "Because these trajectories (from the European here to elsewhere) end up abolishing what yesterday originally occasioned their being: the linear projection of sensibility toward the world's horizons, the vectorization of this world into metropolises and colonies." Abandoning the vectoral thought of metropolitan liberalism, errancy also abandons liberalism's posture of objectivity and pose of disinterestedness as it "strives to know the totality of the world." "The thought of errancy," Glissant insists, "is not apolitical . . . it neither implies nor authorizes any ecumenical detachment."[6] But neither does it imply a fantasy of metropolitan placelessness, an only mildly radicalized Enlightenment dream of knowing or engaging the world from the abstract nowhere of the mind. For if errancy names a sort of roving global politics of interestedness, a total cosmopolitan practice of holding ourselves to the fate of one another, an endlessly circular and radically fanciful determination to *give on and with* "the problems of the Other," then errancy's refusal of detachment (like its geography of address) is also circular.[7] Attached to the problem of the historical other, that is, errancy also attaches itself to the singular, exceptional terrain of the self-in-history. Errancy, interestedness, the politics of the cosmopolitan, Glissant maintains, is and must be "rooted." If it moves toward the future, it does so by doubling back on what has been. If it aspires to the global, then it also has, and should avow, its scenes of departure, its historical grounds of interest and articulation. And this, he argues, is both generally and specifically true, both generally conditional to any elaboration of an errant, relational, interested politics of the globe, and true in a quite specific, even a singular, sense.

For if errancy is always rooted, always hurt into being by a determinate and situated experience of history, then, he further suggests, errancy also has something like an exemplary or originary space of emergence, a first scene. And that space is the Atlantic, that scene the Atlantic abyss. Or let me put it this way: if, by Glissant's terms, errancy is not the abstract and utopic product of an Enlightenment or liberal nowhere of the mind, it is because it is, instead, the strange fruit of the Atlantic abyss, the transverse produce of a singular historical trauma, the engaged knowledge of modernity floatingly rooted in the Atlantic's submarine, exceptional, and alluvial grounds.

Why?

Because, Glissant argues, while the signature characteristic of the modern is to bring into intense and inextricable relation what was once held (or held to be) disparate, it is in the slave cultures of the black Atlantic world that such an experience of living in relation (of giving, willfully or not, "on and with" one another) inescapably enters modern practices of everyday life. For Glissant the paradigmatic modernity of black-Atlantic history is thus a function not only of the abysmal sufferings and disorientations of the slave experience but of the creole, relational cultures that emerge from within the world of slavery. To have been drawn within the networks of trans-Atlantic slavery may have been to become encamped within a permanent state of exception, but slavery's very spaces of exception — its abyssal waters and abysmal plantations — he argues, are also those spaces in which the relational, creole, métissage cultures of modernity are forced into a sustained and intense existence.

This does not mean that Glissant views the Atlantic abyss as without any precedent in his genealogy of a transverse, creole, relational modernity, but it does indicate that he understands trans-Atlantic slavery as paradigmatic or exemplary. "The cultures of the world," he argues, "have always maintained relations among themselves that were close or active to varying degrees, but it is only in modern times that some of the right conditions came together to speed up the nature of these connections."[8] And those right conditions were the atrocious conditions of the barracoon and the plantation: *the* exceptional/ exemplary laboratories of modernity and paradigmatically modern zones of relational encampment; zones now apparent to Glissant not only in the Afro-Americo-Caribbean ghettos, townships, and shantytowns that are the plantation's most immediate successor quarters but in every hybrid, creole, or mixed interstice of the planetary habitus described in the great imaginative tours of the globe that are the *Poetics of Relation*'s late-twentieth-century analogues of Barbauld's romantic flights of fancy to the dim reaches of the world system:

> The disintegration of the [plantation] system left its marks. . . . In the Caribbean and in Latin America the burgeoning shantytowns drew masses of the destitute and transformed the rhythm of their voices . . . In the United States southern blacks went up North . . . toward cities that were becoming violently dehumanized, where nonetheless the Harlem writers, for example, wrote their

Renaissance upon walls of solitude. Thus urban literature made its appearance in Bahia, New York, Jacmel, or Fort-de-France. The Plantation region, having joined with the endless terrain of haciendas or latifundio, spread thin to end up in mazes of sheet metal and concrete in which our common future takes its chances. This second Plantation matrix, after that of the slave ship, is where we must return to track our difficult and opaque sources. . . . . Negro spirituals and blues, persisting in towns and growing cities; jazz, *biguines*, and calypsos, bursting into barrios and shantytowns; salsas and reggaes. . . . This was the cry of the Plantation, transfigured into the speech of the world. For three centuries of constraint had borne down so hard that, when this speech took root, it sprouted in the very midst of the field of modernity.[9]

If, in arguing thus, Glissant can be seen to offer an Atlantic counterclaim to Georg Lucáks's well-known suggestion that it is in the Napoleonic wars, in the vast mobilization of eighteenth- and nineteenth-century citizen armies and their wanderings over the European continent, that modernity comes into a historicist awareness of itself, if, Glissant's argument indicates, it is in the intersection of new world migration and trans-Atlantic slavery, in *that* vast mobilization of human beings into relational exchange with one another, in the dim verges of the plantation system and its circum-Atlantic urban successor zones that a transverse "modernity" finds its moment of beginning, then in advancing such a claim Glissant's *Poetics* is by no means alone. At the very least, it affirms the central argument of Paul Gilroy's *The Black Atlantic: Modernity and Double Consciousness*, a text in which the black Atlantic not only constitutes a "counterculture of modernity" but emerges, once again, as genealogically original to an experience *of* the modern.[10] But while Glissant's *Poetics* is certainly in agreement with Gilroy's *The Black Atlantic* (as it also identifies what Gilroy calls the "fractal," pluriform, expressive cultures that emerge from the history of trans-Atlantic slavery as the paradoxical, relational gift of modernity: the painfully inherited "best element" of modern "exchange"), Gilroy is not unique among Glissant's interlocutors. As the language of "exception" fundamental to Glissant's conception of relational exchange suggests ("For though this experience made you, original victim floating toward the sea's abysses, an exception, it became something shared and made us, the descendants, one people among others. . . . This experience of the abyss can now be said to be the best element of exchange"), Glissant's partners-in-conversation also include Giorgio Agamben, Carl Schmitt, and Walter Benjamin.

And indeed, it is with Benjamin rather than with Agamben or Schmitt that

Glissant's *Poetics of Relation* stages one of its most significant if also one of its most allusive exchanges and debates. For while Glissant shares with Agamben the understanding that the state of exception is foundational to the sovereign emergence of the modern and joins Schmitt in identifying the New World slave plantation as a (or, in fact, *the*) exemplary space in which modernity thus encamps itself, it is Benjamin's counterintuitive reading of the state of exception as both the dystopic type of the modern and the territory or ground of a redemptive "task" and possibility of historical knowledge and experience that most fully accords with Glissant's exceptional poetics of exchange. In understanding the abysmal spaces of the slave ship, slave plantation, and underwater slave burial ground as not only evidencing the exceptional sovereign power of trans-Atlantic capital and trans-Atlantic race terror but also as seeding the alluvial ground of a transverse, relational mode of being in the world whose elaboration is the task of his *Poetics*, Glissant, in other words, shares with Benjamin the paradoxical insight that the labor of an engaged philosophy of history is not to free the present of the violence of the past but to discover in the very brutality of what-has-been the responsibility and promise of a transverse, relational now-being. As Benjamin has it in the eighth of his "Theses on the Philosophy of History": "The tradition of the oppressed teaches us that 'the state of exception' in which we live is the rule. We must arrive at a concept of history that corresponds to this fact. Then we will have the production of the real state of exception before us as a task."[11]

For Benjamin, as I have indicated, the "task of confronting and producing that real state of exception is coincident with a quasi-testamentary theory of the event (or truth event) and with an interested reconceptualization of historical time: a reapprehension of time which insists that the moment of now-being in which we take up the work of historical responsibility (and historical interest) is not ontologically subsequent to, or "after," the violent moments of the what-has-been to which we task or attach ourselves, but exists in a nonsynchronous and long-durational correspondence with these distant moments. For Benjamin, that is, the task of historical responsibility is coincident not simply with the "Theses'" well-known instruction that the work of historical materialism is to "seize hold of a memory as it flashes up at a moment of danger," but with the theory of the image that informs his fuller explication of that "flash" of memory in both the "Theses" and the *Arcades Project*. This is how Benjamin puts it in the "Theses": "The past can be seized only as an image which flashes up at the instant when it cannot be recognized and is never seen again . . . To articulate the past historically does not mean to recognize it 'the way it really was' (Ranke). It means to seize hold of a memory as it flashes up at a moment of danger. Historical materialism wishes to retain that image . . . History is the subject of a structure whose site is not homogeneous empty time, but time filled by the presence of the now [*Jeitzeit*]."[12] And this, one last time, is the formulation he advances in the *Arcades*: "Each 'now' is the now of a particular recognizability. In it, truth is charged to the bursting point with time. . . . It is not that what is past casts its light on what is present, or what is present its light on what is past; rather, image is that wherein what has been comes together in a flash with the now to form a constellation."[13]

The set of rhetorical equations in play here is at once evident and complex. I would parse them so: In response to the knowledge that the state of exception is, in fact, the rule of modern history, the task of historical thought is to avow now-being's responsibility to and correspondence with the past states of exception that have produced it. To acknowledge this task is to assume a vigilance of memory: to hold oneself ready to seize hold of the ruinous past as it flashes up in the form of an image. Seizing that image, the present thus seizes hold of its past and constellates itself with it (or, as Glissant might have it, relates itself to it). To produce the real state of exception (and so realize the relational constellation of now-being with what-has-been-and so, further, fulfill our responsibility *to* and awaken the redemptive promise *of* a materialist conception of history) is, thus, coincident with the task of seizing hold of an image of the past as it flashes up. The crucial link between historical perception (that the state of exception is in fact the rule) and historicist responsibility (the production of the real state of exception as task) is, thus, the "image as it flashes up." The exceptional image is the task. And the task is the interested seizing of that flashing image.

And it is on this point that Benjamin and Glissant are most alike and most dissimilar. For if, on Benjamin's account, what I have been calling the labor of historical witness or cosmopolitan interestedness assumes the form of a responsibility to an image (of the state of exception) flashing up in a moment of epistemological danger (the long dangerous moment of a modern philosophy of time which holds the past to be, indeed, past) then, for Glissant, an errant, relational, interested politics of the globe also begins with a responsibility toward (and the redemptive promise of) an exceptional image, but the nature of that image is not to flash up into awareness but instead to endure as the alluvial bed of modernity. To the extent that the time of the past survives, nonsynchronously, into the present, for Glissant (and this indeed is his fundamental point of departure from Benjamin) that time survives not as that which flashes up but, rather, as that which accumulates: "We no longer reveal totality within ourselves by lightning flashes. We approach it through the accumulation of sediments. The poetics of duration . . . reappears to take up the relay from the poetics of the moment. Lightning flashes are the shivers of one who desires or dreams of a totality that is impossible or yet to come; duration urges on those who attempt to live this totality, when dawn shows through the linked histories of peoples."[14]

At one level the difference between Glissant and Benjamin might be reduced to a mere difference in rhetoric and terminology: where Benjamin speaks of a what-has-been that flashes into awareness, Glissant speaks of a past that accumulates. But rhetoric matters, terminology guards significance. And the care with which Glissant rejects the discourse of the flashing image in favor of a grammar of sediment and accumulation certainly indicates that to his mind there is a meaningful difference between one rhetoric of nonsynchronous time and the other. As the passage I have just cited indicates, Glissant regards the lightning flash as a figure of desire, the not-yet, and the impossible. Accumulation, conversely, exists in his work as a figure of necessity, the unending, and the unavoidable. On his reading, in other words, the flash of the Benjaminian image may illuminate a ruinous past and cast its light on a future which will constellate itself with that past and take some property in it, but that future has not yet come. It is instead dreamed or invoked. The past with which a poetics of duration corresponds does not, however, await the future advent of a coming practice of historical materialism in order to detonate the charge of what-has-been. Rather, for Glissant the what-has-been *is*, and it is *lived*, and it is lived as the total environment linking together the "histories of peoples." Where Benjamin's project may thus be identified as primarily ethical and messianic, Glissant figures his work as primarily ontological and descriptive.

There is another way of putting this, one which attends to the difference between Benjamin's essential *modernism* and Glissant's thoroughgoing determination to articulate a counterdiscourse of *modernity*. The poetics of the moment and the poetics of duration, Glissant indicates, both set themselves off in relation to a totality. The totalizing impulse of the lightning flash is, however, recognizably modernist — recognizably universal in its aspirations but contingent in its mode of realization. The lightning flash might come at any time, in any place, and it might illuminate any image of what-has-been. Its totality is thus at once methodological and utopian. The totality encompassed by Glissant's poetics of accumulation is, by contrast, recognizably modern —

recognizably global in its descriptive ambition but particular in its historicizing range. The modernity it reveals accumulates from a particular time and a particular place. Its relation to totality is thus historiographic and, in the sense in which I used the word in the second section of this book, realist. Where Benjamin's flashing image thus brings to light something to know and something to dream (the total if impossible coming of an ethical and redemptive modernist knowledge of history), Glissant's images reveal something to endure, something which itself endures, or, more resonantly, something which accumulates: time. Though not just any time. Not just an abstract measure of time endlessly and indifferently adding up, but, rather, a modern order of time, the time of modernity: which piles up from an exceptional historical catastrophe.

And that catastrophe is the catastrophe of the Atlantic abyss. Or at least that is the case for Glissant's *Poetics of Relation* which establishes the terms of a sedimented, accumulative philosophy of history not only as the general grammar of a globally interested theory of time but through the inescapably vernacular vocabulary of a determinate experience of history. For even as Glissant engages in what might be understood as an abstract if allusive theoretical debate with Benjamin on the nature of historical time, he consistently articulates his understanding of temporal duration by grounding his conception of sedimentary, alluvial accumulation in a singular historical image.

What image?

By now, there can be no surprise.

The first appearance of Glissant's theory of sedimentary or alluvial accumulation accompanies his initial (re)sighting of the image of the drowning slave in the opening chapter of the *Poetics of Relation*: "Experience of the abyss lies inside and outside the abyss. The torment of those who never escaped it: straight from the belly of the slave ship into the violet belly of the ocean depths they went. But their ordeal did not die; it quickened into this continuous/discontinuous thing: the panic of the new land, the haunting of the former land, finally the alliance with the imposed land, suffered and redeemed. *The unconscious memory of the abyss served as the alluvium for these metamorphoses.*"[15] Glissant's final inflection of his interested philosophy of history (in the last chapter of the *Poetics*) once more associates the accumulative temporality of relation with the image of the drowning ground: "I have always imagined that these depths navigate a path beneath the sea in the west and the ocean in the east and that, though we are separated, each in our own Plantation, the now green balls and chains have rolled beneath from one island to the next, weaving shared rivers that we shall open up. . . . *So what comes over us then is neither flash nor revelation but piling up.*"[16] What should we make of this association of a global philosophy of temporal accumulation with the discrete image of the drowning slave? A number of things, but, minimally, these: if, for Glissant, modernity is the globalization of relation, then a relational modernity also has a ground, and that ground is alluvial, Atlantic, and submarine. If time does not pass (or even recover itself in a lightning flash) but accumulates, then the segment of time we call modernity piles up from a starting point, and that starting point is the ramified system of transatlantic slavery, and that system is crystallized in three enduring images: the image of the plantation, the image of the slave ship, and the image of the drowning slave. These are Glissant's "images," and his *Poetics* may be understood as his response to the weight of these modern images as task.

And in this Glissant is by no means alone.

∗

One of the minor plots of Derek Walcott's *Omeros* is a genealogical plot, a romance narrative that recounts the efforts of Major Plunkett, an expatriate Briton and long-time resident of the island of St. Lucia, to trace a Caribbean genealogy for himself, a labor that will complete itself in his discovery of an eighteenth-century ancestor, a midshipman Plunkett who died in the neighboring seas in the service of the Royal Navy. To that minor plot, Walcott adds what I take to be the major genealogical counterplot of the poem, the anti-romance narrative of the fisherman Achille's encounter with a broken line of descent, or, indeed, of his encounter with brokenness, rupture, aporia, as the figures of his ancestry. Rupture is not, however, simply a figure in the poem. It is the experience of a determinate history, an enduring mode of inhabiting the long aftereffects of the trans-Atlantic slave trade. Over the course of the poem, Walcott repeatedly returns to this plot and counterplot, constantly reworking and recasting the terms of their relationship, perhaps never more starkly than in a moment late in the second book of the poem, an instant in which Achille, casting his line into the water, discovers that where Plunkett has a name to which he can attach his genealogical desire, he has only "noise," but then almost immediately learns that that noise in fact has a name, that where Plunkett has a solitary ancestor, he has the Atlantic:

> His shoulders are knobs of ebony. The back muscles
> can bulge like porpoises leaping out of this line
> from the forge of our memory. His hard fists enclose

its mossed rope as bearded as a love-vine
or a blind old man, tight as a shark's jaws,
wrenching the weight, then loosening it again

as the line saws his palms' sealed calluses,
the logwood thighs anchor against the fast drain
of the trough, and here is my tamer of horses,

our only inheritance that elemental noise
of the windward, unbroken breakers, Ithaca's
or Africa's, all joining the ocean's voice,

Because this is the Atlantic now, this great design,
of the triangular trade. Achille saw the ghost
of his father's face shoot up at the end of the line.[17]

There is little doubt that this is one of the poem's paradigmatic scenes. Shifting attention from Achille, to his own act of epic refashioning ("here is my tamer of horses"), to a collective "we" his epic understands itself to encompass, invoke, and address, ("our only inheritance that elemental noise") and then back to Achille and his uncanny discovery of an Atlantic genealogy, Walcott stages the specter plumbed from the depths of the ocean as more than the ghost of Achille's father, as, also, the poem's own chastening shade and the unsettled ancestor of a living Atlantic citizenry. But if there is something paradigmatic about this ghost and this genealogical scene, then it is something that is paradigmatic of more than Walcott's epic, something paradigmatic of a broader understanding of historical time that *Omeros* shares not only with Glissant's *Poetics of Relations* but with a wide range of black-Atlantic texts similarly haunted by the specter of the Atlantic abyss and the ghosts of trans-Atlantic slavery, a canon of black writing perhaps most famously exemplified by Toni Morrison's *Beloved*, a canon which Walter Benn Michaels suggests has succeeded in establishing a sort of loose hegemony over a late-twentieth- and early-twenty-first-century consensus on the nature of historical time.

As his essay " 'You Who Never Was There': Slavery and the New Historicism, Deconstruction and the Holocaust" makes clear, Benn Michaels is far from sanguine about the influence which he understands such black ghost stories (alongside a set of testimonial holocaust narratives) to have exerted over our contemporaneity's philosophy of history. The particular targets Benn Michaels attacks in the essay — Morrison's *Beloved*, Greenblattian new historicism, poststructural trauma theory, holocaust remembrance, and testimony discourses, all of which he fairly convincingly links to "the ghost story, the story in which the dead speak" — are, therefore, subordinate to his more general critique of contemporary engagements with the persistence of the past. The deep grammar which holds all these discourses together may find its common expression in the figure of the ghost, but its fundamental code, Benn-Michaels argues, is "the effort to make the past present . . . the transformation of history into memory, the deployment of history in the constitution of identity."[18] It is, accordingly, the figure of the past that truly attracts Benn Michaels's animus and inspires his frustration with those holocaust-testimony and slavery-influenced discourses whose central feature, he suggests, is a common fetishization of the past. "Without the idea of a history that is remembered or forgotten," he notes, "the events of the past can have only a limited relevance to the present. . . . It is only when it is re-imagined as the fabric of our own experience that the past can become the key to our own identity. . . . It is only when the events of the past can be imagined not only to have consequences for the present but to live on in the present that they can become part of our own experience and testify to who we are."[19] Benn Michaels's fundamental purpose is to contend that such claims are the product of a mystified thinking, to demonstrate that the past has no more real existence in the present than do the various black and Jewish ghosts through which it has increasingly come to speak its troubled message.[20]

Benn Michaels is an extraordinarily subtle critic, and I find largely convincing the portrait he paints of our ghost-crowded age. Indeed, much of the argument of this book has been that our "moment" can be nothing other than so haunted. But if Benn Michaels is correct in discerning a hauntological impulse in much contemporary writing and thought (and in attributing much of the energy behind this impulse to recent attempts to wrestle with the histories of slavery and the holocaust), he does not, I believe, entirely grasp the import of this ghost-mindedness (certainly not in the case of the slave narratives that provide his critical starting point). And he fails to do so because he demands as the starting postulate of critique the stability of the very categories texts such as Morrison's *Beloved*, Walcott's *Omeros*, or Glissant's *Poetics* exist to complicate or to refuse: the categories of a stable, recognizable, and discrete past and present. Benn Michaels's critique relies on the self-evident, preordained existence of a past and a present, assumes that these are in fact ontologically sound and separate things (rather than complex constructs in their own right), and proceeds accordingly, failing ever to address the possibility that the object of a novel such as *Beloved* is not to conflate these terms but to suspend them, not to make the past present but to reconceive our basic notions of temporality, periodicity, and contemporaneity. To the extent that the past and the present survive as provisionally operative terms within *Beloved*, Walcott's *Omeros*, Glissant's *Poetics* (or, more particularly still, the Guyanese writer Fred D'Aguiar's novelistic recounting of the *Zong* massacre, *Feeding the Ghosts*, and M. NourbeSe Philip's collection of poetry *Zong!* which I have been drawing on in the epigraphs of earlier chapters), they do so not because these ghost stories seek to recapture the past *for* the present, but because they demand a thorough reconceptualization of our notion *of* the present. It is not the status of the past that is at issue in *Beloved*, *Omeros*, *Feeding the Ghosts*, *Poetics of Relation*, *Zong!*, or the broader black-Atlantic philosophy of history such texts exemplify, but, rather, the nature, the extent, the elasticity, the scope, the very *existence* of the present in which Hegel and his heirs have taught us to believe.

Beloved, and the texts for which Benn Michaels makes Morrison's novel a substitute (he draws the phrase "For you who never was there" from the novel), are not concerned with the return of the past. Their interest is in our conception of the contemporary. "All of it is now, it is always now," Morrison's narrative insists as it, like *Omeros* and Glissant's *Poetics*, assumes the burden of addressing the horrors of the middle passage.[21] Writing the "now" under the sign of this "always," *Beloved* codes itself as something written after the "present," as a narrative that emerges on the far side of a progressive, Enlightenment understanding of the present as a delimited, contained, autonomous thing. It writes itself as a narrative in which the present implies more than the delimited now, more than the immediately contemporary, more than the moment; a narrative in which time does not pass or progress, but gathers within an ever more extensive, ever more copious "now" embodied in the ghostly figure of Beloved herself. And it is precisely in this sense that Walcott's *Omeros* shares with *Beloved* not only the literary figure of the ghost but the counter-Enlightenment philosophy of history that specter emblematizes. For Achille inherits more than his father's shade. Inheriting that ghost, he also inherits what Walcott calls "the Atlantic now," a figure best parsed as one in which "the Atlantic" functions both as a noun or a proper name and as an adjectival qualifier of "now." What Achille thus inherits is, therefore, both a geography of history and a form of time, a type of contemporaneity, a complex, enigmatic, Atlantic "now." That "now," like Morrison's own "now," like Glissant's poetics of "duration," again implies a contemporaneity radically distinct from Benn Michaels' self-evident, narrow-band "present" or from those sequentially unfolding "slices" of contemporary time Althusser identifies with a Hegelian and post-Hegelian philosophy of history whose truth claims Benn Michael's seems to have taken at face value. It implies a now that accumulates within itself the moment of loss, the long after-history of loss, and the moment of confrontation with loss.

*

Time does not pass, it accumulates, and as it accumulates it deposits an ever greater freight of material within the cargo holds of a present that is, in this sense, eternally after the Enlightenment present.

Perhaps. But how so?

Walcott's "Atlantic now," Morrison's "all of it is now," and Glissant's sedimentary poetics of duration provide some answers, but clearly they do not exhaust the question. How else then does time accumulate and bring its weight to bear on the Atlantic sedimentation of the modern? How else does the long history of transatlantic slavery interrupt the smooth unfolding of an Enlightenment philosophy of history in which times does not merely pass but progress? I cannot exhaust the question. So let me simply note that in its refusal to progress, time accumulates both variously and unevenly: in the body, in architecture, in the law, in language, in rituals, customs, and ceremonies and, as I have indicated, in images. If this is true for Glissant then it is also true for Walcott's *Omeros*, a poem whose energies are nourished by the epic temporality of its relational images (the very title of the poem operates as something like a hybrid of Benjamin's dialectical montage images encountered in language and Glissant's images of a transverse, creole way of being in the world: "*O* was the conch-shell's invocation, *mer* was / both sea and mother in our Antillean patois / *os* a grey bone, and the white surf as it crashes").[22] Among the most important of these is another image of bone, an image that presents itself to Achille immediately prior to his encounter with the ghost of his father and the Atlantic now, an image prompted by the fisherman's chance remembrance of a drowned friend, which leads his mind to ponder "the nameless bones of all his brothers / drowned in the crossing," which leads him suddenly to see the length of canvas sail he is mending assume the shape of a shroud.[23]

In the lines that immediately follow this vision, Walcott comes close to resolving both the poem's plot and counterplot (and to defining, in negatively utopian fashion, the identity of that "we" for whom the Atlantic dead and the Atlantic now stand as a sole, common, inheritance) in a single complex image:

the tied bundle

huddles like a corpse. *Oui Bon Dieu*! I go hurl
it overside. Out of the depths of his ritual
baptism something was rising, some white memory

of a midshipman coming up close to the hull,
a white turning body, and this water go fill
with them, turning tied canvases, not sharks, but all

corpses, wrapped like the sail, and ice-sweating Achille
in the stasis of his sunstroke looked as each swell
disgorged them, in tens, in hundreds, and his soul

sickened and was ill [24]

Sickened by the image of the drowned, sickened by the image of just what it is
that fills the long modernity of the Atlantic, even as it finds, in the whitewashed anonymity of the Atlantic dead, the union of Achille's and Plunket's
genealogical desires (their joint "inheritance" of an atrocious history), the
poem, like the fisherman, then looks away from this horrific scene, briefly
turns aside from this sudden disinterral of the Atlantic's underwater ceme-
teries, but then looks back again, casts its gaze and Achille's line back into the
water to pull out the ghostly image of the Atlantic now.

What originally stirs in the water and what is then, subsequently, pulled
out of its sediment are not, therefore, exactly the same thing. For if the first
image (of the whitewashed bones of all the dead) links a distant past to a
present moment of danger in a recognizably Benjaminian fashion, then the
second image (of the Atlantic now) is more fully in line with Glissant's errant
vision of the world, more fully an image that marks a past which endures than
one which uncovers an aporetic past with which the present corresponds,
more fully an image of an inherited history than an image of a distant history
reilluminated by a flash of ethical desire and design. It is therefore not the
rupture of death or the moment of drowning that *Omeros* ultimately understands itself to inherit, but the persistence of what death has wrought and the
enduring resolution to live on within the very territory of the abyss, to assume
some property in its fatal waters, and to make of a time that has not passed but
filled the present with its overwhelming, accumulated weight, a modern way
of being in the world. To inherit this "now" is to discover in the image of the
drowned not only the terrible key to a philosophy of history but the secret to
an enduring practice of modern *life*.

And that is precisely the secret that Fred D'Aguiar also discovers when he too finds himself encountering just such an image, or, more precisely, when he finds himself discovering in *such* an image *the* image of the *Zong's* drowned slaves and (following Morrison as much as Walcott and Glissant) assumes that image as both his task and the task of the black-Atlantic historical novel and a black-Atlantic philosophy of history.

*

The sea is slavery. . . . Sea receives a body as if that body has come to rest on a cushion, one that gives way to the body's weight and folds around it like an envelope. Over three days 131 such bodies, no, 132, are flung at this sea. Each lands with a sound that the sea absorbs and silences. Each opens a wound in this sea that heals over each body without the evidence of a scar. . . . Sea refuses to grant that body the quiet of a grave in the ground. Instead it rolls that body across its terrain, sends that body down into its depths. . . . Those bodies have their lives written on salt water. The sea current turns pages of memory. One hundred and thirty one souls roam the Atlantic with countless others. When the wind is heard it is their breath, their speech. The sea is therefore home. . . . The *Zong* is on the high seas. Men, women and children are thrown overboard by the Captain and his crew. There is no fear or shame in this piece of information. There is only the fact of the Zong and its unending voyage and those deaths that cannot be undone. Where death has begun but remains unfinished because it recurs. Where there is only the record of the sea. . . . Those spirits feed on the story of themselves. The past is laid to rest when it is told.[25]

Thus begins and ends D'Aguiar's *Feeding the Ghosts*.

But to say this is to misread both the novel's beginning and its ending. For though the passages I have cited contain the first and last sentences of D'Aguiar's novel, the text neither truly begins nor ends with these words, if only because in assuming the "fact of the Zong" as the subject of his narrative D'Aguiar (like Glissant, Walcott, and Morrison before him) has produced a text informed throughout by a deep awareness of the uncertainty of beginning, the fiction of ending, and the truth of the enduring. That the novel begins somewhere other than with its opening sentences is a function not only of its inevitable historical belatedness (its subsequence to the event to which it "will have to be a witness again")[26] but of its formal commitments to its own belatedness and unoriginality, commitments evident the moment the book is opened and, even before the first sentence of the novel is read, the reader's eye encounters its epigraphs. There are two, one from Walcott ("Where are your monuments, your battles, martyrs? / Where is your tribal memory? Sirs, / in that grey vault. The sea. The sea / has locked them up. The sea is history") and the other from Brathwaite ("The stone had skidded arc'd and bloomed into islands").

We have seen that pairing before. Walcott's "the sea is history" also serves as one of the epigraphs to Glissant's *Poetics of Relation* while Brathwaite's "the unity is submarine" provides the other. Walcott's poem itself alludes to Brathwaite as it transforms the Jamaican poet's "the unity is submarine" into the "subtle . . . submarine" expanse into which Walcott leads his readers. Nor is that submarine world exclusive to Walcott, Brathwaite, Glissant, or D'Aguiar. It is also shared by Kobena Mercer, who in an essay published the same year as D'Aguiar's novel, identifies this underwater burial ground as central to his understanding of an Atlantic "predicament" of memory: "Descendants of enslavers and enslaved alike share in a predicament arising from the unrepresentability of the past. While the former may be unreconciled with a history that has been wiped out of collective memory, the latter, it may be said, are haunted by *too much* memory; ghosted by the floating bodies of lost and unnamed ancestors buried beneath the sea."[27] If it remains unclear whether D'Aguiar's text is as intentionally in conversation with Mercer as it is with Walcott, Brathwaite, and Glissant, then D'Aguiar has indicated that his novel is in dialogue with a wider range of interlocuters than even these intertextual echoes or his epigraphs indicate. Among these are Michelle Cliff's *Abeng*, a novel in which the *Zong* massacre figures as a fleeting background memory, Barry Unsworth's *Sacred Hunger* (another historical novel of the middle passage more than loosely based on the *Zong* massacre), and, most crucially, Turner's *Slavers Throwing Overboard the Dead and Dying*, a painting which not only haunts D'Aguiar's novel, NourbeSe Philip's *Zong!*, and David Dabydeen's collection of poems, *Turner*, but to which Paul Gilroy has directed his attention in both *Small Acts* and *The Black Atlantic*.

Closing his discussion of the canvas in *The Black Atlantic*, Gilroy comments: "Its exile in Boston [where it has been since John Ruskin sold it in 1871] is yet another pointer toward the shape of the Atlantic as a system of cultural exchanges."[28] This seems an apt comment, though to my mind it is less the trans-Atlantic wanderings of Turner's canvas than the circum-Atlantic conversation that has been occupying the attention of D'Aguiar and his fellow British, Guyanese, Jamaican, Canadian, and St. Lucian writers, the circular exchange of images, figures, and epigraphs as he and they have borrowed each other's language to orient their collective gaze on this image of the drowning grounds that truly points to "the shape of the Atlantic as a system of cultural" and communicative exchanges.[29]

As D'Aguiar's novel, like Glissant's *Poetics*, thus stages its "abyssal" descent into "the depths of the sea," what he discovers (and what his epigraphs and allusions would have us understand him to discover) is not only a sign of ending but an archive of the enduring, an array of "underwater signposts" which are *both* the recurring, uncannily resurfacing signs of the racial terror and capital violence of the slave trade *and* the signs of the unification of the disparate, the commonly inherited image and remains of a history that endures as "something shared."[30] Thus, "unity," as the line from Brathwaite predicts: the unity of the creolized where creolization implies both the unification of the disparate and the diasporization of the unified—a gathering in scattering. The singular image of abandonment thereby becomes an image of diasporic survival, an image, as D'Aguiar has it, in which what seemed to figure the loss of home, "is therefore home."[31] What D'Aguiar uncovers in the "subtle submarine expanse" of this underwater, ocean-spanning burial ground is therefore not only a *determination* to survive and endure, but a *proof* of survival and endurance, proof manifest in the form of all these texts to which he alludes, proof manifest in the transverse, circum-Atlantic body of writing his novel evokes before its first sentence is written, proof manifest in this "body" of writing which functions less as testimony to his erudition than as a textual cenotaph to the dead, or, perhaps more precisely, as a textual effigy (as Joseph Roach has taught us to understand that word) through which this past endures as the circulating, cross-Atlantic, writerly exchanges of it.

If the novel's epigraphs thus set D'Aguiar in conversation with his fellow writers, then so too does the novel's opening sentence: "The sea is slavery." We have also seen that sentence before, or nearly so. Walcott's line is almost the same, but not quite: "The sea is history." The sea is history. The sea is slavery. History is slavery. Or so, at least, D'Aguiar seems to suggest in an opening line that once again disavows his text's originality, refuses the illusion of its own capacity to "open," while marking its transformation of the literary history to which it serially opens itself. But perhaps the doubling needs to be read the other way around, or both ways at once. Not only, then, history is slavery. But, also, slavery is history: a statement D'Aguiar's novel would have us read as both literally true and metaphorically untrue—literally true because *Feeding the Ghosts* shares with *Omeros*, *Beloved*, and the *Poetics of Relation* the knowledge that without slavery there is no history of that "sea" all these writers have been struggling to understand, no history of that modern circum-Atlantic world that in some very real senses "begins" with slavery; metaphorically untrue because as all these writers understand neither history nor slavery are, in the colloquially figurative sense of the word, "history." History is never, in this sense, "history," never something that is purely past, done, finished with, distant, all worn out. And neither, D'Aguiar insists, is slavery, certainly not this repeating moment in the history of trans- Atlantic slavery, this moment of drowning, and drowning, and drowning.

This does not mean that the novel somehow understands that these bodies are still falling into the water, still "floating toward the sea's abysses," but that it apprehends that the wound those bodies "opened" in the Atlantic remains open, that more than two centuries after it "occurred," this event retains its negative power to call forth those who find themselves obliged to testify to it, to "be a witness again." There is of course something tautological in offering the fact of D'Aguiar's novel as proof that this past endures "because," as D'Aguiar has it, "it recurs." But if the fact of recurrence, repetition, and the oscillating return of the what-has-been into now-being can serve as an adequate basis for a long-durational history of modern capital (as, following Arrighi, Benjamin, and Jameson, I have argued), then surely it is no more tautological to note that the recurrence of such a repeating event in the testamentary narrative of D'Aguiar's novel (or Walcott's poetry, Glissant's poetics, Philip's verse, or Gilroy's theory) demonstrates in some very real sense that this past is not in fact history, not yet done with, not yet worn out. Or perhaps the argument to make is that history, like capital, *is* tautological, is that which proves itself by appealing to the accumulated sequence of testimonies to itself.

And what, in this regard, does D'Aguiar's conception of history prove? That history is its own future, its own answer, its own predicate; that history is not "history," not a property of the past but the property the present inherits as its structuring material *and* the property (both affective and instrumental) the past holds in the present. The question, D'Aguiar thus suggests, is not whether the present is or is not host to its various "pasts," but whether the now will or will not accept the property it has inherited in its what-has-beens. To all those who say "slavery is history," D'Aguiar's novel responds: precisely, and not at all. Slavery *is* the Atlantic's what-has-been, is what begins this scene of modernity's beginning. But what has begun, he reminds us, does not end. To begin might be difficult; to end, impossible. For no matter how strenuously we might forget what was begun, or wish to call an end to it, what-has-been *is*, cannot be undone, cannot cease to alter all the future-presents that flow out of it. Time does not pass or progress, it accumulates, even in the work of forgetting or ending, even in the immense labor it takes to surrender what-has-been, or to make reparation on it, or to address its ill effects. That the law has changed is immaterial to this *fact*. That the bodies are no longer in the air, in the water, in the pounds claimed by William and John Gregson's trial lawyers is beside the point. That Fred D'Aguiar has written a historical novel and M. NourbeSe Philip, a collection of poetry, or that I have written a book about the *Zong* massacre are equally insignificant in this regard. That past endures *not* because a novelist, a poet, or an academic has paid some present attention to it but because the present from which attention is paid has been made, fashioned, designed by it and by everything else that has been. We cannot, of course, take all these what-has-beens into account. Thought fails before that task. Nor can any of us, even Derek Walcott, I believe, assent to *Omeros*'s assertion that *this*, or any other *such* "past," is our "only" inheritance.

Rather we can learn the lesson of D'Aguiar's novel, the lesson that inheres within the formal determination of a narrative that like Sharp's submission to the Lords Commissioners finds itself obliged to tell the story of the massacre multiple times: first in a synoptic preface, then in a set of harrowing chapters in which each of the murders is counted off one after the other, then again in an account of the ensuing trials, once more through the memory of a solitary survivor, and finally, again in the text's epilogue. Submitting ourselves to that detailed recounting and recounting and recounting, we can learn again the melancholy lesson this structured commitment to recurrence demands of us. And what is that lesson? Turning his eye to the abyss to which the slaves' bodies were abandoned, D'Aguiar puts it this way: "The sea was everywhere and nowhere . . . an end without ending."[32] That is the novel's lesson and its melancholy secret, even if it is a secret spoken in conflict with the text's more recognizably mournful moment of ending. How does the novel end? So: "The *Zong* is on the high seas. Men, women and children are thrown overboard by the Captain and his crew. There is no fear or shame in this piece of informa-tion. There is only the fact of the *Zong* and its unending voyage and those deaths that cannot be undone. Where death has begun but remains unfinished because it recurs. Where there is only the record of the sea. . . . Those spirits feed on the story of themselves. The past is laid to rest when it is told."[33] Ending by laying to rest the past it has found living within its own moment of writing, D'Aguiar's text here imagines an end with ending, a past it can live after, a beginning ended. But everything that lies between D'Aguiar's words of beginning and ending, everything that falls between "The sea is slavery" and "The past is laid to rest when it is told," denies the desire of those final words.

For like Philip's *Zong!*, *Feeding the Ghost*'s fundamental historical burden is to articulate itself as a sustained meditation both on the artifice of beginning and on the impossibility of historical ending, and to do so, entirely appositely, through a rewriting of the resuscitative conceit Sir Walter Scott set at the heart of the historical novel's philosophy of history. While D'Aguiar literalizes that conceit, building the narrative core of his novel on the story of the one jettisoned slave hauled half-alive back onto the deck of the *Zong* and revived by the crew's forcible ministration of food and water, Philip metaphorizes the possibilities of resuscitation by reviving the legal transcripts documenting the massacre (all her poems draw exclusively on the language of those texts). For both D'Aguiar and Philip, however, the labor of resuscitation remains perpetually unfinished and unending rather than preliminary (as it is for Scott). Where Scott provisionally resuscitates the dead, the better to have done with them and the better to bury them, both D'Aguiar and Philip revive the dead, or the words the law draped over the bodies of the dead, the better to acknowledge that the time of dying does not sunder or break itself off from the time of living but fills life with its painful weight.

"This is, not was," Philip insists.[34] To which verdict D'Aguiar adds the testimony of his time-heavy scene of resuscitation: "They fed and watered me by feeding a funnel down my throat. I was not my name. I was not my body. I became my own secret, lost somewhere. Time stood still in my veins. Days slid into nights. Light and dark were the same to me. The *Zong* rose and dipped the same or not at all, I couldn't tell the difference. I did not blink. I was fed. . . . Food and water were forced down me. I was cleaned, stretched and turned. Shadows passed before my eyes but I did not blink. Time became a funnel fed into me."[35] Captivated by and obsessed with this scene of live-giving torture and the torture of living on, *Feeding the Ghosts* not only recognizes itself in this image of force-feeding but indicates that if it is to eschew the classical historical novel's impartial and spectatorial relationship to the history it records, it must do so by electing to become "a witness again." But if to witness is to feed the dead, then, D'Aguiar understands, *Feeding the Ghosts'* work of witness, its labor of resuscitation must be at odds with the burial fantasy of its own words of ending and with the mournfully liberal predispositions of the genre into which it breathes new life.

And so what comes before the end serves paradoxically to confirm the lesson while altering the sense of those final words. For if we recall that telling is also relating, that the past told here is laid to rest when, and only when, it is related, and recall, further, what Glissant has taught us, recall that relation is not about forgetting but about living on within the abysmal, within that real state of exception Benjamin sets before us as the historian's task, then the meaning of D'Aguiar's final words changes. To lay the past to rest thus means not that we should forget it but that we have no choice but to relate it, no choice but to live on within the full knowledge and unending of it. Time does not pass but accumulates. Why? Because what has been begun does not end but endures. Because this fatal Atlantic "beginning" of the modern is more properly understood as an ending without end. Because history comes to us not only as flash or revelation but piling up. Because this is, not was. Because this is the Atlantic, now. Because all of it is now, it is always now, even for you who never was there.

$\mathcal{N}otes$

1. Liverpool, a Capital of the Long Twentieth Century

1 The documents in question are a letter, dated July 2, 1783, sent by Granville Sharp to the Lords Commissioners of the Admiralty requesting them to open an investigation into the murder-by-drowning of 132 slaves aboard the Liverpool-owned slave ship *Zong* in November 1781. Sharp also enclosed accounts of the March 6, 1783 trial in Guildhall, London, in which the *Zong*'s Liverpool owners successfully brought suit against their insurance underwriters to compensate them for the drowned slaves, a petition from the insurance underwriters protesting the verdict, and a shorthand transcription of an appeal held on May 22 and 23, 1783, at the Court of King's Bench (Lord Mansfield, Chief Justice of King's bench presiding). The complete handwritten set of documents are in the National Maritime Museum in Greenwich (hereafter referred to as NMM) and are catalogued as REC/19. For a text of Sharp's letter alone, see *Memoirs of Granville Sharp, Esq. Composed from his own manuscripts and other authentic documents in the possession of his family and of the Africa Institution*, Prince Hoare, ed. (London: Henry Colburn and Co., 1820), 242–244.

2 For the pertinent Lords Commissioners' minute book and record of correspondence, see Public Record Office (hereafter referred to as PRO) ADM 3/97.

3 See Sharp's letter to the Duke of Portland, July 18, 1783, in *Memoirs of Granville Sharp*, 241–242.

4 On the notion of "effective history" and its relation to genealogical critique, see Michel Foucault, "Nietzsche, Genealogy, History," in *The Foucault Reader*, Paul Rabinow, ed. (New York: Pantheon Books, 1984).

5 PRO, ADM 3/97.

6 Ibid.

7 By "exquisite corpse" I refer here not to the use of that phrase by Nicolas Abraham and Maria Torok in their account of cryptonymic and incorporative melancholy in *The Shell and the Kernel*, Nicholas T. Rand, trans. and ed. (Chicago: University of Chicago Press, 1994) — though a melancholy reading of this scene is certainly available and their retheorization of melancholy will be important to my analysis of a series of contemporary *Zong* narratives in the concluding chapter of this book — but to the surreal composite renderings of the human body that Yves Tanguy, Joan Miro, Man Ray, Max Ernst, Andre Masson, and Max Morise collaboratively produced in the early 1920s and called "exquisite corpses." See Dawn Ades, ed., *Surrealist Art* (Chicago and London: The Art Institute of Chicago/Thames and Hudson, 1997), 18–22.

8 Walter Benjamin, letter to Gershom Scholem, May 20, 1935, cited in Susan Buck-Morss, *The Dialectics of Seeing: Walter Benjamin and the Arcades Project* (Cambridge, Mass.: MIT Press, 1991), 49.

9 Walter Benjamin, *The Arcades Project*, Howard Eiland and Kevin McLaughlin, trans. (Cambridge, Mass.: Harvard University Press, 1999), 22.

10 Ibid., 7 and 18.

11 Ibid., 17, 22, and 15.

12 I have drawn these and the other details of the voyage of the *Zong* from a variety of sources. Other than the materials held in the National Maritime Museum and Sharp's letters on the case in the *Memoirs of Granville Sharp*, the more important primary sources include the entry of the plaintiffs and defendants pleadings in the case before the court of King's Bench, Hilary Term, 23 George III, catalogued in the PRO as KB 122/479, and a brief summary of the case in Henry Roscoe, *Reports of Cases Argued and Determined in the Court of King's Bench (1782–1785)* (London, 1831), 232–235. Among secondary sources, the most extensive is Charlotte and Denis Plimmer, *The Damn'd Master* (London: New English Library, 1971) — it is worth noting that the archival basis of the text's account of the massacre is largely limited to the above sources: the majority of *The Damn'd Master* is comprised of a fictitious diary ostensibly kept by one of the sailors aboard the *Zong*. The best brief account of the voyage of the *Zong* is Robert Weisbord's "The Case of the Slave-Ship *Zong*, 1783," *History Today* (August 1969): 561–567. Other historical texts which briefly address the case include David Brion Davis, *The Problem of Slavery in the Age of Revolution, 1770–1823* (Ithaca: Cornell University Press, 1975); Gretchen Gerzina, *Black London: Life Before Emancipation* (London: J. Murray, 1995); and Hugh Thomas, *The Slave Trade* (New York: Simon and Schuster, 1997).

13 For an excellent history of these forts, see Albert van Danzig and Barbara Priddy, *A Short History of the Forts and Castles of Ghana* (Accra: Ghana Museums and Monuments, 1971).

14 Weisbord, "The Case of the Slave-Ship *Zong*," 561–562.

15 Sharp, *Memoirs of Granville Sharp*, 242–244; Weisbord, "The Case of the Slave-Ship *Zong*," 562.

16 Liverpool Record Office (hereafter referred to as LRO), 387/MD/56.

17 Sharp records in his diary entry for March 19, 1783: "Gustavus Vasa, a Negro, called on me, with an account of one hundred and thirty Negroes being thrown alive into the sea, from on board an English slave ship," *Memoirs of Granville Sharp*, 236 ("Vasa," was, of course, Equiano's "Christian" name); *The Morning Chronicle and London Advertiser* seems to have been the first newspaper to cover the trial; discussion of the case in contemporaneous abolitionist writings include James Ramsay, *An Essay in the Treatment and Conversion of African Slaves in the British Sugar Colonies* (London: Phillips, 1784); Thomas Clarkson, *An Essay on the Slavery and Commerce of the Human Species, Particularly the African* (Philadelphia: N. Wiley, 1804); Ottobah Cuguano, *Thoughts and Sentiments on the Evil of the wicked slavery and commerce of the human species* (London: 1787); John Newton, *Thoughts upon the African Slave Trade* (London: J. Buckland, 1788).

18 For a general discussion of the attention given to the case by abolitionist groups and its use in antislavery polemic, see Davis, *The Problem of Slavery in the Age of Revolution*. On the changes effected in insurance law as a consequence of abolitionist agitation regarding the murders and the owners' insurance suit, see Weisbord, "The Case of the Slave-Ship *Zong*," 567.

19 See J. G. A. Pocock, *Virtue, Commerce, and History: Essays on Political Thought and History, Chiefly in the Eighteenth Century* (Cambridge: Cambridge University Press, 1985), especially 37–51; and J. G. A. Pocock, *The Machiavellian Moment: Florentine Political Thought and the Atlantic Republican Tradition* (Princeton: Princeton University Press, 1975), 423–461. I discuss Pocock's work more fully in the following chapters.

20 See Michael McKeon, *The Origins of the English Novel, 1600–1740* (Baltimore: Johns Hopkins University Press, 1987); Catherine Gallagher, *Nobody's Story: The Vanishing Acts of Women Writers in the Marketplace, 1670–1820* (Berkeley: University of California Press, 1994); Lennard J. Davis, *Factual Fictions: The Origins of the English Novel* (New York: Columbia University Press, 1983); and Deidre Shauna Lynch, *The Economy of Character: Novels, Market Culture, and the Business of Inner Meaning* (Chicago: University of Chicago Press, 1998). I discuss the relationship of novelistic discourse to the financial revolution of the early eighteenth century at length in the following chapters.

21 For Marx's basic analysis of exchange value, see the sections on the commodity and commodity exchange in *Capital: A Critique of Political Economy*, translated from the fourth German edition by Eden Paul and Cedar Paul (New York: E. P.

Dutton, 1930); for a suggestive reading of the "general equivalent," see Jean-Joseph Goux, *Symbolic Economies: After Marx and Freud,* Jennifer Curtiss Gage, trans. (Ithaca: Cornell University Press, 1990).

22 Benjamin, *The Arcades Project,* 22.

23 Richard Halpern, *Shakespeare Among the Moderns* (Ithaca: Cornell University Press, 1997), 12.

24 I discuss the form of Benjamin's Convolutes in chapter 6.

25 Buck-Morss, *The Dialectics of Seeing,* 13.

26 For a general discussion of the relation between the two texts, see ibid., 11–24. Lacis records the substance of the conversations she had with Benjamin on this matter as follows: "He was deep in work on *The Origins of German Tragic Drama.* When I learned from him that it had to do with an analysis of German Baroque tragedy of the seventeenth century, and that only a few specialists know this literature — these tragedies were never played — I made a face. Why busy oneself with dead literature? He was silent for a time, and then said: First I am bringing into the discipline of aesthetics a new terminology. In contemporary discussions of drama, the term tragedy and tragic drama are used indiscriminately, just as words. I show the fundamental difference between [them]. . . . The dramas of the baroque express despair and contempt for the world. . . . Second, he said, his inquiry was not merely an academic piece of research; it had a direct connection to very actual problems of contemporary literature. He expressly emphasized that in his work he described Baroque plays in search of linguistic form as phenomenon analogous to Expressionism. For that reason, so he said, I have handled the artistic problematic of allegory, emblem and ritual in such detail. Up to now the aestheticians have evaluated allegory as an art medium of second class. He wanted to prove that allegory was artistically a highly valued means, and more, it was a particular form of understanding truth." Lacis cited in ibid., 15.

27 Fredric Jameson, *The Political Unconscious: Narrative as a Socially Symbolic Act* (Ithaca: Cornell University Press, 1981), 141.

28 See Buck-Morss, *The Dialectics of Seeing,* 8–24.

29 See Ernst Bloch, "Nonsychronism and the Obligation to its Dialectics," *New German Critique,* no. 11 (spring 1977): 22–38.

30 Halpern, *Shakespeare Among the Moderns,* 13.

31 Ibid.

32 Ibid.

33 Louis-Auguste Blanqui, *Instructions pour une Prise d'Armes: L'Éternité par les astres-Hypothese astronomique* (Paris: Société Encyclopedique Française, 1972), 167–169; cited, with Benjamin's comments, in Benjamin, *The Arcades Project,* 25–26.

34 See Giovanni Arrighi, *The Long Twentieth Century: Money, Power, and the Origins of Our Times* (London: Verso, 1994).

35　Arrighi first glosses the notion of the "space-of-flows" so: "John Ruggie has maintained that the chief and most distinctive feature of the modern system of rule has been the differentiation of its subject collectivity into separate, fixed, and mutually exclusive territorial spaces of legitimate domination. Although the substantive forms and individual trajectories of the states instituted by this differentiation have varied over time, their 'species' has been clearly discernible from the seventeenth century to the present day. Today, however, this form of territoriality as the basis for organizing political life seems to be torn apart by a non-territorial, functional space, which has grown within the modern system of rule, but constitutes an institutional negation of that system's exclusive territoriality. Among the main aspects of this implosion . . . [Ruggie] finds it useful to designate the tendency whereby 'transnationalized micro-economic links . . . have created a non-territorial region in the world economy — a decentered yet integrated space-of-flows, operating in real time, which exists alongside the spaces-of-places that we call national economies.' . . . [These] non-territorial spaces-of-flows may have existed unnoticed alongside the national spaces-of-places throughout the history of the modern system" (ibid., 80–81). See John Ruggie, "Territoriality and Beyond: Problematizing Modernity in International Relations," *International Organization* 47, no. 1 (1993): 261–285.

36　Arrighi, *The Long Twentieth Century*, 6.

37　I have adapted these tables from those in the "Figures" section of Arrighi's text. See, in particular, Arrighi, *The Long Twentieth Century*, 364.

38　The general pattern perhaps bears restating. Always beginning with the flight of capital from one center of exchange to another, each cycle originates in a monetary phase: M. That new accumulation of money capital then licenses expanded investment in the production and distribution of commodities: MC. The commodity phase, in its turn, runs its course either once markets have been saturated, or because the profit on the trade in commodities begins to release excessive amounts of money capital, or both, and capital then begins to accumulate once more primarily in financial instruments: CM'. Together these phases define a complete cycle, MCM', which is then repeated by a successor capital state which has arisen to prominence by capturing the mobile money capital its predecessor has "set free."

39　Arrighi, *The Long Twentieth Century*, 79.

40　Benjamin, *The Arcades Project*, 463.

41　Ibid., 25

42　Arrighi, *The Long Twentieth Century*, 79.

43　Jameson, *The Political Unconscious*, 141.

44　The New British history in question emerged from a series of essays J. G. A. Pocock wrote in the mid-1970s and mid-1980s in which he suggested that their never had been, within historiographic writing, such a thing as a British history, only an English history passing itself off as the history of all of Great Britain. In place of this Anglocentric historiography he proposed a complex four kingdoms model (Irish, Scottish, English, Welsh) that would also incorporate what he called the historiography of the Atlantic archipelago, essentially the settler colonies of North America: "I am using 'British History' . . . to denote the plural history of a group of cultures situated along an Anglo-Celtic frontier. . . . The effect is to convince the reader that there once existed a single system, a diversity of Anglo-Celtic cultures grouped around the northern Atlantic — an English, two Scottish, three Irish, and an uncertain number of American — increasingly dominated by the English language and by veneration for, if diverse modes of interpreting, English political norms and institutions. . . . The nature of the subject which might be designated 'British history' ought by this time to be emerging . . . We should start with what I have called the Atlantic archipelago" ("British History: A Plea for a New Subject," *New Zealand Historical Journal* 8 [1974]: 3–21). This initial essay was republished, with responses by A. J. P. Taylor, Michael Hechter, and Gordon Donaldson in *Journal of Modern History* 4 (1975): 601–624, and then followed by Pocock's further explication of his argument in "The Limits and Divisions of British History: In Search of the Unknown Subject," *The American Historical Review* 87, no. 2 (April 1982): 311–336. For further responses, discussions, or elaboration of Pocock's argument or work that situates itself within the new historiography he proposes, see Ian K. Steele, "Exploding Colonial American History: Amerindian, Atlantic, and Global Perspectives," *Reviews in American History* 26, no. 1 (1998): 70–95; Bernard Bailyn, ed., *Strangers in the Realm: Cultural Margins of the First British Empire* (Chapel Hill: University of North Carolina Press, 1991); Karen Ordahl Kupperman, ed., *America in European Consciousness: 1493–1750* (Chapel Hill: University of North Carolina Press, 1995); and the essays on the New British history in a special forum of the *American Historical Review*, especially David Armitage's "Greater Britain: A Useful Category of Historical Analysis?" *American Historical Review* (April 1999): 427–445. For a superb historiographic review of the new Atlantic history which emerged in part in response to Pocock's arguments, see Bernard Bailyn, "The Idea of Atlantic History," *Itinerario* 20, no. 1 (1996):19–44; see also Daniel W. Howe, *American History in an Atlantic Context* (Oxford: Oxford University Press, 1993); Ian K. Steele, *The English Atlantic, 1675–1740: An Exploration of Communication and Community* (Oxford: Oxford University Press, 1986); D. W. Meinig, *The Shaping of America: A Geographical Perspective on 500 Years of History*, vol. 1, *Atlantic America, 1492–1800* (New Haven: Yale University Press, 1986); and David Hancock, *Citizens of the World: London Merchants and the Integration of the British Atlantic Community, 1735–1785* (Cambridge: Cambridge University Press, 1995). While both Pocock's New British history and the Atlantic history that has, in part, emerged from it have proved quite useful to me — indeed, in the sections that follow I adapt his concept of the Atlantic archipelago — I parts ways with Pocock in reading this

Atlantic archipelago both as one that survives the end of the first British empire rather than perishing with it and one that includes not only the Anglo-Celtic and continental American frontiers but also a West-African and a Caribbean territoriality.

45 Among the more influential of which are Paul Gilroy, *The Black Atlantic: Modernity and Double Consciousness* (Cambridge, Mass.: Harvard University Press, 1993); Joseph Roach, *Cities of the Dead: Circum-Atlantic Performance* (New York: Columbia University Press, 1996); a wide range of writings by Stuart Hall, see especially his seminal essay "Cultural Identity and Diaspora," in Jonathan Rutherford, ed., *Identity, Community, Culture, Difference* (London: Lawrence and Wishart), 222–237; Sidney Mintz and Richard Price, *The Birth of African American Culture: An Anthropological Perspective* (Boston: Beacon Press, 1992); Peter Linebaugh, "All the Atlantic Mountains Shook," *Labour/Le Travailleru* 10 (1982): 1–40; Marcus Rediker, *Between the Devil and the Deep Blue Sea: Merchant Seamen, Pirates, and the Anglo-American Maritime World, 1700–1750* (Cambridge: Cambridge University Press, 1987); Jeffrey Bolster, *Black Jacks: African-American Seamen in the Age of Sail* (Cambridge, Mass.: Harvard University Press, 1997); Ira Berlin, "From Creole to African: Atlantic Creoles and the Origins of African-American Society in Mainland North America," *William and Mary Quarterly* 53, no. 2 (April 1996): 251–288; Joan Dayan, *Haiti, History, and the Gods* (Berkeley: University of California Press, 1995); Gretchen Gerzina, *Black London: Life Before Emancipation* (London: J. Murray, 1995); Robert Farris Thompson, *Flash of the Spirit: African and Afro-American Art and Philosophy* (New York: Random House, 1983). See also the essays collected in Ian Baucom, ed., *Atlantic Genealogies*, a special double issue of the *South Atlantic Quarterly* (spring/summer 2001).

46 I have in mind here that disjointed historicity central to Derrida's *Specters of Marx: The State of the Debt, The Work of Mourning, and the New International*, Peggy Kamuf, trans. (London: Routledge, 1994). I clarify my sense of the relation between Derrida's hauntological temporality and Benjamin's philosophy of history in the chapters that follow. In brief, though, I would "figure" that relation by transposing Derrida's specter onto Benjamin's "angel of history" (in the "Theses on the Philosophy of History" in *Illuminations*, Harry Zohn, trans. [New York: Schocken Books, 1968]). Thus the specter, rather than the angel, of history is, as Derrida suggests, defined by its intermittent apparitionality, by its tendency to appear as what reappears. Reappearing, however, the specter of history has, like Benjamin's angel, its "face turned toward the past . . . where we see one chain of events, he sees one single catastrophe which keeps piling up wreckage upon wreckage and hurls it in front of his feet" (Walter Benjamin, *Illuminations*, Harry Zohn, trans. [New York: Schocken Books, 1968], 257). Hauntological temporality, thus conjoined to Benjamin's "now-time," then articulates a time which does not pass, but accumulates, though in such a way that

it is only intermittently that we become aware of what Benjamin calls the what-has-been accumulated within the present. The recent series of renarrativizations of the *Zong* massacre that I discuss in the final chapter of this book (to which series this book also belongs) define, I am suggesting, such an apparitional moment in which the "wreckage" of the past accumulated in the present becomes manifest. I realize, however, that so parabolic an account requires fuller explication. The pages that follow attempt this.

47 Toni Morrison, *Beloved* (New York: Penguin, 1987), 210.

2. "Subject $"; or, the "Type" of the Modern

1 See, in particular, the Capetown sections of *Mason and Dixon* (New York: Henry Holt and Co., 1997). On the ways in which Pynchon's novel defines as its narrative geography a range of circum-Atlantic spaces-of-flow, see my essay, "Globalit Inc, or, The Cultural Logic of Global Literary Studies," PMLA 116, no. 1 (2001): 158–172.

2 See Joseph Roach, *Cities of the Dead: Circum-Atlantic Performance* (New York: Columbia University Press, 1996); Ian K. Steele, *The English Atlantic 1675–1740: An Exploration of Communication and Community* (Oxford: Oxford University Press, 1986).

3 On the importance of port cities to the construction of a circum-Atlantic world, see Franklin W. Knight and Peggy L. Liss, eds., *Atlantic Port Cities: Economy, Culture, and Society in the Atlantic World, 1650–1850* (Knoxville: University of Tennessee Press, 1991); and David Harris Sacks, *The Widening Gate: Bristol and the Atlantic Economy, 1450–1700* (Berkeley: University of California Press, 1991); on Liverpool, in particular, as an Atlantic port city, see S. Mountfield, *Western Gateway: A History of the Mersey Docks and Harbour Board* (Liverpool: Mersey Docks and Harbour Board, 1965); Nancy Ritchie-Noakes, *Liverpool's Historic Waterfront: The World's First Mercantile Dock System* (London: Her Majesty's Stationery Office, 1984); and Robert James Scally, *The End of Hidden Ireland: Rebellion, Famine, and Emigration* (New York: Oxford University Press, 1995), 184–217.

4 Giovanni Arrighi, *The Long Twentieth Century: Money, Power, and the Origins of Our Times* (London: Verso, 1996), 83.

5 Ibid., 134–160.

6 For fuller discussions of the chartered or joint-stock companies and the role they played in the restructuring of seventeenth- and eighteenth-century capital, see ibid., especially 139–140 and 242–247; P. G. M. Dickson, *The Financial Revolution in England: A Study in the Development of Public Credit, 1688–1756* (New York: St. Martin's, 1967); and Hugh Thomas, *The Slave Trade* (New York: Simon and Schuster, 1997), especially 235–261.

7 While he pursues the analogy between chartered company and multinational

corporation, Arrighi allows that the isomorphism is not absolute, largely because transnationals are generally less indebted to state sponsorship, and their attention tends to be less specific to any particular region of the world. Despite such differences in organization and scope, however, Arrighi insists that the comparison holds and so evidences one of those laws of recurrence (or "pendulum-like movement[s]") that he understands to organize the history of capital. See Arrighi, *The Long Twentieth Century*, 242–243.

8 The standard history remains Dickson's *The Financial Revolution in England*; for a brief introduction to the cosponsorship of that revolution by the state's warmaking needs, the emergence of a national bank, stock market, insurance industry, and credit financing, see especially 3–15. I discuss all of these constituent elements of the financial revolution in greater depth in the pages that follow.

9 The best information on the Gregsons' insurance and banking operations is provided in T. C. Barker and J. R. Harris, *A Merseyside Town in the Industrial Revolution, St. Helens, 1750–1900* (Liverpool: Liverpool University Press, 1954), especially 49–57; and John Hughes, *Liverpool Banks and Bankers* (Liverpool: Henry Young and Co., 1906), especially 107–123. Other secondary sources from which I have gleaned information on the business, social, and political doings of the Gregsons and their partners include *Liverpool Registry of Merchant Ships*, Robert Craig and Rupert Davis, eds. (Manchester: Chetham Society, 1967); J. A. Picton, *Memorials of Liverpool: Historical and Topographical* (London: Longmans, Green, and Co., 1875); Richard Brooke, *Liverpool as it was During the Last Quarter of the Eighteenth Century, 1775–1800* (Liverpool: J. Mawdsley and Son, 1853); Thomas Baines, *History of the Commerce and Town of Liverpool and of the Manufacturing Industry in the Adjoining Counties* (London: Longman, Brown, Green, and Longmans, 1852).

10 Insurance practice thus also bears comparison to the eighteenth-century practice of casuistry, particularly as James Chandler has recently taught us to conceive of casuistry as a mode of historicist analysis. See his *England in 1819: The Politics of Literary Culture and the Case of Romantic Historicism* (Chicago: University of Chicago Press, 1998), especially 194–212.

11 Georg Lukács, *The Historical Novel*, Hannah and Stanley Mitchell, trans. (Lincoln and London: University of Nebraska Press, 1962), 35.

12 Jameson suggests that for Lukács, "realist characters are distinguished from those in other types of literature by their *typicality*: they stand, in other words, for something larger and more meaningful than themselves, than their own isolated individual destinies. They are concrete individualities and yet at the same time maintain a relationship with some more general or collective human substance" (*Marxism and Form: Twentieth-Century Dialectical Theories of Literature* [Princeton: Princeton University Press, 1971], 191, emphasis original). Cited in Chandler, *England in 1819*, 255.

13 Chandler, *England in 1819*, 5.

14 See Michael McKeon, *The Origins of the English Novel, 1600–1740* (Baltimore: Johns Hopkins University Press, 1987).

15 I clarify my understanding of a "melancholy realism" throughout the pages that follow. In doing so I have learned a great deal from Michael Rothberg's *Traumatic Realism: The Demands of Holocaust Representation* (Minneapolis: University of Minnesota Press, 2000). As with Rothberg's "traumatic realism," the melancholy realism I have in mind is intimately related to the practice of testimony and to a conception of time which holds the moment of testimony not to fall "after" the moment of the event but to exist in a long-durational continuum with it. The stress I place on the melancholy predisposition to the antimetaphoric and the nominative in the elaboration of such a realism and my broader interest in identifying this representational practice with the type of melancholy historical "interestedness" I examine in the second part of the book have led me not to subsume the appellation "melancholy realism" within Rothberg's superbly nuanced elaboration of "traumatic realism."

16 Lukács introduces his reading of Scott's historicizing accomplishment so: "What is lacking in the so-called historical novel before Sir Walter Scott is precisely the specifically historical, that is, derivation of the individuality of characters from the historical peculiarity of their age" (*The Historical Novel*, 19).

17 Chandler, *England in 1819*, 36–37.

18 Ibid., 123–124.

19 See Benedict Anderson, *Imagined Communities: Reflections on the Origins and Rise of Nationalism*, rev. ed. (London: Verso, 1999), especially 22–36; Chandler, *England in 1819*, 106–107.

20 J. Paul Hunter, *Before Novels: The Cultural Contexts of Eighteenth-Century English Fiction* (New York: Norton, 1990), 167; cited in Chandler, *England in 1819*, 106–107.

21 Another way of framing this is to suggest, following the terms that Chandler uses, that historicism implies both the practice of casuistry (the application of general principles, systematic norms) to a particular instance or case and, *simultaneously*, a "reverse-casuistry" (the derivation of the general principles, systematic norms that are held to account for or explain the case *from* the case itself). That the *Zong* is such a case, one simultaneously apprehensibly by applying to it the general principles of the systems and norms in which it was encompassed, and one which defines the principles of that system, is fundamental to my argument in this first section of the book.

22 Chandler, *England in 1819*, 170.

23 Ibid., 174.

24 Jameson, *Marxism and Form*, 191; cited in Chandler, *England in 1819*, 255.

25 Chandler, *England in 1819*, 256.

26 On the notion of the "ideologeme" see Fredric Jameson, *The Political Unconscious: Narrative as a Socially Symbolic Act* (Ithaca: Cornell University Press, 1981), 141.

27 John Weskett, *A Complete Digest of the Theory, Laws, and Practice of Insurance* (London: Frys, Couchman, and Collier, 1781), 105.

28 Saree Makdisi, *Romantic Imperialism: Universal Empire and the Culture of Modernity* (Cambridge: Cambridge University Press, 1988), 88.

29 Lukács, *The Historical Novel*, 35.

30 Hegel's full comment runs so: "It is not the general idea that is implicated in opposition and combat, and that is exposed to danger. It remains in the background, untouched, uninjured. This may be called the *cunning of reason* — that it sets the passions to work for itself, while that which develops its existence through such impulsion pays the penalty, and suffers loss. . . . The particular is for the most part of too trifling value as compared with the general: individuals are sacrificed and abandoned." Georg Wilhelm Friedrich Hegel, *The Philosophy of History* (New York: Dover, 1956), 33.

31 Thomas, *The Slave Trade*, 247.

32 Unless otherwise noted, I have drawn these and all ensuing figures on Liverpool's involvement in the slave trade; the Gregson's investment in the trade; and details of particular voyages from the superb *The Trans-Atlantic Slave-Trade: A Database on CD ROM*, David Eltis, Steven D. Behrendt, David Richardson, Herbert S. Klein, eds. (Cambridge: Cambridge University Press, 1999).

33 Eltis et al., *The Trans-Atlantic Slave-Trade*.

34 Ibid.

35 Ibid. On the history of the Royal Africa Company, see K. G. Davies, *The Royal African Company* (New York: Longmans, Green, 1957).

36 On the Company of Merchants, see Thomas, *The Slave Trade*, 263–287.

37 Ibid., 264.

38 Eltis et al., *The Trans-Atlantic Slave-Trade*.

39 The pamphlet is among the documents collected in the anonymous *Liverpool and Slavery: An Historical Account of the Liverpool-African Slave Trade, Compiled from Various Sources and Authentic Documents* (Liverpool: A. Bowker and Son, 1884), 112.

40 Thomas, *The Slave Trade*, 249.

41 Baines, *History of the Commerce and Town of Liverpool*, 397–492.

42 Averil MacKenzie-Grieve, *The Last Years of the English Slave Trade: Liverpool 1750–1807* (London: Putnam and Co., 1941), 6.

43 See Eric Williams, *Capitalism and Slavery* (New York: Russell and Russell, 1961); for responses to Williams's argument, see essays by Selwyn Carrington, Joseph Inikori, David Richardson, Barbara Solow, and Gavin Wright in the *Journal of Interdisciplinary History*, 17 (1987); Barbara L. Solow, ed., *Slavery and the Rise of the Atlantic System* (Cambridge: Cambridge University Press, 1991); David Eltis, *Economic Growth and the Ending of the Trans-Atlantic Slave Trade* (New York: Oxford University Press, 1987); and Seymour Drescher, *Capitalism and Anti-Slavery: British Mobilization in Comparative Perspective* (New York: Oxford University Press, 1987). I am indebted to Ian K. Steele's review essay "Exploding

Colonial American History: Amerindian, Atlantic, and Global Perspectives," *Reviews in American History* 26, no. 1 (1998): 70–95, for these references.

44 Slavoj Žižek, *Tarrying with the Negative: Kant, Hegel, and the Critique of Ideology* (Durham: Duke University Press, 1983), 27–28.

45 By which I meant to imply that if we are willing to so expand the calendrical boundaries of our "present" that it stretches all the way back to the late eighteenth century, we tend to be most willing to do so with regard to this discourse; that we are accustomed to recognizing Kant as our rough philosophical contemporary — even if we only express that recognition by our continuing willingness to argue with him; that a "philosophical discourse on and of modernity" which Foucault suggests begins with Kant's 1780s writings on the philosophy of history has become the discursive category through which we naturalize, and so frequently fail to apprehend, the existence of this long contemporaneity. See Michel Foucault, "Kant on Enlightenment and Revolution," Colin Gordon, trans., *Economy and Society* 15, no. 1 (February 1986): 88–96.

46 If we follow Lukács, we cannot only historize the rise of the modern subject and of a modern philosophical discourse on the subject by situating both within this revolutionary moment but, as his famous reading of the popular autohistorization of French culture that accompanied Napoleon's mass mobilization of a citizen army indicates, should "situate" the rise of a historicist sensibility itself within this identical set of historical "circumstances": "The enormous quantitative expansion of war plays a qualitatively new role, bringing with it an extraordinary broadening of horizons. . . . French peasants fight first in Egypt, then in Italy, again in Russia; German and Italian auxiliary troops take part in the Russian campaign; German and Russian troops occupy Paris after Napoleon's defeat; and so forth. What previously was experienced only by isolated and mostly adventurous-minded individuals . . . becomes in this period the mass experience of hundreds of thousands, of millions. Hence the concrete possibilities for men to experience their own existence as something historically conditioned." Lukács, *The Historical Novel*, 24. Both the slave trade and imperialism, it seems fair to suggest, would have produced a similar experience.

47 Žižek, *Tarrying with the Negative*, 22.

48 This is the passage from Hegel's *Phenomenology* which Žižek cites in offering this reading: "In the world of culture (*Bildung*) itself, it [self-consciousness] does not get as far as to behold its negation or alienation in this form of pure abstraction; on the contrary, its negation is filled with a content, either honor or wealth, which it gains in place of the self which it has alienated from itself; or the language of Spirit and insight which the disrupted consciousness acquires; or it is the heaven of faith, or the utility of the Enlightenment. All these determinations have vanished in the loss suffered by the self in absolute freedom; its negation is the death that is without meaning, the sheer terror of the negative that contains nothing positive, nothing that fills it with a content. At the same

time, however, this negation in its real existence is not something alien; it is neither the universal inaccessible *necessity* in which the ethical world perishes, nor the particular accident of private possession, nor the whim of the owner on which the disrupted consciousness sees itself dependent; on the contrary, it is the *universal will* which in this its ultimate abstraction has nothing positive and therefore can give nothing in return for sacrifice. But for that very reason it is immediately at one with self-consciousness, or it is the pure positive, because it is the pure negative; and the meaningless death, the unfilled negativity of the self, changes round in its inner Notion into absolute positivity." Hegel, *Phenomenology of Spirit* (Oxford: Oxford University Press, 1977), 362; cited in Žižek, *Tarrying with the Negative*, 24.

49 See Pocock's introduction to his edition of Edmund Burke's *Reflections on the Revolution in France* (Indianapolis: Hackett Publishing, 1987), vii-1.

50 "Speculation" emerges as perhaps Burke's most vitriolic, contemptuous word in the *Reflections*, and also as the rhetorical figure with which he most effectively links the operations of abstract reason and credit financing. A few examples will suffice to demonstrate its tenor: "Compute your gains: see what is got by these extravagant and presumptuous speculations which have taught your leaders to despise all their predecessors and their contemporaries" (33); "All your sophisters cannot produce anything better adapted to preserve a rational and manly freedom than the course that we have pursued, who have chosen our nature rather than our speculations" (30–31); "This continual talk of resistance and revolution . . . produces in a country like ours the worst effects, even on the cause of that liberty which it abuses with the dissoluteness of an extravagant speculations" (55); "Hypocrisy, of course, delights in the most sublime speculations; for, never intending to go beyond speculation, it costs nothing to have it magnificent. But even in cases where rather levity than fraud was to be suspected in these ranting speculators, the issue was much the same. . . . For, considering their speculative designs as of infinite value, and the actual arrangement of the state as of no estimation, they are at best indifferent about it" (55–56). Burke, *Reflections on the Revolution in France*. On the "general equivalent," see Jean-Joseph Goux, *Symbolic Economies: After Marx and Freud*, Jennifer Curtiss Gage, trans. (Ithaca: Cornell University Press, 1990); on Goux and other post-Marxian readings of exchange, see Gayatri Chakravorty Spivak's essay "Scattered Speculations on the Question of Value," in *In Other Worlds: Essays in Cultural Politics* (New York: Methuen, 1987), 154–175.

51 This is perhaps most clear at the tail end of the famous "choice of inheritance" section of his argument in which, having linked the well-being of the state and the liberty of its subjects to the laws of property, inheritance, and custom (but above all, heritable property), Burke offers in response to his own question ("Compute your gains: see what is got by those extravagant and presumptuous speculations), the following: "Laws overturned; tribunals subverted; industry

without vigour; commerce expiring; the revenue unpaid, yet a people impoverished; a church pillaged, and a state not relieved; civil and military anarchy made the constitution of the kingdom; everything human and divine sacrificed to the idol of public credit; and national bankruptcy the consequence; and to crown all, the paper securities of new, precarious, tottering power, the discredited paper securities of impoverished fraud, and beggared rapine, held out as a currency for the support of an empire, in lieu of the two great recognized species that represent the lasting conventional credit of mankind, which disappeared and hid themselves in the earth from whence they came, when the principle of property, whose creatures and representatives they are, was systematically subverted." *Reflections on the Revolution in France*, 34.

52 That Burke accorded the operations of finance capital a certain priority as an antagonist of liberty is also evident in his long battle against the East India Company and the threat it posed, in Sara Suleri's terms, to submit the imperial state to "the coloniz[ation] of government by speculative finance." See Sara Suleri, *The Rhetoric of English India* (Chicago: University of Chicago Press, 1992), 24–74.

53 Burke, *Reflections on the Revolution in France*, 68. On the guillotine and Revolutionary terror as emblems of the "fatal beauty" hidden within the sublime, see Luke Gibbons, "Subtilized into Savages: Burke, Progress, and Primitivism," *South Atlantic Quarterly* 100, no. 1 (winter 2001): 83–109.

54 Žižek, *Tarrying with the Negative*, 42, emphasis original.

55 Immanuel Kant, "An Old Question Raised Again: Is the Human Race Constantly Progressing?" in *Kant: On History*, Lewis White Beck, ed. (New York: Liberal Arts Press, 1963), 143–144, 147.

56 Anonymous, *Liverpool and Slavery*, 115–116.

57 For detailed histories of the operations of trans-Atlantic credit, see Jacob M. Price, *Capital and Credit in British Overseas Trade: The View from the Chesapeake, 1700–1776* (Cambridge, Mass.: Harvard University Press, 1980); and James D. Tracy, *The Rise of Merchant Empires: Long Distance Trade in the Early Modern World, 1350–1750* (Cambridge: Cambridge University Press, 1990).

58 On the use and history of bills-of-exchange and their relation to the broader history of banking and money, see P. L. Cottrell and B. L. Anderson, *Money and Banking in England: The Development of the Banking System, 1694–1914* (London: David and Charles, 1974); Sir Albert Feaveryear, *The Pound Sterling: A History of English Money* (Oxford: Clarendon Press, 1963); T. S. Ashton and R. S. Sayers, eds., *Papers in English Monetary History* (Oxford: Clarendon Press, 1953); W. R. Bisschop, *The Rise of the London Money Market, 1640–1826* (London: P. S. King and Son, 1910); Pierre Vilar, *A History of Gold and Money*, Judith White, trans. (London: Verso, 1991).

59 J. G. A. Pocock, *Virtue, Commerce, and History: Essays on Political Thought and History, Chiefly in the Eighteenth Century* (Cambridge: Cambridge University Press, 1985), 110.

60 Ibid., 111.

61 Ibid., 112.

62 Ibid., 113. I discuss the South Sea Bubble at length in the pages which follow.

63 Gallagher's understanding of the eighteenth-century "nobody," she indicates in the introduction to her text, is one "deeply impressed by recent accounts of eighteenth-century economic changes that stress the revolution in credit and the proliferation of both debt and 'paper' property." Catherine Gallagher, *Nobody's Story: The Vanishing Acts of Women Writers in the Marketplace, 1670–1820* (Berkeley: University of California Press, 1994), xiv.

64 Ibid., xv; see Brian Rotman, *Signifying Nothing: The Semiotics of Zero* (London: Macmillan, 1987).

65 Gallagher, *Nobody's Story*, 76.

66 Ibid., xv–xvi.

67 Ibid., xvi.

68 Ibid., xvi–xvii.

69 Samuel Johnson, *Rambler*, no. 60, 391; quoted in Gallagher, *Nobody's Story*, 194.

70 Gallagher, *Nobody's Story*, 194.

71 Deidre Shauna Lynch, *The Economy of Character: Novels, Market Culture, and the Business of Inner Meaning* (Chicago: University of Chicago Press, 1998), 5.

72 Ibid.

73 Ibid., 35.

74 Ibid., 93.

75 Ibid., 93–94.

76 Ibid., 98.

77 Ibid., 5, 41.

78 Lynch discusses Hogarth's contribution to the imprinting of typical character on the face and its decoding from the face in ibid., 56–70.

79 *Gore's General Advertiser*, September 9, 1784; quoted in Brooke, *Liverpool as it was During the Last Quarter of the Eighteenth Century*, 288–289.

80 I draw this information from the material in Eltis et al., *The Trans-Atlantic Slave-Trade*.

81 *Printed Report of the Proceedings of the Commissioners of Inquiry into Municipal Corporations* (1833), 53; cited in Brooke, *Liverpool as it was During the Last Quarter of the Eighteenth Century*, 209.

82 The text of the request reads: "To Mr. Robert Williamson, Printer of the Liverpool Advertiser. Sir, — The publishing a list of ships that enter outwards and sail from this port every week we have too much reason to apprehend has been of very bad consequence this war; we, therefore, desire that for future you will omit it in your papers." Quoted in Baines, *History of the Commerce and Town of Liverpool*, 424–425.

83 On the Case family, see Barker and Harris, *A Merseyside Town in the Industrial Revolution*, 48–57. Gregson's daughter married George Case on December 31, 1783; see John Hughes, *Liverpool Banks and Bankers* (Liverpool: Henry Young and Co, 1906), 107–123.

84 Either in partnership with Thomas Case or on his own, Gregson was, by the late 1780s, investing in the outfitting of ships in Liverpool, the purchase of slaves in Africa, their sale in the Caribbean, the brokering of other merchant's slaves in Jamaica, the underwriting of trading vessels, and — when in 1784 he opened the William Gregson and Sons Bank — the business of banking the capital tallies the Atlantic trade was accumulating in his city.

85 On the office and habitual functions of the mid- to late-eighteenth-century Liverpool mayor, and the operations of the Corporation, see Brooke, *Liverpool as it was During the Last Quarter of the Eighteenth Century*, 195–230, 405–410.

86 Ibid., 380; for a full record of John Gregson's activities as mayor, see the *Committee Book of the Liverpool Town Council*, in LRO/352/CLE/TRA/2/11/0.

87 Quoted in Brooke, *Liverpool as it was During the Last Quarter of the Eighteenth Century*, 272.

88 *Gore's General Advertiser*, September 23, 1784; quoted in ibid., 272–273.

89 Quoted in *Liverpool as it was During the Last Quarter of the Eighteenth Century*, 272.

3. "Madam Death! Madam Death!"

1 Pocock traces the earliest personification of credit and the subsequent rise of the figure of "Lady Credit" to a 1706 entry in Defoe's *Review*: "Money has a younger Sister, a very useful and officious Servant in Trade, which in the absence of her senior Relation, but with her Consent, and on the Supposition of her Confederacy, is very assistant to her; frequently supplies her place for a Time; answers all the Ends of Trade perfectly, and to all Intents and Purposes, as well as money herself . . . Her Name in our Language is call'd Credit . . . This is a coy Lass, and wonderful chary of her self; yet a most necessary, useful, industrious Creature: she has some Qualification so peculiar, and is so very nice in her Conduct, that a World of Good People lose her Favour, before they well know her Name; others are courting her all their days to no purpose, and can never come into her Books. If once she be disoblig'd, she's the most difficult to be Friends again with us, of anything in the World; and yet she will court those most, who have no occasion for her; and will stand at their doors neglected and ill-us'd, scorn'd, and rejected, like a Beggar, and never leave them: But let such have a Care of themselves, and be sure they never come to want her; for if they do, they may depend upon it, she will pay them home, and never be reconcil'd to them, but upon a World of Entreaties, and the severe Penance of some years Prosperity" (Defoe, *Review* [facsimile book 6], vol. 3, no. 5, 17–18; cited in J. G. A. Pocock, *The Machiavellian Moment: Florentine Political Thought and the Atlantic Republican Tradition* [Princeton: Princeton University Press, 1975], 452–453). Thereafter, she appears consistently in the *Review* before being taken up by Addison in *Spectator* number 3 and becoming a staple of Augustan rhet-

oric: "She appeared infinitely timorous in all her Behavior; And, whether it was from the Delicacy of her Constitution, or that she was troubled with Vapours . . . She changed Colour, and startled at everything she heard. She was likewise (as I afterwards found) a greater Valetudinarian than any I had ever met with, even in her own Sex, and subject to such Momentary Consumptions, that in the twinkling of an Eye, she would fall away from the most florid Complexion, and the most healthful State of Body, and wither into a Skeleton. Her Recoveries were often as sudden as her Decays, insomuch as she would revive in a Moment out of a wasting Distemper, into a Habit of the highest Health and Vigour" (*The Spectator*, ed. G. Gregory Smith [London: J. M. Dent and Sons, 1961], 11; cited in Pocock, *The Machiavellian Moment*, 455–456). For readings of Lady Credit see Pocock, *The Machiavellian Moment*, 423–461; Patrick Brantlinger, *Fictions of State: Culture and Credit in Britain, 1694–1994* (Ithaca: Cornell University Press, 1996); Sandra Sherman, *Finance and Fictionality in the Eighteenth Century: Accounting for Defoe* (Cambridge: Cambridge University Press, 1996); and Terry Mulcaire, "Public Credit; or, the Femination of Virtue in the Marketplace," in PMLA 114, no. 5 (October 1999): 1029–1042.

2 See Jürgen Habermas, *The Structural Transformation of the Public Sphere: An Inquiry into a Category of Bourgeois Society* (Cambridge, Mass.: MIT Press; 1989).

3 Christian Thorne Miano, unpublished seminar essay.

4 I intend the term "financialized" in the sense used by Gayatri Chakravorty Spivak in *A Critique of Postcolonial Reason: Toward a History of the Vanishing Present* (Cambridge, Mass.: Harvard University Press, 1999). I discuss Spivak's text and her reading of the post-Enlightenment extension of credit networks and epistemologies in chapter 5.

5 On the South Sea Bubble see P. G. M. Dickson, *The Financial Revolution in England: A Study in the Development of Public Credit, 1688–1756* (New York: St. Martin's, 1967), 90–156; the best book-length study of the South Sea affair is John Carswell, *The South Sea Bubble* (London: Cresset Press, 1960); on the South Sea Company's acquisition of the asiento see Thomas, *The Slave Trade* (New York: Simon and Schuster, 1997), 235–242.

6 Defoe, *The Best of Defoe's Review*, William L. Pyne, ed. (New York: Columbia University Press, 1951, 118; quoted in Mulcaire, "Public Credit," 1033; Addison, *Spectator* number 3; quoted in Mulcaire, "Public Credit," 1035.

7 Dickson, *The Financial Revolution in England*, 139.

8 Mulcaire, "Public Credit." Mulcaire's essay suggestively links the "imaginary values" for whom Lady Credit is the discursive emblem to Žižek's "truth of fantasy" in such a way as to suggest that it is precisely the knowledge of the fantastical quality of the values credit represents that accounts for a subjective investment and delight in them and thus to imply that the imaginary is structured not simply like a language but like credit: "To acknowledge that these are imaginary figments, to acknowledge that desire runs on a kind of endless credit,

that it depends on the imaginary status and thus the ultimate inaccessibility of its object, and therefore that one's desires are not expressions of one's autonomous subjectivity but something more like individual currents in a social field generate by the contingent machinery of social institutions such as the marker . . . suggests a small but consequential alteration in Žižek's formulation, from, 'I know very well that this object is unreal, but I will desire it nonetheless' to 'I know very well that this object is unreal; therefore I find it desirable,' because of the way such imaginary desires promise to produce real ideological consequences. For these Whig writers [Addison, Cato, and Defoe], there is no 'but': they know very well that Credit's bags are not really full of gold, and therefore they are charmed by her, precisely because of the charming power to make something out of nothing."

9 Dickson, *The Financial Revolution in England*, 230.

10 LRO 387/MD/54.

11 The best history of the development of credit in the West African slave markets is Joseph C. Miller's *The Way of Death* (Madison: University of Wisconsin Press, 1988).

12 PRO T1/380/12.

13 B. Cruikshank, *Eighteen Years on the Gold Coast of Africa*, 2nd ed. (London: Frank Cass and Co, 1852), 33, 34.

14 Ibid., 42.

15 Ibid., 35.

16 Ibid., 36.

17 Ibid.

18 Ibid., 37.

19 Ibid., 42.

20 The most celebrated eighteenth-century addition to the coinage debates is undoubtedly Swift's *The Drapier's Letters*; for a superb reading of the *Letters*, see Srinivas Aravamudan, *Tropicopolitans: Colonialism and Agency, 1688–1804* (Durham: Duke University Press, 1999), 145–156; see also Peter Laslett, "John Locke, the Great Recoinage, and the Origins of the Board of Trade, 1695–1698," *William and Mary Quarterly*, 14 (1957): 378–385. It is worth noting that among the first items noted in the Committee Book of the Liverpool Town Council during the course of George Case's tenure as mayor of Liverpool (Case was William Gregson's son-in-law) in 1781–82 was an instruction from the mayor to place an advertisement in the newspapers calling for the apprehension of "a group of coiners" who had been operating in the city. LRO, 352/CLE/TRA/2/11/0. Cruikshank, *Eighteen Years*, 42.

21 Cruikshank, *Eighteen Years*, 43.

22 Ibid., 44, 46.

23 The original passage in Arrighi, which I have paraphrased in the text, reads: "Chartered companies were the medium through which the Dutch capitalist

class established *direct* links between the Amsterdam entrepôt on the one side, and producers from all over the world on the other side. Thanks to these direct links, the ability of the Dutch capitalist class to centralize the commercial transactions that mattered in Amsterdam, as well as its ability to monitor, regulate, and profit from the disequilibria of world trade, were greatly enhanced. At the same time, chartered companies played a decisive role in the rise of Amsterdam to the status of world financial center. For investment and speculation in the shares of chartered companies — first and foremost of the voc — were the single most important factor in the successful development of the Amsterdam Bourse into the first stock market in permanent session." Giovanni Arrighi, *The Long Twentieth Century: Money, Power, and the Origins of Our Times* (London: Verso), 1994, 139–140.

24 PRO, T1/450/70–74.

25 Jan S. Hogendorn and Marion Johnson, *The Shell Money of the Slave Trade* (Cambridge: Cambridge University Press, 1986), 156.

26 J. A. Picton, *Memorials of Liverpool: Historical and Topographical* (London: Longmans, Green, and Co., 1875) 165, 379.

27 Ibid., 348.

28 Ibid.

29 Ibid.

30 On Liverpool's Liberty Day celebrations, electoral politics, and Charter, see Richard Brooke, *Liverpool as it was During the Last Quarter of the Eighteenth Century, 1775–1800* (Liverpool: J. Mawdsley and Son, 1853), 195–230.

31 Ibid., 224–230.

32 Ibid., 490.

33 Ibid.

34 Cited ibid., 491.

35 PRO, T1/380/14

36 Brooke, *Liverpool as it was During the Last Quarter of the Eighteenth Century*, 490.

37 Dickson, *The Financial Revolution in England*, 6.

38 Ibid., 145–147; and D. E. W. Gibb, *Lloyd's of London: A Study in Individualism* (London: MacMillan, 1957), 27–33. Much of the detail that follows comes from Gibb's text.

39 Dickson, *The Financial Revolution in England*, 91–92.

40 Gibb, *Lloyd's of London*, 56–57.

41 Ibid.

42 Ibid., 54.

43 John Weskett, *A Complete Digest of the Theory, Laws, and Practice of Insurance* (London: Frys, Couchman, and Collier, 1781).

44 "When goods arrived damaged, the first thing requisite is, to find out the true quantum of the damage or loss, or the diminution in value which they have sustained; and then *to apportion that loss on what would have been the value of the*

goods if they had arrived safe and undamaged." Weskett, *A Complete Digest of the Theory, Laws, and Practice of Insurance*, 25.

45 Fredric Jameson, *Marxism and Form: Twentieth-Century Dialectical Theories of Literature* (Princeton: Princeton University Press, 1971), 191.

46 I discuss both a romantic historicism and the romantic novel's construction of "compensation-for-loss-types" in the second section of the book.

47 Weskett, *A Complete Digest of the Theory, Laws, and Practice of Insurance*, 252.

48 Ibid., 25.

49 Ibid., 25, emphasis added.

50 The initial work of establishing the value of a cargo was a simple matter of agreement, and, so long as the intention of fraud was not suspected, could easily be set higher than market value if the "owner" was willing to pay the correspondingly higher premium; in the case of the total loss of a cargo no valuation was necessary, the amount having already been set by the terms of the contract; the computation of "average" value in the case of total or partial loss was thus the fundamental work on which the fortunes of an insurance underwriter depended.

51 NMM, REC/19.

52 Chandler, *England in 1819*, 195, 209.

53 Ibid., 199–200, 209.

54 Weskett, *A Complete Digest of the Theory, Laws, and Practice of Insurance*, 333.

55 Ibid., 253.

56 Ibid., 105.

4. "Signum Rememorativum, Demonstrativum, Prognostikon"

1 Kant, "An Old Question Raised Again," 137.

2 Ibid., 137.

3 Ibid.

4 See Reinhart Koselleck, *Futures Past: On the Semantics of Historical Time*, Keith Tribe, trans. (Cambridge, Mass.: MIT Press, 1985).

5 Jürgen Habermas, *The Philosophical Discourse of Modernity: Twelve Lectures*, Fredrick J. Lawrence, trans. (Cambridge, Mass.: MIT Press, 1990), 12.

6 Habermas summarizes his sense of the Benjaminian innovation so: "Hence Benjamin proposes *a drastic reversal* of horizon of expectation and space of experience. To all past epochs he ascribes a horizon of unfulfilled expectations, and to the future-oriented present he assigns the task of experiencing a corresponding past through remembering, in such a way that we can fulfill its expectations with our weak messianic power. In accordance with this reversal two ideas can be interwoven: the conviction that the continuity of the context of tradition can be established by barbarism as well as culture, and the idea that each succeeding generation bears the responsibility not only for the fate of

future generations but also for the innocently suffered fate of past generations" (ibid., 14).

7 Kant, "An Old Question Raised Again," 142–143.

8 Ibid., 143, 147.

9 Ibid., 143.

10 Ibid.

11 For Žižek's lengthiest discussion of Badiou, see Slavoj Žižek, *The Ticklish Subject: The Absent Centre of Political Ontology* (London: Verso, 1999), 127–171. The central text to which Žižek refers throughout his reading, Badiou's *L'être et l'événement* (Paris: Editions du Seuil, 1988), has not yet been translated. I rely on Žižek's translations throughout.

12 I discuss the Derridean and Benjaminian cast of Badiou's event theory in the pages that follow. Badiou partially reconciles Althusser to Kant, Žižek suggests, largely by conferring on the sympathy-inducing character of the sublime Kantian "event" a strong Althusserian "interpellative" capacity.

13 Žižek, *The Ticklish Subject*, 166.

14 Ibid., 129.

15 Ibid., 130.

16 Ibid., 137–38.

17 On Derrida's refusal of the ontologization of the spectral see *Specters of Marx: The State of the Debt, The Work of Mourning, and the New International*, Peggy Kamuf, trans. (London: Routledge, 1994), throughout but especially 95–124.

18 While for Kant it will come as a universal, "cosmopolitan," "perpetual peace," this is where Derrida parts ways with Kant and Badiou, since for Derrida the final return of the Truth event must always be held out as a still-open promise: its realization, or "ontologization," equating, to his mind, its necessary betrayal. Derrida, *Specters of Marx*, 4. Žižek glosses the Derridean equation of the ontologization of the "to come" with its inevitable betrayal so: "Deconstructionists [Derrida included] draw the conclusion that the principal ethico-political duty is to maintain the gap between the Void of the central impossibility and every positive content giving body to it — that is, never fully to succumb to the enthusiasm of hasty identification of a positive Event with the redemptive promise that is 'to come.' In this deconstructionist stance, admiration for the Revolution in its utopian enthusiastic aspect goes hand in hand with the conservative melancholic insight that enthusiasm inevitably turns into its opposite, into the worst terror, the moment we endeavour to transpose it into the positive structuring principle of social reality" (*The Ticklish Subject*, 134).

19 Žižek, *The Ticklish Subject*, 131.

20 James Chandler, *England in 1819: The Politics of Literary Culture and the Case of Romantic Historicism* (Chicago: University of Chicago Press, 1998), 207–208; the text by André Jolles that Chandler is discussing is *Einfache Formen* (Darmstadt: Wissenschaftliche Buchgessellschaft, 1958).

21 Žižek, *The Ticklish Subject*, 137.

22 Walter Benjamin, "Theses on the Philosophy of History," in *Illuminations*, Harry Zohn, trans. (New York: Schocken Books, 1968), 255.

23 NMM, REC/19.

24 Ibid.

25 Ibid.

26 Ibid.

27 Ibid.

28 Ibid.

29 Ibid.

30 Ibid.

31 Ibid.

32 Ibid.

33 Ibid.

34 Ibid.

35 Kant, "An Old Question Raised Again," 143.

36 Cathy Caruth, *Unclaimed Experience: Trauma, Narrative, and History* (Baltimore: Johns Hopkins University Press, 1996), 4.

37 For Nicolas Abraham and Maria Torok, the cryptic discourse of the melancholic is a discourse that founds itself on the inability to introject the lost object of desire and a consequent incorporation of that object. As Nicholas T. Rand indicates in his editor's note to Abraham and Torok's *The Shell and the Kernel*, Nicholas T. Rand, ed. and trans. (Chicago: University of Chicago Press, 1994), where introjection implies an acknowledgment of loss which allows the mourner to transform the self "in the face of interior and exterior changes in the psychological, emotional, relational, political, [and] professional landscape," incorporation "is the refusal to acknowledge the full import of the loss, a loss that, if recognized as such, would effectively transform us" (ibid., 127). A form of disavowal, incorporation also implies a secret labor of compensation: "The words that cannot be uttered, the scenes that cannot be recalled, the tears that cannot be shed — everything will be swallowed along with the trauma that led to the loss. Swallowed and preserved. Inexpressible mourning erects a secret tomb inside the subject" (ibid., 130). Within that tomb, Abraham and Torok continue, within that cryptic vault of memory, the mourner hides the terrible, fascinating, strangely exquisite corpse of the lost, violated, and beloved and suffers its serial hauntings.

38 Lynch traces the emergence of this alternate novelistic discourse (one she associates with sentimentality) to a series of late-century narratives in which the action of the text turns on a character's unwillingness to put some object of value into circulation in contradistinction to earlier narratives which "map characterization onto the transactions in which cash [among other objects] changes hands": "This is why these moments in which a coin is *withheld* from exchange are so odd. . . . [For] rather than entering the transactional space of commercial

society and embarking on the project of character reading, [such characters] look to be stalled" (Deidre Shauna Lynch, *The Economy of Character: Novels, Market Culture, and the Business of Inner* Meaning [Chicago: University of Chicago Press, 1998], 114). "In some ways," she continues, "the moments when sentimental narratives seemed momentarily to suspend the logic of exemplarity and exchangeability elicited the romantic rereading that would eventually reinvent mid-century fiction and, personalizing and psychologizing it, recast it in explicitly novelistic forms. In his monumental *History of English Literature* (1873), Taine, for instance, is able to appropriate Sterne's numismatic metaphor in *A Sentimental Journey* to describe the English novel as a tradition that is defined by its concentration on character: 'All these novels are character novels. Englishmen, more reflective than others, more inclined to the melancholy pleasure of concentrated attention and inner examination find around them human medals more vigorously struck, less worn by friction with the world, whose uninjured face is more visible than that of others' " (ibid., 117).

39 Caruth, *Unclaimed Experience*, 8.

40 NMM, REC/19.

41 Ibid.

42 Ibid.

43 Ibid.

44 This text is from John Weskett's *A Complete Digest of the Theory, Laws, and Practice of Insurance* (London: Frys, Couchman, and Collier, 1781); I cite it as evidentiary of what the *Zong*'s insurance contract would have stipulated because while the contract itself has not survived, testimony entered at Mansfield's hearing indicated that the contract was a thoroughly standard policy in all respects. Weskett's 1781 framing of the principle of the "general average" and of the legal restrictions applying to it may thus be taken as describing the terms under which the *Zong*'s policy, drawn up that same year, would have been written. Testimony and argumentation throughout the hearing further indicate that it was exactly the set of stipulations Weskett defines which were at issue before the court.

45 NMM, REC/19.

46 If, that is, we continue to regard the event not as that which marks a moment of absolute rupture but as that which offers its retrospective testimony to a preexisting "situation"; as the mode of appearance of the what-has-been; as the reapparitional appearance of what has been brought to light.

5. *"Please decide"*

1 Fredric Jameson, "Culture and Finance Capital," *Critical Inquiry* 24 (autumn 1997): 246.

2 Ibid., 251.

3 Ibid., 252.

4 Ibid., 258. Jameson summarizes his argument so: "What does all this have to do with finance capital? Modernist abstraction, I believe, is less a function of capital accumulation as such than of money itself in a situation of capital accumulation. Money is here both abstract (making everything equivalent) and empty and uninteresting, since its interest lies outside itself. It is thus incomplete like the modernist images I have been evoking; it directs attention elsewhere, beyond itself, towards what is supposed to complete (and abolish) it. It knows a semi-autonomy, certainly, but not a full autonomy in which it would constitute a language or a dimension in its own right. But that is precisely what finance capital brings into being: a play of monetary entities that need neither production (as capital does) nor consumption (as money does), which supremely, like cyberspace, can live on their own internal metabolisms and circulate without any reference to an older type of content. But so do the narrativized image fragments of a stereotypical postmodern language; they suggest a new cultural realm or dimension that is independent of the former real world, not because as in the modern (or even the romantic) period culture withdrew from that real world into an autonomous space of art, but rather because the real world has already been suffused with culture and colonized by it, so that is has no outside in terms of which it could be found lacking" (ibid., 264–265).

5 Ibid., 252.

6 Spivak refers to this concept throughout her work. It makes its initial appearance in *A Critique of Postcolonial Reason: Toward a History of the Vanishing Present* (Cambridge, Mass: Harvard University Press, 1999) in reference to her reading of *Jane Eyre* and is accompanied by this footnote: "For 'worlding' see Martin Heidegger, 'The Origin of the Work of Art,' in David Farell Krell, ed., *Basic Works, from Being and Time (1927) to the Task of Thinking (1964)* (San Francisco: Harper, 1993), 137–212. Heidegger's idea, that the lineaments of the conflict in the making of the text are set or posited in it insofar as it is a *work* of art, is useful here. What I am doing with these texts is obviously influenced by my sense of how the setting-to-work mode of deconstruction is a reinscription of Heidegger's privileging of art" (*A Critique of Postcolonial Reason*, 115n).

7 Nike Corporation, 1999, http://www.nikeBiz.com/labor/loan.shtml. The ad had its own Web site, but no longer appears on the company's site.

8 Again, this is a phrase Spivak uses throughout *A Critique of Postcolonial Reason*, and again her fullest explication of it comes in a footnote: "In the wake of the Cold War there is a mood of triumphalist Americanism in the United States. 'Democratization,' code name for the transformation of (efficient through inefficient to wild) state capitalisms and their colonies to tributary economies of rationalized global financialization — carries with it the aura of the civilizing mission of earlier colonialisms. Again, the talk is of 'transformation.' And it is now more specifically in terms of gender than anything else. This is the globalized subject. The rationalization of sexuality, the invasive restructuring of

gender relations, poor women's credit-baiting without infrastructural invest-ment in the name of women's micro-enterprise, the revision of women-in-development (modernization) to gender-and-development (New World Eco-nomic Order)—all this is seen as global sisterhood. The Rani of Sirmur is a remote harbinger" (*A Critique of Postcolonial Reason*, 223n). That this description of a "credit-baiting" finance capitalism is a virtual, point-by-point sketch of Nike's microloan program seems evident. That the *Zong* is also "a remote har-binger" of this financializing "now" is what I am arguing.

9 See Ann Laura Stoler, *Race and the Education of Desire: Foucault's History of Sexuality and the Colonial Order of Things* (Durham: Duke University Press, 1995).

10 On the nonequivalent exchange see Slavoj Žižek, *Tarrying with the Negative: Kant, Hegel, and the Critique of Ideology* (Durham: Duke University Press, 1983), 22–27.

11 Giovanni Arrighi, *The Long Twentieth Century: Money, Power, and the Origins of Our Times* (London: Verso), 1994, 83.

12 Jameson, "Culture and Finance Capital," 251, 260.

13 Spivak, *A Critique of Postcolonial Reason*, 99.

14 Ibid., 91 and 91n.

15 Ibid., 153.

16 Ibid., 306.

17 Ibid., 4. Spivak cites this passage from *The Language of Psychoanalysis* by Jean Laplanche and J. B. Pontalis as foundational to her use of the term: "The sense brought to the fore by Lacan . . . [is to be found] for instance, in [what] Freud writes. . . . [about] 'a much more energetic and successful kind of defence. Here the ego rejects [*verwirft*] the incompatible idea *together with the affect* and be-haves as if the idea had never occurred to the ego at all.' . . . The work from which Lacan has most readily derived support for his . . . idea of foreclosure is the case-history of the 'Wolf-Man'" (*The Language of Psychoanalysis*, Donald Nicholson-Smith, trans. [New York: Norton, 1974], 166–169; cited in Spivak, *A Critique of Postcolonial Reason*, 4). It is in part the importance of the Wolf-Man case history which accounts for the link between Lacan on foreclosure and Abraham and Torok on encrypting.

18 Kant, *The Critique of Judgment*, J. H. Bernard, trans. (New York: Hafner Press, 1951), 96 and 105; cited in Spivak, *A Critique of Postcolonial Reason*, 11 and 13.

19 Kant, *The Critique of Judgment*, 215; cited in Spivak, *A Critique of Postcolonial Reason*, 26.

20 Spivak, *A Critique of Postcolonial Reason*, 26–27.

21 Ibid., 123–124.

22 Kant, "An Old Question Raised Again," 143–144; 147. For Mary Louise Pratt's concept of "planetary consciousness," see her *Imperial Eyes: Travel Writing and Transculturation* (London: Routledge, 1992).

23 Žižek, *Tarrying with the Negative*, 28.

24 Kant, incidentally, was aware of this, if somewhat unhappily so: he concludes the essay I have been citing ("An Old Question Raised Again") with a lengthy denunciation of the spread of networks of public credit, which he then suddenly amends, in his final sentence, by "confessing" that it is not just the spectacle of the revolution but the development of such debt financing which "compels [him to recognize] a very imminent turn of humanity toward the better that is even now in prospect" (Kant, "An Old Question Raised Again," 154).

25 Kant, "An Old Question Raised Again," 144.

26 Ibid., 143.

27 Georg Wilhelm Friedrich Hegel, *The Philosophy of History* (New York: Dover, 1956), 33.

28 Spivak, *A Critique of Postcolonial Reason*, 146.

29 Ibid., 132, 146.

30 Ibid., 306.

31 Ibid., 145n.

32 Ibid., 173–174, 175, 190.

33 Ibid., 109.

34 Ibid., 241–242.

35 Ibid., 78.

36 Ibid.

37 Ibid., 421.

38 Žižek, *The Ticklish Subject*, 131.

39 J. A. Picton, *Memorials of Liverpool: Historical and Topographical* (London: Longmans, Green, and Co., 1875), 348.

6. Frontispiece

1 M. NourbeSe Philip, *Zong!* (unpublished manuscript), quoted by permission of the author.

2 The note Eiland and McLaughlin supply to their translation of *Konvolut* is as follows: "In Germany the term *Konvolut* has a common philological application: it refers to a larger or smaller assemblage — literally, a bundle — of manuscripts or printed materials that belong together. The noun 'convolute' in English means 'something of a convoluted form.' We have chosen it as the translation of the German term over a number of other possibilities, the most prominent being 'folder,' 'file,' and 'sheaf.' . . . 'Convolute' is strange, at least on first acquaintance, but so is Benjamin's project and its principle of sectioning. Aside from its desirable closeness to the German rubric . . . it remains the most precise and most evocative term for designating the elaborately intertwined collections of 'notes and materials' that make up the central division of this most various and colorful of Benjaminian texts." Howard Eiland and Kevin McLaughlin,

foreword to Walter Benjamin, *The Arcades Project*, Howard Eiland and Kevin McLaughlin, trans. (Cambridge, Mass.: Harvard University Press, 1999), xiv.

3 Benjamin, *The Arcades Project*, 461.

4 Jacques Derrida, "'A Self-Unsealing Poetic Text': Poetics and Politics of Witnessing," Rachel Bowlby, trans., in *Revenge of the Aesthetic: The Place of Literature in Theory Today*, Michael P. Clark, ed. (Berkeley: University of California Press, 2000), 186.

5 Ibid.; Emile Benveniste, *Le vocabulaire des institutions indo-europeénnes* (Paris: Minuit, 1969), 2:277, cited in Derrida, "'A Self-Unsealing Poetic Text,'" 187. To maintain consistency with her translation of Derrida, I have used Bowlby's translation of the passage from Benveniste rather than that provided in Jean Lallot and Elizabeth Palmer's 1973 translation of Benveniste's text, *Indo-European Language and Society* (London: Faber and Faber, 1973).

6 Paul Celan, "Aschenglorie," in *Atemwende* (Frankfurt am Main: Suhrkamp, 1967), 68, cited in Derrida, "'A Self-Unsealing Poetic Text,'" 181 and throughout. Bowlby lists as an English translation of Celan's poem, Joachim Neugroschel in Celan, *Speech-grille and Selected Poems* (New York: Dutton, 1971), 240, and as a French translation, Andre de Bouchet in Celan, *Strette* (Paris: Mercure de France, 1971), 50.

7 Derrida, "'A Self-Unsealing Poetic Text,'" 200.

8 See Michael Lowy and Robert Sayre, *Romanticism Against the Tide of Modernity*, Catherine Porter, trans. (Durham: Duke University Press, 2001). A brief overview of their argument can be drawn from the following passages from the text's introductory chapter: "Thus we note an important gap [in prior accounts of romanticism]: we find no overarching analysis of the phenomenon that takes its full extent and full multiplicity into account. In what follows we try to fill that gap, starting from a definition of Romanticism as weltanschaung or worldview, that is, a collective mental structure. Such a structure may be expressed in quite diverse cultural realms: not only in literature and the other arts but also in philosophy and theology; political, economic, and legal thought; sociology and history, and so forth. Thus our definition is by no means limited either to literature and art or to the historical period in which the so-called Romantic artistic movements developed"; "Let us note right away, very briefly, the crux of our conception of the Romantic movement: Romanticism represents a critique of modernity, that is, of modern capitalist civilization, in the name of values and ideals drawn from the past (the precapitalist, premodern, past). From its inception, Romanticism can be said to be illuminated by the dual light of revolt and what Gerard de Nerval called the 'black sun of melancholy'" (14; 17–18).

9 Ibid., 17.

10 Primo Levi, cited in Giorgio Agamben, *Remnants of Auschwitz: The Witness and the Archive*, Daniel Heller-Roazen, trans. (New York: Zone Books, 1999), 33, 37.

11 Agamben, *Remnants*, 17.

12 Ibid., 15.

13 Ibid., 18.

14 Ibid., 19.

15 Ibid., 33–34.

16 To be sure, for Badiou, as I have noted, the truth event is necessarily utopic rather than catastrophic. As I intend to suggest, however, the formal characteristics of his "subject" or "some-one" of a truth are in crucial ways homologous with those of Derrida's and Agamben's witnesses.

17 Alain Badiou, *Ethics: An Essay on the Understanding of Evil*, Peter Halliward, trans. (New York: Verso, 2001), 44, emphasis original.

18 Ibid., 44–45, 46–47.

19 Mark Sanders, *Complicities: The Intellectual and Apartheid* (Durham: Duke University Press, 2002), 5.

20 Badiou, *Ethics*, 49–50.

21 Giorgio Agamben, *Homo Sacer: Sovereign Power and Bare Life*, Daniel Heller-Roazen, trans. (Stanford: Stanford University Press, 1998), 12.

22 Ibid., 22.

23 Ibid., 46.

24 See "The National Security Strategy of the United States of America," The White House, Washington, D.C., September 2002. http://www.whitehouse.gov/nsc/nss.html.

25 Carl Schmitt, *Das Nomos von der Erde* (Berlin: Duncker and Humbolt, 1974), 67; cited in Agamben, *Homo Sacer*, 36.

26 See Hannah Arendt, *The Origins of Totalitarianism* (New York: Harcourt, 1968), 267–302.

27 See Agamben, *Homo Sacer*, 24–26.

28 If these are the classical, modern, state-constituted topoi of the state of exception, then in our moment such spaces have also been scrambled and multiplied by the challenge globalization puts to the state. Sovereignty, as Arjun Appadurai has argued, is increasingly without or beyond territoriality, increasingly, by Schmitt and Agamben's terms, exceptional, as it is increasingly multiple, detached from the state, a constitutional power of the corporation, financial markets, the culture industry, and global media. These too, increasingly, are sovereign powers, and their territories of address are all or always straining toward the exceptional; all or always in design constitutive of a legal space of abandonment, whether in the sweatshop, the free-trade zone, an International Monetary Fund austerity economy, beyond the boundary — as James Ferguson's work on the Zambian copper belt demonstrates — of a world bank redline or in one of Appadurai's mediascapes in which the people of the world are solicited to invest affective membership but where few find themselves represented. See Arjun Appadurai, *Modernity at Large: Cultural Dimensions of Globalization* (Minneapo-

lis: University of Minnesota Press, 1986); and James Ferguson, *Expectations of Modernity: Myths and Meanings of Urban Life on the Zambian Copperbelt* (Berkeley: University of California Press, 1999).

29 Žižek, *The Ticklish Subject*, 131.

30 See Orlando Patterson, *Slavery and Social Death: A Comparative Study* (Cambridge, Mass.: Harvard University Press, 1982).

31 It is this relation between the witness and bare life on the one hand, and bare life and sovereignty on another that links the first and third volumes of *Homo Sacer*, the analyses of *Sovereign Power and Bare Life* and *The Witness and the Archive*.

32 Agamben, *Homo Sacer*, 127.

33 See Michael Hardt and Antonio Negri, *Empire* (Cambridge, Mass.: Harvard University Press, 2000).

34 I am thinking primarily of Foucault's discussion of the "care" of life within the context of his elaboration of a theory of biopower in the 1976 College de France Lectures. For a superb reading of those lectures and the relation of Foucault's concept of biopower to colonial racism, see Anne Laura Stoler, *Race and the Education of Desire: Foucault's History of Sexuality and the Colonial Order of Things* (Durham: Duke University Press, 1995), especially 55–94.

35 To name work by only two scholars: Ann Laura Stoler's *Race and the Education of Desire: Foucault's History of Sexuality and the Colonial Order of Things* (Durham: Duke University Press, 1995) and Mahmoud Mamdani's *Citizen and Subject: Contemporary Africa and the Legacy of Late Colonialism* (Princeton: Princeton University Press, 1996) and *Beyond Rights Talk and Culture Talk: Comparative Essays on the Politics of Rights and Culture* (New York: St. Martin's, 2000) productively resituate these problems within a colonial frame.

36 I discuss abolitionist "friendship" discourse in chapter 7.

7. The View from the Window

1 Captain Collingwood had died under uncertain circumstances before either of the trials could take place.

2 NMM, REC/19.

3 As Lynch argues, this romantic "inwardness" — the primary subject of the appropriately titled second portion of her *The Economy of Character* (part two of her book is titled "Inside Stories") — signifies not simply *character's* turning away from property but a way of composing character via an alternate (sympathetic) manner of possessing property: "In the chapters that follow," she notes in the concluding paragraph of the first part of the book, "I will trace how novels' depictions of a protagonists plight with property that is not personal enough operate to 'round' character — to suggest an inner consciousness that seems to exist independent of exchange relations. I will propose, in addition, that novels of manners have served as sites where people, and perhaps women readers

especially, have managed their relations to their things. Our sympathetic identification with the fictional character, which somebody who is nobody, Catherine
Gallagher asserts, gives us a way to be acquisitive without impertinence. Gallagher uses this phrase to emphasize how eighteenth-century conceptions of
sympathy were bound up with conceptualizations of ownership, how feeling
was thought of as a process that aggrandized the self and its properties. Gallagher's account, which we could align with Wordsworth's description of acts of
the imagination as "Possessions . . . that are solely mine / Something within
which yet is shared by none, requires supplementing . . . I suggest that readers
who are invited to imagine the inner life of a complex character, a character
wronged by appearances, are tantalized with what, as consumers who are troubled by luxury yet in thrall to the world of goods, they most fervently seek — a
way to be acquisitive and antimaterialist at once" (Deidre Shauna Lynch, *The
Economy of Character: Novels, Market Culture, and the Business of Inner Meaning*
[Chicago: University of Chicago Press, 1998], 118–119).

4 Pierre Barberis, *Aux sources du realisme: Aristocrates et bourgeois* (Paris: UGE,
1978), 339; cited in Michael Lowy and Robert Sayre, *Romanticism Against the
Tide of Modernity*, Catherine Porter, trans. (Durham: Duke University Press,
2001), 46.

5 Aphra Behn, *Oroonoko: Or, the Royal Slave. A True History*, Catherine Gallagher
and Simon Stern, eds. (Boston : Bedford/St. Martin's, 2000), 35.

6 NMM, REC/19.

7 Ibid.

8 Ibid.

9 Ibid.

10 Ibid.

11 Ibid.

12 Ibid.

13 *Oxford English Dictionary.*

14 John Locke, *The Second Treatise of Civil Government*, J. W. Gough, ed. (Oxford:
Oxford University Press), chapter 5.

15 Georg Wilhelm Friedrich Hegel, *The Philosophy of History* (New York: Dover,
1956), 41, 52. For an insightful reading of the congruences and disjunctions in
Locke's and Hegel's conceptions of property, see Bill Maurer, "Forget Locke?
From Proprietor to Risk-Bearer in New Logics of Finance," *Public Culture* 11,
no. 2 (1999): 365–385.

16 Immanuel Kant, "An Old Question Raised Again: Is the Human Race Constantly Progressing?" in *Kant: On History*, Lewis White Beck, ed. (New York:
Liberal Arts Press, 1963), 147.

17 Ibid., 147.

18 As Ferenc Feher, in somewhat different terms suggests, this is both utterly
consistent with Kant's unyielding insistence that morality must dictate behav-

ior (and compliance with an abstract truth) regardless of the circumstances of events and with his conviction that the primary objective of a properly republican politics must be freedom and not happiness, that is, that republicanism must exist to secure the opportunity to act according to the demands of reason rather than to address social inequalities or social injustices. As Feher further notes, much of Kant's political thought of the 1780s and 1790s might be thought of as driven by his need to derive a political philosophy *not* driven by or beholden to addressing what Marx called *die deutsche Misere*. See Feher, "Practical Reason in the Revolution: Kant's Dialogue with the French Revolution," in *The French Revolution and the Birth of Modernity*, Ferenc Feher, ed. (Berkeley: University of California Press, 1990), 201–218.

19 Kant, "An Old Question Raised Again," 143. Hannah Arendt's observation that Kant's own relation to the Revolution was always that of a "spectator" suggests that this is true not only of the historical subject Kant's posits but of the philosopher himself. See Hannah Arendt, *Lectures on Kant's Political Philosophy*, Ronald Breiner, ed. (Chicago: University of Chicago Press, 1982), especially 44–45.

20 Jacques Derrida, " 'A Self-Unsealing Poetic Text': Poetics and Politics of Witnessing," Rachel Bowlby, trans., in *Revenge of the Aesthetic: The Place of Literature in Theory Today*, Michael P. Clark, ed. (Berkeley: University of California Press, 2000), 200.

21 For a general history of the convention, see Howard Temperley, *British Antislavery, 1833–1870* (London: Longman, 1972), especially 62–92.

22 *Proceedings of the General Anti-Slavery Convention* (London: The British and Foreign Anti-Slavery Society, 1840), 205–206, hereafter referred to as *Proceedings*.

23 The problem of defining some alternate ground of legal standing from which to address the sovereign governments of nations ran throughout the conventioneers' debates and culminated in a lengthy debate on the fifth day regarding "the question, as to the right, or rather the propriety of this Convention addressing foreign governments" (*Proceedings*, 203). One delegate, Dr. Bowring, while indicating that he found it "extremely desirable that you should engage the foreign minister of this country to interest himself in this matter," nevertheless worried that "I know of no means by which you yourselves can regularly enter into communication with governments of a foreign nation" (ibid., 203). To which doubts the Rev. Scales responded: "It is not upon any commercial or political, but simply on moral grounds that we take our stand. We are not merely of this or that nation, but a Convention of all nations, and surely such a Convention might be allowed to break through the trammels of mere etiquette. It occupies ground much higher than that of mere potentates of this world, and therefore is not to be fettered or bound by such ties" (ibid., 204). Joseph T. Price (a delegate from Sawnsen), concurred: "I was, I confess, disposed to entertain some doubts on the question now before the meeting, because I am not aware that we could produce a precedent and show that our British Parliament would

be receivers of petitions from foreigners thus associated. At the same time, I confess, it does appear to me that this is a new description of meeting, such as has not taken place before; and therefore, I think it does merit very grave consideration . . . of being able to present a petition to our own Parliament and Queen" (ibid., 204). Dr. Greville summed up the overwhelming majority opinion in that paean to cosmopolitanism and the rights of the cosmopolitan I cited earlier: "I consider ourselves as of no nation; as assembled from all nations, as representing no nation in particular, but all nations; aiming at one grand moral end, and met for the special purpose of bearing upon all the nations of the world. I do hope that we shall come unanimously to the determination that we have a right to appeal to all governments, and I hope that we shall do so" (ibid., 205–206). On the problems of sovereignty and standing in international law (international human rights law in particular), see Paul Sieghart, *The International Law of Human Rights* (Oxford: Clarendon Press, 1983), especially 3–20. On Human Rights law and the "state of exception," see Anna-Lena Svensson-McCarthy, *The International Law of Human Rights and States of Exception* (The Hague: Martinus Nijhoff Publishers, 1998).

24 *Proceedings*, 5–6.

25 Ibid., 7.

26 Ibid., 7–8.

27 "Spokes*man*" in this instance is quite precise. As Temperley details in his account of the convention, questions of gender were at once central to the convention and sidestepped by it. A number of the emancipist organizations in the United States had sent both men and women to the convention, much to the surprise of the British organizers, who declined to seat the women. A lengthy floor fight ensued until a compromise was reached (one whose irony escaped few of the delegates who spoke on the issue): the women remained, but in a segregated portion of the hall. The problems of suffrage and the franchise thus postponed (or, more accurately, silenced), the male delegates then returned to the business they had set themselves, which meant, as I have indicated, not only a discussion of the best ways to put an end to slavery and the slave trade but extended conversation on what it meant to find themselves thus gathered and of who, gathered together, they understood themselves to be.

28 Though organized as a world antislavery convention, and attended, as I have noted, by delegates from Spain, France, and Switzerland, the conventioneer's world was overwhelmingly Anglophone: British and American.

29 *Proceedings*, 124–126.

30 Ibid., 127.

31 Ibid., 132.

32 Among the list of sentimental or romance abolitionist fiction of the period, Srinivas Aravamudan includes Dorothy Kilner's *The Rotchfords* (1786); Thomas Day's *The History of Sandford and Merton* (1789); Robert Bage's *Man As He Is*

(1792); Elizabeth Helme's *The Farmer of Inglewood Forest* (1796); Hector Mac-Neill's *Memoirs of the Life and Travels of the Late Charles MacPherson* (1800); William Earle's *Obi, or the History of Three-Fingered Jack* (1800); Maria Edgeworth's "The Grateful Negro," from *Popular Tales* (1804); and Mary Sherwood's *Dazee, or the Recaptured Slave* (1821). Romantic abolitionist verse of the moment includes poetry by Thomas Chatterton, Bryan Edwards, William Cowper, Hannah More, Ann Yearsley, Anna Letitia Barbauld, Samuel Taylor Coleridge, Robert Southey, Mary Robinson, and many others. For instructive overviews and anthologies of the abolitionist literature of the time, see Srinvas Aravamu-dan, ed., *Slavery, Abolition and Emancipation: Writings in the British Romantic Period*, vol. 6, *Fiction* (London: Pickering and Chatto, 1999); Alan Richardson, ed., *Slavery, Abolition and Emancipation: Writings in the British Romantic Period*, vol. 4, *Verse* (London: Pickering and Chatto, 1999); and the other volumes in the series.

33 See Dwight A. McBride, *Impossible Witnesses: Truth, Abolitionism, and Slave Testimony* (New York: New York University Press, 2001).

34 Derrida, " 'A Self-Unsealing Poetic Text,' " 200.

35 Thomas Clarkson, *The History of the Rise, Progress, and Accomplishment of the Abolition of the African Slave Trade by the British Parliament*, 2 vols. (London: Longman, Hurst, Rees, and Orme, 1808), 2: 111. I discuss Clarkson's *History*, and this particular phrase, in chapter 10.

36 The phrase "an idea of the sufferings of the Africans" is drawn from Thomas Clarkson, *The History of the Rise, Progress, and Accomplishment of the Abolition of the African Slave-Trade by the British Parliament*, 2 vols. (London: Longman, Hurst, Rees and Orme, 1808), 2:111. It does not refer directly to Turner's painting but is instead, as I discuss at length in chapter 10, central to Turner's own conception of the sentimental economy of his canvas.

8. The Fact of History

1 Thomas Clarkson, *Essay on the Slavery and Commerce of the Human Species, Particularly the African* (London: J. Phillips, 1785), 139.

2 Ibid.

3 Lennard J. Davis, *Factual Fictions: The Origins of the English Novel* (Philadelphia: University of Pennsylvania Press, 1983).

4 Davis's discussion of "probability" draws on one of Fielding's glosses on the role of the novelist that reads, in part, as a revision of Aristotle: "As Fielding points out, since the novelist is not bound by public records, as the historian must be, the novelist must conform to probability more than must a historian: 'As we have no public notoriety, no concurrent testimony, no records to support and corroborate what we deliver, it becomes up to us to keep within the limits not only of possibility, but of probability too.' " Ibid., 200.

5 William Wilberforce, in *Substance of the debates on a resolution for abolishing the slave trade which was moved in the House of Commons 10th June, 1806 and in the House of Lords 24th June, 1806* (London: Dawsons, 1968), 36–37, emphasis added.

6 Ottobah Cuguano's *Thoughts and Sentiments on the Evil and Wicked Traffic of the Slavery and Commerce of the Human Species* (London: 1787).

7 Thomas Cooper's *Considerations on the Slave Trade and the Consumption of West India Produce* (London: 1791).

8 Mary Poovey, *A History of the Modern Fact: Problems of Knowledge in the Sciences of Wealth and Society* (Chicago: University of Chicago, 1998), 28.

9 Ibid., 15.

10 It is accurate to an extent because Poovey does not restrict herself to an account of dialectical idealism or dialectical materialism but attends, more generally, to the fundamental inductive epistemology that underpins these two versions of the dialectic and because, as her way of specifying the operations of such an epistemology, she devotes the bulk of her attention to the ways in which inductive reason has dominated the history of the modern social sciences.

11 Poovey, *A History of the Modern Fact*, 232.

12 For other recent critiques of dominant modernity discourse, see Dilip Gaonkar, *Alternative Modernities* (Durham: Duke University Press, 2001), and Dipesh Chakrabarty, *Provincializing Europe: Postcolonial Thought and Historical Difference* (Princeton: Princeton University Press, 2000).

13 On Hegel's close interest in the Haitian revolution and its importance for his "master-slave" dialectic, see Susan Buck-Morss, "Hegel and Haiti," *Critical Inquiry* 26, no. 4: 821–865.

14 See Peter Linebaugh and Marcus Rediker, *The Many-Headed Hydra: Sailors, Slaves, Commoners and the Hidden History of the Revolutionary Atlantic* (Boston: Beacon Press, 2000.

15 Poovey, *A History of the Modern Fact*, 9.

16 Ibid., 27.

17 Julie Ellison, *Cato's Tears and the Making of Anglo-American Emotion* (Chicago: University of Chicago Press, 1999). For another recent and valuable genealogy of eighteenth-century sensibility and race discourses, see Markman Ellis, *The Politics of Sensibility: Race, Gender and Commerce in the Sentimental Novel* (Cambridge: Cambridge University Press, 1996).

18 Anna Letitia Barbauld, "A Summer Evening's Meditation," 61–78; cited in Ellison, *Cato's Tears and the Making of Anglo-American Emotion*, 106.

19 Ellison, *Cato's Tears and the Making of Anglo-American Emotion*, 104.

20 "The mode of reflective address that reaches beyond the local situation to international subject matter and cosmopolitan audiences is as important to the dynamics of sensibility," Ellison notes, "as the pathos surrounding its familiar types of victims." Ibid., 102.

21 Ibid., 101–102.

22 Adam Smith, *The Theory of Moral Sentiments* (New York: Prometheus Books, 2000), 196–197; cited in Ellison, *Cato's Tears and the Making of Anglo-American Emotion*, 10–11.

23 Anna Letitia Barbauld, "A Summer Evening's Meditation," 61–78; cited in Ellison, *Cato's Tears and the Making of Anglo-American Emotion*, 106.

24 Ellison, *Cato's Tears and the Making of Anglo-American Emotion*, 110.

25 Barbauld, "Eighteen Hundred and Eleven," cited in Ellison, *Cato's Tears and the Making of Anglo-American Emotion*, 112.

26 William Wordsworth, "The Complaint of a Forsaken Indian Woman," cited in Ellison, *Cato's Tears and the Making of Anglo-American Emotion*, 99.

27 That catastrophe is the collapse of a regional weaving economy, bankrupted both by its incorporation within an increasingly national and transnational debt-and-credit financing system and by the stripping away of local manpower as soldiery in Britain's Atlantic wars. Calamity finally overtakes Margaret's family when, sometime in the early 1780s, her husband abandons her for the soldier's "purse of gold" that will allow him to pay off his debts: the poem, though, exchanges that purse and the calamitous system of debt value it represents for the sentimental profit ("the bond of brotherhood") that a "nearer interest" in "sorrow and despair" teaches the reader to draw from a greater investment in the "secret spirit of humanity." See Alan Liu, *Wordsworth: The Sense of History* (Stanford: Stanford University Press, 1989). Wordsworth's "Reconciling Addendum" to "The Ruined Cottage" is in *The Poetical Works of William Wordsworth*, Ernest de Selincourt and Helen Darbishire, eds. (Oxford: Clarendon Press, 1940–49), 5:400.

28 Hannah More, "Slavery, A Poem," cited in Ellison, *Cato's Tears and the Making of Anglo-American Emotion*, 115.

29 William Cowper, "The Task," in *The Poems of William Cowper*, John D. Baird and Charles Rykamp, eds., 3 vols. (Oxford: Clarendon Press, 1995), vol. 2, 4.88–89.

30 Kevis Goodman, "The Loophole in the Retreat: The Culture of News and the Early Life of Romantic Self-Consciousness," *The South Atlantic Quarterly* 102, no. 1, 25–52.

31 Cowper, "The Task," 4.278–80, 4.283–307.

32 Ibid., 1.654, 1.657–662. On Omai's history, see E. H. McCormick, *Omai: Pacific Envoy* (Auckland: Auckland University Press, 1977).

33 This "errant" attribute of a fanciful "poetics" of knowledge, as we shall see, also centrally informs the work of Edouard Glissant, the late-twentieth-century Martiniquan philosopher of "errancy" for whom the melancholy apprehension of the traumatic facts of Atlantic history is also the beginning of a geopolitical knowledge of the modern.

34 Smith, *The Theory of Moral Sentiments*, 196–197.

35 Ibid., 197.
36 Ibid., 4.

9. The Imaginary Resentment of the Dead

1 Adam Smith, *The Theory of Moral Sentiments* (New York: Prometheus Books, 2000), 99.

2 I discuss Kojève in chapter 10.

3 Smith, *The Theory of Moral Sentiments*, 3.

4 Ibid., 55.

5 On what is known as "the Adam Smith problem," that is, the role Smithian sentiment might play in moderating the self-interest of his market actors, see E. J. Hundert, *The Enlightenment's Fable: Bernard Mandeville and the Discovery of Society* (Cambridge: Cambridge University Press, 1994), 219–236.

6 For an excellent study on Smith's contributions to the value theory of the period and its relation to literary value, see James Thompson, *Models of Value: Eighteenth Century Political Economy and the Novel* (Durham: Duke University Press, 1996).

7 Smith, *The Theory of Moral Sentiments*, 4, 3.

8 We might think, to simplify the argument entirely, of the ways in which the contemporary daily consumption of the Dow Jones and NASDAQ averages effects a speculative reification of consciousness analogous to that provided by the daily experience of newspaper reading which, on Benedict Anderson's account, reified and secured the imaginary community of the nineteenth-century nation.

9 See Robert Mitchell, "The Violence of Sympathy: Adam Smith on Resentment and Executions," in *1650–1850: Ideas, Aesthetics and Inquiries in the Early Modern Era* vol. 8 (2003): 421–441.

10 Smith, *The Theory of Moral Sentiments*, 3–4, 4.

11 Edmund Burke, *Reflections on the Revolution in France* (Indianapolis: Hackett Publishing, 1987), 68.

12 Smith, *The Theory of Moral Sentiments*, 99.

13 See Susan Buck-Morss, "Hegel and Haiti," *Critical Inquiry* 26 (summer 2000): 821–865.

14 On the negation or alienation of the self in Smith's model of sympathy, see David Marshall, "Adam Smith and the Theatricality of Moral Sentiments," *Critical Inquiry* 10 (June, 1984): 592–613.

15 Smith, *The Theory of Moral Sentiments*, 119, 123.

16 See Ian Simpson Ross, *The Life of Adam Smith* (Oxford: Clarendon Press, 1995), 424. For Smith's relation to the new rhetoric, see William Samuel Howell, *Eighteenth-Century British Logic and Rhetoric* (Princeton: Princeton University Press, 1971, 536–576).

17   Longinus, "On the Sublime," in *Aristotle's Poetics, Longinus on the Sublime*, Ingram Bywater and W. Rhys Roberts, trans. (New York: Macmillan, 1930), 66.

18   Ibid., 81.

19   J. Jennifer Jones, "Virtual Sublime: Romantic Transcendence and the Transport of the Real," *Dissertation Abstracts International* 63, no. 9 (March 2003): 3205. On the romantic reception of Longinus see also Clarence DeWitt Thorpe, "Coleridge on the Sublime," in *Wordsworth and Coleridge*, Earl Leslie Griggs, ed. (New York: Russell and Russell, 1962); and Thomas Weiskel, *The Romantic Sublime: Studies in the Structure and Psychology of Transcendence* (Baltimore: Johns Hopkins University Press, 1986).

20   Cited in Longinus, "On the Sublime," 75.

21   Longinus's comments here relate directly to the case in which one is speaking of a successor poet's imitation of the sublime effects of his or her predecessors but also describes the listener's adoption, as if it were their own, of the passions such sublime verse describes. Ibid., 81–82.

22   Ibid., 85.

23   Ibid., 100–101.

24   Smith, *The Theory of Moral Sentiments*, 4–5.

25   Longinus, On the Sublime, 83, emphasis original.

26   Smith, *The Theory of Moral Sentiments*, 4–5.

27   Ibid., 8–9.

28   Sigmund Freud, *Mourning and Melancholy in the Standard Edition of the Complete Psychological Works of Sigmund Freud*, ed. James Strachey (London: Hogarth Press, 1933–1974), vol. 16, 249.

29   "The logic of the key in which I hoped to orient this keynote address," Derrida notes in *Specters of Marx*, "was one of a politico-logic of trauma and a topology of mourning. A mourning in fact and by right interminable, without possible normality, without reliable limit, in its reality or in its conception, between introjection and incorporation." Jacques Derrida, *Specters of Marx: The State of the Debt, The Work of Mourning, and the New International*, Peggy Kamuf, trans. (London: Routledge, 1994), 97.

30   Sophocles, *Antigone*, in *Sophocles I: Oedipus the King; Oedipus at Colonus; Antigone*, David Grene, trans. (Chicago: University of Chicago Press, 1991), 207, line 1282.

31   Smith, *The Theory of Moral Sentiments*, 7, emphasis added.

32   Fredric Jameson, *The Political Unconscious: Narrative as a Socially Symbolic Act* (Ithaca: Cornell University Press, 1981), 141, 19.

33   Stephen Greenblatt, *Shakespearean Negotiations* (Berkeley: University of California Press, 1988), 1.

34   In addition to James Chandler's *England in 1819: The Politics of Literary Culture and the Case of Romantic Historicism* (Chicago: University of Chicago Press, 1998), see David Simpson, *The Academic Postmodern and the Rule of Literature: A*

Report on Half-knowledge (Chicago: University of Chicago Press, 1995); Alan Liu, "Local Transcendence: Cultural Criticism, Postmodernism, and the Romanticism of Detail," *Representations* 32 (fall 1990): 75–113; Alan Liu, "The New Historicism and the Work of Mourning," *Studies in Romanticism* 35 (1996): 553–66); Walter Benn Michaels, " 'For You Who Never Was There': Slavery and the New Historicism, Deconstruction and the Holocaust," *Narrative* 4 (1996): 1–16; and the essays collected in "Afterlives of Romanticism," *South Atlantic Quarterly* 102, no. 1 (winter 2003), a special issue edited by Ian Baucom. I consider Benn Michaels's essay and its thoroughgoing skepticism regarding the value of this romantic return in the final section of the book.

35 Smith, *The Theory of Moral Sentiments*, 98–99, emphasis added.

36 See Achille Mbembe, "Necropolitics" *Public Culture* (winter 2003): 11–40.

10. *"To Tumble into It, and Gasp for Breath as We Go Down"*

1 Thomas Clarkson, *The History of the Rise, Progress, and Accomplishment of the Abolition of the African Slave-Trade by the British Parliament*, 2 vols. (London: Longman, Hurst, Rees and Orme, 1808), 2:111. Hereafter referred to as *History*.

2 For a superb history of this image, see Cheryl Finley, "Committed to Memory: The Slave-Ship Icon and the Black Atlantic Imagination," in *Chicago Art Journal* (1999): 2–21.

3 Clarkson, *History*, 2:152–153.

4 Ibid., 2:186–187.

5 Clarkson, *History*, 1:14.

6 See, among others, James Hamilton, *Turner, A Life* (London: Hodder and Stoughton, 1997), 275; Anthony Bailey, *Standing in the Sun: A Life of J. M. W. Turner* (London: Sinclair-Stevenson, 1997), 361–362; *The Oxford Companion to J. M. W. Turner*, Evelyn Joll, Martin Butlin, and Luke Herrmann, eds. (Oxford: Oxford University Press, 2001), 302–303.

7 Clarkson, *History*, 1:264–266.

8 Ibid., 10–13.

9 Ibid., 94.

10 Ibid., 14–15.

11 Ibid., 2:112–113.

12 Ibid., 1:94–95.

13 Henry Fielding, *The History of Tom Jones, A Foundling* (Oxford: Oxford University Press, 1996), 58.

14 James Chandler, *England in 1819: The Politics of Literary Culture and the Case of Romantic Historicism* (Chicago: University of Chicago Press, 1998), 168–169.

15 Saree Makdisi, *Romantic Imperialism: Universal Empire and the Culture of Modernity* (Cambridge: Cambridge University Press, 1998), 88. On the novel and bardic nationalism, see Katie Trumpener, *Bardic Nationalism: The Romantic Novel and the British Empire* (Princeton: Princeton University Press, 1997).

16 Smith, *The Theory of Moral Sentiments*, 99.

17 Fielding, *The History of Tom Jones*, 132.

18 Georg Lukács, *The Historical Novel*, Hannah and Stanley Mitchell, trans. (Lincoln and London: University of Nebraska Press, 1962), 35, 19.

19 Ibid., 34.

20 On Raymond Williams theory of the "residual" and the "emergent," see his *Problems in Materialism and Culture* (London: Verso, 1980), 37–42.

21 Ian Duncan, *Modern Romance and Transformations of the Novel: The Gothic, Scott, Dickens* (Cambridge: Cambridge University Press, 1992), 86.

22 On Turner's work as an illustrator to Scott, see Gerald E. Finley, *Landscapes of Memory: Turner as Illustrator to Scott* (Berkeley: University of California Press, 1980).

23 Cited ibid., 187.

24 Ibid., 32–33.

25 In much the same way that for Finley Turner's "literariness" — or indeed his "knowledge" — entails the "fusion" of his perception of natural objects and his mind's response to these original perceptions, for Hume "sentiment" encompasses the dialectical play of sense impressions and the ideas the mind fashions from those impressions.

26 John Ruskin, *Modern Painters*, in *The Works of John Ruskin: Poetry of Architecture, Seven Lamps, Modern Painters Volume One* (London: The Chesterfield Society, 1905), 44–45, emphasis original.

27 Adam Smith, *Lectures on Rhetoric and Belles Lettres*, ed. J. C. Bryce (Indianapolis: Liberty Fund, 1985), 55.

28 James Chandler, "About Loss: W. G. Sebald's Romantic Art of Memory," *South Atlantic Quarterly* 102, no. 1 (winter 2003): 248–249.

29 Mary Poovey, *A History of the Modern Fact: Problems of Knowledge in the Sciences of Wealth and Society* (Chicago: University of Chicago Press, 1998), 327.

30 Ruskin, *Modern Painters*, 44–45.

31 Ibid., 46.

32 Ibid., 42–43.

33 Ibid., 137.

34 Ibid., 138.

35 Ibid., 383.

36 Kant, "An Old Question Raised Again," 143.

37 For an insightful reading of the ways in which romantic thought (particularly in its relationship to melodramatic discourse) generates a mode of liberalism, see Elaine Hadley, *Melodramatic Tactics: Theatricalized Dissent in the English Marketplace, 1800–1885* (Stanford: Stanford University Press, 1995).

38 Finley, *Landscapes of Memory*, 33, 123, 158.

39 Ibid., 159.

40 Ruskin, *Modern Painters*, 357.

41 Finley, *Landscapes of Memory*, 159.

42 Duncan, *Modern Romance and Transformations of the Novel*, 86, 89.

43 Thomas Babington Macaulay, "Review of Henry Neale's *The Romance of History*," *Edinburgh Review* 47 (May 1828): 364–365; cited in Chandler, *England in 1819*, 158.

11. This/Such, for Instance

1 On Hegel's knowledge and reading of Smith and other Scottish Enlightenment figures, see Terry Pinkard, *Hegel: A Biography* (Cambridge: Cambridge University Press, 2000), 52–53, 174, 483; and H. S. Harris, *Hegel's Development: Night Thoughts (Jena 1801–1806)* (Oxford: Oxford University Press, 1982).

2 Alexander Welsh, *The Hero of the Waverley Novels* (Princeton: Princeton University Press, 1963), 77–85.

3 Alexandre Kojève, *Outline of a Phenomenology of Right*, Bryan-Paul Frost and Robert Howse, trans. (New York: Rowman and Littlefield, 2000), 225.

4 On Hegel's reading of Scott, see Pinkard, *Hegel*, 556–557.

5 Jacques Derrida, " 'A Self-Unsealing Poetic Text': Poetics and Politics of Witnessing, Rachel Bowlby," trans., in *Revenge of the Aesthetic: The Place of Literature in Theory Today*, Michael P. Clark, ed. (Berkeley: University of California Press, 2000), 200.

6 Though it does indicate that another way of defining the eighteenth- to late-twentieth-century durée of our long contemporaneity is by identifying it as the period of the dialectic.

7 Derrida, " 'A Self-Unsealing Poetic Text,' " 180.

8 Ibid., 201.

9 Ibid., 206.

10 Slavoj Žižek, *The Ticklish Subject: The Absent Centre of Political Ontology* (London: Verso, 1999), 133–34.

12. "The Sea Is History"

1 Edouard Glissant, *Caribbean Discourse: Selected Essays*, J. Michael Dash, trans. (Charlottesville: University of Virginia Press, 1989), 66–67.

2 Edouard Glissant, *Poetics of Relation*, Betsy Wing, trans. (Ann Arbor: University of Michigan Press, 1997), 6, 8.

3 Ibid., 5–6.

4 See David Armitage's "Three Concepts of Atlantic History," in David Armitage and Michael J. Braddick, eds., *The British Atlantic World, 1500–1800* (Basingstoke: Palgrave Macmillan, 2002).

5 Glissant, *Poetics of Relation*, 29.

6 Ibid., 20.

7 Ibid., 18.

8   Ibid., 26.

9   Ibid., 72–74.

10 The transatlantic experience of enslavement reveals the condition of modernity in its most intense, accelerated, and brutalizing form, Gilroy argues, because to the extent that modernity can be understood as a way of naming the transition from a customary, "traditional," largely rural and agrarian habitus (what Pierre Nora calls an "environment of memory") to the mechanized, the hyperbureaucratized, the instrumentalized, and the devernacularized, such an experience of modernity (such a shattering of a received Kosseleckian "space of experience" by a novel, abyssal "horizon of expectation") is nowhere more evident, nowhere more rapid, and nowhere more totalizing than in the experience of Africans drawn into the capital machinery of the Atlantic world system: "It is being suggested that the concentrated intensity of the slave experience is something that marked out blacks as the first truly modern people." Paul Gilroy, *The Black Atlantic: Modernity and Double Consciousness* (Cambridge: Harvard University Press, 1993), 221.

11 Walter Benjamin, "Theses on the Philosophy of History," in *Illuminations*, Harry Zohn, trans. (New York: Schocken Books, 1968), 257.

12 Ibid., 255, 261.

13 Walter Benjamin, *The Arcades Project* (Cambridge: Harvard University Press, 1999), 463.

14 Glissant, *Poetics of Relation*, 33.

15 Ibid., 7, emphasis added.

16 Ibid., 206–207, emphasis added.

17 Derek Walcott, *Omeros* (New York: Farrar, Strauss, Giroux, 1990), 129–130.

18 Walter Benn Michaels, " 'You Who Never Was There': Slavery and the New Historicism, Deconstruction and the Holocaust," *Narrative* 4, no. 1 (January 1996): 7.

19 Ibid., 7.

20 For an equally skeptical analysis of recent memory discourse, see Kerwin Klein, "On the Emergence of Memory in Historical Discourse," in *Representations* 69 (winter 2000): 127–150.

21 Toni Morrison, *Beloved* (New York: Penguin, 1987), 210.

22 Walcott, *Omeros*, 14.

23 Ibid., 128.

24 Ibid., 128–129.

25 Fred D'Aguiar, *Feeding the Ghosts* (London: Chatto and Windus, 1997), 3–4, 229–230.

26 Ibid., 5.

27 Kobena Mercer, *Witness at the Crossroads: An Artist's Journey in Postcolonial Space* (London: Institute of International Visual Arts, 1997), 67–68, emphasis original.

28 Gilroy, *The Black Atlantic*, 14.
29 Ibid.
30 Glissant, *Poetics of Relation*, 6, 8.
31 D'Aguiar, *Feeding the Ghosts*, 4.
32 Ibid., 27.
33 Ibid., 229–230.
34 M. NourbeSe Philip, "*Zong!* # 4" (unpublished manuscript, quoted by permission of the author).
35 D'Aguiar, *Feeding the Ghosts*, 215–216.

Index

Armitage, David, 313–14

Arrighi, Giovanni, 23–24, 28, 36, 91, 142; on accumulation, 25, 32, 149; on capital, 36–37, 150–51; general model of, 26, 28, 53; Jameson on, 143–44; on repetition, 29–30; on time, 24–25. See also *Long Twentieth Century, The* (Arrighi)

"Aschenglorie" (Celan), 175–76, 303

Aspinal, James, 10, 38–39

Atlantic cycle, of accumulation, 36, 80–112, 99, 149, 150–51

Atlantic slave trade. *See* Slave trade

Auschwitz, and witness, 301–4. *See also* Holocaust, and witness

Averaging, concept of, 107–9, 138–39. *See also* Insurance

Badiou, Alain, 119, 168, 180, 182, 193–94, 276; on French Revolution, 120–21; on interest, 184; on knowledge, 119–20; on membership and inclusion, 187–88; on the spectator, 182–83; on subject of a truth, 183; on truth event, 119–22; Žižek on, 304

Barbauld, Anna Letitia, 231, 234–35, 315–16

Barberis, Pierre, 198

Behn, Aphra, 68, 198–99

Beloved (Morrison), 322–24, 329

Benjamin, Walter, 4, 106, 145, 158; on allegory, 9, 18–22, 71; on commodity culture, 64; Glissant and, 316–18; Kant and, 114–17; on modernism, 116–17, 319–20; on nineteenth century, 17, 18–22, 22, 25–26; philosophy of history of, 18, 23, 42, 318–19; on repetition, 29–30; on time, 24. See also *Arcades Project, The* (Benjamin)

Benveniste, Emile, 175, 199

Berne, Peter, 85, 86

Bills of exchange, and benefits to Liverpool investors, 62–64

Bisenzone fairs, 36–37

Black Atlantic, The (Gilroy), 31, 34, 316, 328

Blackburn (ship), 48, 49, 75

Blanqui, Auguste, 22

Blanqui, Charles, 29

Bloch, Ernst, 19, 20, 160

Boileau, Nicolas, 253

Bostock, Robert, 85–86, 86, 91

Bradburn, George, 210–11

Brathwaite, Edward, 309–10, 328

Braudel, Fernand, 53

Britain: cycle of accumulation in, 26–27, 37; "Financial Revolution" in, 38. *See also* Liverpool

Bruyére, Jean de la, 198

Buck-Morss, Susan, 18, 247

Burke, Edmund, 65, 158–60, 249

Burke, William, 43, 56–58

Cadell, Robert, 282

Caleb Williams (Godwin), 220

Capital, commodity, 21–23, 28, 71

Capital, finance. *See* Finance capital

Capital, Marx's formula for, 25, 143

Capital accumulation, 25, 36–37, 150–51

Capitalism and Slavery (Williams), 52

Caribbean Discourse (Glissant), 309

Carolina (ship), 48, 75

Caruth, Cathy, 131, 132, 254

Case, George, 77–78

Case, Thomas, 61, 76

Cato, 82

Cato (Addison), 231

Celan, Paul, 175–79, 301–3

Chandler, James, 109, 117, 235, 285; on historicism, 41–46, 260–61; on the romantic type, 280

Characters, 277–78

Ellison, Julie, 230–33, 235, 238, 240
Empire (Hardt, Negri), 190
English Atlantic (Steele), 35
Equiano, Olaudah, 15, 31, 169
Errancy, Glissant on, 312–13, 313–14, 314–15
Essay on the Slavery and Commerce of the Human Species (Clarkson), 211–13, 265, 270–71
Éternité par les astres, L' (Blanqui), 22
Ethics: An Essay on the Understanding of Evil (Badiou), 182
Evident and evidence binary, 227–29

Fable of the Bees (Mandeville), 245
Fancy, and poetry, 233–38
Feeding the Ghosts (D'Aguiar), 34, 324, 327–29, 331–32
Fenelon, François, 253
Fiction, Europe's modern, 225–26. *See also* Novels, eighteenth-century
Fielding, Henry, 216–17, 276–80
Finance capital, 55–57, 66; Arrighi on, 36–37; commodity capital and, 22; contract and, 206; dominance of, 27–28; globalization and, 160–61; insurance and, 99; Jameson on, 142–44; slave trade and, 59; "speculative discourse" and, 22; subject $ and, 55–56; the typical and the average and, 106; world systems and, 27; *Zong* massacre and, 32
Financial revolution, 38, 59, 65–66, 83, 159–60
Finley, Gerald, 283, 286, 290–91
Foe (Coetzee), 163
Foreclosure, 157–59
Foucault, Michel, 148, 184, 190
French Revolution, 65, 227; Badiou on, 120–21; Derrida and, 121; global memory of, 160; Kant on, 115, 117, 157–58; as truth event, 58, 117–18

Freud, Sigmund, 258
"Friends," of slaves, 208–10. *See also* Abolitionism
Frontispiece, 173–75, 177
Frye, Northrop, 225

Gallagher, Catherine, 67–69, 70, 74, 80–81, 215
Genoese cycle, of accumulation, 27, 28, 36–37
Gericault, 268
Gibb, D. E. W., 101–2
Gilbert, Thomas, 10
Gilroy, Paul, 31, 34, 316, 328
Glissant, Edouard, 34, 229; Agamben and, 316–17; Benjamin and, 316–17; Clarkson and, 313; on errancy, 312–15; on "exchange," 311; on image of slaves drowning, 309–10, 320–21, 325; on the modern, 314–15, 319–20; Schmitt and, 316–17; on slave trade, 311–12, 315; on task of historical thought, 318–19; Turner and, 313. *See also* Poetics of Relation (Glissant)
Globalization, and finance capital, 160–61
Godwin, William, 220
Goodman, Kevis, 236–37
Gore General Advertiser, 72–74
Greenblatt, Stephen, 260
Gregson, James, 10, 39, 93
Gregson, John, 10, 39; at masquerade ball, 75; as mayor, 77, 79, 96–97; suicide of, 169
Gregson, William, 10, 39, 41, 72–74; at masquerade ball, 75, 77; number of slaves transported by, 49; shipping records of, 59–60; in slave trade, 48–49; as "typical," 46, 47; wealth of, 93
Gregson family, 11; the Cases and, 76–77; court victory in *Zong* case and,

96–99; fortunes of, 75–76; "free burgess" status for, 76; in insurance business, 39–40; in Liverpool, 38, 48
Greville, Dr., 208
"Guinea cargo," slaves as, 60–61

Habermas, Jürgen, 114
Halpern, Richard, 18, 19, 21, 23
Hardt, Michael, 190, 192
Haussman, Georges Eugene, Baron, 9
Haywood, Solicitor, 131, 199, 200, 202,
    207, 211, 240, 243, 263–64
Hearne, Samuel, 235
Hegel, Georg Wilhelm Friedrich, 47,
    54, 65, 117, 204, 224, 227, 243, 247;
    on history of right, 297–99; Scottish
    Enlightenment and, 298; on the
    "third," 299–300; on the "universal
    and homogeneous state," 33–34;
    Žižek's reading of, 249
Heidegger, Martin, 145
Historicism, 260; actuarial, 42–43;
    Chandler on, 42–46, 260–61; con-
    struction of "type" and, 43–45,
    repeating, 41–42; romantic, 42–43,
    216–17, 260–61; as term, 42–43
History, witness against, 297–305
History of the Modern Fact, A (Poovey),
    223–24
History of the Rise, Progress, and Accom-
    plishment of the Abolition of the Africa
    Slave Trade by the British Parliament
    (Clarkson), 265, 268, 270, 273, 294–
    95
Hogarth, William, 72, 276, 277
Hogendorn, Jan, 92
Holocaust, and witness, 178–79, 185–
    86, 301. See also Auschwitz, and
    witness
Homo Sacer (Agamben), 179–81, 184–
    86, 190
"Humane character," 198–99

Humanity: discourse of, in Zong trials,
    197–200, 202–3; Enlightenment
    image of, 206–7; Kant on, 206–7;
    melancholy and, 206; principles of
    law and, 208; problem of, 195–212;
    of slaves, 196; as term, 203–7; of
    Zong crew, 198
Human rights, politics of, 189–91
Hume, David, 268, 271, 285
Hunter, J. Paul, 44

Imaginary value, and the slave trade,
    17, 94–95. See also Insurance; Value
Imagination: function of, 248–51;
    Longinus on, 256–57
Indebtedness, in Nike advertisement,
    147
Insurance: Atlantic cycle of accumula-
    tion and, 80–112; averaging and,
    107–9, 138–39; contract of the Zong,
    17, 32, 137; finance capitalism and,
    99; Gregson family in, 39–40; in
    Liverpool, 100–103; marine, 100–
    102, 107–8; melancholy and, 135–
    36; slave trade and, 99; types of, 100;
    and the typical, 106–7; underwriters
    of, 102–4; value and, 41, 95–96,
    101–4, 110–12. See also Value
Insurance companies, 99–100
Intensification, in the twentieth cen-
    tury, 141–42
Iraq: human rights and, 192; as state of
    exception, 185–87
Irony, and the "typical," 47–48

Jameson, Fredric, 40, 45, 105, 260;
    Arrighi and, 143–44; on finance cap-
    ital, 142–44; Kant and, 144–45; on
    recurrences, 19–21; on repetition,
    29–30
Jarman, Derek, 144
Jenny (ship), 85

Johnson, Marion, 92
Johnson, Samuel, 69, 80
Jones, J. Jennifer, 254
Journey from Prince of Wale's Fort in Hudson Bay in the Northern Ocean (Hearne), 235
Justice, Lords Commissioners on, 6–7, 7–8

Kant, Immanuel, 155, 167; Benjamin and, 114–17; "fragment of human history" and, 113–14, 144; on French Revolution, 115, 117–18, 157–58; on humanity, 206–7; Jameson and, 144–45; on the modern, 57–58, 58, 116–17; "notion of signs" and, 119; on reading events, 161–62; on sympathy, 131; on truth event, 122; and witness, 222–23; Žižek on, 249. *See also* Truth event
Kelsall, James, 10, 131, 197, 199
Knowledge, Badiou on, 119–20
Kojève, Alexander, 243, 297, 299
Koselleck, Reinhart, 114

Lacan, Jacques, 155–56
Lacis, Asja, 19
"Lady Credit," 80–82
Lee, Nathaniel, 231
Lee, Solicitor, 131, 200–202, 222
Letter, Sharp's, 4; account of *Zong* massacre in, 123–27; blank pages in, 132–33; chronology of events in, 125–27; contents of, 8, 123–26, 132–33; narrative character of, 220–21; novelistic imaginary of, 134; reading, 162. *See also* Sharp, Granville
Levers, and protocols, 152–55
Levi, Primo, 179
Levinas, Emmanuel, 146
Liberal cosmopolitanism, 265–96
Liberty Day, 97–98

Life of Napoleon (Scott), 299
Linebaugh, Peter, 227
Literature, and anti-slavery, 210–11. *See also* Novels, eighteenth-century
Liu, Alan, 235
Liverpool: as capital of long twentieth century, 3–36; London and, 37–38; slave trade and, 48, 50–51; system of credit in, 84–85. *See also* Gregson family
Liverpool Exchange, 51–52, 77–79
Liverpool owners. *See* Owners, of slave ships
Locke, John, 204
Log, of the *Ranger,* 11–14
London, and Liverpool, 37–38
Longinus, 182–83, 253–58
"Long twentieth century," 3–36
Long Twentieth Century, The (Arrighi), 23–24, 24, 142
Lords Commissioners of the Admiralty, 3–8
Lowy, Michael, 33, 178, 193, 222
Lucius Junius Brutus (Lee), 231
Lukács, Georg, 40, 43, 45, 105, 246, 261, 280, 316
Lynch, Deidre, 32, 69–70, 72, 74, 81, 134, 198, 215

Macaulay, Thomas Babington, 294, 295
Makdisi, Saree, 46, 279
Mandeville, Bernard de, 245
Mansfield, Lord, 15, 109, 124, 125, 131, 135, 169, 196, 202, 263
Marine insurance, 100–102, 107–8
Marx, Karl, 25, 121, 152; formula of, of capital, 25, 60, 67, 143, 150
Mason and Dixon (Pynchon), 35
Mbembe, Achille, 262

Slavery, language of, 192–93

Slaves: as "cargo," 60–61; as commodities, 137–38; deaths of, 49;
"friends" of, 208–10; humanity of,
196; human rights and, 191; image of
drowning, 309–10, 320–21, 325–27;
log book descriptions of, 11–14;
melancholy realism and, 233; owners
of, suing for value of, 8; as property,
204–5; purchase of, on credit, 85–92;
value of, 11, 41, 92–93, 150. *See also*
Abolitionism; *Zong* case; *Zong*
massacre

Slave ship, drawing of, 266. See also
Zong (ship)

Slave trade: as commodity trade, 53;
credit and, 71, 83–84, 86–87; evidence of, 16–17; imaginary value
and, 17; insurance industry and, 99;
Liverpool's profits from, 50–51;
material accumulation and, 93–94;
pamphlet on, 59–60, 61; paper
money and, 61–62; spread of finance
capital and, 59; value and, 16–17

Slave traders, 16. *See also* Collingwood,
Luke; Gregson family; Owners, of
slave ships

Small Acts (Gilroy), 328

Smith, Adam, 182–83, 226–27, 234,
238–39, 240–41, 244, 271, 288; on
the dead, 258, 261–63; on function
of the imagination, 248–51; influence of, on Turner, 268; on melancholy, 258–61; on sentiment, 238–
39, 244–45; on the spectator, 252–
53, 257–60; subjects of, 251–52; on
the sublime, 253, 256–57; on sympathy, 256, 267. *See also Theory of
Moral Sentiments* (Smith)

Sophocles, 258

South Africa, apartheid government of,
185–86

Southey, Robert, 231

South Sea Company scheme, 82–83

Spanish cycle, of accumulation, 36–37

Spectacle, sublime, 157–58

Spectator, 81

Spectator(s), 34; of art, 287; Badiou on,
182–83; Clarkson on, 276; figure of,
243–44; historical, 222–23, 242–43;
"idea" of suffering and, 293–94;
Slavers (Turner) and, 291–92; Smith
on, 252–53, 257–58, 259–60; sympathizing with, 281; in *Theory of
Moral Sentiments*, 244–45, 295. *See
also* Witness

Spectator sympathy, 281–82

Specters of Marx (Derrida), 121

Speculative, and the singular, 141–69

Speculative culture, 106

Speculative discourse, 22

Spivak, Gayatri, 33, 145–48, 151–56,
163, 167, 184, 231, 276; on decision,
168; on history of the modern, 151;
native informant of, 155, 164, 243;
on protocol and levers, 152–55; on
reading events, 162–63; on the singular, 163–66. See also *Critique of
Postcolonial Reason* (Spivak)

Stanton, Henry B., 210, 211

State of exception, 173–94

Steele, Ian, 35

Stewart, Dugald, 227

Stock speculation, 83

Stoler, Ann Laura, 148

Stubbs, Robert, 10, 129–30, 199–200,
201

Subject $, 35–79, 151, 158–59, 249. *See
also* Žižek, Slavoj

Subject(s): as alienating, 57; modern,
57–58, 159; in novels, 68–69; of
Smith, 251–52; vanishing, 158–59.
See also Characters

Sublime, the, 253–57

Sublime spectacle, 157–58
Suffering, idea of, 265–96
Sympathy, 195–212; for the dead, 261–
63; the idea of suffering and, 294–95;
Kant on, 131; language of, 267–68;
melancholy and, 257; romantic dis-
course of, 240; Smith on, 256;
Turner and, 287
Sympathy, spectator, 281–82

Tarrying with the Negative (Žižek), 53–
54
Temporal accumulation, 34, 309–33
Testament and testimony, 173–94;
Agamben and, 183; Derrida and,
183; language of, 193; Sharp's letter
as, 174–75, 177
Theoretical realism, 42–43, 71, 133
Theory of Moral Sentiments (Smith), 234,
239–42, 244, 271, 274, 288; the spec-
tator and, 244–45, 295; subject in,
251–52. *See also* Smith, Adam
Things as They Are (Godwin), 220
"Third," 33, 178, 200, 243–44, 299–
300. *See also* Derrida, Jacques; Spec-
tator(s); Witness
Third Critique (Kant), 166
*Thoughts and Sentiments on the Evil and
Wicked Traffic of the Slavery and
Commerce of the Human Species* (Cu-
guano), 221
Time, 24–25. *See also* Temporal
accumulation
Tom Jones (Fielding), 277–78
Torok, Maria, 132, 155, 257
Trust, and system of credit, 89
Truth: artists rendering of, 285–87;
subject of, 183
Truth event, 118–19; Badiou on, 119–
22; French Revolution as, 117–18;
Kant on, 122; modernity and, 113–
40; as symptom, 121–22; *Zong* mas-

sacre as, 119, 121–22, 124–25, 128,
166–67, 246–47, 289. *See also* French
Revolution; *Zong* massacre
Turner, J. M. W., 47, 212, 221, 228,
240–41, 328; Clarkson and, 268,
275–76, 293–94; depicts *Zong* massacre, 274–75; Glissant and, 313;
language of sympathy of, 267–68;
Scott and, 282, 283, 290; "seeing"
Zong massacre, 247–48; sympathy
and, 282, 287; transition in style of,
283–84, 284. See also *Slavers throwing overboard the dead and the dying*
(Turner)
Turner (Dabydeen), 328
Twentieth century: intensification in,
141–42; repeating the eighteenth,
41–42
Type: construction of, 43–46; of the
modern, 35–79; romantic, 279–81;
Zong slaves as, 46

Underwriters, insurance, 101–4
Unsworth, Barry, 328

Value, 17, 94–95; of drowned slaves,
92–93, 137; estimating, 101–4;
imaginary, 17, 94–95; insurance contracts and, 17, 41, 110–12; of slaves,
11, 94; test of, 95–96; in *Zong* case,
11, 96, 105, 264. *See also* Averaging,
concept of; Insurance
"View from the window," 201–2

Walcott, Derek, 34, 310, 321–22, 325–
26, 328–29, 331
Walpole, Robert, 217
Waverly (Scott), 216, 277–79, 280, 282
Wealth of Nations, The (Smith), 239,
245, 274
Wedgwood, Josiah, 267
Welsh, Alexander, 298

Weskett, John, 45–46, 103, 105–8, 110–12

Wilberforce, William, 31, 219, 234, 240

Williams, Eric, 52

Williams, Raymond, 281

Wilson, Edward, 10, 38–39

Witness: and abolitionism, 218–19; Agamben on, 180–82, 184–85, 200; Auschwitz and, 302–4; Derrida on, 33–34, 175–77, 180–85, 200, 211, 299–305; historical, 33; against history, 297–305; the holocaust and, 178–79; identity of, 175–76; language of, 193–94; melancholy and, 300–301; politics of, 189–91; Sharp's account of *Zong* massacre as, 178. *See also* Spectator(s); "Third"

Wordsworth, William, 235, 253–55, 286

World Anti-Slavery Convention, 208, 221, 268

Žižek, Slavoj, 53–54, 66, 81, 149, 159; Badiou and, 119, 120–21, 304; on modern subject, 65; on reproduction of financial revolution, 159–60; subject $, 53–59, 67, 70, 151, 158–59, 249, 251

Zong! (Philip), 34, 324, 328, 331–32

Zong (ship): absence of logbook from, 127–28; British knowledge of the, 15; character of crew on, 198; character of owners of, 199; insurance value of, 11, 17, 32, 41, 137, 150; number of slaves aboard, 11; origin of, 10; owners of, 39; as slave ship, 8; as "typical" atrocity, 47; voyage of, 9–10, 14–15, 32. *See also Zong* case; *Zong* massacre

Zong case, 32, 195–96; attorneys' strategies in, 197–99; as being about value, 96, 105, 137; Clarkson and, 213–15; discourse of humanity in, 197–99, 200, 202–3; discourse over property in, 196–97; as event in history of capitalism, 139; humanity of slaves considered in, 196; as legal case, 109; moment inhabited by, 149; "necessity" in, 136; as property dispute, 135; reading, 32–33, 150; struggle between abolitionists and slave traders and, 16; value in, 264; as vanishing event, 149–50; verdict in, 94, 96; "view from the window" in, 201–2. *See also* Collingwood, Luke; Slaves; Slave trade; *Zong* (ship); *Zong* massacre

Zong massacre: as allegory of middle passage, 274–75; Clarkson's account of, 220–21, 268; as event, 132–33, 134–35; fact of, 222–27; Glissant and, 311; history of, 32; reading, 162, 166–68; representations of, 305; "seeing" event of, 220, 247–48; story of, 219–20; as truth event, 119, 121–22, 124–25, 128, 166–67, 246–47, 289; and the "typical," 108–9; Wilberforce's account of, 220–21. *See also* Collingwood, Luke; Letter, Sharp's; *Zong* (ship); *Zong* case

IAN BAUCOM is associate professor of English at Duke University.
He is author of *Out of Place: Englishness, Empire, and the Locations of Identity*
(Princeton University Press).

LIBRARY OF CONGRESS CATALOGING-IN-PUBLICATION DATA

Baucom, Ian.

Specters of the Atlantic : finance capital, slavery,

and the philosophy of history / Ian Baucom.

p. cm.

Includes bibliographical references and index.

ISBN 0-8223-3558-1 (cloth : alk. paper)

ISBN 0-8223-3596-4 (pbk. : alk. paper)

1. Slave trade — Great Britain — History — 18th century. 2. Slave trade —
Africa — History — 18th century. 3. Slave-trade — America — History — 18th
century. 4. Antislavery movements — Great Britain — History — 18th century.
5. Abolitionists — Great Britain — History — 18th century. 6. *Zong* (Ship)
7. Trials — Great Britain — History — 18th century. 8. Capitalism —
Social aspects — History — 18th century. I. Title.

HT1162.B38 2005

306.3′62 — dc22   2005013577